Exiles fr
European  ations

Refugees in Mid-Victorian England

Edited by
Sabine Freitag

Berghahn Books
New York • Oxford

First published in 2003 by **Berghahn Books**
www.BerghahnBooks.com

Library of Congress Cataloging-in-Publication Data

Flotsam of Revolution (1999 : London, England)
Exiles from European revolutions : refugees in mid-Victorian England /
edited by Sabine Freitag.
p. cm.
Revions of papers presented at the international conference Flotsam of
Revolution: European Exiles in England After 1849 which was held at the
German Historical Institute in London in July 1999.
Includes bibliographical references and index.
ISBN 1-57181-417-5 (alk. paper) -- ISBN 1-57181-330-6 (pbk. : alk. paper)
1. Europeans--England--History--19th century--Congresses. 2.
Immigrants--England--History--19th century--Congresses. 3. Political
refugees--England--History--19th century--Congresses. 4. Political
refugees--Europe--History--19th century--Congresses. 5. England--Ethnic
relations--History--19th century--Congresses. 6.
Revolutions--Europe--History--19th century--Congresses. 7. Great
Britain--History--Victoria, 1837-1901--Congresses. 8.
Europe--History--1848-1849--Congresses. I. Freitag, Sabine. II. German
Historical Institute in London. III. Title.

DA125.A1F59 2003
325'.21'0940942--dc21   2003052059

British Library Cataloguing in Publication Data
A catalogue record for this book is available from the British Library

Printed in the United States on acid-free paper

ISBN 1-57181-417-5 hardback
ISBN 1-57181-330-6 paperback

Contents

Acknowledgements

Under the title *Flotsam of Revolution: European Exiles in England after 1849* an international conference took place at the German Historical Institute in London in July 1999. After the numerous celebrations of 150 years of revolutions in Europe, especially in Germany in 1998, the conference sought to start where for most of the revolutionary protagonists the story ended: in exile. Since 'Flotsam' was defined by the Oxford Dictionary of English as 'People or things that have been rejected and are regarded as worthless', the task of the conference was, as the director at that time, Peter Wende, stated in his opening address, to find out whether the members of this intellectually and culturally rich community in exile were considered 'worthless', either by their host country, or by their countries of origin. How did their story continue, what opportunities for political activity in exile existed for them, and was there any noticeable cooperation between the different national exile groups on the one hand and with politicians and organisations in England on the other?

To discuss and answer these questions participants from all over Europe joined this conference. I am much indebted to the former director of the GHIL, Peter Wende, under whose auspices the conference took place, and to the present director, Hagen Schulze, who has generously supported the publication.

Although this book grew out of a conference it is more than simply a volume of printed conference papers. Many of the papers have been carefully reworked and extended for publication and three contributions have been especially written for this volume. I wish to thank all the contributors for their cooperation and commitment.

My thanks go also to Angela Davis and Jane Rafferty from the GHIL who translated articles into English and checked the spelling throughout the manuscript. I am also very grateful to Ruth Streeter who was the "good spirit" behind the conference organisation.

Frankfurt am Main, February 2003   Sabine Freitag

Notes on Contributors

Sylvie Aprile is Lecturer in Contemporary history at the University of Tours. Her main field of research is French and European history of the nineteenth century. She has published several articles on French revolutionary exiles (*Genèses*, 2000; *Romantisme*, 2000) and prepares an essay on French banishment.

Fabrice Bensimon is Lecturer at the Université Paris 10 – Nanterre. He is the author of *Les Britanniques face à la révolution française de 1848* (2000). He works on British caricature and cartoons, labour history, and cross-channel relationships.

Carol Diethe retired recently from her post as Reader in History of Ideas at Middlesex University. She has published extensively on Nietzsche and on German women writers of the nineteenth century. *Nietzsche's Women* appeared in 1996 and her *Historical Dictionary of Nietzscheanism* in 1999. Further publications include *Towards Emancipation: German Women Writers in the Nineteenth Century* (1998) and *The Life and Work of Louise Otto-Peters, Germany's Founding Feminist* (2002). *Nietzsche's Sister and the Will to Power* will appear shortly with University of Illinois Press. Carol Diethe now lives mainly in Scotland.

Andreas Fahrmeir received his PhD from the University of Cambridge and his Habilitation from the University of Frankfurt. He has since worked as a Research Fellow at the German Historical Institute, London, and as a consultant with McKinsey & Company. He is currently Heisenberg-Fellow at the University of Frankfurt's History Department. His publications include *Citizens and Aliens: Foreigners and the Law in Britain and the German States, 1789–1870* (2000), and *Ehrbare Spekulanten: Stadtverfassung, Wirtschaft und Politik in der City of London, 1688-1900* (2003).

Tibor Frank, MA, PhD, DLitt is Professor of History at Eötvös Loránd University in Budapest, Hungary. A visiting professor at the University of California, Santa Barbara (UCSB, 1987–90), the University of Nevada-Reno (1990-91), and Columbia University in the City of New York (2001), his research focuses on transatlantic studies, with special reference to the relations of Hungary, Austria, and Germany with the US and Great Britain in the nineteenth and twentieth centuries. His current books include *Ethnicity, Propaganda, Myth-Making* (1999), *From Habsburg Agent to Victorian Scholar* (2000), *Ein Diener seiner Herren* (2002), *Roosevelt követe Budapesten* (2002) and *Discussing Hitler* (2002). He is the recipient of the Humboldt Forschungspreis (Humboldt Research Award) for 2002.

Sabine Freitag received her PhD from the University of Frankfurt. She has been a Research Fellow at the German Historical Institute in London from 1996 until

2002. Her main fields of interests are nineteenth and early twentieth century German, British and American history. She is the author of *Friedrich Hecker. Biographie eines Republikaners* (1998) and co-editor of a multi-volume series *British Envoys to Germany, 1815–1866* (2000). She is currently working on a history of criminal law, culture and policy in England, 1870–1930.

Maurizio Isabella works and conducts independent research in Brussels. His publications include 'Una scienza dell'amor patrio': public economy, freedom and civilisation in Giuseppe Pecchio's works (1827–1820), *Journal of Modern Italian Studies* (1999), and 'Italy, 1760–1815', in Hanna Barker and Simon Burrows (eds), *Press Politics and the Public Sphere in Europe and North America, 1760–1820* (2002). He is currently working on the biography of the Milanese exile Giuseppe Pecchio and the Italian exile community in England in the 1820s.

Christine Lattek received her PhD from the University of Cambridge in 1991. She was a Research Assistant and Junior Lecturer at the University of Cologne and at Washington University in St. Louis/USA. She now works as a freelance editor and translator in London. Her recent book *Revolutionary Refugees: German Socialism in London, 1840–1860* will be published in 2003.

Bruce Levine is Professor of History at the University of California, Santa Cruz. His books include *The Spirit of 1848: German Immigrants, Labor Conflict, and the Origins of the Civil War* (1992) and *Half Slave, Half Free: The Roots of Civil War* (1992). His article, 'Conservatism, Nativism, and Slavery: Thomas R. Whitney and the Origins of the Know Nothing Party', appeared in the September 2001 issue of the *Journal of American History*. His next book, tentatively entitled *Confederate Emancipation: Southern Plans to free Slaves during the Civil War*, will be published by Oxford University Press.

Krzysztof Marchlewicz received his PhD from the Adam Mickiewicz University at Poznań where he works as a Research Assistant. His main fields of research are the Anglo-Polish relations in the nineteenth century and the history of Polish emigration to England. He has recently published *Polonofil doskonaly. Propolska dzialanosc charytatywna i polityczna lorda Dudleya C. Stuarta (1803–1854)* (Perfect Polonophile. Pro-Polish Charitable and Political Activity of Lord Dudley C. Stuart) (1803–1854), (2001).

Ivan Pfaff, PhD, studied history in Prague and Brno. His main research interests are the political history of Central Europe in the nineteenth century, especially the Czech enlightenment and national movement. His publications include *The fight of Czech culture against fascism, 1932–38* (1969), *Czech politics and Switzerland, 1848–1918* (1975), *Jalta: Partition of the World or Legend?* (1986), and *Die Sowjetunion und die Verteidigung der Tschechoslowakei 1934–1938: Versuch der Revision einer Legende* (1996).

Pamela Pilbeam is Professor of French History at Royal Holloway College, University of London. Her most recent books are *Republicanism in Nineteenth-Century France, 1814–71* (1995), *The Constitutional Monarchy in France, 1815–48* (1999), *French Socialists before Marx. Workers, Women and the Social Question in France* (2000) and *Madame Tussaud and the History of Waxworks* (2003), published for the bicentenary of the Tussaud exhibition in London.

Bernard Porter is Emeritus Professor of Modern History at the University of Newcastle. He has also taught at Hull and Yale Universities, and been a Fellow of Corpus Christi College, Cambridge, and the Australian National University. His main research interests are imperial and diplomatic history, the British secret services, and nineteenth century British attitudes to continental Europeans. In 1996 he undertook a lecture tour of Germany on the invitation of the *Deutsch-Englische Gesellschaft*, Bonn. He is author of seven books, including (the one with most relevance to this volume) *The Refugee Question in Mid-Victorian Politics* (1979). He is now working on a book on the domestic impact of her empire on Britain.

Iorwerth Prothero is Senior Lecturer in History at the University of Manchester. His research and publications have been mainly on labour and radical movements, initially in London, but subsequently in England and France generally. He is completing a book on religious dissidence in France, and plans after that to write one on the Chartist leader Bronterre O'Brien.

Ansgar Reiss received his PhD from the University of Giessen. He is Lecturer at the University of Regensburg. He has been working for different historical exhibitions in Bavaria. The most recent project is '1803. Wende in Europas Mitte', an exhibition at the Historical Museum in Regensburg in 2003. His book *Radikalismus und Exil. Gustav Struve und die Demokratie in Deutschland und Amerika* will be published in 2003.

John Saville is Professor Emeritus of Economic and Social History at the University of Hull. He has been one of the most influential writers in the field of British Labour History. He has written or edited over 20 books including *1848, the British State and the Chartist Movement* (1987) and *The Consolidation of the Capitalist State, 1800–1850* (1994). Together with Joyce M. Bellamy he edited 10 volumes of the *Dictionary of Labour History* (1972 – 2002) and 25 volumes of the annual *Socialist Register* (with Ralph Miliband, 1964-1989). His political *Memoirs from the Left* will be published in 2003.

1

Introduction

Sabine Freitag

The exile and emigration of political refugees demonstrate in exemplary manner the international dimension of the European revolutions in 1848/49. If it is true that a common European revolutionary culture existed, which maintained political convictions beyond national borders and interests, political exile is the place where this spectrum of shared political and social beliefs and common political experiences can best be examined. For reasons which will be mentioned below, no country other than England and no city other than London offers a better opportunity for analysing the European political exile after 1848/49. The aim of this book is to investigate, within the context of an international comparison, what has so far been treated only within specific national historiographies: the political exile of French, Italian, Hungarian, Polish, Czech and German refugees in England. Only within this context are we able to analysis not only the national pecularities of various exile communities but also their common ground and mutualities, and their interaction – whether active or theoretical – with the host country. The degree of difficulty in adapting to the new situation is of as much interest here as all the forms of political cooperation that existed between exiles from different European countries and between exiles and British organisations and politicians. And finally, the attitude of the host country towards the refugees will come into perspective as well as the refugees' perception of the country which had granted them asylum. In short: this historical survey seeks to stimulate further discussion about 'exclusion' and 'inclusion' within the context of political asylum.

It is nothing new that the term 'political exile' is notoriously difficult to define. Who is entitled to be considered as a political refugee? Using Andreas Fahrmeir's pragmatic compilation in this volume, the most common definitions are: people who flee punishment for the expression of political opinion or for political acts; further, those who fear discrimination or prosecution for their opinions without being political activists; then those who voluntarily leave the oppressive atmosphere of their native countries and live abroad, sometimes with the intention of overthrowing the government of their native state from a distance; and finally even those who leave their country primarily for economic reasons when the economic uncertainty is caused by the political situation at home. As Bruce Levine shows in his contribution (Chapter 14), the group of economically motivated emigrants cannot be considered as purely apolitical because political and economic reasons are often intertwined and some of the so-called economic refugees become politically active only in exile. As new research suggests, it seems disputable whether political and socio-economic motives can be separated neatly when it comes to emigration. Levine, for example, argues that the fact that many German labourers chose North America as their future home can be read as a sign of disapproval of the political system at home, though probably not articulated. When German labourers had the opportunity to become politically involved in the United States they did so, and organised themselves by creating cooperatives and workers' unions, models which they brought from home. On a smaller scale a similar situation could be found in England.

All of the above-mentioned refugees were to be found as exiles in England. The advantage of coming to England was that the exiles could stay relatively close to their home countries or the scenes of revolutionary upheavals, which was ideal if one believed, as many in fact did, that the setbacks of 1849 were merely temporary and their period of exile would be short. If necessary they would be able to return home within a very short time (for example, only 24–36 hours to reach Prussia). In the meantime nearly all their political endeavours were directed towards their country of origin. It was only later, when the prospect of a new revolution receded, that some of those who initially came to England travelled on to the United States.

Contrary to long-held views, as Bernard Porter and Andreas Fahrmeir emphasise in their respective essays (Chapters 4 and 3, respectively), it was not love of England, nor a deliberate decision based on approval of a particular political system, that brought most refugees to the country, but simply a lack of alternatives. In the late 1840s formerly liberal asylum countries like Belgium, France and Switzerland began to change their attitudes towards refugees and became more conservative and hostile by facilitating extradition or simply by making it more difficult to enter their countries. Programmes of financial support such as those which had been organised in France for Polish refugees in the 1830s were stopped, or were not extended to the refugees of

1848/49, and the protection against extradition for political offences was rescinded. The combination of financial and political pressure and deportations left the political refugees who wanted to stay in Europe no alternative but Britain. Britain was, as Bernard Porter put it, very much a last resort. Britain not only had liberal asylum legislation, but also lacked any regulations that curbed the stream of refugees. The unique character of British policy on asylum and immigration in the nineteenth century became obvious when the Belgian Foreign Office asked the British government for some information about the number and present whereabouts of certain refugees in Britain. The British Foreign Office had to admit that refugee lists did not exist: they did not seem necessary because everybody could enter the country freely without any restriction. Even when, out of an exaggerated fear of subversive foreign influence, the British parliament passed a temporary Aliens' Act in 1848 (which lapsed, as planned, in 1850) that authorised the government to expel those individuals considered likely to cause political unrest, not a single deportation resulted. In fact, as John Saville stresses in his essay (Chapter 2), between 1823 and the Aliens' Act of 1905 no foreigner was ever refused entry into Britain, or expelled, whatever his or her status or political opinions.

For a long time exile has been described mainly in terms of 'exclusion'. At first sight there seems every reason to do so. Exiles live in artificial and psychologically very stressful circumstances: they no longer belong to their home country, nor yet to the host country. And since the host country often treats them as aliens, this is exactly how the refugees feel. Assimilation takes time and many refugees of 1848/49 remained unintegrated for years. They hoped that they would soon be able to return to their mother country. Every refugee faces difficulties in structuring and organising a new life away from the familiarity of the old one. It is only natural that the first people they make contact with in exile are often fellow countrymen living in similar circumstances. A common language is the most important means of creating a sense of solidarity and communal spirit. Those who were unwilling or unable to learn English stayed isolated and restricted their environment to communication with compatriots. They often took refuge behind an exaggerated esteem of their own culture, as did, for example, the German governess Amalie Bölte and Amalie Struve, wife of the revolutionary Gustav Struve. They could not acclimatise to English life and came to see England as inferior to Germany.

But a common language does not always guarantee the harmonious cohesion of an ethnic exile community. Exile also means factions, mistrust, helplessness, controversies and splits within an apparently homogeneous exile group of one nationality. In reality there was not one single homogeneous exile group that was not split into several factions because of personal rivalries or political arguments over different concepts of exile politics and programmes. It seems that the peculiar circumstances of exile caused these splits and deepened the gap between different political factions. But one must bear in mind that these factions often already existed before they met in exile. Feeling like a fish out of water, being forced into idleness and inactivity after an exciting time of political engagement at home, many political exiles became frustrated and looked for opportunities to play an important role again, even though these possibilities were very limited. Particularly in intellectual circles the psychological crisis of the émigré society produced tensions and the main problem persisted over the years: there were 'too many chiefs and too few Indians'. Everybody wanted to play a leading role. When a fund-raising tour to the United States was launched the German exile group split over how to use the money even before they actually got it. In the end, as Sabine Freitag describes in Chapter 11, two separate representatives were sent to America, which did not really help to win over the confidence of fellow German-Americans.

For women in particular, as Carol Diethe shows in Chapter 15, it was difficult to cope with the new situation. Focusing on the German émigré women Jenny Marx, Johanna Kinkel and Malwida von Meysenbug, she explains what difficult conditions they faced in exile. Each headed a political household which was visited by numerous exiles every day. In the belief that their exile was only temporary, they educated their children with the aim to returning to their countries of origin, only to realise with the passage of time how 'English' their children had already become. Jenny Marx used up her own creative energies in the daily struggle for money, whereas Johanna Kinkel and Malwida von Meysenbug were able to use their experience of exile in literary form.

An exception was Jeanne Deroin, the French feminist, suffragette and political activist, whose personal life and political thinking Pam Pilbeam examines in her paper (Chapter 16). Having been treated badly by the French authorities for her liberal and emancipated convictions, Deroin was imprisoned for six months and decided to emigrate to England after she was warned that she was likely to be rearrested for her persistent political agitation. She left France for

England in 1852 and never went back, spending the rest of her life – over forty years – in self-imposed exile in London.

Are there any national characteristics in the way exile groups behave in the host country? Fabrice Bensimon (Chapter 6), for example, demonstrates that French refugees had huge difficulties in adjusting to their situation. One of the most famous examples of an exile who did not want to assimilate or become too close to the host country was Alexandre Ledru-Rollin. Just a few weeks after fleeing to England he published a critical account of his host country, *De la décadence de l'Angleterre* (published the same year in English under the title *The Decline of England*, London 1850) which was understandably widely resented by the English. They criticised him for 'biting the hand that feeds him'. Ledru-Rollin argued that the whole country was led by the two aristocracies – land and finance – which worked as parasites to exploit the country's great masses. Describing British economy and society in negative terms he also stressed French culture as superior and in his account he confirmed long-held traditional stereotypes: the English were stiff, ate poor food and were too materialistic. With his open and harsh critique Ledru-Rollin was an exception. French, but also German, Hungarian or Italian refugees usually did not want to irritate the English authorities nor the English public and tended not to criticise them openly.

Exile is not a static situation but one marked by fluctuation and change. Even exile groups from the same country could change during a relatively short period of time, as happened in the case of the Polish emigrants. Krzysztof Marchlewicz (Chapter 7) compares the activities and political goals of the 'great emigration' which had been in England since the 1830s, with those of the group who arrived after 1849. After 1849 the social composition of Polish emigrants changed, the number of non-noble origin was considerably higher and their political orientation moved to the left. Previously dominated by conservative, aristocratic circles, they now had a much higher proportion of artisans, workers and simple soldiers with a socialist-communist background. The older generation based in the 'Hotel Lambert' was still hoping for support from the Western powers in the struggle for Polish independence, in order to set up a constitutional monarchy along British lines. The strongest faction after 1849, however, the Polish Democratic Society, was working towards an independent Republic of Poland with a single-chamber parliament elected on the basis of universal suffrage. The London revolutionary commune, the Polish People, which was supported by

Polish workers and artisans, by contrast, aimed to set up a Slavic federation within a world-wide Socialist republic, in which private property would be abolished, and land and industry communally owned. The only common denominator between all Polish factions was the desire for an independent Poland.

Exile is not only a history of isolation and failure to assimilate. Analysis of the many forms of political cooperation that existed between exiles from different European countries is long overdue. Under what circumstances was such cooperation successful? And when did international cooperation come to an end and national interests regain central importance? Ledru-Rollin, for example, repeatedly attempted to organise a European association of democrats (always excluding Britain), which may be interpreted as an attempt to create an 'imagined community' in the face of the threatened loss of the real one.

One of the most famous examples of cooperation between European exiles was Giuseppe Mazzini's Central European Democratic Committee. Its members included Ledru-Rollin, the Polish republican Alfred Darasz, and the German republican and leftist Hegelian, Arnold Ruge. The internationalism of the European exiles was based on the vision of a 'springtime of nations' and Mazzini's committee was the symbol of this vision. It attempted to bring together all democrats in exile who were not committed to the socialist-communist bloc. The committee was able to draw up a manifesto which extolled the idea of popular sovereignty in a democratic 'Europe of People'. The manifesto presented common interests which were acceptable to all European exiles: abolition of monarchies, universal franchise, freedom of association, education free of charge and a progressive tax system. On these general terms, leaving out the special circumstances of every country, international cooperation was possible. The plan to create national committees in every European country was never realised. When Ledru-Rollin, who edited their common newspaper *Le Proscrit*, started his own journal the committee slowly began to collapse. Arnold Ruge resigned in autumn 1851 and even though Stanisław Worcell was elected as a new Polish member after the death of Darasz in 1852, the committee faded away in spring 1853. Lack of influence and struggles over the direction of the committee brought its work to an end.

There are two reasons why contacts between refugees and the British were limited: first of all, most exiles were really only interested in liberating their own countries and therefore concentrated their political efforts on means which helped to support their aims. Secondly, most refugees had to struggle just to stay alive and were often distracted by everyday work to earn a living. Nevertheless contacts existed and it seems that for those involved the exchange was fruitful and stimulating. Some refugees had prominent friends who supported them, but this was the exception. Where links existed there was often a great affinity between the class the refugees came from and the class that supported them. While Lord Dudley Coutts Stuart managed to organise support for the first wave of aristocratic Polish emigrants through the London Literary Association of the Friends of Poland, the more radical Polish Democratic Society received assistance from English radicals led by William James Linton and Joseph Cowen jur. Indeed, after 1849 the Polish immigrants were increasingly seen as a threat and English radical circles became their only source of support.

British intellectuals were also very much interested in French refugees, in particular those from the working class. Some English radicals gained renewed political inspiration from their contacts with French refugees. Even though concern for and contact with foreign refugees was not, as Iorwerth Prothero shows in Chapter 13, a characteristic of mainstream Chartism, contacts did exist with the minority rationalist wings, moral reformers who had continental experience and contacts, and the social-democratic elite. Although here shared political views fostered political exchange and cooperation, the republican and socialist opinions of the French refugees incurred the strong emnity of the conservative and liberal circles who were interested in social stability and feared their radical rhetoric would have a negative influence. Where solidarity with the French existed in conservative circles it was only because French refugees were seen as victims of a political regime that was not much liked in Britain. However, the suppression of the revolutionary upheavals meant the arrival in London of refugees who were often very poor, so that practical help became more important than intellectual stimulation.

The liberal Italian exiles who came to England after the uprisings of 1821, 1832 and 1848 managed, as Maurizio Isabella demonstrates in Chapter 5, to develop the closest contacts with the British establishment and contributed at a very early stage to shaping British politicians' understanding of the Italian question. Usually the men of the first emigration wave – intellectuals, men of letters and conservative aristocrats – were anglophile. For them the British constitution appeared to be one that would satisfy the demands of the liberal aristocrats for governing their countries and more generally for defending the interests of the propertied classes. Radical Italian refugees, who were able to observe the condition of the English working class, criticised the British commercial system on account of the dangerous effects of mechanisation and the great social inequality of the English society it produced. Not surprisingly, English republicans, radicals and Chartists represented the 'natural' social environment for the Italian democrats. Henry Holland was undoubtedly the most famous English politician known to sympathise with the Italian cause. Even though politically not a radical he was in favour of Italian independence and shared most readily the Italian exiles' anti-Austrian feelings. The small community of liberal exiles who came to England after 1849, far fewer than in the 1820s and 1830s, continued to find sympathetic political supporters and friends in Palmerston, Russell and Gladstone. It may have been the language used by the Italian exiles in public lectures and publications that managed to offer a consistent image of a homogeneous and cohesive nation struggling for freedom, in which the British could safely reaffirm, as Isabella states, their own political beliefs by supporting the Italian cause.

Even though contacts and common actions between foreigners and the British were limited, the simple mechanisms of mutual perception revealed a great deal about the construction of national identity. Mutual perceptions were often irrational or untrue but could nevertheless serve as a self-affirmation of one's own community. There were great national differences in the mutual perception of refugees and Englishmen.

The French, for example, remained sceptical of British hospitality and were afraid that they would soon be extradited. When the Aliens' Act was introduced in 1848 they thought that it was mainly directed, as Bensimon shows, against them. Some French refugees even suspected the British government of deliberately starving them since it refused any financial support for refugees. In truth it was the free market system that was starving them. Traditional mistrust on both sides shaped relations between the British and the French. With an inadequate knowledge of the language and unable to find well-paid work, most French refugees never considered staying permanently in Britain. The British attitude towards the French was no less ambivalent. Government and ruling classes regarded the French as troublemakers with subversive tendencies. The events of 1789, 1830 and 1848 had shown the French to be unstable and incapable of sticking to one opinion or one political system. The British public, however, did not share the view of the authorities, the press, and some political circles who, for obvious reasons, were trying to promote both anti-French and anti-socialist feelings. According to Bensimon no demonstrations against French refugees were ever recorded.

The Czech perception of Great Britain was, as Ivan Pfaff demonstrates in Chapter 9, the complete opposite. Czech intellectuals uncritically idealised English nobility, admired British industrialisation and commerce and the British constitution. Britain seemed to be a suitable model for their own future state. The Austrian authorities were uneasy about the clear reference to liberal Britain as a model for Czech politics. Even though Czech exile politics in Britain after 1849 was nothing but a small episode in nineteenth-century Czech history, it nevertheless demonstrates how, for the first time, Czechs opened up to the political ideas of Western Europe, where they hoped to find some ideas for their own future constitutional state. The British perception of the Czech situation, on the other hand, was plain ignorance. English intellectuals and politicians, like Thomas Carlyle or Lord Palmerston, had little feeling for the situation of the Czechs, in contrast to that of the Poles. There was no understanding of the demands of a nation of whose very existence Europe seemed unaware. If they wanted to preserve their own nationality, Palmerston advised František Rieger, the Czechs should join Russia in order to prevent 'Germanisation'. Czech national identity was not something British politicians or the British public really cared about. If the Czechs entertained any hopes of British intervention in their cause they soon became disillusioned. Like many other European exiles, the Czechs came to the conclusion that their host country had offered them asylum not so much for themselves as for the sake of its own self-esteem.

The attitude towards refugees always says something about the host country's political climate and *Zeitgeist*. Bernard Porter suggests that the British public tolerated the refugees partly because their aversion to regulations was even greater than their dislike of the influx of foreigners. In general there were few points of contact between the English people and the refugees, and so the British public were not able to develop any real understanding of their problems. It was generally thought that the refugees' struggle for existence absorbed most of their political energies and that hard work would eventually render them harmless. Meanwhile politicians like Palmerston used the refugees for political purposes, as John Saville shows in his contribution. Palmerston deliberately used the immigrants as instruments of his foreign policy to demonstrate

Britain's political superiority and domestic stability, which did not appear to have been threatened by the influx of political refugees. The myth of Britain's internal political stability, Saville argues, was created at a time when there could be no question of its existence in reality. Even though fears existed of Irish insurrection, prompted by the revolutionary upheavals on the Continent, neither the British government nor British ruling classes entertained any doubts that they were in the right. It was not until the Kennington Common Rally was broken up by the police on 10 April 1848 that they took their refuge behind some sort of conspiracy theory. Because of the ideological affinities between the continental socialists and communists in exile and the English Chartists they saw the refugees as the real instigators of the mass demonstration.

Even in a modern and cosmopolitan city like London exile was a sort of limbo for the refugees because it was impossible for them to participate directly in the future development of their home countries. What ways and means were left to them for sustaining their involvement with their home countries? With their political illusions increasingly shattered, political exiles in England became aware that their planned short stay would turn into long-term residence. Therefore their first priority was to make a living and many settled down to teaching, lecturing and journalism in the following years. But many still believed in the importance and efficiency of exile propaganda in influencing a process which ultimately had to develop within the home country itself.

One of the most significant exile activities was the publication of newspapers and journals, which was also one of the most important sources of income for exiles. In the beginning the idea was always to distribute these papers in the home country, but usually they were not allowed to enter that country, were seized at borders, or sometimes censored so heavily by the authorities that the original objective was totally lost. As Sylvie Aprile shows (Chapter 10), the newspaper _L'Homme_ represented a milestone in the history of the international press. Edited by French exiles in Jersey, its columns were open to exiles from the whole of Europe. The political programme of a 'république universelle et social' within a 'United States of Europe' ruled out the Anglophobia that was typical of many French exiles. Aprile also demonstrates the problems faced by the editors. It was a complicated process to distribute the journal in France itself, and in addition the newspaper was unable to report on events in France, which was what exile readers were most interested in. The influence of _L'Homme_ on the Continent was limited, but nevertheless the cooperation of authors from different European countries was the beginning of an international press. It helped to create a forum that sought to transcend national borders and deepen awareness of the existence of political matters which were central to the whole of Europe.

Collecting money for another revolution, for weapons and propaganda material, was the main goal of another form of exile politics, which Sabine Freitag describes in her essay: the fund-raising tour to North America by Gottfried Kinkel, Amand Goegg and Lajos Kossuth. America was supposed to be the natural ally of all democratic refugees who were forced into exile. But financial support from the USA ceased after the collectors left the country and all three fundraisers returned from their journey disappointed by the amount of money they had raised. However, even though the action itself was not a success in financial terms, newspaper reports of the event nevertheless brought Germany's difficult political situation to readers' minds on both sides of the Atlantic for the first time. When Gottfried Kinkel was forced to explain how he intended to use the money collected discussions about the German situation were unavoidable. What became clear was that the political situation in Germany was different and far more difficult than the Hungarian, Polish, or even the Italian struggle for national independence from foreign occupation. In Germany it was not a question of foreign occupation, but the insurmountable task of overcoming the huge variety of political and social conditions within the German Confederation. A future democratic and republican Germany would have to get rid of more than thirty kings, grand dukes and dukes, and the discussions about the final form of its political organisation and social and economic structures showed a wide range of ideas and concepts from many different 'schools'. These schools were to make their mark in exile too.

Whereas moderate liberal democrats such as Arnold Ruge and Gottfried Kinkel first had to create a forum for their exile politics, German socialists and communists could make use of an infrastructure that already existed in London, and they were rapidly integrated. As the universal claims of socialist theories went beyond national borders and characteristics, the refugees from the 1848 revolution were able to contribute to an internationalisation of the radical workers' movement. Cooperation with French Blanquists and English Chartists seemed, as Iorwerth Prothero shows, an obvious move in the attempt to create a common anti-democratic-bourgeois bloc. But different opinions on exile politics even in German socialist circles, as Christine

Lattek demonstrates in Chapter 12, led to factions and splits. While the former soldier and socialist August Willich emphasised the need for military training to harden his cadres for the inevitable battles, Karl Marx, who came to London in 1849 after being expelled from France and Belgium, thought education and propaganda alone would allow the proletariat to develop its class consciousness and would enable them to build up an organisation strong enough to survive the years of struggle ahead. The classic struggle between theory and practice led to a split. Emphasising the importance of action and distrusting any intellectual influence and leadership, August Willich and his political companion Karl Schapper insisted that the proletariat should take its affairs into its own hands, both in the present organisation and in the coming revolution, so that the party of the intellectuals could no longer lead the people by the nose. Strangely, historians have neglected the history of the Willich-Schapper league and concentrated almost exclusively on Marx's development, although for a while the league was the more prominent one in German workers' circles in London. But its increasingly unrealistic schemes for revolution, its anti-intellectualism and exaggerated desire to act soon made it obsolete. The league collapsed when Willich emigrated to the United States. Meanwhile Marx transferred the Central Authority to Cologne. In 1864 he and his supporters founded the First International Working Men's Association (IAA, Internationale Arbeiterorganisation) which later established a branch in New York chaired by the German refugee Friedrich Sorge as honorary secretary. After 1870 there were some contacts between German workers' associations in London and the rapidly rising Socialist party of August Bebel in Germany. All in all many German 'economic' refugees were able to contribute to an internationalisation of the radical workers' movement in England. Although the theories of Marx and Engels, refugees in their own right, did not make an immediate practical impression on British politics their journalism indirectly fostered the steadily growing number of local workers' associations.

Bruce Levine's paper allows a comparison to be drawn between the fate of the craftsmen and workers who went to America and those who went to Britain. German immigrants in America, especially in big cities such as Chicago, had a greater impact on the country's labour and social policy than those in England. Though they felt the lack of state welfare in cases of economic crisis and unemployment bitterly, the initiatives they set up following the German model, such as cooperatives and societies of producers and consumers, did not succeed in America's profit-oriented market society. But some of the organisational forms and institutions which they supported, such as workers' unions, associations, strikes, mass demonstrations, unemployment benefits and laws regarding maximum hours and minimum wages, brought wide circles of American and other foreign-born workers together, and allowed them to grow into a political power. They changed the outlook of organised labour. Many German labourers managed to band together to advance some of their crucial common interests, insisting that the fight for democracy was as important in the economy as it was in politics.

Lacking the support of institutions or organisations, significant exile politics frequently depended on individual politicians. The cases of Giuseppe Mazzini, Lajos Kossuth and Julian Harney illustrate that the success of exile politics largely depended on the integrative force of the individual personality. Mazzini, like no other, was able to enlist the support of the English authorities, reforming politicians and members of society for the cause of an independent Italy, as Maurizio Isabella illustrates. Mazzini established a theory of anti-socialist republicanism and attempted to bring together all the democrats in exile who were not committed to the socialist-communist cause. Thanks to Mazzini's fundamental and personal contribution, the Italian cause gained increasing popularity in England. Mazzini also played a central part in rallying the moderate Chartists around a republican and reformist programme. He provided, as Isabella demonstrates, disillusioned and demoralised Chartists, especially from the younger generation, with a new and appealing programme of moral regeneration. Julian Harney was, as Iorwerth Prothero shows, a key person on the Chartists' side, linking together foreign refugees and Chartists in a political network by means of his personal contacts and never-failing enthusiasm. Lajos Kossuth, as Tibor Frank documents in Chapter 8, was the most prominent figure within the Hungarian exile community. As the Hungarians in exile in London were not a unified group, unity had to be conjured up by reference to Kossuth. This became their quasi-programme. Spiritualism, which had come into fashion since the 1830s, also contributed to Kossuth's ultimate status as a secular saviour.

'The history of the emigration in London is not described completely if one does not add a history of the secret police. Emigration and political police are two branches growing on the same revolutionary tree.' This statement by the German exile and spy Edgar Bauer, quoted in Christine Lattek's contribution, emphasises another important part of exile history. In England refugees were policed very 'mildly'. Police surveillance of the refugees, initially ordered by the authorities, was gradually relaxed as it became obvious that they did not pose a threat to Britain in the years after 1848. Refugees had, as Porter argues, much more to fear from their own police spies than from the little detective department in Scotland Yard which was set up to keep a watch on them. If there was any surveillance left it was usually carried out by spies for the despotic continental powers like Austria or Prussia who wanted to know what plans were entertained by their former subjects. Austrian spies sent abroad operated completely separately from the diplomatic apparatus. While foreign governments were puzzled as to how Britain could be so cavalier about her own domestic security, Britain was more concerned about the embarrassment some refugees were causing to her diplomatic relations with Austria and France than with their actual behaviour in the country itself.

For different reasons refugees and their persecutors shared one common expectation: both sides reckoned on a new revolutionary outbreak. For quite a while keeping an eye on refugees became an important business. Every assassination attempt, such as, for example, the one on the Austrian Emperor Francis Joseph in February 1853, could be interpreted as the detonator. The most famous example, which seemed to prove the dangerous situation fostered by British tolerance, was Felice Orsini's attempt to murder Emperor Napoleon III in Paris in 1858 with the support, so it was said, of exiles in England. Foreign governments were inclined to see a connection between the political struggle against their states and British hospitality. A particularly paranoid delusion was that the British government was actually cultivating foreign revolutionaries in order to undermine their neighbours. This was far from true. Nevertheless continental governments saw these incidents as evidence of a well-connected network of a European revolutionary party working against Vienna and Paris, even though the number of alleged conspirators was tiny. Moreover, they were isolated and watched each other with endless mistrust and vigilance. How the exile climate was influenced by mutual suspicion is described in the contributions by Bernard Porter, Christine Lattek and Tibor Frank.

As already mentioned, exile is not a static situation but determined by many changes. How long does the exile remain an exile? Over the years, for many refugees London ceased to be a waiting-room and turned into a permanent home. Successful integration and assimilation into the host country could put an end to exile, could change an exile into an emigrant who settled for good. This was the case for many refugees who stayed in England. Even if the parents' generation continued to be conscious of their immigrant status, their children often did not. This put a more or less 'natural' end to exile. Political changes in the home country and amnesties could also put an end to exile and could encourage people to return. Of course, the actual reasons for returning – as Ansgar Reiss shows in Chapter 17 – were as varied as the individuals themselves. Lajos Kossuth, Gottfried Kinkel, Guiseppe Mazzini and Karl Marx, for example, never returned to their home countries. Some of them preferred to stay in exile simply because they did not want to corrupt their status as political martyrs. Others, like the Hungarians Gyula Andrássy or Ferenc Pulszky or the German Lothar Bucher, succeeded in reintegrating themselves into the new political situation of the old fatherland. To this day, there is no international comparison of prominent returnees. In general, however, it can be said that few returnees were able to play an important political role after their return. Compromise with the new authorities was often the price of successful reintegration. In the case of Lothar Bucher, who returned to Germany to become a close ally of Bismarck, the price was the complete denial of his own past and political convictions. It seems, as Reiss's contribution suggests, that the successful reintegration of political refugees depended on how, when founding a national state, the different nations dealt with their own past. Were they able to integrate the 1848/49 period as an important stepping-stone towards building their national state, or did they see it as a disruptive, senseless and dangerous episode which should be suppressed and was best forgotten? Where the revolution could be interpreted as an important part in the creation process of the nation-state (whether by bringing a number of small states together or by bringing about separation from a transnational state like Austria), its political protagonists were later made welcome. If the enemy of revolution or unification was seen beyond the country's borders, for example in Italy, Hungary or Poland, internal integration of former émigrés was much easier. Ultimately, they had all wanted what was best for the nation. However, in countries such as Germany or France, where the refugees had been seen as internal political enemies, things were quite different. They were never acknowledged as the political midwives of democratisation or unification. The price for being allowed to return to their home country was – more or less – denial of their own political past. But another reason for the fact that so few refugees became prominent figures in later years in their home country was that their exile fell into a period that was marked by the most radical social change in the wake of industrialisation. On their return the exiles were confronted with very different societies. A new generation was taking over and this was not conducive to returnees re-assuming an important political role.

In many cases the coordinated action of continental governments against the refugees had discredited their political aims in the long run. Since it was not only reactionary states that acted against the refugees but also more liberal ones, it became impossible for the European democratic elite to establish itself as a real power. Exile always weakens those who have to leave. If we measure the failure or success of political refugees in the nineteenth century only by their ability to influence politics at home, they failed. They had limited opportunities and failed to make a real impact. The refugees were not able to cross the bridge and win over a broader group of supporters at home.

On the other hand, exiles were able to enrich the political and cultural landscape of the country that granted them asylum. While exile propaganda failed to reach people at home, as originally intended, some exile journals, for example *Hermann* or the *Londoner Deutsches Journal,* managed to survive and transformed into quite successful journals in the United Kingdom. Moreover, exile could function as a kind of substitute political platform where freedom of the press and of association could be practised while forbidden at home. In exile refugees preserved and cultivated forms of political participation and developed independent concepts which were not to become political reality until many years later.

Exile also creates continuity. The workers' movement is a good example. Many economic refugees were able to contribute to an internationalisation of the radical workers' movement in England. But in the case of Marx it was only after his death that he had any considerable impact on the numerous socialist groups which were formed during the 1880s and 1890s. Perhaps, as Sylvie Aprile stresses in her paper, it is not appropriate to judge the success or failure of a movement in terms of a successful revolution and the establishment of European republics. In this respect exile politics was a failure. But the richness of the press, the discussions about a future Europe and the degree of international cooperation deepened mutual understanding in a European context and showed, at the same time, under what circumstances people from different nations were able to leave behind national interests to support political concerns of interest to all.

I

Englishmen and Refugees

2

1848 – Britain and Europe

John Saville

The revolutionary days in Paris in late February 1848 set in motion a greater political turbulence in Europe than any other event between 1815 and 1914. A revolution in France immediately brought back the still vivid memories of Jacobinism and of French troops pouring over the boundaries of European states: memories greatly encouraged by an understanding of the resentment that remained among many of the French at the territorial rearrangements of the 1815 treaties. The presence of radicals such as Ledru-Rollin, Louis Blanc and Armand Marrast in the new Provisional Government – the most vigorous critics of the pacifism of the July Monarchy – confirmed the uncertainty and the fears common to most of Europe. On the day that the Republic was declared the Austrian Ambassador circulated the wholly false rumour that 50,000 French troops were about to move into Italy. Throughout most of the German states the military were mobilised, and on 4 March 1848 Prussia ordered her troops on the Rhine to be put on the alert. When news of the Paris uprising reached Russia, the bastion of European reaction, it was rumoured that the Tsar conveyed the news to a group of officers by shouting: 'Saddle your horses, gentlemen, a republic has been proclaimed in France.'[1]

The reactions of military power were in line with intense diplomatic activity. King Leopold of Belgium was among the more disturbed. He sent some of his own more private precious possessions to England for safekeeping and he actually contemplated abdicating from the throne. Prussia and Austria conducted intense discussions in Vienna, and Metternich, hoping to benefit from Italy's fear of France, offered Sardinia a defensive alliance. It was an offer that was declined, since Sardinia feared Austria as much as it distrusted France. It was to England that Sardinia appealed for help against any possible French aggression, and it was the stability of England in these early tumultuous days that was at the centre of most of the diplomatic manoeuvres in the capitals of Europe.[2]

Lamartine, who had become Foreign Secretary in the Provisional Government, was deeply conscious of the European attitudes to France and of the fears of aggression that the revolutionary upheaval engendered. In the very early days he drafted a minute emphasising that France was not considering any military action, and a few days later, conscious that a much more emphatic statement was required, he circulated round the courts of Europe the famous *Manifesto to Europe.* This set down the principles upon which the new republican government would base its foreign policies. Its central theme was the desire for peace and fraternity.

There were problems, however, for the most sophisticated draughtsman. Lamartine was the foreign minister of a government which included representatives of the radical groupings in Parisian politics and he could not avoid reflecting certain of their most fervent beliefs. Thus he was obliged to denounce the treaties of 1815 as a major humiliation to France and the French people at the same time as he emphasised that a military solution to these and other problems was not contemplated. The *Manifesto* also insisted that France would 'protect' legitimate movements of nationality, with Poland and Italy being the most obvious examples.

The *Manifesto* was seriously considered in all foreign chancelleries and the conclusions were by no means always sympathetic towards France. There was a typical reaction, however, from Palmerston who phrased his robust analysis in a letter to Clarendon, the Lord Lieutenant in Dublin (more commonly known as the Viceroy):

> The circular is evidently a piece of patchwork put together by opposite parties in the Government, the one warlike and disturbing, the other peaceful and conciliatory. I should say that if you were to put the whole of it into a crucible, and evaporate the gaseous parts, and scum off the dross, you would find the regulus to be peace and good fellowship with other Governments.[3]

Three years later, early in 1851, Richard Cobden asked Palmerston why the British Ambassador in Paris enjoyed a salary of £10,000 with a further sum of £4,000 for upkeep and outfit of the Embassy. The occasion for the question was the Report of a Select Committee on Official Salaries, and the background to Cobden's question was the knowledge that official salaries at home, and elsewhere abroad, were all below these figures. Palmerston replied later to the question by pointing out that the Paris Embassy inevitably had a great deal of hospitality to dispense, and then he continued with an important statement of his understanding of England's general policy towards France:

> I think our relations with France may be considered the keystone of our foreign policy. France is the country among the great powers that is nearest to us, with which we have the most important relations, and with which we are most likely to come into collison if pains are not taken to avoid it, and with which a collison must inevitably be attended with the gravest consequences. I, therefore, think that a perfectly good understanding with France, as long as it can be maintained without any sacrifice of interest and of honour, is the first object at which, in regard to foreign relations, the British government should aim.[4]

This statement by Palmerston needs, of course, important additions and qualifications. There was a traditional rivalry between the two powers that was rarely if ever absent from at least popular sentiment. During these middle decades of the century popular opinion, which went right up the social scale, included the strongly held belief that France was waiting for the opportunity to invade Britain from across the English Channel. There were several national scares, analysed by Cobden in a pamphlet of 1862, none of which had any serious substance.[5]

Palmerston's main concern following the February revolution was to discourage France, in all ways open to him, from becoming involved in any military operations, especially in any disputes between Austria and Italy. Palmerston was fortunate in his Paris Ambassador, Lord Normanby, whose appraisal of the July Monarchy had been highly perceptive, and whose reports from revolutionary Paris are a pleasure to read. Normanby was on very friendly terms with Lamartine, and the relations between these two have usually been underestimated by historians of the period. Normanby agreed with Palmerston that Lamartine's protestations concerning his peaceful policies were acceptable.[6]

There were, inevitably, problems for the British government, with Ireland, by definition, being among the most serious. Ireland had been immediately stimulated by the revolution in France: the famine was still exerting its terrible effects and the possibility of Irish insurgence was never far from the mind of any government at Westminster. The Chartists, naturally enough, had sent a delegation to Paris to congratulate the Provisional Government, and Normanby made an immediate protest at the way its members had been received by certain of the more radical ministers. Lamartine apologised for the 'indiscretions' of some of his colleagues, and there the matter ended. But when the Irish sent their delegation – they picked St Patrick's Day (which for English readers is 17 March) – Lamartine himself received them, and in his speech referred to 'Ireland's soon hoped-for constitutional independence'. Even worse, the Irish presented an Irish flag to be flown 'by the side of their brothers'. Normanby was furious, especially at the acceptance of the flag, and insisted upon a statement that would put matters in a more agreeable manner to the British. The outcome, in Normanby's summary to Palmerston, was not wholly satisfactory to the British Government.[7]

There was an incident in early April which illustrates the strength of historical understanding in national memories. In early April Smith O'Brien presented an address on behalf of the people of Ireland in which he referred to the close relations of the oppressed Irish people and France, and remarked specifically on the welcome asylum France had given Irish refugees in the late seventeenth century and the early decades of the eighteenth. He then continued with a statement which would infuriate the English. It was reported in full in *Le Moniteur,* 4 April 1848. The most calculated inflammatory passage read:

> Dans les temps passé, au moment le plus extreme de l'Irlande, vos pères ont accuelli avec hospitalité nos guerriers exilés, et le champs de Fontenoy peuvent dire comment cette hospitalité a été acquitée par l'effusion du sang Irlandais, coulant pour soutenir la gloire de la France.[8]

War in Europe and insurgency in Ireland were the two most important problems for Palmerston and his senior colleagues in the British government. Their problems were exacerbated by the attitudes of the Queen and the Prince Consort. Victoria liked Louis-Philippe and was naturally wholly in opposition to republicanism. It was her suggestion, with which Palmerston agreed, that Louis-Philippe should be given financial help on his arrival in England, and £1,000 was taken from the secret service funds and handed over as coming from an anonymous donor.[9] Palmerston, it should be noted, who was very pleased to see the removal of Guizot and Metternich from office, was always civilised towards them both when they settled in England. The conflicts with Victoria over the revolutionary movements in Europe continued throughout his tenure of office – within accepted constitutional limits, it must be added. Victoria was always conscious of her constitutional position, and of both the strengths and the limitations of her place in respect to the powers of her ministers. There is a well-known letter from Russell, the Prime Minister, which is a striking illustration of the self-confidence, too often arrogance, of the great Whig landowners and aristocracy within the English constitutional polity. The extract below was written on 29 February, six days after the revolution in Paris:

Lord John Russell presents his humble duty to your Majesty, and has the honour to transmit a short note from Lord Normandy, which is very satisfactory.

Lord John Russell declared last night that your Majesty would not interfere in the internal affairs of France. But in repeating this declaration to Mr. Cobden, he added that the sacred duties of hospitality would be, at all times, performed towards persons of all opinions. Both declarations were generally cheered. In extending this hospitality to members of the Royal Family of France, it is only to be observed that no encouragement should be given by your Majesty to any notion that your Majesty would assist them to recover the Crown. In this light it is desirable that no Prince of the House of Orleans should inhabit one of your Majesty's palaces in or near London.[10]

It was not the Prime Minister whom Victoria found most difficult, but Palmerston, for she took the view of him, common to many in Europe, that he was generally supportive of their revolutionary/radical movements. His radicalism was, of course, much exaggerated. He did not welcome the revolutions in Germany, although he had always advocated constitutional reform. It was France and then Austria and Italy which caused more unease. He was always insistent upon the importance of a strong and united Austria and always concerned that France should not extend its influence. It was for these reasons that after the exile of Metternich Palmerston suggested to Vienna, in Austria's own interests, that Lombardy should be ceded to Sardinia. If Austria insisted on retaining Lombardy it was likely that Charles Albert of Sardinia would take it by force. France would probably be of assistance and France, for Palmerston, could not be trusted. Palmerston, it should be noted, had no real interest in the unification of Italy, and the victory of the Austrians at Custozza did not change his mind.[11] Victoria, as on so many European issues, had no sympathy with Palmerston, and both she and members of her Court were involved in constant intrigues against him.

Normanby's brother, Charles Phipps, was equerry to the Prince Consort, and there was much gossiping in the letters between Paris and London. Normanby's wife was a great political chatterbox and she happily fed the rumours and prattle that were always in circulation. There was an occasion when those intriguing against Palmerston thought that the Lord Lieutenancy of Ireland was a possible exit for him, but he was an effective, tough-minded politician and very difficult to move around. So the Queen had to carry on with a Foreign Secretary whom she wholly mistrusted. She told her doctor that having to read one of Palmerston's dispatches before dinner made her feel bilious. Her dislike of Palmerston was not, perhaps, of the intensity of the paranoia she was later to display towards Gladstone, but she was younger and in her case age certainly did not soften her prejudices. Her attitudes towards Palmerston were reproduced in other courts. Prince Albert and King Leopold of Belgium had long amused themselves by referring to Palmerston as Pilgerstein, and when Palmerston was finally dismissed for welcoming Louis Napoleon's assumption of the Imperial crown on 2 December 1851 – in a private comment to the French Ambassador in London – the crowned heads of Europe rejoiced in their several ways.

There is one aspect of British policy towards Europe that is sometimes taken for granted, or more often, perhaps, ignored. In the quotation, given earlier, from Lord John Russell's letter to Queen Victoria, he commented to Cobden 'that the sacred duties of hospitality would be, at all times, performed towards persons of all opinions'. During the early revolutionary years in France there had been enacted in 1793 an Aliens' Bill by which control of undesirable immigrants into Britain could be regulated, and this was repealed in 1826. There was similar legislation in 1848, soon after the February days, and this remained on the statute book for about two years. But the central fact of British policy on these matters was that between 1823 and the Aliens' Bill of 1905 no foreigner was ever refused entry into Britain, or was expelled, whatever his or her status or political opinions. There were undoubtedly more pleasant places than London in which to find yourself. Paris was one such place, for London was too often clouded by fog and the reception by the natives was rarely of a warm, welcoming kind. London, however, was the one place at any time one could be expected to be left alone by the local security forces. They would have information on the political radicals, often of a detailed kind, but people would not be expelled at the request of another government.[12]

This was not an agreeable policy to certain groups in British society, and to British governments at times it was a serious diplomatic problem. The decade following 1848 was a difficult period in these matters for the British governments, with the Orsini affair as the high point.[13] In the years which followed, including the aftermath of the Paris Commune, public and populist opinion remained unchanged, and mostly relaxed. It was the swelling tide of Jewish immigration from Eastern Europe, and the worsening international situation that was the background to the Aliens' Act of 1905.

Historians of 1848 invariably make reference to the famous demonstration on London's Kennington Common on 10 April 1848, underline its quite extraordinary impact on public opinion throughout the country, including the removal of the Royal Family from London to the Isle of Wight, and then record its complete failure. And that usually is all, although there will sometimes be a reference to the unrest in Ireland which, like the revolutionary movements on the Continent, were almost all to fail by the autumn of 1848.

What is too often omitted in the accounts of 1848 in Britain is the fact that the Kennington Common meeting of 10 April was never intended to be anything but a demonstration to accompany the Charter with its great list of signatures to be delivered to the House of Commons. The panic which preceded 10 April was the product mainly of the media, the press largely aided by the pulpit, against the background of the revolutionary events in Europe. What is quite striking if you read the national and especially the provincial press – the latter much more important than in the twentieth century, with many towns having at least half a dozen local newspapers – is the solidarity of the middle classes with their aristocratic politicians.[14]

This was to be a crucial factor in the political alignments confronting the Chartist movement. The 1840s up to 1848 had been years of quite bitter dissension between the industrial middle class and the landed groups. The debates over factory legislation, the Corn Laws, the imposition of income tax and then its rise from seven pence in the pound to one shilling (12 pence) at the beginning of 1848): these were among the important issues dividing the propertied classes. The closing of their ranks, largely in reaction to the February events in France, was illustrated by the huge response to the call for special constables.[15] The editorial columns of almost all the national and local newspapers immediately reflected the fears now so widespread.

In certain of the older historical texts of this period it is sometimes suggested that the repressive forces available to the government in London were not especially effective, and earlier decades offer some evidence for this assessment. By 1848, however, the internal security forces on the mainland of Britain had gained much by way of practical experience. There had been two previous periods of intense Chartist agitation: the first 1839–40 in South Wales in particular, and the second in the Midlands and parts of Scotland in 1842. The experience gained of crowd control, and the collaboration between the military and the police forces had become well established and efficient in most areas by 1848.[16]

Lenin, whose understanding of revolutionary situations was not that of an innocent, always insisted that a prime factor in the achievement of revolutionary success was the disintegration of, or serious divisions among, the ruling party or groups.[17] On this important test it must be emphasised that in neither London nor Dublin was there the slightest evidence of any failure of morale among the leading political personalities. There was never doubt in anyone's mind that they were in the right. Reading the correspondence between government ministers offers clear evidence both of the recognition that the revolutionary events on the Continent could have serious consequences inside Britain, and especially in Ireland, and the understanding that the British government was in complete control of their own situation. It was understood that they must walk carefully and above all in England there must be no bloodshed. For twenty years after the Peterloo massacre of 1819, leading politicians would write to each other and often the quite commonly used phrase was 'Remember Peterloo'. During the early months of 1848 the importance of not shedding blood was quite often referred to. Ireland was, of course, different. The comment quoted below is one of many that could be given for that year. It is taken from a letter from Clarendon, the Irish Viceroy, to Sir George Grey, the Home Secretary, and written on 7 April 1848:

> There is so much loyal and good feeling in the Country, such mighty interests at stake, the circumstances of Europe are so grave, the future is so menacing, that I feel sure you will not appeal in vain to the 'Haves' in England against the 'Have-nots'. But this is not the time for stickling about constitutional forms or party consistency.[18]

The press were wholeheartedly on the side of vigorous action. Even more important was the attitude of the senior figures in the legal administration. There had been occasions in the decades after 1789 when the legal system had failed the authorities, mainly, it should be noted, through the jury system – which is why, of course, great trouble was always taken in Ireland that juries were of right-minded citizens; that is, most Catholics had to be excluded. (It was a practice known as 'packing' the jury.) In the 1790s and the 1830s, the two decades especially to be noted, there are well-known examples of juries in England absolving defendants put on trial by the government. But not in 1848. There is not one example of a jury throwing out the prosecution's case against any Chartist prisoner. More important perhaps: there is not one example of any of the eight senior judges offering the slightest criticism of the prosecution's case against the Chartists being sentenced; and all repeated in legal language their strong and unequivocal support of government action.[19]

Ernest Jones was arrested in early June and charged with seditious behaviour and unlawful assembly. Along with him were five other prominent London Chartists and they were all found guilty. Jones was awarded two years. The Attorney-General prosecuted. Jones and his comrades were treated like common criminals, there being no difference within the English system between political offenders and ordinary criminals. According to the story which Jones often told of his experiences in prison, he was kept in solitary confinement, his only reading was the Bible, and he was punished for refusing to pick oakum.[20] Two of his comrades died in prison and one shortly after. It is worth noting that the Chartist trials in Scotland in this year were more humane than in England – their legal system was different – and in both countries it mostly depended upon the attitudes of the presiding judge or judges. The English system has always been biased against political dissidents but this is hardly unique among the nations.

There was never to be a potentially revolutionary situation in England during 1848. It was industrially a much more advanced economy than anywhere in Europe, and its middle class, allied with the powerful landlord class, presented a defence of property that had no parallel in Western and Central Europe. Russia, of course, was *sui generis*. Ireland had more potential given its virtual colonial status but in 1848 the aftermath of the famine, the emigration to the USA, and the relative political weakness of its home leadership all contributed to failure. And weakness in leadership in England was undoubtedly an important factor after the arrest of Ernest Jones, although the degree to which he would have adopted an uncompromising revolutionary stance is a debatable question.

'The Springtime of the Nations': the wonderful hopes and radical visions of a future society which the February days had articulated were to be rapidly disappointed, indeed overwhelmed by the conservative forces throughout Europe. The one immediate change was the elimination of serfdom throughout the Habsburg Empire, but by the end of 1849 almost all the crowned heads of Europe had returned, and France herself was soon again to have an emperor. The half-century which followed was, however, to witness remarkable changes in social and political structures. The rapid growth of industrial capitalism evidenced in Western and Central Europe by the spread of the railway network, was accompanied by the intensification of nationalist sentiment. The important moves towards the unification of Italy in the 1860s went alongside the massive growth in the economic power of Prussia. Germany emerged as the most powerful nation in Europe after the defeat of France in the Franco-Prussian war of the early 1870s. There came about a different balance of power within the continent of Europe which, in the quarter-century before 1914, began to alter the contours of world politics.[21] In his long Introduction of 1895 to Marx's *The Class Struggles in France, 1848–1850*, Friedrich Engels asked the following question of those turbulent days: 'Was there not every prospect then of turning the revolution of the minority into a revolution of the majority?' He went on to answer his own question:

> History has proved us, and all who thought like us, wrong. It has made it clear that the state of economic development on the Continent at that time was not, by a long way, ripe for the elimination of capitalist production; it has proved this by the economic revolution which, since 1848, has seized the whole of the Continent, and has caused big industry to take real root in France, Austria, Hungary, Poland, and recently, in Russia, while it has made Germany positively an industrial country of the first rank – all on a capitalist basis, which in the year 1848, therefore, still had great capacity for expansion.[22]

During the very early days of the Provisional Government in Paris Lamartine and the majority of his ministerial colleagues had rejected the demand by certain radical groups that the Red Flag should replace the traditional tricolour flag of France. The symbolism of their rejection was to be confirmed rather more conclusively, and certainly more speedily, than most contemporaries would have presumed, or hoped for.

Notes

1 The literature on the revolutions of 1848 is voluminous. There is an excellent listing of memoirs and contemporary reminiscences in the bibliography to Priscilla Robertson, *Revolutions of 1848. A Social History* (Princeton, NJ, 1952; reprint 1967). There are two classic essays by Karl Marx, *The Class Struggles in France, 1848–1850* and *The Eighteenth Brumaire of Louis Bonaparte*. There are various editions, with an Introduction by Engels to both in the later editions, of which the 1895 Introduction to *The Class Struggles* is the most important. 1848 has inevitably been much written about by French historians; see for a selec-

tion Georges Weill, *L éveil des nationalitiés et le mouvement libéral, 1815 – 1848* (Paris, 1930); idem., *Histoire du Parti Républicaine en France, 1814 – 1870* (Paris, 1928); Elie Halévy, 'English Public Opinion and the French Revolutions of the Nineteenth Century', in A. Colville and H. Temperley (eds), *Studies in Anglo-French History* (London, 1935); Jean Dautry, *1848 et la deuxieme république* (3rd edn, Paris, 1977) with a beautifully drawn map of the location of the barricades of June 1848 in the central districts of Paris (p. 166). Among other works, Roger Price, *The French Second Republique: A Social History* (London, 1972) offers a bibliographical addition to Robertson (above) and is especially helpful for periodical literature. The most useful account for Anglo-Saxon readers of the relations between England and the Continent is probably Lawrence C. Jennings, *France and Europe in 1848: A Study of French Foreign Affairs in Time of Crisis* (Oxford, 1973). The periodical literature is essential for a full understanding of the revolutions: for France the main journals in English are *French Historical Studies* and *French History*, and see, among others, *La Revue Française de Science Politique.*

2 J.A.S. Grenville, *Europe Reshaped,* 1848 – 1878, Part One (Sussex, 1976) provides a summary of European diplomacy, with Chapters VI and VII on the aftermath of the French and European revolutions.

3 Evelyn Ashley, *The Life and Correspondence of Henry John Temple, Viscount Palmerston, 1846 – 1865,* (London, 1876), 2 vols., II., p. 76. There is a note in Ashley which explains that 'regulus' is the pure metal left after melting. See also Jasper Ridley, *Lord Palmerston,* (London, I970), *passim.*

4 *Hansard,* 1850, CIX, 26 February – 26 March, Col. 548.

5 Richard Cobden, *The Three Panics: an Historical Episode* (3rd edn, London, 1862) reprinted in Vol. 2 of *The Political Writings of Richard Cobden* (London, 1903).

6 The Marquis of Normanby, *A Year of Revolution: From a Journal Kept in Paris in 1848,* 2 vols. (London, 1857). Publication of Normanby's *Journal* provoked Louis Blanc to write a furious critique: *1848. Historical Revolutions: inscribed to Lord Normanby* (London, 1858; reprint New York, 1971). Louis Blanc begins a Preface with a panegyric to the English principle of asylum to all foreign citizens, and then proceeds to criticise Normanby for a book which was 'teeming with errors'.

7 The Chartist delegation is reported in Public Record Office (PRO) FO 146/342, no. 162, 15 March 1848, and there is an account of the delegation's visit in the *Northern Star,* 18 March 1848. The Irish delegation's visit is discussed in correspondence between Palmerston and Normanby: FO 146/ 342 (18 March); FO 146 / 329, no. 17 (22 March); FO 146/ 1342 (1 April).

8 As noted in the text, it was the reference to the battle of Fontenoy, fought in May 1745, that especially angered Normanby. The role of the Irish in the battle has been a matter of historical dispute among English historians. For some quite remarkable differences of emphasis, which certainly must reside in political differences, see the examples in Note 90, p. 240, in John Saville, *1848: The British State and the Chartist Movement* (Cambridge, 1987).

9 Robertson, *Revolutions of 1848*, p. 38.

10 *The Letters of Queen Victoria* (ed. A. C. Benson and Viscount Esher, London, 1907), II, 29 February 1848. The published letters of Queen Victoria all illustrate the Queen's dislike of Palmerston. See also: H.C.F. Bell, *Lord Palmerston* (London, 1936), II, pp. 419 and 434 ff; B. Connell, *Regina v. Palmerston. The Correspondence between Queen Victoria and her Foreign and Prime Minister, 1837 – 1865* (London, 1962).

11 During the confused political and military situation in north Italy, Piedmont, under Charles Albert, was defeated by the Austrian Marshall Radetsky, on 24 July 1848, at Custozza. An armistice was concluded between Austria and Piedmont early in August 1848: Grenville, *Europe Reshaped*, Part 2.

12 The definitive text on British asylum in the nineteenth century is Bernard Porter, *The Refugee Question in Mid-Victorian Politics* (Cambridge, 1979).

13 Ibid., *The Refugee Question*, Ch. 6.

14 For a sensible statement of the old-fashioned interpretation of the Chartist and radical movements before 1850, E.L.Woodward, *The Age of Reform, 1815 -1870* (Oxford, 1938), Ch. 3; and for accounts which incorporate the considerable research of the past decades: James Epstein and Dorothy Thompson (eds), *The Chartist Experience: Studies in Working Class Radicalism and Culture, 1830 -1860* (London, 1982); Dorothy Thompson, *The Chartists* (Aldershot, 1984); Owen Ashton, Robert Fyson and Stephen Roberts (eds), *The Chartist Legacy* (Woolbridge, 1999).

15 For the striking response to the call for special constables all over England, following the February days in France, Saville, *1848: The British State, passim*. It should be noted that in previous years the answer to the summons for special constables had always been somewhat patchy in different areas of the country. The response was partly dependent upon the level of anticipated violence in the particular locality or region, partly on the record of the police or military in previous years. For an erudite and interesting analysis of the ordinary people of Paris by the summer of 1848, see Charles Tilly and Lynn H. Lees, 'The People of June 1848', in Roger Price (ed.), *Revolution and Reaction: 1848 and the Second French Republic* (London and New York, 1975).

16 The literature on public order is also considerable. The most useful and comprehensive introduction is still F. C. Mather, *Public Order in the Age of the* Chartists (Manchester, 1959). Among the periodical writing: O. Teichman, 'The Yeomanry as an Aid to Civil Power, 1795–1867', *Journal of Social Army History Research*, 19 (1940), pp. 75–91; L. Radzinowicz, 'New Departures in Maintaining Public Order in the Face of Chartist Disturbances', *Cambridge Law Journal* (1960), pp. 51–80; R.D. Storch, 'The Policeman as Domestic Missionary: Urban Discipline and Popular Culture in Northern England, 1850–1880', *Journal of Social History*, 9/4 (Summer 1976), pp. 481–509.

17 N. Lenin, *State and Revolution* (various editions). For a lively introduction, the essays in Robin Blackburn (ed.), *Revolution and Class Struggle: A Reader in Marxist Politics* (Hassocks, 1977).

18 7 April 1848: *Clarendon Papers*, Letter Book, Vol. 2, Bodleian Library.

19 Saville, *1848: The British State,* Ch. 6.

20 Ernest Jones published a summary of his prison and other experiences in a pamphlet in 1868: *Ernest Jones. Who is He? What Has He Done?*, the substantial details of which had been spoken about or printed many times. See John Saville, *Ernest Jones. Chartist* (London, 1952). Dr Miles Taylor, Lecturer in Modern History, Kings College, University of London, is undertaking research for a biography of Ernest Jones, and evidently there is much in Jones's own accounts, especially of his prison experiences, that has to be seriously revised.

21 Eric J. Hobsbawm, *The Age of Capital: 1848 – 1875* (London, 1975), *passim.*

22 Karl Marx, *The Class Struggles in France, 1848 to 1850* (Moscow, 1952), p. 19 of the Introduction by Engels.

3

British Exceptionalism in Perspective:
Political Asylum in Continental Europe

Andreas Fahrmeir

In late April 1848, the Bavarian Ministry of the Interior learned that the British parliament was debating an Aliens' Bill. The ministry was sufficiently concerned by this to enquire 'if and how many of the Bavarian subjects present in England will return to the fatherland, which routes they will use and whether they are likely to be supplied with the necessary funds for travel.'[1]

It is not quite clear what prompted this interest: the sense of responsibility a paternalistic state felt for its subjects, fear of a sudden influx of people who had acquired British ways and might make the domestic situation yet more volatile, or the desire to prepare for additional expenses in good time. In any case, the reply from London, dispatched on 8 May 1848, was reassuring. According to the Bavarian minister, the bill merely authorised the government to deport 'such individual foreigners, who plan to foment unrest, or whose actions give rise to suspicions of such aims. Thus, in so far as Bavarian citizens keep quiet, they can reside unhindered in England now as before, and I do not hear of a single one of them who would have to fear deportation.'[2] In Munich, the Ministry of the Interior remained to be convinced. On 24 May, it closed the file with the remark that it would have to be seen whether Britain would expel Bavarian subjects.[3] As it turned out, the Bavarian Embassy was right, and the Ministry of the Interior was wrong: the 1848 Aliens' Act[4] did not lead to a single deportation.[5]

This episode demonstrates that in the early months of 1848, it was by no means clear that Britain would become one of the main countries of long-term residence for the refugees displaced by the failure of the European revolutions of 1848, besides the United States of America. At this time, Britain was still primarily fulfilling her more traditional role of welcoming conservative politicians, such as Metternich or Louis-Philippe, fleeing countries where revolution appeared to triumph. In fact, Britain became the ideal country of asylum in Europe not only because of the liberal attitudes of her politicians, but also because the more attractive alternatives which had hitherto existed diappeared one by one.

In order to describe the history of political asylum in Europe in the first half of the nineteenth century, it is necessary to address the question of who is entitled to be considered a 'political refugee'. The term is notoriously difficult to define. It can cover people who flee punishment for the expression of political opinions or for political acts; those who fear discrimination or prosecution for their opinions without being political activists; those who wish to leave the oppressive atmosphere of their native countries and live abroad, possibly intending to further the overthrow of the government of their native state from a distance; or even those whose ability to make a living is curtailed by a difficult economic situation caused by political uncertainty.[6] There will probably be considerable disagreement about which actions can be considered political and which are simply 'criminal': for instance, shoplifting could always be justified as a protest against an oppressive economic order, whereas tyrannicide can be classified as murder. In the final analysis, the definition depends to a large extent on the time and place under consideration. For practical purposes, however, political refugees are people who commit acts or subscribe to opinions which are considered criminal in their own country, but held to be legal (or even laudable) in the country which considers them refugees.

In the light of this very pragmatic definition, a country can become an ideal place of exile for several reasons. It can provide political asylum, that is to say, undertake to protect refugees from prosecution by their native state by allowing them to remain and possibly by supporting them economically. As people who leave their homes because of their political opinions are unlikely to abandon their goals as soon as they leave, it is obviously a great advantage if the country of exile allows them to continue their political activities without hindrance.

As refugees are, first and foremost, foreigners desiring to live abroad, they are subject to ordinary immigration laws, controls and restrictions. An ideal place of refuge can thus also simply have a very generous immigration policy. In particular, it is important that the host country does not limit the residence of foreign paupers; otherwise, only refugees of independent means, or those who can find private charity to support them, could feel safe. It is even better if the host country also provides financial support for resident foreign nationals. After 1826, Britain was the only country to fulfil the latter condition. No other country – not even the USA – allowed all foreigners to immigrate freely into her territory in the nineteenth century. All states granted permission for certain individuals to immigrate according to more or less explicit and systematic rules.[7]

However, almost all European countries had granted temporary or permanent political asylum to some individuals between 1789 and 1848. After 1789, the French émigrés had been allowed to migrate to German states such as Baden,[8] the Archbishopric of Mainz,[9] or Austria.[10] When Napoleon demanded that Freiherr vom Stein be dismissed from Prussian service, he was welcomed by Austria and found a job in the Russian administration a few years later.[11] France in turn welcomed people with revolutionary sympathies, but not others. As article 120 of the 1793 constitution stated, the French people 'grants asylum to foreigners banished from their fatherland for the cause of liberty. It refuses it to tyrants.'[12] 'Political asylum' was thus a result of individual decisions by various governments to allow foreigners whose political persuasions they shared to enter and remain. There was no general definition of political refugees or of political asylum. Needless to say, there was also no bureaucracy which recognised and certified 'refugee status'.

At the time, Britain did not act differently from other European countries. The Aliens' Acts in force between 1793 and 1826 allowed the expulsion of foreigners. To be sure, according to the *Parliamentary Papers*, this happened only to 671 people between 1793 and 1823[13] – in addition to at least 1,700 cases in which the deportees had to be allowed to return because no other country was willing to accept them.[14] With few exceptions, deportations were ordered for political reasons,[15] with the result that Britain became predominantly a place of exile for anti-revolutionary refugees. Of course, it was not always easy to predict the development of refugees' political views, so that some decisions appear curious in retrospect. The Vicomte de Chateaubriand, whose main achievement so far had been an abortive attempt to discover a route across the United States in an ox-cart, was allowed to stay and contemplate the beauties of Westminster Abbey until Napoleon was prepared to give him a post in the diplomatic service.[16] Chateaubriand's later superior, Foreign Minister Talleyrand, by contrast, had been told to leave Britain soon after arriving there.[17]

After the end of the Napoleonic Wars, the acceptance of refugees continued to depend primarily on the political attitudes of the country they wished to enter. Moreover, the country in question had to be able and willing to resist demands by neighbouring states to return or expel refugees, a question not of ideology, but of power. When a radical Prussian colonel called Massenbach fled to the independent city-state of Frankfurt-on-Main in 1817, threatening to publish Prussian military secrets, it was clear that the Frankfurt senate had little choice but to turn him over to the Prussian authorities, however reluctant it might be to do so.[18] By contrast, larger states, or states which were assured of diplomatic backing, could allow themselves far greater liberties. This was true even within the German Confederation, where the Federal Diet managed to enforce a degree of cooperation in the pursuit and punishment of political offenders. In 1837, for instance, Prussia offered employment to the seven professors who had been dismissed from the University of Göttingen for what their monarch considered political insubordination.

In the 1830s, the status of political refugees appeared to improve somewhat, and some attempts at defining 'refugee status' were being made. The 8,000 to 10,000 people leaving Poland after the failure of the 1830 uprising[19] found that even conservative states felt obliged not to approve extradition for political offences. Even the likes of Prussia or Saxony were reluctant to turn over refugees to the country from which they had fled, if that country was Russia, the exiles included a substantial proportion of 'respectable' members of the higher ranks of society, and public opinion was predominantly on the refugees' side. However, this did not mean that most states had abandoned the idea of requesting or granting extradition for political reasons altogether. In fact, the obligation to extradite political offenders between the roughly forty states of the German Confederation was actually incorporated into the law of the Confederation in 1832.[20]

In Belgium and France, by contrast, the principle that extradition for political offences could not take place was either included in extradition law and treaties in the 1830s, or was declared to be a part of government policy.[21] Britain went one step further and refused to consider extradition treaties with countries other than the USA and France, because she feared that they could be abused for political purposes.[22]

But whereas Polish refugees were allowed to stay temporarily in the states adjacent to Poland, there was no intention of granting them permanent residence permits. After the Russian Tsar announced an amnesty, the pressure on the remaining refugees increased considerably. In fact, most of them had already decided to move further west, to France. Even though they were probably not entirely aware of what awaited them, they could hardly have made a better choice. France not only provided them with a safe haven, but also with financial assistance. The subsidy individual refugees received reflected, in the first instance, the recipients' social status, classed in one of five groups, each equivalent to a military rank. It was also influenced by personal circumstances such as age, infirmity, or the number of dependents, as well as by nationality – Polish refugees receiving higher payments than Italian or Spanish ones.[23]

Gérard Noiriel has argued convincingly that this French policy was neither due to a revolutionary tradition of asylum based on the 1793 constitution, nor an expression of some sort of revolutionary solidarity. Not even the memory of the Franco-Polish alliance in the Napoleonic Wars was decisive, though it played a part. The reason invoked most frequently in parliamentary debates was the monarchical tradition of hospitality. The demand for refugees to be treated generously found support not least among aristocratic deputies, some of whom still recalled their own days as 'proscrits' in exile. Finally, the French practice merely continued the treatment of refugees from Spain in the 1820s, who had been supported by Louis XVIII's governments in the name of Bourbon solidarity.[24]

French generosity doubtless raised refugees' expectations elsewhere. The complaints of exiles in London in the 1830s about the British government's refusal to grant them financial assistance, apart from that available in the poorhouse, are only understandable given the availability of state aid for refugees across the Channel.[25]

However, aid did not come without conditions. In the first place, individuals had to establish that they were indeed political (not economic) refugees of a sort the French government would wish to support. In the case of German refugees, for instance, the source for that information was as likely as not the government of their native state, which was unlikely to write favourable reports on political opponents in exile. In such cases, the chances of applications for relief being successful were extremely slim.[26] Moreover, in return for its generosity the French government expected conformity on the part of the refugees. They had to reside in the locations assigned to them – provincial towns, far away from Paris. They also had to desist from political activity. If they refused to do either, the subsidy would be withdrawn and expulsion would likely follow.

The strict surveillance of refugees in France was partly an attempt to avoid international complications of the sort which troubled

Switzerland around the same time. The political activities of the 'young Europe' and 'young Germany' groups were of sufficient concern to Switzerland's neighbours for them to demand action with increasing stringency. International pressure, in combination with growing Swiss doubts as to whether granting hospitality to political radicals was really so much of a good thing, proved successful in the long run: in 1836, for instance, some 130 foreign refugees, 110 of them German, twelve Italian and eight Polish were expelled from Switzerland.[27]

Even by the 1830s, therefore, Britain was the only European country to allow refugees to continue their political activities, although they would have to support themselves. But the British government does not appear to have accepted this situation with enthusiasm. On occasion, it did attempt to use the limited means available to it to discourage refugees from travelling to Britain, even if the British public approved of their causes. True, there were no restrictions on entry to Britain as such, and, once on British soil, foreigners had an absolute right to remain there.[28] The British Foreign Secretary for much of the period in question, Viscount Palmerston, was passionately opposed to the extradition of refugees for political offences.[29]

Yet, the following episode shows the limits of British generosity, and may explain the scepticism of the Bavarian Ministry of the Interior when it was told that the Aliens' Act was not designed to have much immediate effect. In spring 1833, the Saxon government was preparing to expel all Polish refugees who had not obtained or sought an amnesty from the Russian Tsar. Bavaria and Austria refused transit visas to such refugees, and Prussia was prepared to grant them only if they could obtain a British or French visa. In response to a request for instructions from the British minister in Dresden, Palmerston wrote that visas could not be issued 'to those Poles who, having no means of maintaining themselves here, would soon after they arrive [in Britain] find themselves in distress; nor to any whose character and conduct have not been entirely unobjectionable'[30] – difficult conditions for people involved in a revolution. In the end, after a few additional despatches had left Dresden for London, but no further guidance was forthcoming, the British minister decided to refuse a British visa to only one of the seven remaining applicants.[31]

Thus, on the eve of the 1848 revolution, refugees could reasonably expect that they would not be turned over to the countries from which they had fled, provided they did not remain within the

German Confederation. However, the right to reside in another country depended on a considerable degree of agreement between the refugees and the host countries' governments.

True, the extradition of political offenders was explicitly prohibited in the respective laws of Western European countries, but there were as yet few precedents which defined clearly which sorts of crimes were 'political'. Moreover, nothing prevented the extradition of political refugees for nonpolitical crimes: the formulas in extradition treaties merely stipulated that requests for the extradition of individuals for political offences could not be complied with, and that the fact that extradition had taken place was a valid defence against charges of a political nature.

Refugees were normally subject to the usual immigration rules. They had no right to enter foreign countries, particularly if they did not have money, and, except in Britain, their political activities could be curtailed at will by the police simply by refusing to renew residence permits. Indeed, immigration laws usually made the expulsion of foreigners who could not support themselves mandatory. From the point of view of governments, invoking such laws had the additional benefit of forcing refugees to depart without giving their cases an explicitly political dimension.[32] The sole concession was that until the 1870s paupers about to be expelled were allowed to choose which border they wanted to cross in Western European states, particularly in Belgium.[33] Whether they were allowed to cross the border they chose was, however, up to the state they wished to enter.

All things considered, for the 'flotsam of the revolution' of 1848/49 the prospects for finding a safe country of long-term residence in Europe were not particularly good. Whatever its long-term effects may have been, in the short term the revolution had been unsuccessful more or less across the board. In the majority of states, refugees faced governments who had just consolidated their power after surviving revolutionary upheavals or at least serious disturbances, and who were unlikely to regard the sort of political activists whom they blamed for their plight with much affection. Furthermore, in the course of 1848, all governments had tended to blame the machinations of evil foreigners for their problems.[34] This was perhaps particularly pronounced in German states, but it was the case elsewhere as well. The motive for passing the British Aliens' Act of 1848 was itself an exaggerated fear of subversive foreign influence. In addition, the revolution seemed to unleash pent-up anti-immigrant hostility in many states: the British government noted in 1848 that some 3,000 British labourers had been forced to flee across the Channel to escape xenophobic rioting in France.[35]

At first sight, the most welcoming destinations for refugees were France, Switzerland and Belgium. They were relatively close to the scenes of revolutionary upheaval, which was ideal if one believed, as many of the refugees did, that the setbacks of 1849 were merely temporary and their period of exile would be short. Moreover, tradition indicated that these three countries would be relatively sympathetic to refugees. This turned out to be a miscalculation.

The French government was far less hospitable to the refugees of 1849 than it had been to those of the 1830s. Government assistance was not forthcoming; poor exiles were advised to join the Foreign Legion or offered one-way tickets to Belgium or Britain. Domestic developments in France made the political climate frostier for left-wing refugees in the course of 1849, and expulsions increased noticeably. Finally, France also narrowed the definition of political crimes, placing the refugees who remained in a state of uncertainty, if not outright peril. On 20 June 1849, Louis Napoleon assented to the extradition of six persons suspected of complicity in the murders of two members of the Frankfurt National Assembly, even though the two had been killed in the context of a political demonstration.[36] As Gérard Noiriel notes drily, under the Second Republic, France no longer welcomed refugees. On the contrary, the ministers concerned now suspected that applicants for asylum wished to avoid conscription or take advantage of France's public education system.[37]

With France adopting a restrictive asylum and immigration policy, pressure on smaller states, such as Belgium and Switzerland, was sure to increase. Switzerland had been generous in granting entry to persons fleeing Germany and other countries, and had supported them financially. However, the precedent of 1836, the expulsion of refugees who would not go home after an amnesty, or at least keep quiet, was soon repeated. This time, the Swiss authorities went further. In order to ensure that certain persons would not disturb the peace in Europe again, they offered to pay them one-way fares to the USA, as well as some pocket-money. The money was to be handed over by Swiss representatives in France or Britain only when the refugees had actually boarded a ship to North America.[38] Belgium pursued a similar policy, but apparently without resorting to financial incentives in quite the same way. Refugees could stay only if they ceased to engage in political activity. Those who did not do so were expelled sooner or later.

Finding one country after another shutting its doors to them, those refugees who could not, or would not, accept one of the amnesties offered after 1849, and who did not wish to live under political supervision or abandon their political aims, had little choice but to take what had originally seemed like an unpalatable option: travel to countries which offered no financial assistance, and where most refugees could not expect to be welcomed enthusiastically, but which provided freedom from fear of extradition, which did not order expulsions, and which did not force them to take advantage of offers of free one-way tickets to the USA, even if they were available. There was only one country in Europe which met these conditions, and which is therefore the topic of this volume: Britain.

Notes

1 Bayerisches Hauptstaatsarchiv München (henceforth: HStAM), MA 28073, Ministry of the Interior to Foreign Ministry, 25 April 1848 ('ob und wie viele von den dermalen in England sich aufhaltenden bayerischen Unterthanen in das Vaterland zurückkehren, welche Reise-Routen sie einschlagen werden, und ob dieselben wohl mit den erforderlichen Reisemitteln versehen seyn dürften.').

2 HStAM, MA 28073, Bavarian Embassy, London, 8 May 1848 ('solche einzelnen Ausländer wegzuschicken, welche Unruhen anzustiften ... versuchen, oder aber sich durch ihr Betragen einer solchen Absicht verdächtig machen würden. In sofern also Bayerische Unterthanen sich ruhig verhalten dürfen sie jetzt wie früher in England ungehindert verbleiben, und ich höre auch von keinem einzigen derselben welcher weggewiesen zu werden befürchten sollte.').

3 HStAM, MA 28073, Ministry of the Interior to Foreign Ministry, 24 May 1848.

4 11 Vict, c. 20.

5 *Parliamentary Papers*, 1850, XXXIII, p. 227.

6 See, e.g., the recent definitions in Wolfram Siemann, 'Asyl, Exil und Emigration der 1848er', in Dieter Langewiesche (ed.), *Demokratiebewegung und Revolution 1847 bis 1849: Internationale Aspekte und europäische Verbindungen* (Karlsruhe, 1998), pp. 70–91, esp. pp. 73–6.

7 See, e. g., Andreas Fahrmeir, *Citizens and Aliens: Foreigners and the Law in Britain and the German States, c. 1789–1870* (Oxford and New York, 2000), Ch. 3; Frank Caestecker, 'Der Migrant', in Ute Frevert and Heinz-Gerhard Haupt (eds), *Der Mensch des 19. Jahrhunderts* (Frankfurt/Main, 1999), pp. 228–60, 366f.; idem., 'Migratiecontrole in Europa

gedurende 19de eeuw', in Jan Art and L. François (eds), *Docendo Discimus: Liber amicorum R. von Eeno* (Ghent, 1999), pp. 241–55.

8 Sabine Diezinger, *Französische Emigranten und Flüchtlinge in der Markgrafschaft Baden, 1789–1800* (Frankfurt/Main, 1991).

9 Wilhelm Wühr, 'Emigranten der französischen Revolution im Kurfürstentum Mainz', *Aschaffenburger Jahrbuch*, 2 (1955), pp. 61–97.

10 Helmut Gebhardt, *Die Grazer Polizei 1786–1850: Ein Beitrag zur Geschichte des österreichischen Sicherheitswesens im aufgeklärten Absolutismus und im Vormärz* (Graz, 1992), pp. 94f.

11 Hellmuth Rößler, *Reichsfreiherr vom Stein* (Göttingen, 1964), pp. 73f., 83.

12 'donne asile aux étrangers bannis de leur patrie pour la cause de la liberté. Il le refuse aux tyrans.'

13 *Parliamentary Papers* 1816, XIII, p. 281; *Parliamentary Papers* 1818, XVI, p. 205 (where it is, incidentally, incorrectly claimed that there were no deportations by Secretary of State's warrant in 1814); *Parliamentary Papers* 1824, XVI, p. 495.

14 *Parliamentary Papers* 1816, XIII, p. 281.

15 Deportations for economic reasons are mentioned in James Picciotto, *Sketches of Anglo-Jewish History* (London, 1956), pp. 212, 469.

16 François René Vicomte de Chateaubriand, *Mémoires d'Outre-Tombe*, ed. by Maurice Levaillant and Georges Moulinier (Paris, 1951), 2 vols, I, pp. 341–432.

17 Simon Schama, *Citizens: A Chronicle of the French Revolution* (London, 1989), p. 684.

18 Bernd Häußler, 'Der Geheimnisträger wähnte sich zu Unrecht in Sicherheit: die "Freie Stadt" Frankfurt, Preußen und die Massenbach-Affäre', *Frankfurter Allgemeine Zeitung*, 19 November 1992, p. 46; Heinrich von Treitschke, *Deutsche Geschichte im neunzehnten Jahrhundert* (6th edn., Leipzig, 1906), II, p. 410.

19 See e. g. Edmond Privat, *L'Europe et l'odyssée de la Pologne au XIXe siècle* (Paris, 1918); Annelise Gerecke, *Das deutsche Echo auf die polnische Erhebung von 1830* (Wiesbaden, 1964).

20 *Protokolle der deutschen Bundesversammlung* (1832), § 231, p. 953

21 Siemann, 'Asyl', p. 77; Herbert Reiter, *Politisches Asyl im 19. Jahrhundert: Die deutschen politischen Flüchtlinge des Vormärz und der Revolution von 1848/49 in Europa und den USA* (Berlin, 1992), pp. 28–33.

22 See Nicholas Adams, 'British Extradition Policy and the Problem of the Political Offender, 1842–1914' (PhD, Hull, 1989), and Fahrmeir, *Citizens*, Ch. 4.

23 Gérard Noiriel, *La tyrannie du national: le droit d'asile en Europe 1793–1993* (Paris, 1991), pp. 47f.

24 Ibid., pp. 38f.

25 Reiter, *Asyl*, pp. 118f.

26 Noiriel, *Tyrannie*, p. 72

27 Reiter, *Asyl*, pp. 104–111, esp. 110f.

28 Public Record Office London (PRO), HO 45/6849/1, Foreign Office to Home Office, 15 October 1859.

29 See e.g. PRO, London, FO 68/36, Francis Forbes to Viscount Palmerston, Dresden, 17 June 1833, no 24; Reiter, *Asyl*, p. 38.

30 PRO, London, FO 68/36, [Viscount Palmerston] to Francis Forbes, Foreign Office, 28 May 1833, no. 2, draft, cypher.

31 PRO, London, FO 68/36, Francis Forbes to Viscount Palmerston, Dresden, 23 September 1833, no. 38.

32 See, e.g., Sophie de Shaepdrijver, 'Vreemdlingen in *Villette*: de buitenlandse aanwezigkeit in het negentiende-eeuwe Brussel', in Hugo Soly and Alfons K. L. Thijs (eds), *Minderheden in Westeuropese steden (16de-20ste eeuw) / Minorities in Western European Cities (Sixteenth – Twentieth centuries)* (Brussels and Rome, 1995), pp. 115–34, at 127f.

33 On Belgian immigration policies see Frank Caestecker, *Alien Policy in Belgium, 1840–1940: The Creation of Guest Workers, Refugees and Illegal Immigrants* (New York, 2001).

34 Ilja Mieck, 'Ausländer und Immigranten in Berlin 1848', in Ilja Mieck, Horst Möller and Jürgen Voss (eds), *Paris und Berlin in der Revolution 1848 / Paris et Berlin dans la révolution de 1848. Gemeinsames Kolloquium der Stadt Paris, der Historischen Kommission zu Berlin und des Deutschen Historischen Instituts (Paris, 23.-25. November 1992) / Colloque organisé par la Ville de Paris, l'Historische Kommission zu Berlin et l'Institut Historique Allemand (Paris du 23 au 25 novembre 1992)* (Sigmaringen, 1995), pp. 216–28.

35 PRO, London, HO 45/2166.

36 Reiter, *Asyl*, pp. 157–61.

37 Noiriel, *Tyrannie*, pp. 56, 69.

38 Reiter, *Asyl*, p. 223.

4

The Asylum of Nations:
Britain and the Refugees of 1848

Bernard Porter

Every civilised people on the face of the earth must be fully aware that this country is the asylum of nations, and that it will defend the asylum to the last ounce of its treasure, and the last drop of its blood.[1]

Times change. That proud boast could not be made today. Britain is one of the least generous of European nations towards those seeking political asylum on her shores. Generally she locks them up, before sending the majority of them back to where they came from. Most are presumed to be 'bogus'. That means they are only pretending to be victims of oppression; in reality they are just greedy for the better standard of life that Britain is believed to offer. Why that should be regarded so reprehensibly by a culture that almost fetishises material self-improvement in every other circumstance seems curious, but there it is. 'Refugees' have become the new populist scapegoat of the British political right and the tabloid press. But, as *The Times* quotation that heads this chapter indicates, it was not ever thus. In the middle of the nineteenth century, refugees from continental Europe's civil and national struggles were not always loved by their hosts. But they were always tolerated, never expected to prove their political credentials, and never – ever – sent back.

This was, broadly speaking, why they came. It was not – usually – because they liked the place. Some hated it. Letters home by exiles record all manner of unhappiness and resentments. Some refugees put their disapproval of everything around them into books, the most notorious of which at this time was Alexandre Ledru-Rollin's *De la décadence de l'Angleterre*, which he wrote just a few weeks after fleeing there, and which was widely resented by the English, understandably, as a classic instance of 'biting the hand that feeds...'[2] Many exiles only went there after other, more congenial refuges had turfed them out. This was especially true of the 1848 influx. Britain was very much a last resort, therefore. But it was also the *best*. The reason for that was that the right of asylum there was not a privilege, to be *granted*, by a liberal Home Secretary, say, but just as capable therefore of being withheld or withdrawn; but an absolute, automatic *right*.

That right was not enshrined in law. It was stronger than that. Quite simply, British governments could not prevent refugees entering the country, or extradite them when they were there, because there were no laws that would empower them to do so. And because in Britain people's freedoms at that time were secured by the *absence* rather than the presence of laws – 'With us,' wrote one contemporary, 'everything is lawful that the law does not prohibit', in contrast to certain continental countries where 'the maxim appears to be, that nothing is lawful but what law permits'[3] – that was the end of the matter. This it was that made Britain so peculiarly secure a refuge for political refugees during most of the nineteenth century; or, indeed, for any foreigner who wished to visit or settle there, for any reason at all, including self-improvement.

In retrospect this appears remarkable. Not many modern nations have deliberately eschewed the right to control who lives within their frontiers. And these particular refugees, it should be remembered, were particularly fiery ones. In this they differed from earlier waves of exiles to Britain – the Huguenots, for example – and from those who encamped to the USA. If they went on there it generally meant they had given up the struggle at home. They had shaded into the rather different category of *immigrants*. Britain's refugees had not. One of the attractions of England to them was that it was *near*. It was a temporary expedient, like a footballer stepping into touch for repairs. That made them the more dangerous. Many contemporaries – especially continental conservatives – could scarcely believe that Britain *could* tolerate them. On several occasions in the nineteenth century European governments demanded the return of their exiled dissidents, clearly under the illusion that Britain could comply. When she did not, they sometimes suspected that it was because Britain *wanted* them there, plotting against Britain's enemies themselves subversively. One French propagandist blamed the entire 1848 revolutionary movement on Britain, working through the refugees. Her own immunity proved it. If you want to know the identity of an incendiary, he wrote, look to see whose house is still standing.[4] When it finally dawned on the continentals that Britain *could* not expel the revolutionaries, they

predicted dire consequences for her. Eventually the diseases that she
was harbouring would infect her too. Predictions of this could be quite
circumstantial. Foreigners were behind the Kennington Common
Chartist demonstration of 10 April 1848.[5] Continental socialists were
conspiring with American Catholics to put a communist on the Papal
throne.[6] Karl Marx was plotting to murder Queen Victoria.[7] French
revolutionaries were planning to turn the opening of the Great Exhibition of 1851 into the first fusillade of the British revolution. (Because
it was held in Hyde Park, some of them had devised the cunning plan
of disguising themselves as trees.)[8] There seems to be quite genuine
puzzlement in many of the friendly warnings that came to London
from foreign offices and police ministries abroad in the wake of the
1848 revolutions. How could Britain be so cavalier with her own
domestic security? Could it really be so?

Was it really so? Of course, there are one or two caveats that need
to be made to the cloudless picture of an absolute right of asylum
painted here so far. The 'Royal prerogative' is one. The monarch was
supposed to have a residual right, stretching back to the Dark Ages,
to expel people if he or she wanted, which in modern times could
be transferred to government ministers. Some contemporary legalists
argued this. But then in that sense the monarch had the right to do
many things. Whether this translated into a practical power was
doubtful. In normal circumstances it certainly did not. Using the
prerogative in this way would have provoked a constitutional crisis,
possibly even rebellion. In 1858 a government fell for attempting
much less than this: not expelling anyone but launching a prosecution in an English court against a refugee who was implicated in the
Orsini bomb plot against Napoleon III.[9] Maybe it was comforting for
governments to know that the prerogative was there, buried under
all the centuries of precedent, if the refugees in Britain so misbe-
haved as to alienate the native population entirely from them: if Karl
Marx, for example, *had* killed the Queen. But it would have needed
something as shocking as that. Secondly: there were extradition
treaties with one or two countries, including France, which in principle enabled Britain to surrender immigrants for trial in their own
countries for crimes committed there. The problems with that were,
firstly, that there were so few extradition treaties at this date;
secondly, that it was very difficult to activate them, largely because
British magistrates did not trust foreign courts to treat the extradi-
tees fairly (only one extradition application was successful in the
French treaty's first ten years);[10] and thirdly, that 'political' crimes,

which were deemed to include politically *motivated* crimes, like assassination, were exempted in any case. So extradition treaties were particularly impotent against refugees.

Thirdly, there was the 1848 Alien Act. This is a quite serious caveat. It really did allow the government to expel newly arrived (only) foreigners, if a minister had 'Reason to believe, from Information given to him... in Writing, by any Person subscribing his or her Name and Address thereto' that they threatened the 'Peace and Tranquillity of any Part of this Realm'.[11] It was passed easily by both Houses of Parliament in April-May 1848, as the result of a temporary panic about all the Frenchmen who were suddenly appearing in London at that time. The Home Secretary, Sir George Grey, was less panic-stricken than some, but even he felt that 'we have a right to protect ourselves against foreigners – to prevent foreigners interfering with us – taking upon themselves to be the apostles of [republican] principles, and coming to us as propagandists.'[12] It was part and parcel of a number of defensive measures that reveal, as John Saville has shown, the steel that lay behind the Whig government's otherwise apparently laid-back response to the revolutionary threat of 1848.[13] On the other hand, it was hedged around with safeguards: the right of a refugee to know the accusation against him, right of appeal to the Privy Council with facilities for summoning witnesses, and so on. This was far more than Britain's present-day legislation gives them; and it was never actually *used*. No refugee was refused entry or expelled under it. The 1848 Act lapsed, as it was intended to, in 1850.

Thereafter governments had to resort to more informal means to counter the refugee 'threat'. This is the fourth caveat that needs to be applied to the notion of 'absolute' asylum in the middle of the nineteenth century, but it is really a very trivial one. The refugees were *policed*; but only mildly. Around 1850 a separate little detective department in Scotland Yard was set up to keep a watch on them. Its head was a man called John Hitchens Sanders, whose main purpose, certainly his main contribution, was to reassure the government, and through it, foreign governments, that the refugees were not up to very much harm.[14] He was rather protective of the refugees, therefore, than the reverse. (They had far more to fear from their own police spies.) He was also used to tempt some of the Hungarians to move on to America, by offering them free passages and money for clean suits so that the Americans would let them in;[15] and on one occasion to expel a number of particularly violent Frenchmen from the island of Jersey. (Jersey had its own laws, which made this possible, but not their removal back to France. Most of them simply decamped to London or even Guernsey.)[16] The reason for this, it should be noted, was not any particular fear of the refugees on Britain's part, but the embarrassment they were causing to her diplomatic relations with Austria and France. That was, of course, a particularly sensitive matter at the time of the Jersey expulsions: in the middle of the Crimean War.

It is arguable that these exceptions do not alter the general picture very much. They show that there were some apprehensions beneath the surface of British politics, and a preparedness to act less liberally if the situation ever arose; but overall the virginity of Britain's asylum policy remained pretty well intact. (By this metaphor the 1848 Act could be regarded as a marriage with tyranny that was never consummated.) The next question, then – and the main one to be discussed in this chapter – is *why*? How was Britain able to remain so chaste? And why did she bother to?

✱✱✱

One canard must be shot down at the start. There is no evidence, or even sign, that British governments deliberately cultivated foreign revolutionaries in order to undermine their neighbours. That was a paranoid delusion. Nor did Britons even particularly *like* them. Some they did like, hugely; the most celebrated examples are Lajos Kossuth and Giuseppe Garibaldi, who both made triumphal progresses through England in 1851 and 1864 respectively, to the great embarrassment of the governments of the day, again for foreign policy reasons; but they were both fêted not as refugees (neither came with the intention of settling there), but as freedom fighters whose heroic reputations and adventures had gone before them.[17] There were some other genuine refugees who were welcomed by select sections of the indigenous population: Italian *literati*, for example, who could always be sure of a flattering reception among the 'Holland House' set of aristocratic Whigs; Polish counts whom Lord Dudley Stuart especially cultivated; the Hungarians who were looked after by the radical capitalist Joseph Cowen in Newcastle upon Tyne; and the Germans – Schapper, Engels, Marx – who were taken up by George William Harney and his extreme Chartists. But even taken all altogether these made up a small minority.

Most of the refugees in England were ignored or despised. Very few Britons could be found to befriend the French, especially after

Ledru-Rollin's slap in the face (Louis Blanc may have been an exception).[18] The zealous and violent ones of all nationalities were very generally reviled. Popular stereotypes saw the French as excitable, the Germans as dirty, the Italians as underhand, and the Poles as somewhat promiscuous revolutionaries, joining in other people's revolutions not on principle but just for the fun of it, rather like football hooligans. All poor refugees were seen as what today would be called 'scroungers', unwilling to earn an honest penny, preferring to beg or even rob instead.[19] There were a number of quite notorious criminal refugees, at least one of whom, the multiple murderer Emmanuel Barthélemy, ended up in Madame Tussaud's Chamber of Horrors after his execution. (This was after he had stabbed two Englishmen to death in 1854. The previous year he had shot a fellow refugee in Egham, but was let off on that occasion by a judge on the grounds that, being French, he probably did not realise that you were not allowed to kill people in England.)[20] Lastly, it must be borne in mind that the vast majority of ordinary British people probably never came across a refugee during the whole of their very restricted lives, knowingly at any rate, and had _no_ opinions about them to speak of. The same considerations that made Britain's refugees temporary residents only – their continued activism – also took away any incentive for them to mix with their hosts. Usually they lived in ghettos, nearly all in the Leicester Square area of London, protected by political and social life-support systems of their own. So _that_ was not why they were tolerated. It would be more likely to have the opposite effect.

The reason why they were _claimed_ to be tolerated was on principle. However inconvenient it might be to have all these dirty, lazy, immoral, hirsute, pipe-smoking, garlic-smelling firebrands in England, it was better than enacting oppressive laws to keep them out. Such laws might prevent some small harms, but they could also be abused: by foreign tyrannies to tighten the noose around the necks of noble patriots, for example, and by frightened domestic governments to block the spread of new ideas. Any restrictions on the choice of people to travel and live where they liked were, quite simply, illiberal. They would need to be justified by overwhelming necessity, which it was difficult to imagine short of war. In Victorian Britain – apart from that little wobble in April 1848 – that necessity was not thought to arise. Generally speaking the presence of foreign revolutionaries in Britain was not believed to pose any domestic danger at all. The reason for this, and the second element in the 'principled' or liberal rationale for absolute asylum at the time, lay in Britain's current political and economic situation. She was a 'free' country. Free countries were impervious to harm by revolutionaries and other conspirators. As Palmerston picturesquely put it in April 1852:

> A single spark will explode a powder magazine, and a blazing torch will burn out harmless on a turnpike road. If a country be in a state of suppressed internal discontent, a very slight indication may augment that discontent, and produce an explosion; but if the country be well governed, and the people be contented, then letters and proclamations from unhappy refugees will be as harmless as the torch upon the turnpike road.[21]

The implication of that, of course, was not only that Britain – the turnpike road – was safe from conflagration, but that continental conflagrations were the Continent's – the powder magazines' – own fault. So her neighbours could not blame Britain even if their revolutionaries *were* plotting against them from the safety of her shores. If they had been free too, they could not have been harmed. We have seen already that there is no evidence of Britain deliberately using the refugees to subvert foreign countries; but there can be little doubt that people like Palmerston took some pleasure, or at least consolation, in using them to *embarrass* them. They were an effective weapon in his patriotic armoury, at least among his own constituency, who revelled in this pungent mix of radicalism and xenophobia.

Palmerston probably believed all this. It is true that he took a more vigorous line over the refugees in 1848, and was the prime minister who was toppled in 1858 for seeking to strengthen the laws against them; but most of his animus against them arose, again, from his diplomatic concerns, and even in the eye of the 1848 storm – those few weeks in the spring when the Chartists, encouraged by events in Paris, were massing for their last great lunge against the establishment – he was confident that the authorities could cope. '[T]he Constables Regular and Special', he wrote to his minister in Paris the day after the Kennington Common rally of April 10, 'had sworn to make an example of any whiskered & bearded Rioter whom they might meet with, and I am convinced would have mashed them to jelly.' 'Whiskered and bearded' at that time is code for 'foreign'. (The English were clean-shaven). So it was just as well that they never showed up.[22] Most other Britons appear to have shared his confidence. After April 1848, certainly, they felt Britain to be uniquely secure among

European Countries, their sense of safety enormously bolstered by the fiasco, or presented fiasco, of Kennington Common. Their reception of the refugees has to be seen in that light. No longer were they a menace; instead they were walking proof, every one of them, of Britain's superiority and consequent resilience. The wilder they were, the worse they behaved, the more trouble they caused, the more risible they appeared – the more they underlined that superiority, and Britain's magnanimity in putting up with them. If they were not wild, did not cause trouble, and the rest of it, that too indicated Britain's superior political virtue: her genius in being able to tame these beasts.

What is interesting, and surely significant, is how many of the refugees themselves went along with this. Engels famously wrote (in 1844) that 'England is undeniably the freest, in other words the least unfree, country in the world'.[23] Johanna Kinkel in a letter home of 1854 drew the same inference as the British from this: their political freedoms, and the fact that 'The Police hinder no one in the development of his talents', meant that 'people here are not bitter and angry'.[24] Consequently they were not combustible. Even Marx gave up trying to combust them after a while. That too seemed to bear out the British analysis: that in England there was simply nothing for them to work on. This may have been the refugees' main significance to the British themselves, in fact: to boost their national *amour propre*.[25] That may have had material repercussions. After 1848 the myth grew rapidly, and became almost an essential ingredient of her national self-image, that she was a peculiarly and inherently stable polity, due to her 'liberty', which, as 1848 showed, doused even the hottest firebrands coming from abroad. That became a difficult myth to argue against, and consequently to counter in any practical way. If it was not true originally, in 1848, belief in it made it so.

✳✳✳

But of course there were other reasons why the refugees were not thought to pose a threat to Britain in the years after 1848. One is that they did not *try* to. Most of them, even the promiscuous Poles, were really only interested in liberating their own countries, and not the British working classes, who they thought, quite reasonably, should take responsibility for themselves. There are almost no examples of refugees taking any significant active part in British radical politics at any time before the 1880s. (The main exception is Major Bartolomei Beniowski, who helped with the Newport rising of 1839.)[26] Some were apparently deterred by their assumption that the British government would turf them out if they did get involved, even though this was untrue.[27] In 1848, of course, that briefly became a quite reasonable fear, and consequently possibly a real deterrent. There is evidence that refugee leaders of all nationalities worked hard to curb their more violent followers, in order to avoid provoking the authorities into amending their asylum policy. When they suspected British police spies were present at meetings they launched into paeans of gratitude to the Queen and her ministers, and accusations against the 'wild men' of being foreign police *agents provocateurs*.[28] For their part the British authorities, not wishing to provoke their own liberal compatriots with anti-refugee measures, were happy to accept these assurances.[29] It was a kind of tacit bargain between the two sides, which owed less to British 'liberty' *per se* than to mutual fear of its being compromised.

The *kind* of liberty it was may also have had a bearing. It is well known, and we have seen already in connection with Britain's asylum 'laws', that it was a negative rather than a positive one. The ideal was that people should be left alone, rather than empowered. That of course left them free from state interference, like alien laws, but at the mercy of the market. Johanna Kinkel put her finger on this in her letter back to Germany of 1854; the English were wonderfully free politically, she wrote, and with a surprisingly tolerant police: 'But – one must work terribly hard here.'[30] Many of the refugees found this demoralising. 'The life here', wrote Alexander Herzen, 'like the air here, is bad for the weak, for the frail, for one who seeks welcome, sympathy, attention; the moral lungs here must be as strong as the physical lungs, whose task it is to separate oxygen from the smoky fog.'[31] Most refugees had to struggle just to stay alive. Many of the chapters in this volume confirm this. Some of them, as Fabrice Bensimon shows, suspected the British government of deliberately starving them,[32] but that was no more justified than the charge from the other side that it actively encouraged them.

In truth, it was the free market system that was starving them. Earlier in the century, before the full rigours of 'political economy' took hold in Britain, monies had been periodically voted by parliament for distressed Polish, Spanish and even French refugees; but they petered out in mid-century, were only for old stagers not new arrivals, and in any case were never as generous as the monies the French, for example, paid to their Poles.[33] Private charity was never sufficient. Even with his fees for journalism and Engels's generous patronage, Marx lived in squalor for his first few years in London.[34] Dudley Stuart's famous 'Polish balls', an annual society charity dance for the Poles' relief, could only aid a fraction of them. Others were reduced to stealing umbrellas from his anteroom while his butler's back was turned.[35] The more democratic refugees were the worst off of all, with only the support of the working classes, who could not afford – or did not want to – even Stuart's scale of munificence. When Harney tried to organise a fund for them in 1852 he raised only £69 11s. in a year, too little even to be divided among the various committees that took care of the separate nationalities; which convinced him, probably rightly, 'of the absolute indifference of the great mass of the British people to the claims of the political exiles'.[36] It may also have marked what several refugees saw as the Englishman's criminalisation, almost, of poverty;[37] at least among able-bodied men, who if they could 'find no employment ... in this busy hive of industry', as *The Times* put it in October 1850, were 'unworthy of compassion'.[38] It was a hard world: a terrible one for those who were reduced to begging and stealing, but difficult even for the lucky ones who managed to find work. No wonder so few of them stayed in Britain – just a few thousand in the early 1850s, according to police estimates[39] – despite her theoretical tolerance.

This must also, surely, go some way to explaining their political emasculation after they arrived in England, and consequently Britain's *ability* to tolerate them. It was not just the hard work and poverty that ground them down, but the whole materialistic culture of Britain: the emphasis on the practical, and the disregard of the kind of woolly theorising which, it was thought, lay behind the most ludicrous revolutionary schemes. This is what Herzen meant by his description of the moral 'fog' he found in England. It may have been a far more effective prophylactic against the spread of such doctrines than the Victorians' much more vaunted 'liberty'.

That was certainly the view of some perceptive Britons at the time. An example is a Scot called Samuel Laing, who was typical in many ways. He was a radical businessman, and *also* an author, which was an unusual combination in mid-nineteenth century Britain: businessmen usually had better things to do with their lives than engaging in intellectual pursuits. On the other hand, he is probably more representative of contemporary British culture than many intellectuals. He was not in Britain when the European revolutions broke out, as it happened, but, quite fortuitously, on a tour of Germany.

(In a sense he was a refugee the other way: one of mainland Britain's more characteristic kind, escaping from the tyranny of the market rather than of the state. His business had just been ruined, and he found it cheaper to live abroad.) He was in the real eye of the storm. And he thought he saw there the whole root of the trouble. Germans, he wrote in an account of his observations he published in 1850, had too much leisure. They worked fewer hours, and at a lazier pace. The middle classes among them also began work, serious, practical work, that is, much later in life than in Britain, wasting their early years being turned into 'philosophers, theorists [and] dreamers' by 'men of speculative ... minds, professors, scholars', while their English contemporaries, without any serious universities to go to, were forced 'from their sixteenth year, in[to] the counting-house, warehouse, or workshop, giving their minds entirely to their trade or business, thinking of nothing else, and strangers to philosophy, literature, or refined accomplishments'. Too much thinking, thought Laing, was 'dangerous to the state'. As proof of this he cited specifically the Frankfurt parliament, 'composed', he wrote, 'of philosophers, men of high literary reputation for profound learning and talent', who none the less 'made a very sorry figure in 1848'. In Britain by contrast, 'in our free and competition-driven social state, the young man has far less spare time, and far more important and manly occupations for the little time he has to spare'. That stopped him from going wrong.[40] It also stopped the Frankfurt philosophers from going wrong any *longer* when they fled to England, and found they too had to buckle down to useful tasks. That may be why they were, from a British point of view, 'safe' there. It was not so much the *freedom* as the *discipline* that the market system imposed.

Notes

1 *The Times*, 28 February 1853, p. 4.

2 It was immediately translated into English as *The Decline of England* (London, 1850), and met with universal ostracism. Alexander Herzen's *My Past and Thoughts* (New York, 1968 edn.), vol. III, is another critical account. See also Ivan Pfaff's contribution to this volume (Chapter 9), on the Czechs' inability to adjust to the English lifestyle.

3 Samuel Laing, *A Tour in Sweden in 1838* (London, 1839), p. 89.

4 Charles de Bussy, *Les Conspirateurs en Angleterre, 1848–1858* (Paris, 1858), pp. 2, 35, 178. For further examples see Bernard Porter, *The Refugee Question in Mid-Victorian Politics* (Cambridge, 1979), pp. 47–50, 84–5.

5 See for example Mrs Hardcastle (ed.), *Life of John, Lord Campbell* (London, 1881), II, p. 236.

6 Cutting from *New York Herald*, 29 March 1851 in Public Record Office (hereafter cited as PRO) HO 45/3518A.

7 See Robert Payne, *Marx* (London, 1968), pp. 234–40.

8 See Forbes' (British minister in Dresden) despatch to Palmerston, 23 April 1851, copy in PRO HO 45/3518; Bloomfield (St Petersburg) to Palmerston, 19 February 1851, PRO FO 65/391; Magenis (Vienna) to Palmerston, 6 April 1851, PRO FO 7/389. Alarmism was not confined to foreigners. A letter to the police from one 'G. Graham, aeronaut', dated 8 April 1851, gives a lurid account of a plot to use the cover of the Exhibition to overthrow the government, by refugees abetted by Catholic priests. The police were sceptical, sensing an ulterior motive behind it: Graham had recently patented an anti-riot shield: PRO MEPO 2/43.

9 This affair is dealt with in detail in Porter, *The Refugee Question*, Ch. 6.

10 Information given to Parliament, 8 June 1852: *Hansard's Parliamentary Debates*, 3rd series, vol. 122, c. 193.

11 11 & 12 Vict. c.20.

12 Grey in House of Commons, 17 April 1848: *Hansard*, 3rd series, vol. 98, c. 560.

13 John Saville, *1848: The British State and the Chartist Movement* (Cambridge, 1987), p. 127.

14 See Porter, *Refugee Question*, pp. 151–61 *et passim*, and idem., *Plots and Paranoia: A History of Political Espionage in Britain, 1790–1988* (London, 1989), pp. 91–5.

15 PRO MEPO 2/43 is the Police file on this.

16 See Porter, *Refugee Question*, pp. 163–7.

17 Enthusiasm for Kossuth and Garibaldi waned the longer they stayed. Sabine Freitag's chapter in this volume shows that exactly the same happened to Kossuth when he moved on to America (Chapter 11).

18 See Fabrice Bensimon's contribution to this volume (Chapter 6).

19 For refugee petty crimes, see Porter, *Refugee Question*, p. 43, fn. 125.

20 See *The Times*, 22 March 1853, p. 7; 7 December 1854, p. 10; 5 January 1855 p. 9; 11 January 1855 p. 9; 17 January 1855, p. 10; 23 January 1855, p. 8; and Charles Hugo, *Les Hommes d'Exil* (Paris, 1875), pp. 30, 38–42.

21 Palmerston in House of Commons, 1 April 1852: *Hansard*, 3rd series, vol. 119, cc. 511–12.

22 Palmerston to Normanby (private), 11 April 1848, in Palmerston Papers, GC/NO f. 474.

23 Quoted in Rosemary Ashton, *Little Germany: Exile and Asylum in Victorian England* (Oxford, 1986), p. xii.

24 Ibid.

25 Alexander Herzen later charged that England 'maintained its right of asylum for the sake of its own self-respect, and not for the sake of those who sought it': Herzen, *My Past and Thoughts*, III, p. 1052.

26 See Henry Weisser, *British Working-Class Movements and Europe, 1815–48* (Manchester, 1975), pp. 101–3.

27 See Herzen, *My Past and Thoughts*, III, p. 1121; Alvin R. Calman, *Ledru-Rollin après 1848 et les proscrits français en Angleterre* (Paris, 1921), pp. 185–6; and Sylvie Aprile's chapter in this volume (Chapter 10).

28 See for example Police Reports of 1 November 1851, in PRO HO 45/3518, and 25 January 1852, in PRO HO 45/4302; and Chapter 10 in this volume.

29 See Porter, *Refugee Question*, p. 157.

30 Ashton, *Little Germany*, p. xii.

31 Herzen, *My Past and Thoughts*, III, p. 1025.

32 See Chapter 6 in this volume.

33 The Polish grant started in 1834: see *Hansard*, 2nd series, vol. 22, cc. 659 *et passim*. The financial details can be gleaned from a Treasury Return of 1841 reproduced in the Irish University Press reprint of British Parliamentary Papers, *Emigration*, vol. 20, p. 436; and from almost annual debates and questions noted in *Hansard*. Earlier there had been grants to those fleeing from the French revolutionary terror: M. Wilmot, *The French Exiles* (London, 1960), pp. 223–5; and for the relief of American loyalists after 1814: *Hansard*, 1st series, vol. 30 (1815), Appendix, p. lix.

34 Ashton, *Little Germany*, p. 22.

35 See the police court reports of the cases of Racibuski, twice arrested for this offence, in *The Times*, 26 March 1851, p. 8, and 17 January 1852, p. 7.

36 *Reynolds's Newspaper*, 8 August 1852, p. 13 and 14 May 1853, p. 9.

37 See Ugo Foscolo in 1823: 'The English are a humane people, but will have nothing to do with one who wants bread', quoted in 'Anglomane' [Anthony Gallenga], 'Foscolo and English hospitality', *Fraser's Magazine*, vol. 31 (April 1845); and (later) Alexander Herzen: 'The Englishman has no special love for foreigners, still less for exiles, whom he regards as guilty of poverty, a vice he does not forgive': Herzen, *My Past and Thoughts*, III, p. 1112.

38 *The Times*, 28 October 1850, p. 4. The situation was probably similar,
   or worse for them, in America. At the conference which gave rise to
   this volume I remember an American contributor seeming genuinely
   puzzled that more of the 48-ers who went to the United States did not
   set up investment banks.
39 This is based on the policeman Sanders's estimates, the fullest of which,
   dated 19 March 1853, is in PRO HO 45/4816. These may not be reliable. But again they must have reassured his superiors. Without some
   kind of count the refugee numbers would almost certainly have been
   exaggerated.
40 Samuel Laing, *Observations on the Social and Political State of the European People in 1848 and 1849* (London, 1850), pp. 200–3, 352.

II

Emigré Communities

5

Italian Exiles and British Politics before and after 1848*

Maurizio Isabella

"You will not then be dissuaded from returning to Naples, Belmonte," said the dark Englishman at last, after a silence of some minutes:" Yet to what avail? There are lives and liberties enough in peril without adding yours."

"Yet I must go," replied Belmonte, "I can bear this life no longer: idle, aimless, a useless cumberer of a foreign soil, it were better to die at once than thus to live."

"To die! Yes, it might be so," said Mowbray earnestly, "but not to waste your life in the prisons of Naples. To live, if life it can be called, cut off from the land of the living – that would be an existence a thousandfold more useless, more hopeless, than yours is here."

"So be it," said the Italian while his eyes flashed with a sudden light, "so be it, Yet, must I go – though it be to prison or to death, I will meet them on my native soil, My heart yearns to breathe once more the air of Italy, even if it be just to look on her blue heaven, and to die." He paused.

A sudden moisture dimmed the eyes of Mowbray, whilst a look of the sympathy that sought not, nor needed words, passed between the younger Italian and the other Englishman.

C.G. Hamilton, *The Exiles of Italy, Edinburgh*[1]

I

Most of the extensive scholarship devoted to exiles in *Risorgimento* historiography was traditionally confined to describing the biographical details of the exiles, heroes condemned to live far from their homeland, but none the less struggling for the independence of Italy, the main goal of their existence. This approach was directly influenced by the patriotic literature the exiles themselves had produced since the 1830s. Poems like Pietro Giannone's *L'esule*, memoirs and biographies of exiles such as Giuseppe Pecchio, Carlo Beolchi, Guglielmo Pepe or, after the unification, Giuseppe Mazzini and Giovanni Arrivabene, contributed to the link between patriotism and exile in the readers' imagination.[2] It was above all with Atto Vannucci's widely read *I martiri della libertà italiana dal 1794 al 1848* that exiles acquired a central role in the Italian *Risorgimento*. Vannucci compared Italian patriots to the Christian martyrs in language borrowed from popular religious literature, and pointed explicitly to exile as one of the previous generation's sacrifices for the fatherland, alongside imprisonment and death.[3] The Piedmontese patriot Santorre di Santarosa, who had died in 1825 in Greece, where he had gone to fight for independence after living in exile in England, provided an early Romantic example of this martyrdom for freedom.[4] In line with this tradition, Italian historians long studied exiles from an exclusively Italian perspective, and attached little importance to foreign influences. The relations that existed between Italian exiles and the British political scene was for a long time a relatively neglected field of research.[5] It was only in 1954 that the need for a different approach was established by Alessandro Galante Garrone and Franco Venturi. These two historians recognised that the exiles themselves had played a primary role in discussing foreign political models, in assimilating and spreading progressive ideas which were thus absorbed into Italian culture. Likewise, European intellectual elites and political circles outside the peninsula became aware of the existence of an Italian question.[6]

The purpose of this chapter is to show how the exiles' direct observation of British political institutions, society, and its economy, the most advanced in Europe, stimulated debates about the features of the Italian nation. Vice versa, the British were faced with a national discourse which helped define their own identity as a political community. The study of the Italian exile community in Britain can therefore contribute to our understanding of the processes leading to the definition of both the Italian and British national identities, and cast some light on the development of political ideas in both countries.[7]

In attempting to assess the contribution made by the exiles to the development of Anglo-Italian political and intellectual relations, the moderate and the democratic refugees who made up the exile communities will be discussed separately. The liberal exiles who came to England after the uprisings of 1821, 1832 and 1848 managed to develop the closest contacts with the British establishment and contributed at a very early stage to shaping British politicians' understanding of the 'Italian question'. For this reason we have to go back to the first and second wave of Italian exiles if we wish to understand the context in which the Whig-liberal British political elite gave 'moral support' and sympathy to the cause of Italian patriots. The early waves of Italian exiles were mainly made up of men of letters and conservative aristocrats, members of secret societies who in 1821, 1831 and 1848 had called for administrative reforms and constitutional charters in Turin, Milan, Naples and the Central Provinces of the Papal State. It should be noted that, in reality, especially until 1848, a certain degree of ideological fluidity characterised the political positions held by exiles, who were often divided on grounds of personal friendship or dislike rather than along 'party' lines. In the 1830s and 1840s some exiles who had gone to England as Mazzinians abandoned their republican allegiances to espouse British constitutionalism. One such case, for instance, was the Piedmontese Antonio Gallenga who, an exile in London from 1839 and once a fervent admirer of Mazzini, in 1848 came to adopt moderate political views and looked to the British parliamentary system as a model for a federal and independent Italy.[8] In a number of cases moderate *Carbonari*, on the other hand, were attracted by the magnetic personality of Mazzini and by his ideas after he settled in London in 1837.

The roots of the extraordinary and almost unique popularity of the Italian cause in England are to be identified in the literary, romantic dimension of the British interest in Italy. This was influenced by travel literature, the writings of Byron and Shelley, and the passion for Italian language and literature, which were linked to an admiration for a glorious cultural and civic past and concern for the contemporary scenario of decadence and political oppression.[9] The success of the campaign waged by the exiles to promote their programme was facilitated by the fact that most of them were men of letters who shared the same Romantic culture as the British aristocratic circles to which they had easy access, and literati friends such as Samuel Rogers and Charles MacFarlane.[10] Most of the moderate exiles ended up teaching Italian literature either privately or in public institutions.[11] The study and teaching of Italian literature enabled the exiles to reaffirm their political programme, as for them literature and patriotism went hand in hand.[12] The slant which the famous Dante scholar Gabriele Rossetti gave to his interpretation of the *Commedia*, whose *Commento* he published in London in 1826, reflected the politics of the Carbonari. Rossetti implicitly drew a parallel between his generation of exiled patriots and the poet: member of a secret society, exiled, a passionate lover of freedom.[13] Antonio Gallenga, in his *Italy, Past and Present*, published in 1848, presented a similar national interpretation of Dante, and added a long survey of the writers of the day which highlighted the moral allegiance to the nation displayed in their historical novels, essays and patriotic poems.[14]

The most popular patriotic Italian book in England was probably Silvio Pellico's *Le mie prigioni*, republished in London by the Piedmontese immigrant Pietro Rolandi, whose London bookshop made Italian literary works available to both British readers and Italian exiles from 1826 to 1863.[15] Pellico's political effectiveness and immense popularity stemmed from the convincing contrast between the brutality of the Austrians' behaviour and the author's religious sensibility, shaped according to a model of piety centred on Christ which appealed to Anglicans and Nonconformists alike. *Le mie prigioni* become paradigmatic in the construction of the anti-Austrian Black Legend. Andryane's *Memoirs* (based on the author's imprisonment, translated into English by the Piedmontese exile Fortunato Prandi with Sarah Austin in 1841), as well as the numerous articles on Italian affairs published by the exiles in the British press, reinforced the anti-Austrian propaganda which focused on the cruelty and barbarity of the Austrian judicial system.[16] Henry Brougham's discussion of Austrian rule in Lombardy in his *Political Philosophy* provides a good example of how this rhetoric was adopted by Whig-liberal circles:

> The hateful rule of foreigners, whose language and manners are strange to them, is not by any means the only grievance of the Milanese. No man of a certain station is secure against the workings of private enmity or the caprices of an absolute court ... the Prisons of Silvio Pellico would remain as a memento of the deeds done by arbitrary power in what is deemed its mildest exercise.[17]

Although Brougham conceded that Austrian administration had been far better than that of its predecessor, the Spanish government, and rightly claimed that after the Restoration, Austrian rule was still the mildest in the Italian peninsula, he reaffirmed the Whigs' belief that only a written constitution could properly defend the rights of citizens against the abuses of government, a conviction shared with the Italian liberal circle.[18]

Exile gave the moderates a chance to gain first-hand experience of the workings of the British political system, idealised by the Italian liberal elites after 1815. After the Restoration Italian liberals were generally anglophile: the British constitution, in fact, appeared to be the one that would best satisfy the demands of the liberal aristocrats to govern their countries and more generally to defend the interests of the propertied classes. Between the 1820s and 1840s, the exiles published several political pamphlets with proposals for a federal constitution for northern Italy, or for constitutional reform in Naples. In most cases, the model proposed for Italy was based on the British system.[19] Although in the 1820s the exiles cooperated and developed close contacts with members of Bentham's circle such as John Bowring, Edward Blaquiere and Leicester Stanhope, there is no evidence of Bentham's influence in their constitutional proposals (as was the case in many of the Spanish exiles' constitutional plans). Indeed, their understanding of the British constitutional model was more often influenced by the writings of Constant, Mme de Staël, Guizot and the doctrinaires. Generally speaking, they seemed to approve of the 1832 reform and would have agreed that the most obvious flaws of the constitution had to be redressed.[20] Nevertheless the exiles, who read Macaulay's and Henry Hallam's constitutional histories, tended to provide an enthusiastic and uncritical account of English political life and institutions, as opposed to Austrian or Bourbon rule in Italy. Giuseppe Pecchio's *Un'elezione di membri del parlamento in Inghilterra*, and *Osservazioni semi-serie di un esule sull'Inghilterra*, (significantly republished in Rome in 1848 during the liberal government), offered the Italian public a vivid description of English political life and institutions which, according to the author, fostered civic virtues and patriotism in the same way that republican life had done in the Italian medieval cities.[21]

British commercial society was widely criticised in Italy by the moderates on account of the dangerous effects of mechanisation, which they predicted would lead to even greater inequality in the distribution of wealth and hence trigger social unrest. Life in England, however, affected the exiles' appraisal of the impact of economic growth on society. Pecchio and Gallenga, in fact, praised the English model of development based on mechanisation, industrial development, international trade and increasing opportunities for all sectors of society to improve their material conditions. Giuseppe Pecchio's *L'anno mille ottocento ventisei dell'Inghilterra*, published soon after the 1826 commercial crisis, provided a convincingly optimistic analysis of the functioning of an advanced commercial society which, in spite of temporary setbacks, managed to reconcile freedom and productivity, and guaranteed a better standard of living for the majority of the population. Pecchio was convinced that the Italians had to take the British socioeconomic example as a model in successive generations, though he conceded that the unique characteristics of Italian society, climate and stage of development might require some alternative strategies in order to reach similar results.[22]

In the context of these discussions the definition of Italian national character emerged by comparison with the English one. Indeed, in the wake of Montesquieu, Pecchio maintained that the English were active, abstemious, industrious and good fathers thanks to the influence of their climate. Therefore while the English workers could sustain up to sixteen hours of work per day, Italians could not do more than eight. Pecchio, however, believed that the laziness typical of southern people could be addressed thanks to education and free political institutions, and Italians could regain the virtues of patriotism, modesty and industriousness they had possessed when citizens of the free medieval republics of Venice, Genoa and Florence, with independence. After all, in Pecchio's words, England was a new Florence. Italians, in order to regain their identity, had therefore to acquire some of the qualities typical of the citizens of contemporary England, and therefore to become more "British", but also had to revive those original republican virtues which they had lost after centuries of despotic rule.[23]

In his book *Italy, Past and Present*, Antonio Gallenga rejected Vincenzo Gioberti's idea of Italian primacy, presented in his *Del primato morale e civile*. This was based on the premiss of the superiority of the Italian social, economic and moral model, and depended on his belief in the supremacy of the Roman Catholic Church and its values. Gallenga felt that it was absurd to accept a principle which explicitly condemned the social and economic transformations taking place in Britain, while it was leading the world in material progress and technological innovations: 'ours is the age of coal, and Italy has not a lump of the precious material. Her people had not the least share in the world-upsetting inventions of the nineteenth-century.'[24]

II

As early as the 1820s, it was the Holland House circle which opened the doors of the Whig establishment and English politics to the Italian exiles. Through Henry, Lord Holland, in fact, the Italian exiles mixed with the other heirs of the Foxite tradition such as Lord John Russell, Sir James Mackintosh, and other intellectuals and politicians such as Henry Brougham, Macaulay, Horner, the editor of the *Edinburgh Review* and its journalists. Henry Holland was undoubtedly the English politician who most readily shared with the Italian exiles their anti-Austrian feelings. He justified his hatred of the despotic 'ultra-Metternich and Apostolick faction' above all by pointing to the way in which they ruled Lombardy and their influence on the Italian peninsula, considered as particularly backward.[25] The attraction between Holland House and the Italian exiles also depended on the fact that Whig aristocrats and Lombard, Piedmontese and Neapolitan liberal noblemen were part of the same liberal, upper-class cosmopolitan set, and they had already met in Milan, Florence and Geneva before 1821. Moderate Italian exiles shared the same political culture with them and, when the rise of the republican party in Italy in the 1830s in their view made revolutions dangerous and undesirable, they looked to the diplomatic pressure of English liberal governments to support their demands for reform. After all, even though they spoke as if the Italian nation actually existed, the moderates' demands for constitutional charters in the Italian states and their rejection of Mazzini's 'absurd' idea of national unification were compatible with the Whigs' support for gradual reform and local autonomy. The 1831 and 1848 revolutions provide good examples of how the exiles took advantage of this connection to promote the interests of the Italian liberal-conservative elites with the British government.

In 1831 and 1832, when Lord Holland and Lord Palmerston, at that time respectively Chancellor of the Duchy of Lancaster and Foreign Secretary, took an interest in the Italian peninsula and in the reform of the Papal State, it was the Lombard exile Giuseppe Pecchio who played a fundamental part as intermediary between the British government and those revolutionaries who had been responsible for the 1831 uprising in the *Legazioni*. An economist and a journalist for the most important liberal-Romantic Italian journal, the Milanese *Il Conciliatore*, the aristocratic Pecchio had settled in England in 1823 after leading the failed 'salon revolution' against the Austrians in 1821, organised with his circle of liberal friends.[26]

By 1831, Pecchio was a well-known writer and had become the most influential and best connected exile; the majority of Italian exiles living on the Continent looked up to him as the leading Italian figure in England.[27] In 1832, thanks to his contact with Lord Holland

and Lord Melbourne, he managed to obtain English citizenship.[28] Fully integrated as he was into upper-class society and married to a wealthy English lady, Pecchio had become more sceptical as to the possible success of any revolutionary plans during an unfavourable international situation.[29] In fact, in 1831 he refused to join any of the committees set up by exiles either in London or Paris – he was invited to become president of the London Committee – on the grounds that private action would prove more effective than public assemblies.[30] Unpublished documents in the Holland House papers reveal how successful Pecchio was in pursuing this discreet political strategy of informal diplomacy.

Pecchio's main concern initially was to convince Lord Holland, whose marginal role in the government did not prevent him from creating a 'parallel foreign policy' and interfering in Palmerston's affairs, that the revolutionaries in the Central Provinces, 'propriétaires et des classes les plus respectables', were very moderate.[31] Indeed, the Bolognese leaders demanded administrative reforms and were more concerned with security against popular unrest than with radical revolutionary plans.[32] Hopeful that the French government would prevent any intervention by Austria to crush the revolutionary government, Pecchio insisted to Lord Holland that the revolutionaries' wish to establish an Italian federation would contribute to strengthening the balance of power in Europe, by creating a northern Italian federation which would serve as a barrier between 'two eternal rivals' [Austria and France].[33]

Holland's reaction to Pecchio's request for support for the revolutionaries' plan was cautious and, in spite of his sympathy for the Italians, Holland reaffirmed the Whig belief in gradual institutional reform as opposed to revolution.[34] Lord Palmerston shared a similar view:

> in my heart and as an individual, I would rather see an independent state erected in Italy by a successful revolt against the Pope and the Austrians, than the restoration of precisely the old order of things by German bayonets. But it surely is of great importance to the general peace of Europe to prevent the French and Austrians from coming to blows in Italy.[35]

However, very much to Pecchio's satisfaction, the British government took part in the negotiations with the Austrian, French, Prussian and Russian diplomats in Rome. These led to a Memorandum containing suggestions for administrative and judicial reform, which was submitted to the newly elected Pope Gregory XVI. The Romagnoli were by then resigned to accepting Papal government on the condition that administrative changes were made. Unfortunately, the Papal government did not follow the Memorandum's recommendations, maintaining control by ecclesiastic hierarchy over public administration.[36] Yet Pecchio's action in favour of his friends in the *Legazioni* continued and even intensified. At the beginning of 1832, Pecchio made available to Holland and Palmerston two long *Mémoires* about the situation in the *Legazioni* which voiced the frustration of the liberals. The documents complained about the intervention by the Austrian government, and the failure of the Papal government to implement the reforms suggested in July 1831.[37]

The contacts between the British government and the Italian exiles were known in diplomatic circles and greatly worried Metternich.[38] At this point, Palmerston decided to intervene directly with the support of France, and sent the minister Seymour to Rome to persuade the Holy See to implement substantial changes in the administration. In March 1832, the British minister proposed to the Papal government a second Memorandum, whose content was based on suggestions made to Palmerston by the Romagnoli, thanks to Pecchio's mediation. Lord Palmerston commented to Holland:

> The heads of required improvements which are pointed out in Sig. Pecchio's letter will serve as useful hints to me in giving instructions to Seymour. But you know well that it would be impossible for us, for a great many good and substantial reasons to become guarantors of the improvements which the Pope may be persuaded to make.[39]

The Memorandum called for a general amnesty, the abolition of the Holy Inquisition, the secularisation of the administration and an independent judiciary, the establishment of lay Commercial and Provincial Councils to administer communes and Provinces, in addition to a Central Council in Rome.[40] This new diplomatic initiative was destined to fail in the face of opposition from Austria and the Holy See. None the less it represented a turning-point in British foreign policy towards the Papal state, which had for centuries been marked by abstention from any official contact, let alone any direct involvement in the Papacy's internal affairs.[41]

In the late 1830s and 1840s Antonio Panizzi took over from Pecchio, who died in 1835, as the point of reference in English political circles for Italian matters. An assistant librarian and, from 1837, Curator at the British Library, Panizzi also became a British citizen.[42] In 1848 and

1849, Antonio Panizzi became the most active exile in voicing the demands of the Lombard liberals to the British government. His activity in England must be seen in the context of the tensions between liberals and democrats which characterised the 1848 revolutions throughout the peninsula. Using the argument of the potentially destabilising effect of the republican movement, the Italian moderates tried to ensure the support of British diplomacy for constitutional regimes. Between April and May 1848, when the Lombard provisional government was racked by disputes between republicans and liberals, Panizzi urged Pompeo Litta and Giovanni Berchet to work for the prompt annexation of Lombardy to Piedmont, and to send an envoy to London. He also informed them that he had advised his English friends in the government to recognise the new Kingdom as the best move against any dangerous French republican influence in Italy.[43] As a matter of fact, in 1848 Palmerston seemed to favour the creation of a state of Northern Italy under the Piedmontese constitutional monarchy, which could become a useful buffer state between Austria and France, and advised Austria to withdraw from Lombardy. In May Palmerston refused to accept the Austrian offer of a separate constitution for Lombardy within the Empire as the basis for negotiation, and kept Panizzi informed of the government action in the mediation between Piedmont and Austria. Panizzi continued to work in favour of the Lombard moderates as their informal ambassador until the end of the war and the defeat of the revolutionary movement.[44]

The cause of the liberal government in Rome was promoted in London by another well-established exile, the poet and librettist Count Carlo Pepoli. Pepoli had first arrived in England in 1832 from Bologna, where he had been a member of the provisional commission which governed the city during the uprising. In London he married a woman from a wealthy British family, Elizabeth Fergus of Kirkcaldy, and taught Italian literature. In 1848 he left London for Rome to become a member of the newly established parliamentary assembly granted by Pius IX.[45] But by the beginning of 1849, with the crisis of the liberal regime in Rome, he was already back in London, where he was to spend the next ten years. Soon after his return Pepoli had a number of meetings with Palmerston in an attempt to save the already faltering constitutional regime in Rome, repudiated by the Pope, who had fled Rome, where he was threatened by the Republicans already gathering *en masse*, to take refuge in Gaeta. In a letter to Palmerston, to which he attached a confidential memorandum addressed by the Roman minister Muzzarelli to the Sardinian minister Gioberti, Pepoli asked the British minister to send a British agent to promote a reconciliation between the Pope and the liberal government, 'the only line of conduct by which the republican movement could be kept in check, life and property secured, and complete anarchy avoided'. Pepoli acknowledged with gratitude the interest shown by the British government in the Papal state in 1832 with the Memorandum, and in 1848 with Lord Minto's mission, and tried to convince Palmerston that there was still room for a compromise with the Pope, badly advised by reactionary cardinals who called for Austrian intervention.[46] However, the pressure exerted on Palmerston came too late and at a difficult political moment. After Lord Minto's mission to Turin, Florence and Rome, promoted to encourage the liberal parties and support constitutional regimes, Palmerston's priority had been to prevent any possible French or Austrian intervention in the Papal State until the beginning of 1849, when he became anxious that revolutionary forces might take control.[47] Indeed Pepoli's attempt to involve the British government in rescuing the liberal government while maintaining the Pope's authority, was overtaken by events: only two weeks later the Republic was proclaimed in Rome.[48]

It is undeniable that the moral support provided by Holland, Palmerston and Russell often left the liberal exiles dissatisfied, because their British friends' primary concern remained the maintenance of a European balance of power to offset the risk of a European war. Although their overall attitude did not change after 1849, in the 1850s the Whigs and Gladstone came to consider the Neapolitan and Papal administrations beyond reform, and the expulsion of Austria from Italy only a question of time.[49] The small community of liberal exiles who came to England after 1849, far fewer than in the 1820s and 1830s, continued to find sympathetic political supporters and friends in Palmerston, Russell and Gladstone. With Panizzi they constituted the 'Italian liberal monarchical party' in England, whose point of reference was the Sardinian minister D'Azeglio.[50] Panizzi and the Neapolitan James Lacaita were especially good friends of Gladstone – Lacaita and Gladstone first met during the latter's trip to Naples – and both contributed to his interest in political conditions in Naples, which resulted in the publication, in 1851, of his famous *Two Letters to the Earl of Aberdeen*. The letters, an uncompromising condemnation of Bourbon rule, attacked the inhuman conditions in which moderate intellectuals such as Poerio were detained in prison, and evoked a vast response not only in Britain but also in continental Europe, and marked Gladstone's conversion to liberalism. Lacaita became private secretary to Lord Lansdowne and to Gladstone, after his appointment in 1858 as Lord High Commissioner in the Ionian Islands. In the 1850s Panizzi and, to a lesser extent, Lacaita, continued to play a privileged intermediary role as exponent of the Piedmontese moderate party in London, and were used to this end by both Cavour and Russell, until the unification of Italy.[51]

III

The democrats dominated the Italian exile community after 1849. In 1851 the Italian community in London, concentrated in Holborn, numbered some 1,600 people. The majority of the Italian refugees and immigrants lived an obscure existence as artisans, cooks, waiters and organ grinders. Most of those who had left Italy for political reasons seemed to have come from Rome, the last republican city to capitulate, after a spell in Switzerland or France. The privilege of mixing with the upper classes and in middle-class political and intellectual circles was confined to the small group of exiles who enjoyed a similar social background.[52] In spite of the exiles' republicanism, the upper classes renewed the sympathy they had shown for the Italian revolutionaries after 1821 and 1832. On his arrival in London, Pisacane recalled that 'every lady wanted to give a party for us', and that 'the English aristocracy considers us men hostile to their party, but pays tribute to our intelligence.'[53] Similarly, despite their political differences, many moderate exiles were ready to support the newly arrived democrats – the Mazzinian Francesco Crispi, for instance, was helped by the liberal Scalia brothers, who, like him, were of Sicilian origin.[54] In general, however, the English republicans, radicals and Chartists represented the 'natural' social environment for the Italian democrats.

Mazzini, who returned to London in February 1851, was already well known in reformist and radical circles. His friendship with some of his most fervent admirers, such as William Linton, William Lovett, the Ashurst family and James Stansfeld, in fact dated back to his first period of exile, between 1837 and 1848.[55] Admittedly, during that period Mazzini's fame had been limited. It was only the scandal of the opening of his private letters in 1844 that made him a celebrity thanks to the extensive coverage the event received in the press.[56] This period was otherwise crucial for his intellectual and political development because of the lasting impression the Chartist movement made on him. Although Mazzini had condemned the violence of certain demonstrations, such as the Birmingham riots in 1839, he supported the Chartist programme and thought that given its deep social and economic inequalities, British society was in a pre-revolutionary state. He also admitted that had he been English, he would have liked to have been a leader of the extraparliamentary radical movement. It is no coincidence that at the end of the 1830s Mazzini decided to relaunch the *Giovine Italia* and open it up to the working classes, whose role in the development of a national movement he had neglected.[57]

Immediately before 1848, however, increasing interest in the national questions in Europe among Chartists and radicals greatly facilitated Mazzini's advocacy of his own ideas. This emphasis on internationalism was part of a new political strategy developed to counteract the weakening of their movement at home, which from the mid-1840s onwards had started to lose momentum.[58] In middle- and working-class radical circles these ideas of international brotherhood went hand in hand with the reaffirmation of the more traditional values of English radical patriotism, based on the virtues of the Puritan revolution, the English ancient liberties, popular sovereignty and the example of Cromwell's Commonwealth.[59] After 1849 Mazzini's political personality was appropriated by the supporters of radical politics and likened to that of national radical heroes like Milton or Cromwell. The republican experiment in Rome had contributed to making Mazzini a charismatic figure who embodied the virtues of the heroic revolutionary and the wise political leader, who possessed the moral rectitude of a spiritual father to whom people with different allegiances showed respect and devotion. As a consequence he became a political symbol used in rites marking the social events of radical circles and clubs in which they celebrated the anniversaries of the European revolutions and praised universal brotherhood. In 1849 Edward Truelove's son was given the name of Mazzini in a secular ceremony at the John Street Institution, and many more children were christened Mazzini in the aftermath of the Roman revolution, demonstrating that his fame had reached the most politicised sectors of the working classes.[60] The prestige he enjoyed explains why both moderate Chartists and republicans on the one hand, and socialist exiles on the other tried to demonstrate that Mazzini endorsed their political agenda and could be considered 'one of us'.[61] In spite of the criticism they levelled at some aspects of his political thought, whether it be its intense religiosity, its excessive nationalism, or its condemnation of Benthamite individualism and utilitarianism, political refugees of other nationalities and English radicals supported the Italian question and worked alongside him.[62] This was the case with one of his closest collaborators, the secularist George Holyoake, a propagandist of the co-operative movement. While disliking the religious element of Mazzini's message and dismissing his attacks on French socialism, Holyoake as editor of the *Leader* and the *Reasoner* published Mazzini's writings and in 1852 launched his 'Shilling Subscription in aid of European Freedom'.[63]

This process of 'appropriation' was in turn encouraged by the appeal that a number of aspects of Mazzini's thought held for radicals. The intense religious dimension of Mazzini's message, with its distinctive puritanical touch, was familiar to many radicals, whose culture was heavily influenced by Dissent. Mazzini's patriotism in fact was not only based on civic virtues and republican values, but stressed an austere morality and a sense of duty towards the community and the nation, as opposed to the mere assertion of personal rights, and the need for a moral regeneration in order to establish a fair society.[64] A large section of Mazzini's *Society of the Friends of Italy* was made up of Nonconformists or Unitarians.[65] For William Adams, Mazzini was 'the greatest teacher since Christ'.[66]

Furthermore, his programme contributed to the development in the 1850s of a new broad liberal platform which would continue to appeal to the middle and working classes throughout the era of Gladstone's liberalism. As Gregory Claeys suggests, after 1848 and the political defeat of Chartism, Mazzini played a central part in rallying the moderate Chartists around a republican and reformist programme. This rejected the socialist element acquired by Chartism in the 1840s and restored some of its more traditional concerns, namely an emphasis on local communities and a critique of central government control, as well as the importance attached to education and to republican values, as expounded in Mazzini's *Thoughts upon Democracy in Europe* and the *Duties of Man*.[67] Mazzini's repeated attacks in the press on French socialist exiles such as Louis Blanc, before the revolutions and after Napoleon's coup d'état in December 1851, helped to inhibit the spread of socialism in England. Mazzini in fact rejected the idea of class struggle while recognising the pressing social concerns of the working classes.[68] In the words of one enthusiastic supporter, William Adams from Cheltenham, Mazzini provided disillusioned or demoralised Chartists, especially those of the younger generation, with a new and appealing programme of moral regeneration:

> Chartism was not satisfying. We were Chartist and something more ...
> Higher aspirations entered our heads, suffused our thought, coloured our
> dreams. 'Happiness' we had been told, 'is a poor word. Find a better' ...
> We had found a programme, but we wanted a religion. It came to us
> from Italy.[69]

Later in life, Adams recalled that Mazzini's followers organised
weekly meetings in their homes, during which the works of revolutionary leaders were read, essays were debated, and national and
international projects were discussed.[70] The Chartist artisan and
wood engraver William Linton was probably Mazzini's most devoted
English follower. Linton's monthly *English Republic*, first published
in 1851, bore Mazzini's unmistakable hallmark. In the *English Republic* Linton placed the emphasis on universal suffrage. While stressing
the importance of solidarity among citizens and the need for some
social reform, he condemned the direct and 'dictatorial' intervention
of the state in the economy, which would violate individual liberty,
along with the social experiments of Fourier and Owen, and
embraced Mazzini's brand of nationalism. Mazzini's *Duties of Man*
were published in the pages of Linton's periodical. Linton's definition of the English nation owed much to both the radical tradition
and Mazzini's national idea.[71]

With Linton the republican Joseph Cowen, an industrialist from
Newcastle, became one of the most fervent supporters of Mazzini's
idea of virtue as a citizen's moral commitment to the community. In
1854, with the collaboration of Harney and Linton, he launched a new
monthly, the *Northern Tribune*, which fully endorsed Linton's Mazzinian brand of republicanism. In pure Mazzinian terms the *Northern
Tribune* said: 'Capital has its duties as well as its rights, and there
ought to be closer than a mere money-bond between masters and
men.'[72] Outside the Newcastle region, where Mazzini's following was
particularly strong, it was also possible to find occasional admirers of
his ideas in Wales and even in Ireland. In Belfast in 1856 the preacher
D. Maginnis committed himself to organising public meetings to raise
money for Mazzini's 'shilling collection'. Maginnis was in contact with
Linton and agreed with his political principles, although he believed
that a republic could only be established through the gradual enlightenment of the people. He organised Sunday evening lectures in his
chapel on 'Polities of Religion' to disseminate republican ideas and
advocate universal suffrage.[73] For his followers Mazzini's teachings
represented not a revolutionary but an educational programme to
establish a new morality and way of life.[74]

Mazzini's fundamental and personal contribution to the increasing popularity of the Italian cause in England was enhanced by his ability to mobilise and organise public opinion. Mazzini realised that the democrats had more to gain by seeking and campaigning for the direct support of a wide spectrum of the public than by developing selective contacts with government circles. This implied a rejection of the approach adopted by moderate exiles such as Pecchio, Panizzi and Pepoli. The establishment of the *Society of the Friends of Italy* in 1851 was in line with this strategy. Middle-class liberals, free traders, parliamentary reformers, radicals, intellectuals, Chartists, Dissenters and secularists were among the 800 members who joined the Society throughout the country.[75] In his first address to the *Friends*, Mazzini urged his audience to whip up support for the freedom and independence of Italy through letters, articles in the press and pamphlets, and with petitions which would put pressure on parliament. Mazzini believed that as Britain's mission in the world was to promote peace, prosperity and the principle of nationality, its government should act to enforce the principle of nonintervention in Italy, thus bringing to an end foreign influence (namely French and Austrian) over Italian politics.[76] Members of the *Society* like George Dawson, in turn, considered that the very principles of English patriotism – which he dated back to Cromwell's Protestant patriotism – called for the active support of the Italian national cause.[77] The *Society* produced material for propaganda and was successful in raising money and creating a network of representatives who organised public events in northern England and southern Scotland. Although its membership was quintessentially middleclass, Mazzini attached great importance to disseminating its publications among workers.[78] When the *Society* disbanded in 1853, following the failure of the Milan uprising which had temporarily weakened Mazzini's popularity, English Mazzinians such as James Stansfeld, William Ashurst and Joseph Cowen established a new organisation, the *Emancipation of Italy Fund Committee*, which was aimed at targeting the English working classes. The Genoese workers had, in fact, asked its founders to appeal to English workers for solidarity in their struggle for Italian freedom. Workers from Newcastle enthusiastically responded to the appeal. Mazzini proudly wrote that thanks to his activism in England, 'the people of Italy replaced an aristocracy whose memory dated back to the patrician emigration of 1821.'[79]

Undoubtedly, anti-Catholic prejudice worked in favour of the Italian cause in England.[80] In 1851, the appointment by the Pope of a Catholic

Hierarchy in England sparked a fierce reaction in public and reinforced the traditional English hostility towards the Papacy.[81] Not surprisingly, the foundation of Mazzini's *Friends of Italy* coincided with this event. For the Italian exiles as well as for English public opinion, religious and political regeneration in Italy was inextricably linked to the reform of the Catholic Church and the abolition of the temporal power of the Pope. In particular, the Evangelical Italian exiles contributed to popularising the image of the oppressive nature of the Papal government with its corrupting influence on Italians. The moral and spiritual message of their newspaper *L'eco di Savonarola*, which first appeared in London in 1847, combined the beliefs expressed by Mazzini in his *Duties of Man*, and the Bible. Its collaborators included the Mazzinian evangelicals Salvatore Ferretti, Camillo Mapei, and Filippo Pistrucci, director of Mazzini's School. The motto of the publication was a quotation from Savonarola: 'Italia renovabitur'.[82] One of the most famous exiles from the Roman republic, the Barnabite Father Alessandro Gavazzi, built his fame on the anti-Catholic lectures he delivered after 1851 in England, Wales and Scotland: violent attacks on the spiritual and temporal power of the Papacy, the role of monks, nuns and the Jesuits in Italian society, and the Holy Inquisition. These public addresses were attended by hundreds of people, including Palmerston and Russell.[83] In an article published in 1853 in the *Westminster Review*, Aurelio Saffi cited as evidence of Italy's moral and civil regeneration the unconvincing argument that Italy was no longer a Catholic country as the overwhelming majority of the population had freed itself from the negative influence of Catholic superstition and bigotry.[84] Saffi (like Gavazzi and Mazzini) did not, however, call for the establishment of a Protestant Church in Italy, but instead advocated a new form of religious expression in keeping with the Italian tradition of universal spirituality.

Among Mazzini's closest collaborators, who included exiles such as Maurizio Quadrio, Giacomo Medici and Federico Campanella, Aurelio Saffi certainly did the most to uphold the Italian cause and Mazzini's ideas in Britain. Saffi had been one of the *Triumviri* who led the government of the Roman Republic with Mazzini.[85] Between 1855 and 1856, he gave a series of public lectures on Dante and Machiavelli in Manchester. The following year he spoke about the Italian *Risorgimento* at a number of conferences in London, Edinburgh and Glasgow. Saffi's aim was not to explain to the public the 'Italian question' in the light of party politics, but to convince British public opinion that Italy's primary need was to gain independence from foreign rule; only after their emancipation should the Italian people choose the form of government they wished.[86] In Glasgow, where more than 1,600 people listened to him in the City Hall, Saffi noted with satisfaction that the audience included both the wealthy and the working classes. His speeches in Hawick and Paisley were received with such enthusiasm that in Hawick the crowd carried his carriage through the streets.[87] At Oxford, where from 1853 he taught Italian language and culture at the Taylor Institute, he introduced his students to the Mazzinian creed. Several of them, such as Frederic Harrison and James Bryce, later acknowledged this intellectual debt which had helped to shape their political views.[88]

In spite of Mazzini's 'hegemonic' influence among the Italian exiles, some Italian democrats who opposed Mazzini's revolutionary strategy for the unification of Italy promoted the Italian cause independently. Felice Orsini, a Mazzinian conspirator until 1854, came to believe that unification could be achieved only with the support of Piedmont. After escaping from Mantua prison in 1856, he settled in England, where his public lectures on the state of Italy brought him considerable popularity. In Birmingham and other smaller centres he persuaded his audience to send petitions to parliament condemning the occupation of the Papal State by foreign troops. The adventure-packed memoirs of his experience as a revolutionary and prisoner in the Austrian prisons, *The Austrian Dungeons of Italy*, which was published in London in 1856, sold 35,000 copies.[89]

For other patriots, exile represented a crucial intellectual experience, as thanks to their contacts with French émigrés and English Chartists in London, they came to embrace those social democratic ideals violently attacked by Mazzini. For them the condition of the working classes in England was evidence of the need for a more radical political programme than the one supported by Mazzini. Luigi Pianciani's journalistic activity represents an interesting example of the dissemination of socialist ideas among Italians in England. A former colonel in the republican army of Rome, Pianciani became, after 1851, increasingly critical of Mazzini's purely political approach to revolution, which alienated the working classes from the struggle against despotism. In 1854, he settled in Jersey, where he wrote extensively for the social democratic weekly *L'Homme*, which he edited between March 1854 and June 1856.[90] *L'Homme* included articles by Mazzini, Hugo, Herzen, Kossuth and Blanc, and Mazzini criticised its political orientation as eclectic and unfocused. Although he did not go so far as to commend the abolition of private property,

Pianciani believed that in a postrevolutionary and unified Italy, political reforms would have to be coupled with serious social reforms to enable the working classes to gain control of the means of production.

Another exile who went on to develop an original intellectual profile independently of Mazzini was Carlo Pisacane, one of the officers in charge of the defence of Milan and Rome during the revolutions.[91] While in England between November 1849 and June 1850, he seemed to have remained isolated from the Mazzinians. Instead, he mixed with English radical and democratic circles – as a guest of Mathilde Ashurst Biggs he met James Stansfeld and Jacob Holyoake – and benefited intellectually from these contacts. Thanks to his contacts with English radicals Pisacane discovered the works of Godwin, Owen, Malthus and Ricardo, and through Holyoake he met Louis Blanc. These experiences contributed to his conversion from republicanism to socialism. During his exile, observation of the condition of the working classes and of the social inequalities of English society, as well as of the political conditions on the island, reinforced his belief that a social revolution was badly needed.[92] Pisacane harshly criticised the British constitutional model, which he believed was instrumental in perpetuating the exploitation of the working classes, and dismissed Lord Russell as the 'coryphaeus of a hypercritical liberalism'.[93] He also devoted much of his time in London to writing his *Della Guerra Combattuta*, a reassessment of the events of the Roman Republic and of the reasons for the military defeat inflicted on the defence, in which he voiced his critique of Mazzini's programme. Pisacane was later to develop an analysis of capitalism which was influenced by the writings of Proudhon. It went so far as to question the very concept of property, proposing, as it did, a communist model of society.[94]

IV

Towards the end of the 1850s two events highlight how the Italian exiles continued to be the object of public attention. In 1858 the Orsini case provided tangible evidence of the relationship between the struggle against despotism in Europe and freedom in Great Britain. Orsini's attempt to murder Emperor Napoleon in Paris with the support of other exiles in England further increased his fame. The British government's attempt to pass the 'Conspiracy Bill', which would have weakened the rights of political refugees, and the imprisonment of Edward Truelove (accused of writing a pamphlet in favour of Orsini which condemned Napoleon's policy in Italy), threatened to undermine the right to free speech. The hostile reaction of middle- and working-class radicals imbued these events with great political significance nationally.[95]

Great public enthusiasm greeted the arrival in 1859 of the last group of political exiles to reach England, the sixty Neapolitan liberal and republican 'Forty-Eighters', released after almost ten years of imprisonment. The exiles were lionised by the Whig grandees and warmly welcomed by Mazzini's working-class supporters as living symbols of Bourbon despotism. *The Times* informed its readers about their arrival, and the *Illustrated News* published portraits of Poerio, Spaventa, Castromediano and Pica.[96] The contrasts between parties and individual exiles became apparent in the organisation of financial support for the Neapolitans. However, these differences did not seem to alter the public's perception of the Italian cause. By this stage the exiles had helped to make the Italian 'question' uncontroversial: it appealed to the English liberal upper classes because Austrian rule in Italy and the methods of government adopted by the Papal State and the Kingdom of Naples were considered unacceptable by their standards, and to the radical middle and working classes who could identify with the republican patriots' quest for independence and freedom. As Biagini suggests, the Italian *Risorgimento* was a perfect political cause for the English middle and working classes, providing, as it did, concrete examples of heroism (the defence of Rome in 1849) or exciting events (Orsini's adventurous life) to stir the imagination. Its success lay also in the fact that it did not introduce any element of class antagonism which might have challenged the social harmony underpinning English popular liberalism.[97] Indeed, the language used by exiles in public lectures and publications presented a consistent image of a homogeneous and cohesive nation struggling for freedom, which excluded any class tension, overrode the division between parties, between town and country, between cities, regions, north and south. In Mazzini's words: 'Twenty five million Italians writing the same language ... honouring the same national geniuses ... excited by the sacred tricolour national flag and by the holy and mysterious words of fatherland, Italy and Rome'.[98] The British could safely reaffirm their own national identity and political beliefs by supporting the Italian cause.

Notes

* I should like to thank Professor Derek Beales and Dr Eugenio Biagini for their helpful comments on earlier versions of this paper.

1 C.G. Hamilton, *The Exiles of Italy* (Edinburgh, 1857), p. 3. I am indebted to Dr Lucy Riall for kindly drawing my attention to this novel.

2 Pietro Giannone, *L'esule* (Paris, 1829, then Florence, 1868), Camillo Ugoni, *Vita e scritti di Giuseppe Pecchio* (Paris, 1836), Carlo Beolchi, *Reminiscenze dell'esilio* (1831), Guglielmo Pepe, *Memorie* (Lugano, 1847), Giuseppe Mazzini, *Note biografiche* (Milan, 1861), Giovanni Arrivabene, *Memorie della mia vita* (Florence, 1879).

3 Atto Vannucci's book was published in 1848 in Florence, then republished in Florence in 1860, in Leghorn in 1849 and Turin in 1850. The French translation appeared in Geneva in 1860. Similar texts are *Panteon dei Martiri della libertà* (Turin, 1852), and M. Ricciardi's *Martirologio italiano* (Florence, 1860). On this feature of the *Risorgimento* language see Alberto M. Banti, *La nazione del Risorgimento* (Turin, 2000), pp. 170–5; Cosimo Ceccuti, 'Le grandi biografie popolari nell'editoria italiana del secondo ottocento', *Il Risorgimento* 47 (1995), pp. 110–23.

4 See, for instance, Giuseppe Mazzini, 'Santa Rosa', *Apostolato Popolare*, 1 (10 November 1840), now in Mazzini, *Scritti editi e inediti*, 25 (Imola, 1916), pp. 33–7.

5 Emilia Morelli, *L'Inghilterra di Mazzini* (Rome, 1965); Margaret Wicks, *The Italian Exiles in London, 1816–1848* (Manchester, 1937); Harry W. Rudman, *Italian Nationalism and English Letters* (London, 1940).

6 Alessandro Galante Garrone, 'L'emigrazione politica italiana nel Risorgimento', *Rassegna Storica del Risorgimento* 41 (1954), pp. 223–42; Salvo Mastellone, *Storia ideologica d'Europa da Sieyès a Marx* (Florence, 1974), pp. 192–3. On exiles in London and Paris until 1845 see the excellent work of Franco Della Peruta, *Mazzini e i rivoluzionari italiani* (Milan, 1974). For an attempt to study early political emigration to England in an international context see also Maurizio Isabella, 'Gli esuli italiani in Inghilterra e il movimento liberale internazionale tra filellenismo e americanismo', *Annali della Fondazione Einaudi*, 28 (1994), pp. 413–65. A useful bibliography is in Maria Adelaide Fonzi Columba, 'L'emigrazione', *Bibliografia dell'età del Risorgimento* (Florence, 1972), pp. 425–69. A study on the relationship between exile and Italian nationalism can be found in Donna R. Gabaccia, 'Class, Exile, and Nationalism at Home and Abroad: The Italian Risorgimento', in Donna R. Gabaccia, and Fraser M. Ottanelli (eds), *Italian Workers in the World. Labour Migration and the Formation of Multiethnic States* (Champaign-Urbana, 2001). An original

assessment of the importance of post 1848 exile for the development of the Southern Question can be found in Marta Petrusewicz, *Come il Meridione divenne una Questione. Rappresentazioni del Sud prima e dopo il Quarantotto* (Catanzaro, 1998).

7 On nationalism see Benedict Anderson, *Imagined Communities: Reflections on the Origin and Spread of Nationalism* (London, 1991). On the Italian case see Banti, *La nazione del Risorgimento*; on England see Roberto Romani, *National Character and Public Spirit in Britain and France, 1750–1914* (Cambridge, 2002), and Margot Finn, *After Chartism: Class and Nation in English Radical Politics, 1848–1874* (Cambridge, 1993).

8 Tony Cerrutti, *Antonio Gallenga: An Italian Writer in Victorian England* (Oxford, 1974), p. 113.

9 Paul Ginsborg, 'Il mito del Risorgimento nel mondo britannico', *Il Risorgimento* 48 (1995), pp. 384–99; Charles Peter Brand, *Italy and the English Romantics* (Cambridge, 1957); Maura O'Connor, *The Romance of Italy and the English Imagination* (London, 1998).

10 Charles MacFarlane, *Reminiscences of a Literary Life* (London, 1917), p. 197.

11 Antonio Panizzi first taught at Liverpool before being appointed Professor at University College in London in 1828; Gabriele Rossetti became Professor at King's College in London; Evasio Radice taught at Trinity College, Dublin. (Wicks, *The Italian Exiles*, passim).

12 Giuseppe Pecchio wrote that literature was 'a powerful tool capable of defeating despotism.' Giuseppe Pecchio to Giuseppe Giglioli, 17 February 1833, in Costanza Giglioli Stocker, *Una famiglia di patrioti emiliani, i Giglioli di Brescello* (Milan / Genoa / Rome / Naples, 1935), p. 85.

13 Pompeo Giannantonio, *Gabriele Rossetti dantista*, in Gianni Oliva (ed.), *I Rossetti tra Italia e Inghilterra* (Rome, 1984), pp. 21–32.

14 Cerrutti, *Antonio Gallenga*, pp. 70–8; Aldo Garosci, *Antonio Gallenga: Vita avventurosa di un emigrato dell'Ottocento* (Turin, 1979, 2 vols), I, pp. 167–75.

15 Mario Nagari, *Pietro Rolandi da Quarona Valsesia, 1801–1863* (Novara, 1959).

16 See, for instance, Pecchio, *Qu'est que c'est l'Austrie?*, in Paolo Bernardelli (ed.), *Giuseppe Pecchio: Scritti Politici* (Rome, 1978), pp. 525–43, originally appeared in the *Edinburgh Review* (1824). This description of Austrian rule in Italy had a lasting influence on Italian historiography. For a reassessment of Austrian rule in Italy see David Laven, 'Law and Order in Habsburg Venetia, 1814–1835', *Historical Journal* 39 (1996), pp. 383–403.

17 Henry Brougham, *Political Philosophy* (1842–43, 2 vols), I, p. 679. Similar comments can be found in John Cam Hobhouse, *Italy: Remarks*

made in Several Visits from the Year 1816 to 1854 (London, 1859, 2 vols), I, pp. 9–13, II, p. 258.

18 Brougham, *Political Philosophy*, p. 662.

19 A useful list of these projects is in Franco della Peruta, *La federazione nel dibattito politico risorgimentale*, in idem, *Conservatori, liberali e democratici nel Risorgimento* (Milan, 1989), pp. 309–39. See also Carlo Ghisalberti, 'Il sistema costituzionale inglese nel pensiero politico risorgimentale', *Rassegna Storica del Risorgimento* 66 (1979), pp. 25–37. Among many examples of the British constitutional model applied to Italy see Francesco Romeo, *A Federative Constitution for Italy* (London, 1822); Giuseppe Pecchio, *Catechismo italiano* (Lugano, 1830), now in Bernardelli (ed.), *Scritti Politici*, pp. 547–66; Guglielmo Pepe, *L'Italie politique et ses rapports avec la France et l'Angleterre* (Paris, 1839).

20 On the constitutional ideas of the Spanish exiles in England see Vicente Llorens Castillo, *Liberales y Romanticos: Una emigracion espanola en Inglaterra, 1823–1834* (Mexico City, 1954). On the Italian exiles and Bentham's circle see Isabella, 'Gli esuli italiani in Inghilterra'. On the influence of French liberalism, Alessandro Galante Garrone, *L'albero della libertà: Dai giacobini a Garibaldi* (Florence, 1987), pp. 98–122.

21 Both published in Lugano, 1826 and 1831 respectively. Now both in *Scritti Politici*, pp. 229–75 and pp. 357–510.

22 *L'anno mille ottocento ventisei dell'Inghilterra* (Lugano, 1827), now in Bernardelli, *Scritti Politici*, pp. 279–354. An analysis of his political and economic ideas is contained in Maurizio Isabella, 'Una scienza dell'amor patrio: public economy, freedom and civilization in Giuseppe Pecchio's works (1827–1830)', *Journal of Modern Italian Studies* 4 (1999), pp. 157–83.

23 G.Pecchio, *Osservazioni semi-serie di un esule sull'Inghilterra*, (Lugano, 1831), now in Bernardelli, *Scritti Politici*, pp. 362–63. On definitions of national character in the nineteenth century see now the important Romani, *National Character*.

24 Antonio Gallenga, *Italy, Past and Present*, (London, 1848, 2 vols), II, pp. 337, 351.

25 Leslie Mitchell, *Holland House* (London, 1980); Peter Mandler, *Aristocratic Government in the age of Reform: Whigs and Liberals, 1830–1852* (Oxford, 1990).

26 Maurizio Isabella, 'At the Origins of the Italian Risorgimento: Revolutionary Activity and Politico-economic Thought of Giuseppe Pecchio (1785–1835)', PhD dissertation, University of Cambridge, submitted in October 1997.

27 Pecchio to Camillo Ugoni, 10 December 1828, in Mario Lupo Gentile, 'Giuseppe Pecchio nei moti del '21 e nel suo esilio in Inghilterra', *Rivista d'Italia* 13 (1910), pp. 317–50, p. 338.

28 Pecchio to Henry Holland, 21 March 1832, *Holland House Papers*, BM, 51836; Pecchio to Panizzi, 2 August 1832, Add Man. 36714, BM.

29 Pecchio to Panizzi, 2 November 1830, in Luigi Fagan (ed.), *Lettere ad Antonio Panizzi di uomini illustri, 1823–1870* (Florence, 1880), p. 85.

30 Camillo Ugoni to Panizzi, 30 October 1830, in Fagan, *Lettere*, pp. 91–3; Della Peruta, *Mazzini e i rivoluzionari italiani*, pp. 42–3.

31 Pecchio to Holland, 16 February 1831, *Holland House Papers*, BM 51836.

32 Steven C. Hughes, *Crime, Disorder and the Risorgimento: The Politics of Policing in Bologna* (Cambridge, 1994), pp. 107–35, esp. p. 111.

33 Pecchio to Holland, 6 March 1831, *Holland House Papers*, BM 51836.

34 Pecchio to Panizzi, 19 April 1931, in Fagan, *Lettere*, pp. 96–8.

35 Palmerston to Holland, 20 March 1831, *Holland House Papers*, BM 51599A.

36 On the diplomatic negotiations see Alan J. Reinerman, *Austria and the Papacy in the Age of Metternich* (Washington, 1989, 2 vols), II, pp. 35–80. As Pecchio was later to acknowledge, 'Moi meme, vulcanique que je suis, j'avais toujours preché à mes compatriots de la Romagne qu'il valait mieux de s'entendre et de s'arranger avec le Pape que d'avoir un seconde invasion Autrichienne', Pecchio to Holland, 22 March 1832, *Holland House Papers*, BM 31836.

37 These documents were also sent to the French government, addressed to the Foreign Secretary Sebastiani. They can be found in the Public Record Office, Foreign Office, 43/25, dated January and February 1832.

38 Narciso Nada, 'La polemica fra Palmerston e Metternich sulla questione romana nel 1832', *Bollettino Storico Bibliografico Subalpino* 59 (1954), pp. 89–153, esp. p 105.

39 Palmerston to Lord Holland, 18 March 1832, *Holland House Papers*, 51599A. Emilia Morelli erroneously attributes to the Roman patriot Francesco Guardabassi the role played by Pecchio in the events, in Emilia Morelli, *La politica estera di Tommaso Bernetti, segretario di stato di Gregorio XVI*, (Rome, 1953), p. 75.

40 On this diplomatic event see Charles Webster, *The Foreign Policy of Palmerston, 1830–1841* (London 1969, 2 vols), I, pp. 200–7; Reinerman, *Austria and the Papacy*, II, pp. 149–77.

41 Giorgio Candeloro, '*Dalla restaurazione alla rivoluzione nazionale 1815–1846*', in *Storia dell'Italia moderna* (Milan, 1988), II, p. 230; Noel Blakinston, *The Roman Question* (London, 1961). Pecchio complemented his political action with an attempt to influence public opinion.

In fact he provided the *Edinburgh Review* with the material for a long article on the situation in Italy, 'Political Condition of the Italian States', probably written by Macaulay or William Empson under the influence of both Pecchio and Panizzi. In the article, published in July 1832 and written as a review of Sismondi's works, the author advocated the reform proposals included in the Memorandum, as a basis for the regeneration of the Papal State. (Pecchio to Panizzi, 24 August 1832, Add Man 36,714, BM.)

42 Giulio Caprin, *L'esule fortunato Antonio Panizzi* (Florence, 1945); Constance Brooks, *Antonio Panizzi Scholar and Patriot* (Manchester, 1931); Maurizio Festanti (ed.), *Studi su Antonio Panizzi* (Reggio Emilia, 1979–80); Enzo Esposito (ed.), *Antonio Panizzi. Atti del convegno di Studi, Rome, 21–22 aprile 1980* (Salerno, 1982).

43 Brooks, *Panizzi*, pp. 81–8. The letter of 13 April 1848 is published at pp. 208–11.

44 On Palmerston and Northern Italy in 1848–49 see Ottavio Barié, *L'Inghilterra e il problema italiano nel 1848–49* (Milan, 1965); George J. Billy, *Palmerston's Foreign Policy: 1848* (New York, 1993), pp. 85–109.

45 On Carlo Pepoli see entry 'Pepoli Carlo', in *Dizionario del Risorgimento nazionale* (Milan, 1930–33, 3 vols), III, pp. 838–39; and Margaret Wicks, *The Italian Exiles*, pp. 175–78. In England he published *Prose e versi di Carlo Pepoli* (London, 1837, 2 vols).

46 Count Pepoli to Palmerston, dated Kennington, 24 January 1849, *Broadland Papers*, General Correspondence, PE/50, 1–2, University of Southampton. The Memorandum provided an encouraging, if unrealistic, description of the relationship between the liberal government in Rome and the Pope in Gaeta.

47 Giuseppe Monsagrati, 'Alle prese con la democrazia. Gran Bretagna e U.S.A. di fronte alla repubblica romana', in Ester Capuzzo (ed.), supplement to *Rassegna Storica del Risorgimento, Numero speciale per il 150° anniversario della repubblica romana,* 86 (1999), pp. 287–306.

48 Giorgio Candeloro, *La rivoluzione nazionale (1846–1849),* in *Storia dell'Italia moderna* (Milan, 1995), III, pp. 307–43, 373–77.

49 Derek Beales, *England and Italy, 1859–1860* (Cambridge, 1961), pp. 93–6.

50 This community included the Sicilians Luigi and Alfonso Scalia – Luigi in 1848–9 had been the Sicilian emissary to London – the Lombard Count Carlo Arrivabene Valenti Gonzaga, who had fought in the Sardinian army in 1849, and Giuseppe Devincenzi. In 1856 Palmerston sent Luigi Scalia to the Paris Peace Conference, where the Sicilian aristocrat presented a memorandum about conditions in Sicily to the Foreign

Secretary Lord Clarendon. On the Scalia brothers see Tina Whitaker Scalia, *Sicily and England: Political and Social Reminiscences, 1848-1870* (London, 1907). On Carlo Arrivabene see entry 'Arrivabene', in *Dizionario Biografico degli Italiani* (Rome, 1962), IV, p. 331; on Giuseppe Devincenzi see Emilia Morelli, *Alcune note sull'esilio di Giuseppe Devincenzi*, in *Atti del secondo convegno. Giuseppe Devincenzi nel Risorgimento e nella politica post-unitaria* (Teramo, 1974), pp. 39-49.

51 On Lacaita see Charles Lacaita, *An Italian Englishman Sir James Lacaita, KCMG* (London, 1933); Maria Avetta, 'Studi cavouriani I: Una"vexata quaestio" alla luce dei carteggi cavouriani', *Rassegna storica del Risorgimento* 21 (1934), pp. 49-71. On Panizzi's role between the British and Piedmontese government in the 1850s see Emilia Morelli, 'Panizzi e il decennio di Preparazione', in Esposito, *Atti del convegno di studi su Antonio Panizzi*, pp. 13-49; on Panizzi and Gladstone see M.R.D. Foot, 'Gladstone e Panizzi', in Festanti, *Studi su Antonio Panizzi*, pp. 121-31; D.M. Schreuder, 'Gladstone and Italian Unification, 1848-1870: the making of a Liberal?', *English Historical Review* 85 (1970), pp. 475-501.

52 Lucio Sponza, *Italian Immigrants in Nineteenth-century Britain: Realities and Images* (Leicester, 1988), p. 32.

53 Pisacane to his brother, 23 December 1849, in Aldo Romano (ed.), *Epistolario* (Milan / Genoa, 1936), p. 105-6.

54 On Crispi's exile in England see Christopher Duggan, *Creare la nazione: Vita di Francesco Crispi* (Bari, 2000), pp. 138-50.

55 Francis Barrymore Smith, *Radical Artisan: William James Linton, 1812-97* (Manchester, 1973); Joel Wiener, *William Lovett* (Manchester, 1989); L. Hammond and B. Hammond, *James Stansfeld: A Victorian Champion of Sex Equality* (London, 1932).

56 On Mazzini's exile before 1848 see Salvo Mastellone, *Introduzione* to Giuseppe Mazzini, *Pensieri sulla democrazia in Europa*, (Milan, 1997), pp. 7-79. General works are Denis Mack Smith, *Mazzini* (New Haven / London, 1994); Roland Sarti, *Mazzini: A Life for the Religion of Politics*, (Westport, Conn., 1997); Emilia Morelli, *L'Inghilterra di Mazzini* (Rome, 1965). An assessment of Morelli's work on Mazzini is now in Franco Della Peruta, 'Il Mazzini di Emilia Morelli', in idem, *L'Italia del Risorgimento: Problemi, momenti e figure* (Milan, 1997), pp. 349-67.

57 In 1840 Mazzini set up a Mutual Aid Society in London and published the *Apostolato Popolare* to educate Italian workers in his political and social creed. (Della Peruta, *Mazzini e i rivoluzionari italiani*, pp. 333-6); Mazzini to Nicola Fabrizi, 1838, in *Scritti*, XIV, pp. 409-11; 'Is it Revolt or a Revolution' (*Tait's Edinburgh Magazine*, 1840), now in *Scritti*, XXII, pp. 375-403,

58 Finn, *After Chartism*, pp. 57–8. A general work on Mazzini and English radicalism is William Roberts, 'Mazzini's Thought in the Development of British Culture Politics and Society', in Giuliana Limiti (ed.), *Il mazzinianesimo nel mondo*, (Pisa, 1996, 2 vols), II, pp. 1–76; idem, *Prophet in Exile: Joseph Mazzini in England, 1837–1868* (New York / Berne / Frankfurt / Paris, 1989), pp. 49–75.

59 Finn, *After Chartism*, pp. 10–11.

60 *English Republic*, III (1854), pp. 1–2. Finn, *After Chartism*, p. 129; Rudman, *Italian Nationalism*, p. 88.

61 Gregory Claeys, 'Mazzini, Kossuth and British Radicalism, 1848–1854', *Journal of British Studies* 28 (1989), pp. 225–62.

62 Miles Taylor, *The Decline of British Radicalism, 1847–1860* (Oxford, 1995), pp. 194–6.

63 Joseph McCabe (ed.), *Life and letters of George Jacob Holyoake* (London, 1908, 2 vols), I, pp. 228–43. George Holyoake, *Sixty Years of an Agitator's Life* (London, 1909, 2 vols); Pia Onnis, 'Battaglie democratiche e Risorgimento in un carteggio inedito di Giuseppe Mazzini e George Jacob Holyoake', *Rassegna Storica del Risorgimento* 22 (1935), pp. 885–926.

64 Eugenio Biagini, *Liberty, Retrenchment, and Reform: Popular Liberalism in the Age of Gladstone, 1860–1880* (Cambridge, 1992), pp. 46–50. Mazzini developed these themes in his *Duties of Man*. On Mazzini's patriotism see Maurizio Viroli, *For Love of Country: An Essay on Patriotism and Nationalism* (Oxford, 1995), pp.144–55. On Mazzini's religiosity see Ettore Passerin D'Entreves, 'Le religioni del progresso nell'età romantica e il Vangelo politico-religioso di Giuseppe Mazzini', *Vita e Pensiero*, 52 (1965), pp. 248–68, and 354–58; on Puritan and non-Conformist politics see Eugenio Biagini, *Presbiteri e politica: Sociabilità politica e cultura religiosa*, in idem, *Progressisti e Protestanti. Aspetti della tradizione liberal-laburista in Gran Bretagna* (Manduria / Bari / Rome, 1995), pp. 183–207.

65 Finn, *After Chartism*, pp. 166–7.

66 William E. Adams, *Memoirs of a Social Atom* (London, 1903, 2 vols), I, p. 263.

67 Claeys, 'Mazzini, Kossuth and British Radicalism, 1848–1854'.

68 On Mazzini and socialism see Franco Della Peruta, *I democratici e la rivoluzione italiana* (Milan, 1974), pp. 253–89.

69 Adams, *Memoirs of a Social Atom*, I, p. 262. On Adams see also Owen R. Ashton, *W.E. Adams: Chartist, Radical and Journalist, 1832–1906* (Tyne and Wear, 1991).

70 Adams, *Memoirs*, p. 267.

71 On Linton's critique of socialism see the article 'Are the Socialists republican?', *English Republic*, II (1852-3), now reprinted in Smith, *Radical Artisan*, pp. 223-6 On Linton's patriotism see Finn, *After Chartism*, pp.114-16, 125.

72 On Cowen see Nigel Todd, *The Militant Democracy: Joseph Cowen and Victorian Radicalism* (Tyne and Wear, 1991). The quotation is from the *Northern Tribune*, I (February 1854), p. 63.

73 Maginnis to Linton, 23 December 1856, *Linton Collection*, IV/8, Feltrinelli Foundation, Milan.

74 See, e.g., Adams, *Memoirs of a Social Atom*, pp. 266-7.

75 Finn, *After Chartism*, pp. 166-71; O'Connor, *The Romance of Italy*, pp. 77-87.

76 *Discorso di Giuseppe Mazzini letto alla società degli amici d'Italia in Londra la sera dell'11 Febbraio 1852* (Rome, 1952), p. 13.

77 Finn, *After Chartism*, pp. 168-189.

78 'It strikes me that the republishing of this and together with the first addresses to the Friends of Italy, in a popular form, for one penny...would perhaps do some good...I should like to be read by the working classes.' Mazzini to Holyoake, 26 July (no year, but probably around 1855), in Fondo Holyoake, Plico 3,30, Museo del Risorgimento, Milan.

79 Giuseppe Mazzini, *Agli italiani, Marzo 1853*, in Terenzio Grandi and Augusto Comba (eds), *Scritti politici di Giuseppe Mazzini* (Turin, 1972), pp. 713-14. On the *Fund* see O'Connor, *The Romance of Italy*, pp. 89-90.

80 Ginsborg, 'Il mito del Risorgimento nel mondo britannico', p. 394.

81 Taylor, *The Decline of British Radicalism*, pp. 202-4.

82 Valdo Vinay, *Evangelici italiani esuli a Londra durante il Risorgimento* (Turin, 1961); Giorgio Spini, *Risorgimento e protestanti* (Milan, 1989); Camillo Mapei, *Italy, Illustrated and Described, in a Series of Views with an Introductory Essay on the Political, Religious and Moral State* (Glasgow, 1847).

83 Basil Hall, 'Alessando Gavazzi: a Barnabite Friar and the Risorgimento', *Studies in Church History* 12 (1975), pp. 303-56

84 Aurelio Saffi, 'Religion in Italy', *Westminster Review* 4 (1853), pp. 311-41.

85 On Saffi see Paul Ginsborg, 'Aurelio Saffi: il decennio di esilio',unpublished paper prepared for the conference on Aurelio Saffi held in Forlì in 1990. I am indebted to Professor Ginsborg for generously providing me with a copy of his paper. See also Giovanni Quagliotti, *Aurelio Saffi* (Rome, 1944); Aurelio Saffi, *Ricordi e Scritti di Aurelio Saffi* (Florence, 1892-1905).

86 See Saffi to Stansfeld, 20 October 1856, *Scritti*, IV, pp.382–87. The original is in Museo del Risorgimento, Milan, Fondo Holyoake, Plico 1, f.6. The two lectures are published in *Scritti*, IV, pp. 338–436.

87 Ibid., *Scritti*, IV, pp. 437–41.

88 Finn, *After Chartism*, pp. 199–200.

89 Leopoldo Marchetti and Elena Larsimont Pergameni (eds), *Felice Orsini, Memorie politiche* (Milan, 1962), pp. 259–61. On the English translation of Orsini's bestseller see E.A. Daniels, *Jessie White Mario, Risorgimento Revolutionary* (Athens/USA, 1972), pp. 46–7.

90 Franco Della Peruta, 'Luigi Pianciani e il socialismo', in idem, *L'Italia del Risorgimento*, pp. 189–212.

91 On Pisacane's exile see Luciano Russo, *Carlo Pisacane: Vita e pensiero di un rivoluzionario senza rivoluzione* (Milan, 1993), pp. 44–52. On Pisacanes's political ideas the most recent works are Cesare Vetter, *Carlo Pisacane e il socialismo risorgimentale* (Milan, 1984), and Leonardo La Puma, *Il pensiero politico di Carlo Pisacane* (Turin, 1995). Pisacane died in 1857 on the unfortunate expedition of Sapri, organised with the support of Mazzini.

92 Pisacane's comments of the English political system are in his *Saggi: la Rivoluzione*, now in Aldo Romano (ed.), *Carlo Pisacane, Saggi storici-politici-militari sull'Italia* (Milan / Rome, 1957), p. 84.

93 Della Peruta, *I democratici e la rivoluzione italiana*, p. 467.

94 Russo, *Carlo Pisacane*, p. 232.

95 The pamphlet was entitled 'Tyrannicide. Is it Justifiable?', and was written by William Adams. On the Orsini case in England see Bernard Porter, *The Refugee Question in Mid-Victorian Politics* (Cambridge, 1979), pp. 170–99.

96 Paolo Emilio Imbriani, *Voci di esuli politici meridionali. Lettere e documenti dal 1849 al 1861 con appendici varie* (Rome 1965); Paolo Romano, *Silvio Spaventa Biografia politica* (Bari, 1942); pp. 90–2; Mazzini to Saffi, 14 March 1859, in *Scritti editi e inediti* 63 (Imola, 1933), p. 198.

97 Biagini, *Liberty*, p. 372.

98 *Discorso di Giuseppe Mazzini letto alla società degli amici d'Italia* pp. 10–11. On the language of the nation used in *Risorgimento* literature see Banti, *La Nazione del Risorgimento*. Saffi's lectures are a typical example of this language (see especially Saffi, *Scritti*, IV, pp. 410–12, where Saffi denies the existence of any class tension in Italian cities); Luigi Mariotti (pseudonym of Antonio Gallenga), *Latest News from Italy* (London, 1847). For the English reception of this image of the Italian nation see the historical introduction of Mrs. C.G. Hamilton, *The Exiles of Italy*, pp. VII-XXXII.

6

The French Exiles and the British

Fabrice Bensimon

A significant French community spent some years, in some cases more than two decades, in Britain, mostly in London and in the Channel Islands. The purpose of this article is not to study the various aspects of their politics, their debates and discussions, sometimes their feuds and clashes. An assumption about the French exiles is that they were quite cut off from the British, and that, unlike the Italians, for instance, they seldom had relationships, especially friendly links, with them. I do not intend to disprove this view. Instead, I shall focus on the type of interaction that their presence in Britain provoked. Inevitably they met Englishmen for various reasons: political, but also ordinary, everyday reasons, like making a living, finding lodgings, and so on. Although there was a relatively small number of Frenchmen, they were observed by various groups of British people: the authorities, some newspapers and journalists, a few intellectuals, some radical activists, etc. What did these observers think of them, and how did they judge them? The exiles themselves observed and commented upon Britain and the British. What were their views on their host country and its people? How did a small, politically minded, mostly male community interact with a nation which had reasons both for accepting and for rejecting this group? To deal with these issues, it is necessary to refer to the broader framework of Anglo-French relations in the middle of the nineteenth century. As it is impossible to treat such a large topic exhaustively, I shall focus on a few characters and events that illustrate general features of this relationship. I shall first deal with the French attitudes, before commenting upon those of the British.

French attitudes

Living in Britain

Some Frenchmen, such as Louis Blanc, left the Continent as early as August 1848. Most of the French exiles left after the coup of 2

December 1851, many of them being *proscrits*. In 1852, there may
have been about 4,500 French people in Britain. Most did not stay
long. By 1853, the number had decreased to 1,000,[1] and by 1859 to
400; for various reasons, some went back to France, and some
emigrated elsewhere. By the late 1850s and the 1859 'amnesty', most
of the refugees had left. However, some, such as Louis Blanc or
Ledru-Rollin, stayed until the fall of Louis Napoleon, in 1870. But in
the 1860s, this group was far smaller, ageing, and appeared to be
less a centre of interest in British political life.

There were various political groupings among the refugees. For a
while, Ledru-Rollin and Delescluze were close to Mazzini and
Kossuth. There was also, further left, the Revolutionary Commune,
grouped around Félix Pyat. Between these two, a number of Frenchmen (Pierre Landolphe, Martin Nadaud, Jules Leroux) formed a
group of 'Independents', who considered Louis Blanc to be their
leader. But Louis Blanc did not get involved, and the group broke
up. Subsequently, several refugees including Louis Blanc tried to
unite the all of the French exiles in London, but these plans failed.
The 1859 amnesty put an end to all such attempts for good.

The living conditions of the refugees varied greatly. Most lived in
conditions comparable to those that can be observed in other refugee
communities, where making ends meet was extremely hard. Britain
was seldom the country of choice: it was a destination imposed by
the constraints of geography, and political opportunities or lack of
them. Very few refugees could speak English. And except for the
richest, the most educated or the most famous among them, finding
the means of subsistence was terrible and difficult. Some French
tailors, shoemakers and cooks, especially, could find a job. Shoemaker Thierry set up a shop in Regents Street. Pottier, formerly a
hatter, opened a tavern in Fitzroy Square which served as a rallying
point for the newly arrived refugees. But the members of most other
trades (masons, carpenters, mechanics or printers) found it
extremely hard, and nearly starved. Former deputy Rouet lost all his
savings in a music-hall business.[2] Gustave Lefrançais, a refugee who
had founded the first union of socialist teachers in France, only spent
a year in London. He did not have enough money to pay for lodgings, and he mostly slept outdoors, or spent part of the night in one
of the pubs near the docks. The squalor suffered by the refugees,
and their socialist beliefs, convinced some of them that the British
government was deliberately letting them starve. Pierre Leroux was
a socialist thinker whose wife and children lived in a slum, 'with no

air to breathe', as he said, 'and almost no bread to eat.'[3] He denounced Britain's so-called 'hospitality': 'political liberty but also the liberty to die of starvation.'[4] Delescluze, who could not bear the 'dry and cold hospitality' of England, went back to France where jail awaited him.[5] The French refugees found a confirmation of their views in the press – a refugee read in *The Times*: 'The prince-president is quite wrong to spend so much to send the Republicans to Africa and Cayenne; let him just cast them on our shores, and with the help of our fogs, the wretchedness in which we let them die and languish will soon get him rid of them.'[6]

Sometimes, the French refugees who had some education were able to give French lessons, especially with the help of British people, either the acquaintances of well-known refugees such as Louis Blanc, or some Chartists who had set up committees. But even French lessons were not easy to arrange – or to keep – for a number of reasons. First, even teaching French required some knowledge of English, which many refugees did not have – Lefrançais explained that he taught French by using the various objects in his pupil's living-room! Second, the English people interested in French lessons were more likely to be middle- or upper-class anti-socialists than working-class Chartists or radicals. And there was the competition from French servants, who were more respectable. Pierre Leroux found that his lessons were cancelled when his socialist ideas were revealed to two of his pupils. Martin Nadaud, by contrast, concealed his origins as a mason,[7] when he found a job as a teacher in a Wimbledon school. A great difficulty was that even if they concealed their political opinions, their appearance gave a great deal away. There was a stereotype of the French republican, which may be seen in some of the cartoons in *Punch*:[8] a beard, a moustache, a long worn-out jacket, seditious pamphlets, etc. This stereotype of the subversive French republican sometimes made things more difficult, or was felt to make things more difficult, by some of the French refugees. Louis Blanc reported that until the Crimean War, a moustache was a definite attribute of French socialists!

The French view of Britain and the British

How did the French view their host country? There was, among the French republicans, a traditional hostility to Britain on several grounds. There was hostility to English Protestantism, even if many of the republicans were atheists, hostility to the exploitation of the English working class, hostility to materialism, and support for the

Irish Repealers. Ledru-Rollin best illustrated this stand. Less than a year after he had arrived in England, he published his *Decline of England*. Ledru-Rollin argued that the basis of British wealth was rotten, as the country was led by the two aristocracies – land and finance – which worked as parasites to exploit the country's great masses. After a description of the society and economy of the country, the *Decline* ended with various statistics, namely, tables showing the cost of the royal family, the price of officers' commissions, and rates of drunkenness broken down by trade.[9] Ledru-Rollin's book was largely a copy of others. Published a year before the Great Exhibition, it was not even approved of by the other refugees who could witness their host country's wealth, and who thought it was a bad idea to criticise the country in which they were trying to live. And among the British, Ledru-Rollin's popularity, which had already been quite low since the revolution, when he had been the villain of the British press, suffered seriously as a result of the pamphlet.

Paradoxically, this text has remained the best-known French report on Britain. But there are sources which cast a much more favourable light upon Britain and the British. Of course, one has to be cautious about the genuineness of the French publications – French refugees did not want to irritate the English authorities. The French had their national stereotypes of the British. Some of these were the usual ones relating to national character: the British were supposedly stiff, they were individualistic, they were conformists. There were also the usual stereotypes about poor food and bad weather. Louis Blanc complained about what he called 'the despotism' of public opinion in Britain. Above all, there were two main stereotypes. One was that the British were cold – Victor Schoelcher said England was 'the coldest country on the earth in all meanings.'[10] And the other was that the British were too materialistic, that is, too keen on money. Charles Hugo wrote about London: 'These three million alarmed beings have one purpose: money.'[11] As stated earlier, many refugees resented the country and the authorities for leaving them in dire straits, but they seldom extended this hostility to the English people.

There were also more positive views. The French refugees were impressed by economic developments, the rhythm of the cities, and the activity of harbours like London, Glasgow and Liverpool. All in all, it seems that whereas the upper- and middle-class Britons found very little to admire in France and the French (except culture), the French refugees often admired the wealth and industry of the 'great mid-Victorian boom'. The socialist Nadaud wrote that he was convinced by the benefits of imperialism when visiting the harbour of Liverpool.[12] Overall, the French refugees were both appalled by the poverty in London (their own but also that of the English and of immigrant communities), and impressed by Britain.

And many – although not all – also appreciated the British, whom they held in genuine esteem. For instance, Lefrançais, who suffered so much in London, praised the English character.[13] Nadaud became a total Anglophile. When he worked as a mason, he appreciated the friendliness of the local workers; as a tourist in Lancashire during the 1853–4 strike, he was impressed by their solidarity; and when he became a teacher, he became very fond of the well-off young public school gentlemen. He liked England so much that after the 1859 amnesty he only briefly went to France and soon returned to Wimbledon where he remained until 1870. Another example is Simon Bernard: after his acquittal, Bernard – a Fourierist, an avowed conspirator – praised English liberty and the English jury system.

All in all, it seems that the French refugees who eventually managed to acquire some knowledge of English (or rather those who stayed long enough to do so), although they seldom made great friends or married in England, did have some positive opinions and stereotypes of the English. This was largely linked to their political beliefs. Like many other exiles, the French views were a mixture of patriotism and internationalism. When they exchanged ideas with the English, Germans or Hungarians, organised common banquets and toasts, or set up common committees and associations, they unknowingly laid the foundations of the first International of the following decade.

It is now interesting to look at the opposite view, that is, how the British considered these *proscrits*.

British attitudes

The authorities
The general pattern described by Bernard Porter applies to the way the British authorities considered the French refugees. The authorities did not like the French refugees. To use one of Palmerston's phrases, they considered them to be the 'scum' of society. They were aware that the *proscrits* were most unlikely to pose any serious threat to British stability. But as the refugees were a regular bone of

contention with the continental authorities, the British cabinet spent some money and energy on the surveillance of their activities. Bernard Porter has studied the efficiency of 'special agent' John Sanders, who, from 1849 to 1859, spent most of his time spying on the refugees.[14] On some occasions, the British authorities tried to limit the activities of the French refugees, especially when these were likely to lead to a diplomatic incident with France. This was the case on two main occasions. The first one was in Jersey (Sylvie Aprile in this volume (Chapter 10) deals more extensively with this particular community.) The authorities wanted some refugees to leave the island, as they considered the refugees in Jersey to be too violent, too close to France and thus tempted to organise a plot, and too integrated into the island society because of the community of language. A speech by Félix Pyat in September 1855 provided the pretext. The speech, which was printed in the refugee newspaper *L'Homme,* directly attacked the emperor, but also Queen Victoria. Pyat's speech referred to the Anglo-French alliance in the Crimea in images which were traditional in French political discourse, but far less familiar in Victorian England. Referring to the alliance, he argued that the Queen had sacrificed her chastity in the alliance.[15] *The Times,* which argued for the expulsion of the Jersey refugees, did not even mention the quotation or the images, which were taboo: 'But Englishmen cannot be forgetful of the plain laws of morality ... Our readers will sufficiently judge of its character without wading through its blasphemies, its obscenities, and its instigations to murder ... No feeling of decency or of respect for the usages of the country which has sheltered them restrains for a moment the ruffiantly rhapsodist ... the most striking feature of their mind is their fiendish malevolence.'[16] In addition to appearing as quite rude, Pyat's speech fitted in with a few stereotypes of the French as being sexually licentious and profligate, violent as well as vulgar. A meeting of the Jersey inhabitants was organised, probably on the initiative of the Lieutenant-Governor who wanted to get rid of the French refugees, and about forty of them, including Victor Hugo, were eventually expelled. However, this was not such a great setback as most of them went to London or to Guernsey.

The other significant attack on the French refugees was the Orsini affair in 1858. In this case the consequences could have been far more serious for the French refugees, especially for those who were involved in the attempted murder of Louis Napoleon. But threats from the French authorities provoked a reaction in Britain. This led to the failure of the 'Conspiracy to murder' Bill which Palmerston wanted adopted, and to the acquittal of Simon Bernard who was tried for complicity to murder. There was both a popular reaction against the Palmerston government's attempts to restrict the liberty of the refugees, and a parliamentary one against the supposed dictates of the French authorities. Radical MP Joseph Roebuck argued: 'If our ancestors reacted with contempt and defiance to the menaces of *Napoléon le Grand*, should we, their descendants, quail before the threats of *Napoléon le petit*?'[17] Tens of thousands of people attended meetings or demonstrated against Palmerston's bill. I will come back to their motivation, but the authorities had to step down.

National character and stereotypes

Of course, among the Britons who demonstrated in support of the refugees, very few knew any, and not many had ever heard of the various types of socialism and republicanism they discussed in emigration. The British ruling classes and newspapers such as *The Times* (let alone openly xenophobic ones such as *John Bull*) had absolutely no sympathy for the French refugees. They had several reasons for this. They considered most of the French refugees to be subversive, dishonest socialists and believed that there were only a 'few honourable exceptions.'[18] In the years after the 1848 revolution in particular, there was a strong feeling that such men could have toppled Britain's stable order, and this made the members of the British ruling classes particularly distrustful of the French socialists. The British throne had not been subverted in 1848, but this had been a serious worry. And the French socialist symbolised the fears felt at the time by many in the dominant orders of society. The 1830s and 1840s were probably the period when modern Britain came closest to a revolution, and that dreadful experience was still present in people's minds. In this respect, French republicans embodied the revolutionary tendency of France, with the bloody consequences of its recent history. In a private letter from 1849, the Whig historian Macaulay wrote that had he been in Cavaignac's place, the June days would have been even worse for the red republicans.[19] This type of hostility to French socialists was shared by many among the elite. And although in the same circles there was a strong hostility to Bonaparte because of his despotism and because of the painful memories attached to his name, this is why many people in the ruling classes, ranging from Palmerston to an arch-liberal like Walter Bagehot, secretly or publicly approved of the 1851 coup. Of course, a big difference was that, as refugees, the French socialists were no longer a threat. But except in a few liberal or Francophile circles, they found little access to the upper layers of society (and only the most respectable of the refugees were admitted). Pierre Leroux wrote pages complaining about John Stuart Mill's refusal to guarantee Leroux's rent payment, and we will see that Mill was one of the very few who maintained a regular relationship with one refugee. And while a number of middle-class English radicals tapped the resources of their social networks and their associations, it seems that most of them declined to deal with the French republicans and socialists and focused their efforts on the nationalists.

Their socialist beliefs were not the only reason why many French refugees did not make acquaintances among the London elite; more simply, most of the refugees were poor, and thus unlikely to enter such milieux, and had few language skills. But this was also true of the other refugee communities.

To understand relationships between peoples, one has to take various parameters into account. Competition, rivalry and diplomatic ups and downs are decisive elements. And these played a crucial part at a time when France and Britain were thought to be comparable military powers. Another element is the popular image and representation of the other nation.[20] A series of stereotypes applied to the French in general. These were popular stereotypes, but they also largely prevailed in more educated circles. One has to bear in mind that the idea of 'national characters' was deeply rooted in the mid-nineteenth century – especially as applied to the French.[21] One observation was that they were prone to revolutions. This was often explained by their supposed fickleness – during the 1789 revolution, they had got rid of the monarchy and proclaimed a republic, before submitting to a despot. Then, monarchy had been reestablished, and fifteen years later, the incorrigible Parisians had overthrown it again, to put on the throne another dynasty, which they had overthrown again in 1848 for a new republic. Obviously, these French people could not stick to any definite opinion. They changed their minds all the time, and this was why their political history compared so unfavourably with Britain's, which had been stable for more than a century and a half.[22] Another stereotype was that the French were excitable and violent. This violence was mentioned on a number of occasions, for instance, at the opening of the Great Exhibition, when various people, including the Duke of Wellington, insisted on the risk of a plot by the French.[23] This 'scare' is laughed at by *Punch*.[24]

Other occasions were Félix Pyat's speech in 1855, and Emmanuel Barthélémy's shooting of two Britons in December 1854. He ended up in Madame Tussaud's Chamber of Horrors. Other stereotypes also applied to the French. There was the idea that they were proud and expansionist, and this largely explains the successive invasion scares of the mid-nineteenth century. There was also the idea that the French liked posing, that they were a bit theatrical. And other stereotypes (largely inspired by reality!) specifically applied to the refugees: that they were pipe-smokers, heavy drinkers, more likely to talk than to act.

And finally, the French refugees lived as a community, mostly in impoverished streets and cafés in Soho, and seldom thought of making friends with Britons.

The London elite
As a result of these various factors, only a very few of the leading members of the refugee community (who also turned out to be the more educated, the better off, those of a middle-class background) managed to have social relationships with members of the London middle or upper classes. Louis Blanc best managed to achieve some kind of integration in these circles. Various sources show that from the beginning of his stay in London he was entertained for dinner in leading circles, for example, by Thomas Carlyle,[25] George Eliot,[26] Herbert Spencer,[27] etc.[28] When, in 1860, Blanc delivered lectures on eighteenth-century France, they were a great success with participants such as Dickens and Thackeray. Louis Blanc established a very cordial relationship with John Stuart Mill.[29] Throughout the 1850s and 1860s Mill and Blanc regularly met and discussed various issues, although Mill was often in France. Mill never addressed Louis Blanc with words other than 'Mon cher monsieur Louis Blanc'; he often congratulated the Frenchman for his articles on England as well as for his history of the French Revolution, and said that if he had modified his *Principles of Political Economy*, it was because of the actions of the Luxembourg Commission in 1848. Similarly, Louis Blanc often quoted Mill's writings with approval in the articles he sent to continental newspapers.[30] But this relationship was the exception rather than the norm. It can be explained both by the fact that Mill was a Francophile and that Blanc was a very, very moderate socialist. George Eliot met Pierre Leroux in 1851 and had a passionate discussion on problems ranging from social organisation to the origins of Christianity. She described him as 'a dreamy genius',[31] but there is no mention of any other encounter between the two.

The best known of the French refugees, Ledru-Rollin, did not attract (or seek, it seems) any British friendship. His publication, one year after he had arrived, of *De la décadence de l'Angleterre* (*Decline of England*) probably contributed to his isolation, as did his open support for the cause of Irish repeal of the 1800 Act of Union. However, Ledru-Rollin eventually had contacts with several Britons, including writer William Thackeray and Julian Harney. But these relationships were more occasional contacts than true links.

Radical circles

In working-class radical circles, there was a keen interest in the French refugees and their ideas. In the decade that followed 1848, Chartism, although no longer a mass political movement, was still alive in various towns where groups of agitators and propagandists were active. Men such as Ernest Jones, Julian Harney, William J. Linton and G. W. M. Reynolds continued their political activity on political principles close to those of the Chartists in the late 1830s and in the 1840s. As Margot Finn has shown,[32] the political programme of this tendency was largely influenced by the 1848 continental revolutions. Until 1848, Chartism had focused on political reforms. But the 'year of revolutions' led some leaders of the movement, such as Julian Harney and Ernest Jones, to integrate the republican and socialist programme into theirs.[33] The post-1848 radical movement in Britain tried to reconcile socialist beliefs and democratic demands. The *Northern Star* gave long accounts of Louis Blanc's books. Various newspapers existed, which all bore testimony to the Chartist's evolution towards a programme that was inspired by the French experience: 'The Charter, and much more.' Holyoake edited *The Reasoner*, Harney *The Democratic Review* which purported to 'justify the red republicans',[34] and *The Red Republican* which did so even more clearly,[35] and Linton *The English Republic* (1851–55). This evolution was largely helped by frequent contacts between English Chartists and exile socialists.[36] In London, the same presses printed both English and refugee radical papers and works. A business run in Fleet Street by Holyoake served as a cultural centre, providing assembly rooms, a bookshop and a library.[37] Several English radicals made friends with their continental (including French) counterparts, for example, Holyoake and Blanc. There was a social life, with ceremonies, funerals, processions, symbols, martyrs and catchwords that were recognised by all. The Chartist commemorations of the 1848 February revolution or of Robespierre's birthday typified the annual events orchestrated by English radicals. An illustration which is a poster for a 'tea party' on Robespierre is a good example.[38] Holyoake named his own son Maximilien Robespierre in June 1848. The first names of G. W. M. Reynolds's sons were respectively Kossuth, Mazzini and Ledru-Rollin.

Public opinion

What about the rest of the people, that is ordinary Britons, who never met a single refugee? I agree with Bernard Porter when he says that there was not much sympathy for the refugees.[39] At the same time, it seems that English public opinion did not follow the authorities, the press, and some political circles which tried to promote anti-French as well as anti-socialist feelings against the refugee community. As we have seen, this was the case on several occasions: during the 1848 revolution, before the 1851 Great Exhibition, on the occasion of the Pyat speech in 1855 and on the Orsini affair in 1858. On all occasions, this nationalist propaganda failed. Except for the Jersey affair in 1855, no demonstrations against the refugees have been recorded.[40] And at the same time, there were large popular reactions in their defence, for example, at the time of the Orsini affair, when protest defeated the 'Conspiracy to murder' Bill, and when public opinion led a jury to acquit Simon Bernard in the Orsini affair. It has been argued that xenophobia against France and Louis Napoleon served as a catalyst for the 1858 protest, when hostility to France led to a defence of the refugees. This is possible. But this xenophobia could have been directed against the French refugees, and it was not. The prime motive of the protesters was probably hatred of continental despots, which was widespread in England. By demonstrating in support of the refugees, the English protesters were defending what they considered the fundamental right of the victims of political oppression to organise and be active in England. Thus, the French refugees were seen as a bunch of agitators by the authorities, as a group of insolent brawlers by *Punch*, the *Illustrated London News* and *The Times*, and as the victims of a nonliberal regime by many ordinary people.

Conclusion

Overall, it seems that the republican, socialist opinions of the French refugees brought them strong enmity only among the conservative and liberal circles that had some interest in social stability. The reaction of ordinary Britons was indifference in most cases, sympathy in some. Some English radicals found renewed political inspiration in their contacts with the refugees. Several tried to help and sometimes did give them crucial relief.

As for the French refugees themselves, they were not in England by choice, and most suffered from the material hardships entailed by life in exile, by being far away from their relatives and friends – and above all from the place where they thought they could be useful to their cause – and by their difficulties in communicating with the local people. This is why returning home was the main priority for most of them. Some of those who stayed did manage to find a stable position and a social network. Or vice versa: they stayed because they had found some kind of stability and the means necessary for survival. And despite the traditional hostility between the two nations, they both liked, and were liked by, many local people they met. This was largely explained by their dual identity: Frenchmen, certainly, but Frenchmen who were the victims of the French regime, a regime which even at times of alliance such as during the Crimean War, never gained much sympathy among ordinary Britons.

Notes

1 About 800 in London, 100 in Jersey, and another 100 in the rest of the country.

2 Alexandre Zévaès, 'Les Proscrits français en 1848 et 1851 à Londres', *La Révolution de 1848*, 20 (1923), p. 351.

3 'Je pensais à ma femme et à mes enfants enfermés depuis deux mois, sans air et presque sans pain, dans un taudis à Londres'. Pierre Leroux, *La Grève de Samarez, poème philosophique* (Paris, 1863), I, p. 237.

4 'O hospitalité de l'Angleterre : tu te montras là ce que tu es : la liberté politique, mais aussi la liberté de mourir de faim. Quel secours Albion donna-t-elle à tant de victimes ? Aucun, absolument aucun.' *Ibid.*, p. 305.

5 Alexandre Zévaès, 'Les Proscrits français en 1848 et 1851 à Londres (fin)', *La Révolution de 1848*, 21 (1924), p. 105.

6 'Le prince-président – écrivait le *Times*, il y a quelques jours – a bien tort d'envoyer à grands frais les républicains en Afrique et à Cayenne ; qu'il se contente donc de les *jeter sur nos côtes*, et, nos brouillards aidant, *la misère dans laquelle nous les laissons mourir et s'étioler* l'aura

bientôt débarrassé d'eux.' Gustave Lefrançais, *Souvenirs d'un révolutionnaire* (Paris, 1972), p. 164. [I have not been able to find the extract translated from *The Times* by Lefrançais. The above text is therefore the translation of a translation, and not the original text.

7 Martin Nadaud, *Mémoires de Léonard ancien garçon maçon*, (Paris, 1976), p. 439.

8 *Punch*, 20 (April 1851), p.174.

9 Alexandre Auguste Ledru-Rollin, *Decline of England*, London 1850.

10 Louis Blanc, *Lettres d'Angleterre* (Paris, 1865–6), I, p. 281 (letter of 25 June 1863); 'L'Angleterre, le pays le plus froid de la terre en tout sens'. Victor Schoelcher, *La Correspondance de Victor Schoelcher*, edited by Nelly Schmidt (Paris, 1995), p. 255.

11 'On a dit de Londres : une immense ville sans grandeur. Rien de plus vrai. Trois millions d'habitants qui vont, viennent, circulent, spéculent, fourmillent et ne vivent pas. Trois millions d'hommes pressés et pas un passant. [...] Ces trois millions d'êtres effarés n'ont qu'un but : l'argent. Tous brûlent le pavé à la poursuite des affaires. *Time is money*. Dans la Cité on a le spectacle d'une ville en déroute.' Charles Hugo, *Les Hommes de l'exil* (Paris, 1875), p. 324.

12 Martin Nadaud, *Mémoires*, p. 420.

13 'la volonté de fer qui caractérise vraiment le peuple anglais', Lefrançais, *Souvenirs*, p. 170.

14 Palmerston wrote to Clarendon about the 1848 Provisional Government: 'But what a state for a nation of thirty-three millions to be in, to be so despotically governed by eight or nine men who are the mere subordinates of 40,000 or 50,000 of the Scum of the Faubourgs of Paris. There is no other nation that would submit unresistingly to such a Tyranny, but the French are children in regard to all Serious affairs.' Letter of Palmerston to Clarendon, 22 April 1848, quoted in Herbert C.F. Bell, *Lord Palmerston* (London, 1936), I, p. 424; Bernard Porter, *The Refugee Question in Mid-Victorian Politics* (Cambridge, 1979).

15 '*Yes, you have sacrificed* ALL: – *the Queen's dignity!- the woman's delicacy...* – ALL – EVEN CHASTITY – for the love of that Ally.' Quoted in Bernard Porter, *The Refugee Question in Mid-Victorian Politics* (Cambridge, 1979), p. 24.

16 *The Times*, 17 October 1855, p. 6. See also ibid, p. 7 (account of the meeting of the Jersey inhabitants against the refugees on 22 October 1855, p. 6).

17 3 P D 148, cc. 766 and 771 (5 February 1858) Quoted in Porter, *The Refugee Question*, p. 118.

18 *The Times*, 22 October 1855, p. 6.

19 'Had I been in Cavaignac's place at that time I would have made such an example of the rabble of the Faubourg St Antoine that the ears of all the world should have tingled.' Letter to Margaret Trevelyan, 26 June 1849, in *The Letters of Thomas Babington Macaulay,* edited by Thomas Pinney (Cambridge, 1977), V (January 1849 – December 1855), p. 75.

20 See François Crouzet, 'Problèmes de la communication franco-britannique aux XIXe et XXe siècles', in François Crouzet (ed.), *De la Supériorité de l'Angleterre sur la France* (Paris, 1985), pp. 428–50.

21 In a series of essays on France in 1852, Walter Bagehot wrote: 'I need not prove to you that the French *have* a national character'. Walter Bagehot, *The Collected Works of Walter Bagehot,* edited by Norman St John-Stevas, *The Historical Essays* (London, 1968), V, p. 522.

22 *Punch,* 34 (20 March 1858), p. 117.

23 See Porter, *The Refugee Question,* p. 86.

24 *Punch,* 20 (May 1851), p. 193.

25 See the very positive description of Louis Blanc by Carlyle, e. g. in James Froude, *Thomas Carlyle, A History of His Life in London, 1834–1881* (London, 1884), I, p. 452.

26 E.g. Letter of George Eliot to Mr. and Mrs. Charles Bray, 27 April 1852: 'We had a brilliant soirée yesterday evening. W. R. Greg Foster (of Rawden), Francis Newman, the Ellises and Louis Blanc were the stars of the greatest magnitude'. George Eliot, *The Letters of George Eliot,* edited by Gordon S. Haight (London / Oxford, 1954), II, p. 21.

27 Cf. Herbert Spencer's *Autobiography* (Osnabrück, 1966, 1st edn 1904), I, pp. 459–60 on the language skills of Louis Blanc.

28 For instance, Charles Greville, who lived in aristocratic Whig circles rather than among socialist intellectuals, mentioned a dinner with Louis Blanc in his diary for October 1848: 'He is very gay, animated, and full of information, takes in very good part anything that is said to him, and any criticisms on his revolution and the Provisional Government.' Charles C.F. Greville, *The Greville Memoirs. A Journal of the reign of Queen Victoria from 1837 to 1852,* edited by G.L. Strachey and R. Fulford (London, 1885), III, p. 235 (entry for 20 October 1848).

29 There are numerous sources for the esteem John Stuart Mill had for Louis Blanc, e.g. 'I feel an entireness of sympathy with them [the Provisional Government] which I never expected to have with any government ... I also sympathise very strongly with such socialists as Louis, who seems to be sincere, enthusiastic, straightforward, and with a great foundation of good sense and good feeling, though precipitate and *raw* in his practical views'. Letter to John Pringle Nichol, 30 September 1848, in F. Mineka (ed.), *The Earlier Letters of John Stuart Mill,*

1812–1848 (Toronto, 1963), p. 739–40. See also John Stuart Mill, *Auto-biography* (London, 1873), p. 231. See also idem., 'Vindication of the French Revolution of February 1848', in John M. Robson (ed.), *Essays on French History and Historians* (Toronto, 1985).

30 E.g., see Blanc, *Lettres d'Angleterre*, I, pp. 284, 286; II, p. 242. Louis Blanc sent articles to *Le Temps* in France, *L'Etoile Belge* in Belgium, and *Europa* in Germany (Léo Loubère, *Louis Blanc. His Life and his Contribution to the Rise of French Jacobin-Socialism,* (Chicago, 1961), p. 154).

31 George Eliot to Sara Hennell, 21 January 1851, *The Letters*, II, p. 5.

32 Margot C. Finn, *After Chartism: Class and Nation in English Radical Politics, 1848–1874* (Cambridge, 1993), p. 361. For a concise introduction, see Margot Finn, '"A Vent Which Has Conveyed Our Principles": English Radical Patriotism in the Aftermath of 1848', *Journal of Modern History*, 64 (1992), pp. 637–59.

33 Gregory Claeys, *Citizens and Saints: Politics and Anti-Politics in Early British Socialism* (Cambridge, 1989), pp. 268–74.

34 *The Democratic Review: Of British and Foreign Politics, History, and Literature* (June 1849), p. 1; quoted in Finn, "A Vent Which Has Conveyed Our Principles", p. 643.

35 On Harney's move toward socialism, see A. R. Schoyen, *The Chartist Challenge: A Portrait of George Julian Harney* (London, 1958), in particular chapter 7, 'From Green Flag to Red'.

36 Finn, *After Chartism*, p. 102.

37 Ibid., p. 117.

38 See Punch illustration: 'Robespierre: Tea Party'. Source: Bishopsgate Institute, London, G.J. Holyoake Diary, 1853, in Finn, *After Chartism*, p. 123.

39 See Bernard Porter's contribution in this volume, Chapter 4.

40 One exception was the meeting of the Jersey population after Pyat's speech and article, but this was obviously not spontaneous, but orchestrated by the Lieutenant- Governor of the island.

7

Continuities and Innovations:
Polish Emigration after 1849

Krzysztof Marchlewicz

The nineteenth century was a time of rapid social and demographic change for Poland. It witnessed the Industrial Revolution, national uprisings and emigration, especially between the pivotal years of 1795 (Third Partition of Poland) and the outbreak of the First World War in 1914. Dissatisfaction with the political state of the country, a lack of opportunity for activity to change it legally and fear of repression meant that for most of this time there were large groups of Polish exiles whose aim was to change the political status of their homeland. The first massive emigration occurred after the defeat of Kościuszko's Insurrection and the Third Partition of Poland in 1795, when several thousand people emigrated. With the creation of the Duchy of Warsaw in 1807, and the Kingdom of Poland in 1815, the number and role of Polish exiles was somewhat reduced. The next waves of emigration took place only after the failure of the November Uprising in 1831, the defeat of the Cracow Uprising in 1846, the suppression of the European revolutions of the late 1840s, and, finally, the failure of the January Uprising in 1864. It is estimated that because of these as many as 30,000 people left the country and settled in France, England, Belgium, Switzerland, Turkey and the USA.[1] Living in the hope of returning to a free Poland, they conducted lively political, literary and scientific activities, whose significance in maintaining Polish national consciousness cannot be overemphasised. The fact that the Polish national anthem was created in exile and was originally sung by the soldiers of the Polish Legions formed alongside the French Army in Lombardy at the end of the eighteenth century has become symbolic.

In considering the Polish 'political' emigration to England after 1849 it should be remembered that it was not unusual to see quite significant groups of Poles arriving in Britain. When participants in the European revolutions of the late 1840s arrived in Western Europe, there was already a large population of Polish emigrants there, consisting mainly of the soldiers of the 1831 Uprising. In France there were several thousand Poles, and nearly 500 lived in Britain. Because of the presence among them of many distinguished Poles,[2] as well as the unusual length of their political activities in exile, this emigration has been termed the 'Great Emigration'. The majority of Polish historians also include in this group the wave of refugees from 1849, correctly observing that among them were many emigrants from 1831 who had participated in the European revolutions and had then gone into exile again. The Great Emigration is considered to have ended in 1864, when the defeat of the January Uprising in Poland sent a completely new wave of emigrants to the West of Europe. This new wave dominated the old centres of Polish emigration.

This essay will look at the history of the Great Emigration in Britain, or, to be more precise, at the history of this emigration after 1849, when the post-November exiles from Poland were joined by several hundreds of veterans of the new European upheavals. Presenting basic information about the Poles living in Britain in the 1850s, this essay will consider how 'the Flotsam of Revolution' changed the image of the old Polish emigration, and will show what the newcomers and the émigrés already settled in England at that time had in common, and what differentiated them. What was new in the activities of this augmented Polish émigré community, and what can be seen simply as a continuation of activities from before the 'Springtime of Nations'?

✳✳✳

We have at our disposal approximate data concerning the population of Polish emigrants in Britain between 1831 and 1857 (see Table 7.1). These come from the pamphlet *O Towarzystwie Literackiem Przyjaciół Polski. Odezwa do Rodaków* [On the History of the Literary Association of the Friends of Poland. An Appeal to the Countrymen] which was published in London in 1857 by the Polish secretary of the Association, Karol Szulczewski.[3] This list is all the more valuable, since it not only gives the overall number of Poles residing in Britain for every year, but also states how many had arrived or left Britain at this time. From this it may be seen that in 1848 more Polish refugees actually left than arrived here. Among those leaving were those who, counting on the improved situation of Poles in Austria and Prussia, were returning to their country, and those hoping to participate in the revolutionary struggles in other European countries. The sudden suppression of the Polish national revival in Poznań and Cracow meant that some of them found themselves back in England as early as the summer of 1848. These were but the vanguard of subsequent waves of Polish revolutionists, who arrived in Britain at a later period. The summer of 1849 saw the arrival of some members of the Polish Democratic Society (PDS), expelled from France because of their contacts with the Republican left. In 1850 they were joined by approximately 150 Polish participants in revolutions in Germany who had sought asylum in Switzerland until this time. On 5 June 1850 a ship with 101 Poles aboard docked in Southampton. These were veterans of the Hungarian Uprising, who, after its suppression, had been interned in Turkey.

Table 7.1 Polish refugees in Britain 1831–57. Data of the Literary Association of the Friends of Poland.

Year	Arrivals	Departures	Deceased	Grand Total in England
1831	2	–	–	2
1832	30	19	–	13
1833	22	2	–	33
1834	545	123	2	453
1835	76	72	2	455
1836	162	28	5	584
1837	115	27	7	665
1838	54	47	7	665
1839	44	93	7	609
1840	29	51	7	580
1841	18	33	5	560
1842	14	21	7	546
1843	11	18	14	525
1844	47	34	6	532
1845	14	21	9	516
1846	15	28	10	493
1847	15	22	10	476
1848	14	45	12	433
1849	116	62	13	474
1850	262	197	1	538
1851	464	204	10	788
1852	163	169	16	766
1853	107	59	8	806
1854	70	65	7	804
1855	88	127	12	753
1856	18	120	12	639
1857	182	68	7	746

(Source: K. Szulczewski, *O Towarzystwie*, p. 38, appendix no. 6). It should be remembered that the LAFP figures are rather understated.

A further 250 of their companions landed in Liverpool on 4 March 1851 and an additional 61 disembarked in Southampton on 6 July 1851.[4] Taking individual cases of emigration into account, it appears that by the end of 1851 at least 650 Poles who had participated in the revolutions of 1848–9 had arrived in England. In the following years Polish refugees continued to arrive. In all probability there were also participants in the upheavals of the late 1840s among them, but these groups were not as large as in the previous period. It should be stressed that not all the newcomers remained in Britain permanently. The catastrophic financial situation of most of the refugees and the serious difficulties they faced in getting a job caused many to leave. We know that of the 101 people who had landed in Southampton in June 1850, forty-six soon afterward sailed to the USA. Of those arriving on two transports that had docked in Liverpool and Southampton in 1851, a similar decision was made by more than sixty individuals.[5] Over the next few years, they were followed by about 200 more Poles. Considerably fewer emigrated to other European countries, and some left for Turkey in the mid-1850s to take part in the war against Russia. This continuous inflow and outflow of immigrant waves meant that the population of Polish emigrants in Britain was very uneven during the 1850s. After growing rapidly in the period 1849 to 1851, it fluctuated between 600 and 900 exiles, as can be seen in Table 7.1.[6]

Around 1851 the newly arrived refugees probably outnumbered the Poles who had been settled for years in Great Britain. Although both groups had been forced to emigrate for the same reason – fighting for an independent Poland – there was much to divide them. This observation certainly applies to the social and professional makeup of the old and new emigration. Polish historians accept that three-quarters of the 1831 emigrants were of noble origin, while one quarter were of bourgeois or peasant background. For good reason, then, this emigration has been described as the elite of the nation in exile. Jerzy Zdrada has written:

> The majority of emigrants were from among the military, and a decided majority of these were officers who comprised approximately 70 % of the whole. Finding themselves abroad was the majority of Polish intelligentsia from the Russian Partition: politicians, university professors, school teachers, students, writers, journalists, officials of the Insurrectionist government and clergymen.[7]

The arrival in England of over 200 Polish soldiers released from internment camps in Prussia in 1834 meant that the emigration in Britain lost some of its elite character. However, on the eve of the 1848–9 revolutions, the majority of emigrants were still of noble origin or members of the above-mentioned professional groups.[8]

The wave of émigrés reaching England after 1849 came from a different social milieu. We do not have any precise figures, but it is known for certain that the percentage of people of non-noble origin was considerably higher than in the case of the 1831 emigration. In addition, the professional structure of the new emigration was not as elite as that of its predecessors. There were far fewer landowners, clergymen, writers, lawyers and other representatives of the learned professions among its ranks, and many more craftsmen and workers.[9] The proportion of officers to privates among the refugees was also different. The majority of veterans of revolutionary struggles arriving in Britain after 1849 were simple soldiers.[10] Often, they were so young that they did not have any qualifications for employment.

The generation gap, although it applied only to some of the newly arrived refugees, was another important reason why the integration of the old and new immigration took time. Mutual contacts were made none the easier by the differences in political and military experience of the refugees of 1831 and those of 1849. A factor unifying these groups was the presence among the new wave of immigrants of a large group of exiles from 1831 who had abandoned their temporary residence in Western Europe in 1848 to take part in revolutions on the Continent. After their defeat, they returned as immigrants to England.[11]

The Poles who arrived in Britain after 1849 found themselves in a much worse financial situation than the refugees who had been there for a longer time. The vast majority of the new arrivals had no funds whatsoever and for various reasons could expect no help from families left behind in Poland. The universal lack of a knowledge of the English language among the newcomers did not help in looking for work. Thanks to the Poles already settled in England and their British friends, some immigrants were able to find employment. The Working Classes Committee founded in Liverpool in 1851 (composed mainly of local Chartists and Radicals) found various jobs within a short time for about 150 refugees recently arrived from Turkey.[12] Although their incomes were not very high, they could count themselves among the lucky ones. The rest were left to the charity of various individuals and institutions.

Table 7.2 Annual grants voted by the House of Commons for the relief of
the Polish refugees 1834–57.

Year	Total sum of the grant	Number of refugees receiving allowances
1834	£10,000	488
1835	£10,000	466
1836	£10,000	477
1837	£10,000	462
1838	£10,000	646
1839	£15,000	553
1840	£13,000	488
1841	£12,000	?
1842	£10,900	488
1843	£10,500	423
1844	£10,000	405
1845	£ 9,700	?
1846	£ 9,400	?
1847	£ 9,100	?
1848	£ 8,700	?
1849	£ 7,390	?
1850	£ 3,791	211
1851	£ 3,000	209
1852	£ 3,000	?
1853	£ 3,000	192
1854	£ 3,000	189
1855	£ 3,000	181
1856	£ 3,000	?
1857	£ 2,740	147

(Sources: *Appeal of the Literary Association of the Friends of Poland to the
Inhabitants of Great Britain and Ireland in behalf of the Polish Refugees*
(London, 1840), p. 23; K. Szulczewski, *O Towarzystwie*, p. 37, appendix no.
5; J. Paszkiewicz, *Lista emigrantów polskich w Wielkiej Brytanii*, pp. 62–3;
Reports of the Annual Meetings of the LAFP, [19th], p. 13, [21st], pp. 7–8 and
[22nd], pp. 7–8.)

The assistance, however, was not great. From 1834 the British government paid Polish political exiles a small monthly pension, but from
the end of the 1830s the authorities allowed new names to be added
to the list of pensioners only in exceptional cases. As a result, the
number of Poles receiving regular support from the Treasury system-
atically decreased. The funds voted by parliament to this end also
decreased (see Table 7.2). As far as I know, none of the immigrants

arriving in England after 1849 was included on the government list. In 1850 the cabinet of John Russell provided £1,200 for transport from Turkey and an additional £100 for immediate help to the Poles who had arrived in Southampton. Somewhat later, pressed by the Literary Association of the Friends of Poland (LAFP), the prime minister also agreed to cover the costs of transporting Polish emigrants to the USA. In the years 1851 to 1857, the government spent approximately £2,500 to this end.[13]

Those immigrants who decided to remain in England could therefore expect support only from private sources. The organisation most active in supporting the Poles was the London Literary Association of the Friends of Poland, which, nevertheless, had to contend with growing problems. At the end of 1848, the leader of the Association, Lord Dudley Coutts Stuart, wrote to his friend, Prince Adam Jerzy Czartoryski: 'It is true that the sympathy, which once existed [here toward the Poles] has diminished. The chief reason is the persuasion, in the public mind, that the Poles are connected with the revolutionary movements all over Europe.'[14] Stuart expressed a similar opinion to Czartoryski in 1850:

> There is scarcely any sympathy remaining for the Poles. The Tories and Conservatives hate them as the promoters of anarchy all over the world; the colder Liberals think they belong to times gone by, to ancient history; the warmer ... feel their interest still more engaged by the Hungarians.[15]

Because a large part of British public opinion held this attitude, the Association, whose funds came from public collections, was forced to limit the scale of its help. The annual expenses of the LAFP for aid to the Poles, which during the 1830s and 1840s had only rarely fallen below £1,000, were much lower after 1849. Recognising its inability to provide allowances to all immigrants and seeing no possibility of finding work for them, the Association began to organise further emigration for the Poles in the 1850s. Emigrants deciding to leave for America or Australia received their travel expenses from the LAFP and sometimes also letters of recommendation to trusted persons at arrival points. This initiative was met with vehement protest, particularly from members of the Polish Democratic Society. They felt that every emigrant leaving Europe weaked the Polish national movement, which would delay the restoration of an independent Poland.[16] In order to stop the wave of further emigration, the PDS increased its own aid campaign for Poles remaining in England. Money for this came from subscriptions from Poles with a source of income, and from collections organised by British friends.[17]

The conflict between the LAFP and the Poles supporting it on the one hand, and the PDS members on the other, was neither the first nor the last conflict within the Polish émigré community in England. Its entire history – like that of the Great Emigration in other European countries – was marked by virulent partisan conflicts, which appear to be common to most political emigrations. Quarrels among the Poles began as early as 1831, caused by different opinions on the reason for the defeat of the last uprising. The scope of discussions soon expanded to the problem of methods to be used to achieve independence, and political visions for the reborn Poland. The first political parties of the Great Emigration were formed during heated polemics. And though many of these organisations were short-lived, it was not long before the overall division of the emigration into right, centre, moderate left and radical left was accomplished.

The main force on the right was that of the camp around Prince Adam Jerzy Czartoryski, former Russian foreign minister and one of the leaders of the Polish government during the November Uprising. Although the headquarters of this conservative group was in Paris, many followers of Prince Adam lived in Britain, finding support among the British members of the LAFP. Their ultimate goal was to build an independent Poland within the borders of 1771, that is, before the First Partition. They hoped to achieve this on the Greek model, by provoking an uprising in Poland and prompting the intervention of Western powers on the side of the Poles. The political ideal of the Hotel Lambert[18] was the British constitutional monarchy, upon which they wanted to model the future Polish state. Prince Adam's circle was aware that some social reforms were necessary in Poland, but detailed discussion of this matter was left for later, in line with their motto: 'First to be and then to consider how to be.'

The centre party on the émigré political scene in England consisted of immigrants who accepted some of the views of Czartoryski's followers as to the methods to be adopted in the struggle for an independent Poland, but did not share the ideas of the Hotel Lambert on the future of the Polish state. They saw the need for a broad land reform and were repelled by the project to put Czartoryski on the regained Polish throne, popularised by some of the Prince's followers. On the other hand, 'the half-measures' group – as they were sometimes called – feared radical reforms promised by the socialists and democrats. Their own organisations were the

Union of the Polish Emigration (Zjednoczenie Emigracji Polskiej – headquarters in Brussels) and the Committee of the Whole Polish Emigration in London (Komitet Ogółu Emigracji Polskiej w Londynie), usurping the right to represent all Poles residing in Britain. Until 1848 the Committee tried to keep an equal distance between Czartoryski's group and the left, whereas it was itself composed of both liberal monarchists and republicans.

The role of the moderate left in the Great Emigration was taken by the previously mentioned Polish Democratic Society (Towarzystwo Demokratyczne Polskie). Founded in 1832 in Paris, it quickly became one of the largest emigrant organisations, whose ranks included Poles living in France, Belgium, Switzerland, Italy and England. Like the Hotel Lambert, the PDS sought ways for Poland to regain its independence, and they put their faith in an armed uprising. However, in contrast to the Czartoryski group, they did not put much stock in the help of Western powers. They also quickly worked out a programme of social reforms, demanding the rebuilding of an independent Poland as a democratic republic, with a one-chamber parliament, a president chosen in popular elections, strong local self-government and free, state-run education. Unlike the radical left, the PDS recognised the good points of private ownership of land and the means of production, and did not postulate the total nationalisation of the economy.

And, finally, on the radical left wing of the Great Emigration was a group of secessionists from the PDS, who in 1835 formed the so-called Polish People's Communes (Gromady Ludu Polskiego). They were active mainly in Britain, in particular in London, Portsmouth and on the Isle of Jersey. Their utopian-socialist programme – most fully presented in Zenon Świętoslawski's work *Laws of the Universal Church* (*Ustawy Kościoła Powszechnego*, 1844) – abandoned the notion of rebuilding the Polish state, aiming instead to create a Slav federation within a world wide republic, in which all the means of production would be owned in common and the upbringing of children would be left to the state. One of Świętoslawski's curious ideas was that Cairo should be the capital of this 'ideal state' and Polish its official language.[19]

What were the relative strengths of these four emigrant blocs in the 1830s and 1840s, and how did the situation change after 1849? Before 1849 the Hotel Lambert group could expect the support of more or less one quarter (approximately 150) of the Poles residing in England. The sway held by the socialists of the Polish People's

Communes was similar, though it must be remembered that in the second half of the 1840s this organisation's activities had begun to wane. Numerically weaker in this same period was the PDS, which never had more than several dozen members in Britain before 1848. The decided majority, however, was connected with 'the half-measures' group. At various times, this circle included from 100 to 250 members.

After 1849, far-reaching changes occurred within this constellation. The old centre group disintegrated, and the majority of its members joined the ranks of the PDS and Czartoryski's supporters. The latter also began to play a decisive role in the Committee of the Whole Polish Emigration in London. There was a visible decline in the influence of the leaders of the Polish People's Communes. Although some historians estimate that there could have been as many as 200 Poles with socialist leanings in England after 1849,[20] no more than several dozen refugees joined specific initiatives undertaken by Polish socialists in Britain in the 1850s. The group moving into the lead at that time was the PDS. This was connected partly with the presence in London of the Society's chief officers, who, upon expulsion from France, had settled there in 1849. A tremendous revitalisation of the PDS came with the arrival in Great Britain of several hundred Polish participants in struggles in Hungary and Germany. The outlook of the vast majority of these excluded any cooperation with émigré conservatives and they joined the PDS *en masse*. Thus in the 1850s the Society's membership grew to several hundred, and it had active sections in Bradford, Halifax, Leeds, London, Manchester, Newcastle, Nottingham, Rochdale, Sheffield and on Jersey.[21]

After 1849 only the weakened socialists, the PDS and the Hotel Lambert remained on the political scene of Polish immigration in Britain, whose centre of gravity had moved strongly to the left. In the first months after the failure of the European European revolutions, the Hotel Lambert was hardly notable for any particular activity. This was to a large extent the result of the inaction of its Paris headquarters. Having painfully experienced the defeat of his plans, Czartoryski for some time considered retiring from public life and handing over leadership of his camp either to his son, Prince Wtadystaw Czartoryski or to his nephew, Count Wtadystaw Zamoyski. The problems of the Hotel Lambert group in England were heightend by the crisis of the LAFP, as it gradually lost supporters and found it increasing difficult to gather funds for its work. Even political friends of Prince Adam such as Lord Dudley Coutts Stuart or Dudley Ryder, the Second Earl of Harrowby, complained that the good climate for pro-Polish efforts in Whitehall and the City was already a thing of the past.

Only a new crisis in Russian-Turkish relations enlivened the activity of the Czartoryski camp on the Thames. The outbreak of the Crimean War renewed their hopes that Paris and London would want to raise the Polish Question. In the mid-1850s Prince Adam and Count Zamoyski visited London on several occasions, offering the governments of Aberdeen and Palmerston the military service of the Poles in return for British support for their aspirations for independence. This proposal was accompanied by a public campaign organised by the LAFP and Hotel Lambert followers in England, whose purpose was to obtain the support of British society for the restoration of Poland. These actions resulted in London granting permission for the formation in Turkey of Polish military units financed by England (1855). The war, however, was near its end, and despite Palmerston's bold plan to take Finland, the Kingdom of Poland and the Caucasus away from the Russians, none of the Coalition partners was willing to fight for such goals. At the Congress of Paris the Polish Question was not raised, which was a serious defeat for the Hotel Lambert. After 1856 the activities of this group slowly faded from the scene in England. The political heirs of Czartoryski, who died in 1861, renewed it for some time during the January Uprising (1863–64), fruitlessly attempting to convince the British authorities to intervene on behalf of the Poles.[22]

The work of the Hotel Lambert group in Britain during the 1850s may be described as a continuation of its earlier actions calculated to keep up the interest of European governments in Polish affairs, building support for the Poles in the West and working towards a good climate for Polish political aspirations. After 1849 the external conditions had changed, but the programme and methods of Czartoryski's group, such as press campaigns, public meetings and instigation of pro-Polish debates at Westminster, remained the same. The socialists and the PDS also continued their previous activities in many areas. However, an additional element may be observed, that is, unusually intensive cooperation with the other European immigrants in England after 1849.

Following the formal disbanding of the Polish People's Communes in 1846, the socialists were for a long time unable to form a new organisation. Of the two traditional centres of their activity – the island of Jersey and London – the former was more active. In March 1849 Zenon Świętosławski returned from the Continent to St Helier and soon surrounded himself with a group of like-minded Poles.[23]

They formed close links with republican refugees from France, Hungary and Italy (Victor Hugo, Charles Ribeyrolles, Pierre Leroux, László Teleki, Lazar Messaros and Luigi Piancini), at that time staying on the Channel Islands. The result of cooperation among this international group was the creation of the Comité Révolutionnaire des Démocrates Socialistes Réfugiés à Jersey. At the end of 1852 Świętoslawski established the Universal Printing Establishment (Imprimerie Universelle) in St Helier, which published various pamphlets by Polish republicans, Hugo and Herzen, and, after 1853, also the emigration journal *L'Homme* edited by Ribeyrolles and Félix Pyat.[24] A small yacht purchased by Świętoslawski served to smuggle these publications to France. The British authorities put an end to the activity of this centre of republican thought at the request of Paris during the Crimean War. In 1855, thirty-nine exiles, headed by Hugo, were ordered to leave Jersey. Among them was Świętoslawski, who managed to move his printing equipment to London where he once again started up the Universal Printing Establishment at 178–179 High Holborn.

From that moment the capital of Britain became the centre of the Polish socialist movement for several years. Although Polish socialist organisations, such as the Permanent Council of Poles in London (Rada Nieustająca Polaków w Londynie) and the Society of Polish Emigration (Towarzystwo Emigracji Polskiej), had been active in London as early as the first half of the 1850s, they were of no importance. Two Poles, Colonel Ludwik Oborski and Wergiliusz Dąbrowski, joined the International Committee only in 1855. After reconstituting the Committee as the International Association in 1856, Polish emigrants retained a strong position in the new organisation and formed one of its four national sections. It was probably on this occasion that Polish socialists finally organised themselves into a group called The Polish People – Revolutionary Commune of London (Lud Polski – Gromada Rewolucyjna Londyn), whose aims were the abolition of private property and the creation of a world-wide socialist republic. This group, among whose leaders were Zenon Świętoslawski, Jan Kryński, Ludwik Oborski and Henryk Abicht, was not very long-lived. In 1858 it was compromised by allowing itself to have been lured into a correspondence with the Prussian chief of police in Poznań, E. Barensprung, who exposed its aims and methods by presenting himself as the president of a non existent Polish revolutionary committee. The waning activity of the International Association brought with it also the end of its Polish section. By 1861, when the owner of the bankrupt Imprimerie Universelle left London, the Revolutionary Commune of London probably no longer existed. Świętoslawski himself died on Jersey in 1875, having gone mad after receiving the news of his son's death in the January Uprising.[25]

Of course, the socialists had a monopoly neither on activity among the Poles living in England, nor on contacts with other emigrant groups. As has been mentioned, the largest Polish organisation in Great Britain at that time was the PDS. At its head was Centralisation, whose most active members were Stanisław Worcell, Wojciech Darasz, Jan K. Podolecki, Antoni Żabicki and Ludwik Bulewski. They coordinated the Society's ongoing activities and supervised the work of the PDS publishing house at 38 Regent Street, where, among other things, the Society's newspaper, *Demokrata Polski,* was edited.[26] Centralisation organised delivery of its publications and sent its emissaries to prepare a new uprising in Poland. The London authorities of the PDS were most active at the time of the Crimean War. Like the Hotel Lambert, the democrats had great hopes on its outbreak, although each group had different plans. Centralisation sharply criticised Czartoryski's project of forming Polish military units alongside the Coalition forces in the East, feeling that all efforts should be concentrated on preparing an uprising in Poland. It appeared, however, that the PDS did not have enough influence in Poland to achieve this goal. What was worse was that some of the Society's members (particularly those from France) did not agree with the position of the London authorities and unsuccessfully attempted to create a 'democratic legion' in Turkey. In this situation Centralisation concentrated on conducting a propaganda campaign in England, calculated to gain British support for Polish aspirations for independence. This was organised in opposition to a similar action by the Hotel Lambert, which the PDS exposed as a campaign by Polish conservatives who were connected with the undemocratic governments of France and England.

Polish democrats had the support of some Italian, German, Hungarian and French exiles, with whom Centralisation had maintained close contacts since the very beginning of its stay in London. As early as 1849, the PDS articles began to appear in *Le Proscrit* (later – *La Voix du Proscrit*), published by French emigrants. In 1850 the Society's activists, together with Italians, Frenchmen and Germans under the leadership of Giuseppe Mazzini, Alexandre Lédru-Rollin and Arnold Ruge respectively, formed the Comité Central démocratique européen, which was joined later by Lajos Kossuth and Dumitru Bratianu. The Poles were represented on the

Committee successively by Darasz, Worcell and Bulewski, who all belonged to the PDS leadership. Centralisation also cooperated with a small group of Russian emigrants. It had particularly close ties with Alexander Herzen, who in 1852 helped finance the Society's London publishing house and opened the Free Russian Publishing House alongside it. The PDS availed itself of the help of its foreign friends in the years when hopes for a solution to the Polish Question were high during the Crimean War. Kossuth, Mazzini, Ruge, Herzen and Lédru-Rollin were present at the meetings organised by the Polish democrats. The PDS often received organisational assistance from English radicals led by William James Linton and Joseph Cowen jr. These efforts all turned out to be fruitless. The uprising in Poland never materialised, and the Polish Question was not on the agenda of the Western powers. After 1856, PDS activity in Britain began to wane, although the organisation was not formally disbanded until 1862.[27]

✱✱✱

It is difficult to present the rich history of the Polish emigration in England after 1849 in such a condensed form. Many aspects of its activities have had to be neglected; others could only briefly be mentioned. In conclusion, we should return for a moment to the question posed at the beginning of this essay and consider what can be called new in the activities of the Polish emigration in Britain in the 1850s, and what was a continuation of their activities from before the 'Springtime of Nations'?

Noticeable elements of continuity occur in the programme and organisational shape of the main refugee circles. Among the Poles living in England we see almost the same organisations functioning after 1849 as before the revolutions of the late 1840s. These groups used much the same methods, and tried to implement programmes whose basic principles had been developed in the 1830s and 1840s. New immigrants thus entered a framework created by the immigrants of 1831, and they usually respected the authority of the former leaders. Only gradually, as the dominant personalities of the old emigration died, did the younger generation begin to take over the leadership of some organisations.

A new quality that appears in the life of the immigrants after 1849 was a distinct shift to the left of the political opinions of the majority of exiles. The wave of participants in the revolutions of the late

1840s brought with it a more radical approach to the problems of Poland and Europe, which increased the popularity of leftist groups. Another new quality was the changed political climate around the Poles in Britain itself. Although the British authorities still did not try to limit the number of immigrants wanting to settle in England, the universally shared sympathy towards the Polish Insurrectionists of 1831 became a thing of the past. Most British politicians and much of public opinion came to see the Poles as a threat to the social order and believed that they should be watched carefully, not given support. The effect of this attitude was to make the material situation of Polish exiles in the 1850s much worse. The only circles on whose solidarity and help the new immigrants could count were those of some English radicals.

Another new quality was the cooperation between the Poles and immigrants of other nationalities. It should, of course, be mentioned that this was not entirely new, as is shown by Ludwik Oborski's contacts with the Deutscher Arbeiterbildungsverein and The Fraternal Democrats in the 1840s, and those between the PDS activists and Mazzini and The People's International League.[28] During the 1850s, however, this cooperation expanded and intensified considerably. It encompassed new areas and reached much deeper into the ranks of given groups, not remaining limited only to the leadership. For some circles it even became one of the most important methods of implementing their programmes. This, it seems, justifies calling it a new quality in the life of the Polish emigration.

Since neither of the two qualities mentioned in the title of this essay appears to outweigh the other, it seems that the 1850s may be described as a new chapter in the history of the same Great Polish Emigration to England between 1831 and 1864.

Notes

1   S. Kalembka, 'Polskie wychodźstwa popowstaniowe i inne emigracje polityczne w Europie w XIX wieku' [Polish Post-insurrectional Exiles and Other Political Emigrations in Europe in the Nineteenth Century], in *Polska XIX wieku. Państwo, spoteczeństwo i kultura* [Nineteeth-century Poland. State, Society, and Culture], edited by S. Kieniewicz (Warsaw, 1982), pp. 200–25. An outline of Polish history at that period is given in *The Cambridge History of Poland,* edited by W.F. Reddaway, J.H. Penson, O. Halecki, and R. Dyboski, Volume 2: *From Augustus II to Pilsudski (1697–1935),* (2nd edn, Cambridge, 1951), pp. 112–460.

2 We shall mention only the famous Polish poets, Adam Mickiewicz, Juliusz
   Słowacki and Zygmunt Krasiński; the composer, Fryderyk Chopin; the
   generals, Henryk Dembiński, Wojciech Chrzanowski and Józef Bem; the
   politicians, Prince Adam Jerzy Czartoryski, Stanisław Worcell, and Zenon
   Świętoslawski.
3 K. Szulczewski, *O Towarzystwie Literackiem Przyjaciół Polski w Anglii.
   Odezwa do Rodaków* [On the History of the Literary Association of the
   Friends of Poland. An Appeal to our Countrymen] (London, 1857), p. 38.
   The LAFP was founded in 1832 by the poet Thomas Campbell
   (1777–1844), who was deeply moved by the defeat of the Polish Uprising.
   Despite its name, for many years, it was primarily concerned with charitable work on behalf of Poles who reached England. It consisted mainly
   of representatives of the English middle class and aristocracy, and its
   leader for many years was Lord Dudley Coutts Stuart (1803–54).
4 See S. Kalembka, *Wielka Emigracja. Polskie wychodźstwo polityczne w
   latach 1831–1862* [The Great Emigration. Polish Political Exiles between
   1831 and 1862] (Warsaw, 1971), pp. 364–5; also *Report of the Nineteenth
   Annual Meeting of the Literary Association of the Friends of Poland*
   (London, 1851), pp. 1–13; and a brochure published by the LAFP *Sprawa
   młodej emigracyi polskiej po wypadkach 1848 w latach 1850–1851 do Anglii
   przybyłej* [The Case of New Polish Emigrants who arrived in England after
   the Events of 1848, in 1850, and 1851] (London, 1852), pp. 3–27.
5 Kalembka, *Wielka Emigracja.*, pp. 365–6; *Report of the Nineteenth*, pp.
   3–11.
6 It should be remembered that the LAFP figures are somewhat understated.
7 J. Zdrada, *Wielka Emigracja po Powstaniu Listopadowym* [The Great
   Emigration after the November Uprising] (Warsaw, 1987), p. 11.
8 A great deal of information about the status of Polish exiles who arrived
   in England in the nineteenth century may be found in an article by J.
   Paszkiewicz, 'Lista emigrantów polskich w Wielkiej Brytanii
   otrzymujących zasiłki od rządu brytyjskiego w latach 1834–1899' [List of
   Polish Refugees receiving Pensions from the British Government between
   1834 and 1899], in *Materiały do biografii, genealogii i heraldyki polskiej*
   [Sources on Polish Biography, Genealogy, and Heraldry] (Buenos Aires /
   Paris, 1964), II, pp. 59–109. It is based on British Treasury records in the
   PRO (ref. T. I/4099, T. 5081–5097, PMG/53/2–8).
9 I. Koberdowa mentions that of 140 Poles, who after the failure of the revo-
   lutions in Baden and Italy, sought asylum in Switzerland and then left for
   England, over fifty were craftsmen or workers; see I. Koberdowa, *Pierwsza
   Międzynarodówka i lewica Wielkiej Emigracji* [The First International and
   the Left Wing of the Great Emigration] (Warsaw, 1964), pp. 9–10.

10 Among the 124 Polish veterans of the Hungarian Uprising who in the spring of 1850 sailed from Turkey to England, there were somewhat over thirty officers; see *Sprawa młodej emigracyi*, p. 24.

11 A good example here is the life of Colonel Ludwik Oborski – a veteran of the Napoleonic Wars and an officer in the Armies of the Duchy of Warsaw and the Kingdom of Poland, who, after the failure of the 1831 Uprising emigrated to France. Following the defeat of the Savoy Expedition, undertaken along with Mazzini's followers in 1834, he emigrated to England. In 1848 he left England, taking part in battles with the Prussian Army in Poznań province (1848), and subsequently led one of the divisions of the Insurgent Army in Baden (1849). After the failure of the Baden Uprising, he returned to London, where for many years he took an active part in the life of immigrant society; see B. Cygler, *Pułkownik Ludwik Oborski – szermierz wolności (1789–1873)*, [Colonel Ludwik Oborski – An Advocate of Freedom] (Gdańsk, 1976).

12 The Secretary of the Committee was a local businessman, James Spur. He was supported by the radical, Joseph Cowen, well known for his later activity, who headed a similar Committee which he had founded in Newcastle; see P. Brock, *Z dziejów Wielkiej Emigracji w Anglii* [On the History of the Great Emigration to England] (Warsaw, 1958), pp. 112–13; also B. Limanowski, *Stanisław Worcell* (Warsaw, 1948), pp. 310–12.

13 *Report of the Nineteenth*, p. 11; Szulczewski, *O Towarzystwie*, p. 37.

14 Stuart to Czartoryski, Isle of Wight, 12 September 1848, Prince Czartoryski's Library, Cracow, Ms 5518 I, pp. 475–6.

15 Stuart to Czartoryski, London, 18 April 1850, Prince Czartoryski's Library, Cracow, Ms 5519 I, pp. 295–6.

16 The position of the LAFP on this matter is explained in the pamphlet *Sprawa młodej emigracyi;* the PDS's position in its main journal *Demokrata Polski* (1 May 1851).

17 Brock, *Z dziejów Wielkiej*, pp. 112–14; Limanowski, *Stanisław Worcell*, p. 310.

18 This name comes from the residence bought by Czartoryski in 1843 on the Island of Saint Louis in Paris.

19 Polish literature on the programmes of the main political groups of the Great Emigration is too extensive to be presented here even in the most abbreviated form. An outline of the problems connected with the issue are presented by S. Kalembka, *Koncepcje dróg do niepodległości i kształtu Polski wyzwolonej w myśli politycznej Wielkiej Emigracji* [Roads to Independence and Ideas on the Future Poland in the Political Thought of the Great Emigration], in *Rozprawy z dziejów XIX i XX wieku* [Studies in XIX and XX Century History] edited by S. Kalembka (Toruń, 1978), pp. 33–45.

Among the literature in English the following may be mentioned: M. Kukiel, *Czartoryski and European Unity 1770–1861* (Princeton, 1955); P. Brock, 'The Birth of Polish Socialism', *Journal of Central European Affairs*, 3/XIII (1953), pp. 213–31; idem, 'Polish Socialists in Early Victorian England: Three Documents', *Polish Review*, 1–2/VI (1961), pp. 33–52; idem, 'The Political Program of the Polish Democratic Society', *Polish Review*, 2/XIV (1969), pp. 89–105 and 3/XIV (1969), pp. 5–24.

20 Koberdowa, *Pierwsza Międzynarodówka*, pp. 18–19.

21 Ibid, p. 12. See also H. Rzadkowska, *Działalność Centralizacji londyńskiej Towarzystwa Demokratycznego Polskiego 1850–1862* [Activities of the London Centralization of the Polish Democratic Society 1850–1862] (Wrocł aw, 1971), p. 46.

22 Various aspects of the activities of the Hotel Lambert during this period are discussed in detail by M. Handelsman, *Adam Czartoryski* (Warsaw, 1948–50), III, part 1 and 2.

23 They included, among others, Roman Czarnomski, Jerzy Mikułowski, Roch Rupniewski and Franciszek Zychoń.

24 A full list of UPE (Universal Printing Establishment) publications may be found in Brock, *Z dziejów Wielkiej*, pp. 163–7. In this are listed, among others, the brochures of A. Hercen, *La Russie et le Vieux Monde* [1854]; G. Mazzini, *Du devoir d'agir. Au parti national* [1854]; L. Piancini, *De la Revolution et de l'Italie* [1854] and V. Hugo, *Discours de l'exil 1851–1854* [1855].

25 See Brock, *Z dziejów Wielkiej*, pp. 82–110; W. Knapowska, 'Lud Polski – Gromada Rewolucyjna Londyn' [The Polish People – Revolutionary Commune of London], *Kwartalnik Historyczny*, 2/LXII (1955), pp. 63–97.

26 This periodical was certainly one of the most important titles among the publications of the Great Emigration. Between 1837 and 1849 it was published in Poitiers and Paris. After a break, publication resumed in Brussels in 1851, and in 1852 it was moved to London. *Demokrata* was published intermittently to 1862.

27 See P. Brock, 'Polish Democrats and English Radicals 1832–1862. A Chapter in the History of Anglo-Polish Relations', *Journal of Modern History*, 2/XXV (1953), pp. 150–6; Kalembka, *Wielka Emigracja*, pp. 366–406; H. Rzadkowska, *Działalność Centralizacji*, pp. 8–150.

28 Cygler, *Pułkownik Ludwik Oborski*, pp. 108–9; Koberdowa, *Pierwsza Mię dzynarodówka*, pp. 26–30; H.G. Weisser, 'The British Working Class and the Cracow Uprising of 1846', *Polish Review*, 1/XIII (1968), pp. 9–10.

8

Lajos Kossuth and the Hungarian Exiles in London

Tibor Frank

Few emigrations have been immortalised in so many diaries, letters, novels, official documents, and spy reports as that of the refugees reaching London after the international wave of revolutions in 1848. It would be no exaggeration to say that there is literally a whole library recording the national and social composition of the groups who sought asylum in the British capital: their political allegiances, their plans and deeds, their conflicts and quarrels, their dreams and disillusionments. According to the British government's official records, there were 4,380 political refugees in Britain in 1853. Of these 2,500 were Poles, 1,000 were French and 260 were Germans.[1] In addition to immigrants officially considered 'political refugees', there were, however, many other émigrés: according to the German Eugen Oswald, the number of exiles who attended the funeral of one Italian patriot was estimated by contemporaries as about 10,000.[2] Many were genuine revolutionaries and freedom fighters disappointed in their aspirations and forced into exile, who hoped that Britain would realize their dreams. But, according to contemporary descriptions, there were also many who – in Johanna Kinkel's dismissive words – bore the title 'revolutionary' as though it were 'the exclusive appellation of some kind of office.'[3] For many of these, as Alexander Herzen remarked, 'revolutionary' signified an occupation and 'position in society'. As fish now out of water, all they could hope for was the outbreak of another revolution. It was then that the craze for levitation and spiritism spread like wildfire among the fanatics, the obsessive and those who had lost heart – a symptom of the psychological crisis of émigré society, which often took refuge in the irrational.[4]

Agents and Spies

The émigrés set up various groupings, organisations, clubs and secret societies of their own. They brought with them the factionalism of their respective homelands, formed ever new groups, and obstinately tried to sustain them. In addition to the constant conflicts, Britain's alien and unfriendly atmosphere contributed to their bad humour. The refugees felt that the host country had offered them asylum not so much for themselves as for the sake of its own self-esteem.[5] In the spring of 1853, serious debates had taken place in the British parliament on the issue of asylum, and, in reply to a question from Lord Lyndhurst, the Prime Minister had raised the prospect of taking legal steps against those who abused the country's goodwill with regard to their refugee status. The Austrian ambassador to London also urged such a policy, and reported to Foreign Minister Count Karl Ferdinand Buol-Schauenstein with satisfaction on the ever-increasing political tensions over the asylum issue. In the end the government did not dare to restrict the rights of the refugees. 'In the present conditions', reported the Hungarian exile Jácint Rónay, 'the British people would regard any infringement of the right to asylum as injurious to their own liberty, and the most sensible measures would somehow fail.'[6] The official British position remained the same throughout the Victorian era, namely that as long as foreign organisers 'did not threaten Britain's public order', the government could not get at them. The party in power invariably reacted with great caution to official requests, emphasising that the British public was highly sensitive to the problems of asylum, and that possible violations of asylum rights could easily lead to the government's fall. Even in 1888 an Austrian diplomat who (on instructions from Foreign Minister Count Gustav Kálnoky) inquired about the possibility of anarchists being expelled was turned away with the answer that the circumstances recalled those surrounding the fall of the Palmerston government forty years earlier, in which infringement of the right of asylum had played a decisive part.[7]

Nevertheless, the British government did what it could against the refugees. When in 1850 the Austrian ambassador to London raised the matter of the refugees with the Home Secretary, the British politician rejected the possibility of heavy-handed intervention, but expressed a readiness to accept that 'all those persons sent to London for the purpose of watching the refugees and recommended by the ambassador' would 'be put into touch with the London police.'[8] This meant that although the British government was unwilling to act against the continental émigrés openly – because it did not dare to do so – it was not averse to offering a helping hand to their persecutors. In this way an international network of agents, which settled on the émigrés like a lethal parasite – a veritable host of observers, 'correspondents' and spies filtering through to London – could operate in a relatively unhindered manner.

Austrian agents sent abroad performed their work separated strictly from the diplomatic apparatus. This is known from an exchange of letters between Minister of the Interior Baron Alexander von Bach and Prime Minister Prince Felix Schwarzenberg at the end of 1851.[9] One source of the conflicts between Buol and police chief Baron Johann von Kempen was precisely that the latter attempted to bring his people into contact with embassies. Just days after Kempen's appointment Buol felt it necessary – on 10 June 1852 – to point out to the head of the Supreme Police Authority that he should either establish direct postal links with his London agents (in this case one Emil Elias Lattes and an agent by the name of Förster), or convey sealed documents to them via the embassy. 'In order to avoid compromising situations, which are not wanted, embassies should, where possible, refrain from all other contact with individuals of this kind', the Foreign Minister emphasised.[10] However, it seems that Kempen's people did not take the Foreign Minister's request seriously. In fact, scarcely one year later Buol felt it necessary to instruct his Paris and London embassies not to admit Kempen's agents. These agents were to send their reports to a 'Mr. Arnold' by way of the ordinary post. In order to signify that it was from one of Kempen's confidants, a telegram in cypher should be signed with an M above a line and two asterisks side by side underneath the line thus: $\underset{**}{\underline{M}}$

In case of need a coded report could be forwarded to the imperial ambassador in Brussels, who would pass it on to Vienna, similarly in cypher.[11] As early as May 1853 Colloredo, the Austrian ambassador to London, mentioned the Foreign Minister's 'emphatic, repeated instruction' that the embassy should not accept secret reports from their authors, but should convey these 'directly to Vienna, to the Imperial Royal Supreme Police Authority.'[12]

It was not merely personal and political conflicts between the heads of the two departments and concern about discrediting 'official' Austria that was behind this concern to separate the foreign affairs and police apparatuses. Vienna worried at least as much about the vulnerability of agents' identities and secrets. This was all the more necessary since the émigrés watched each other with endless mistrust and vigilance,

suspecting an agent in almost everyone. Soon after his arrival in
Britain, Lajos Kossuth gave a speech to the Hungarian émigrés:

> During my sojourn in England [the former governor-president's words
> were noted down by Sándor Mednyánszky, who was present] I have been
> besieged by three kinds of letters: those asking for autographs, those from
> officials, and those making accusations. The last kind come only from
> émigrés, and are the most numerous. I admit that if after these I wanted
> to look about me, I would find only spies, because there is no one among
> you untainted by slander of some kind.[13]

But the suspicions went even further. Kászonyi noted that the Hungarian émigrés, however few there were, were divided into factions. Each
suspected the others and was jealous of them, imagining that it saw
spies everywhere. A captain by the name of Lóránd was the oddest of
them all. He asserted in all seriousness that, as agents of the Austrian
government, Kossuth himself and Mazzini received certain sums, otherwise neither would have been able to make a living. With regard to
himself, however, he said that he was a victim of the Austrian police,
who were contriving constantly to harm him: for example, his land-
lady had been bribed to steal, on a daily basis, his sugar, tea and coal.
They knew when he went out and where he went; at night they put
paint on the railings in front of the house so that he would soil his
coat on them; every omnibus driver and every conductor was an
Austrian spy, and, moreover, those sitting next to him always knew
where he was going and where he had come from.[14]

This paranoid reaction indicates something of the psychological situation in which the émigrés were living in the London of the early 1850s.
Of course, the more sensible of them knew that it was not their own
little secrets that interested the Vienna police. To the protagonists of
Kászonyi's London émigré novel *Die Lorette* it was clear that with
Kossuth's arrival in the British capital they had become participants to
some extent in a major conspiracy, people of whom even the Austrian
emperor would take heed, along with 'Napoleon, the queen of Spain,
Tsar Nicholas, and even the kings of Belgium, Holland and Sardinia
…' 'The spies are nosing round us', says Colonel Guido Zengei, one
of Kászonyi's protagonists, 'in order to discover our goals, and having
been informed, governments on the Continent deny us passports and
visas, and by so doing restrict our activity to Britain.'[15] For the émigrés,
spies and agents represented everyday enemies. The Germans compiled
a list of German police agents operating in London, and Hans Ibeles,
the hero of Johanna Kinkel's novel of the same name, could have
studied exact descriptions of all of them, as well as the disguises they

used to deceive the exiles.[16] As *Die Lorette* shows, the Hungarian émigrés in London sometimes organised real hunts in order to expose individual agents. According to Herzen's memoirs, spies were 'identified, unmasked and beaten up', although the Russian revolutionary adds with resignation that they performed their tasks with complete success nonetheless.[17]

At the time, teaching was the usual source of income for continental émigrés in London. The diaries of German and Austrian refugees show language teaching to have been the most frequent career. Eugen Oswald taught German and French and edited German readers; Malwida von Meysenbug worked as a German governess; Arnold Ruge gave lectures on German literature; and even Count Worcell, a Pole, was undeterred by language teaching.[18] Herzen remarked ironically that 'the Germans taught music, Latin, and literature and art of every sort to pay for their daily beer.' Many who had never taught before, or had never even taken any lessons themselves undertook to give lessons. The competition pushed down the rates horribly.[19]

Teaching among the London Germans features centrally in Johanna Kinkel's émigré novel *Hans Ibeles in London*. The main protagonists almost all teach, and, moreover, in very difficult circumstances. Looking for work was a bitter business and teachers needed to have a wide circle of acquaintances if they 'wished to stay afloat on the sea of competitors that was London'. At least three years were necessary for a teacher to acquire a reputation, while to secure a position in a school amounted almost to a miracle. Private lessons were the rule, and the émigrés soon realized that 'they could not be choosy: they had to teach anyone'.[20]

Kossuth and the Hungarian Community in London

The Hungarian events of 1848–9 have generally been associated, inside and outside Hungary, with the name of Lajos Kossuth (1802–94). A lawyer by training and a patriot by devotion, Kossuth was the leader of the opposition in pre-March Hungary and became first a member of Count Lajos Batthyány's revolutionary government and, subsequently, head of state of the short-lived Hungarian republic of 1849.

The Hungarian revolution and War of Independence, which began on 15 March 1848, proved to be the longest in Europe. Unable to put it down alone, the Habsburgs requested the support of Russian Tsarist troops whose intervention resulted in the Hungarian surrender on 13 August 1849 at Világos (today Siria in Romania).

After the surrender Kossuth fled the country never to return, spending the rest of his remarkably long life in exile. He went first to Turkey
where he was interned at Kyutahia, to be rescued by the USA in 1851.
After a brief stay in Britain he went to the USA for six months and
returned to Britain in mid-1852. He stayed there until 1861, when he
settled for good in Italy.

As a former head of state and acknowledged leader of the émigré
Hungarians, Kossuth enjoyed an exceptional reputation among his
compatriots and in the wider, international community of exiles. He
spoke several languages and devoted his very considerable political
talents to focusing international attention on the cause of Hungary.
With single-minded determination he grasped every opportunity to
identify, discuss and promote the Hungarian issue in all the countries
he visited or lived in – including Turkey, Great Britain, the United States
and Italy – and became the internationally recognised spokesperson for
Hungarian independence and national sovereignty. It is not an exaggeration to say that Kossuth reestablished his nation on the political
map of Europe from where it vanished after the collapse of the
medieval kingdom of Hungary after the battle of Mohács in 1526.

Kossuth's methods included political negotiation, diplomacy and
traditional statesmanship, but he increasingly used more modern
methods of public relations and political marketing, such as public
addresses, lectures and journalism. A much admired orator in both his
native Hungarian and in English, he was able to mobilise public sentiment and marshal emotional support for his homeland on two
continents. His astonishing command of English came from his early,
lonely studies in Hungary, partly during his prison term of 1837–40 in
Buda, and resulted in feverish activity as a public speaker in both
Britain and the USA. In America alone he gave some 600 talks during
his relatively brief stay of about six months in 1851–2, several of which
were recorded among the great speeches of the nineteenth century.

Rescued from his captivity by the US government, Kossuth first came
to England in late 1851. When he arrived, England was experiencing
one of those brief, feverish outbursts of public sentiment so characteristic of the British. 'We are great hero worshippers', Charles Greville
wrote to Henry Reeve of *The Times,* 'and there is something romantic
and imposing in the Hungarian war ... However like other things of
this kind, the fever soon subsides and Kossuth a week after his departure will be forgotten.'[21]

This was not to happen for quite a time. To express the sentiments
of 'Englishmen of all parties', the journalist and author Douglas

William Jerrold proposed a subscription for 'a testimonial taking the form of a fine copy of Shakespeare inclosed in a shrine ...'.[22] Harriet Beecher Stowe remembered how this idea actually emerged: 'There are those here in England who delight to get up slanders against Kossuth, and not long ago some most unfounded charges were thrown out against him in some public prints. By way of counterpoise an enthusiastic public meeting was held, in which he was presented with a splendid set of Shakespeare.'[23] Harper's *New Monthly Magazine* was quick to report the background of the 'penny subscription [that was] commenced to represent Kossuth with a copy of Shakespeare's works, in a suitable casket.' The *Magazine* quoted Douglas Jerrold as saying:

> It is written in the brief history made known to us of Kossuth, that in an Austrian prison he was taught English by the words of the teacher Shakespeare. An Englishman's blood glows with the thought that, from the quiver of the immortal Saxon, Kossuth has furnished himself with those arrowy words that kindle as they fly – words that are weapons, as Austria will know. There are hundreds of thousands of Englishmen who would rejoice thus to endeavour to manifest their gratitude to Kossuth for the glorious words he has uttered among us, words that have been as pulses to the nation.[24]

Kossuth was excited about the presentation. In a hitherto unpublished letter, dated 3 May 1853 and now held by the Folger Shakespeare Library in Washington, he revealed to his political friend Charles Gilpin, MP, the political character of his interest in Shakespeare.

> It is Tuesday already; and I have yet no communication about the 'Shakespeare presentation meeting['], at which you desired my presence from Friday next. – Will it be indeed or not? What hour of the day? What is its particular character? A large open meeting or a private one of a committee? Is it indeed to have a political character or not? Am I expected to be present and to speak? What will be the address which I am expected to answer? – about all this I know nothing yet.[25]

The presentation took place in London's Tavern Hall on 6 May 1853. In a major speech, carefully written for the occasion, Kossuth gave the fullest and most spirited version of his encounter with Shakespeare:

> And there I sat musing over it [i.e. Shakespeare]. For months it was a sealed book to me, as the hieroglyphs were long to Champolion, and as L[a]yard[']s Assyran monuments still are. But at last the light spread over me and I drank in full cups with never quenched thirst, from that limpid source of delightful instruction, and of instructive delight. Thus I learnt the little English I know.[26]

By then his story was complete, finished and polished, openly serving political purposes. As he added to his audience of Londoners, he acquired not only his English language skills from the poet, but also his knowledge of politics as well:

> But I learnt something more besides, I learned politics. What? politics from Shakespeare? Yes, Gentlemen. What else are politics than philosophy to the social condition of men? And what is philosophy but the knowledge of nature and the human heart? And who ever penetrated deeper into the recesses of these Mysteries than Shakespeare did? He furnished me the materials, contemplative meditation wrought out the rest.[27]

What was originally a private myth now came to be the foundation of a *topos*: Shakespeare's name became identified with Kossuth's long preparation for his role as an exiled spokesman for his country. In his 1853 speech in the Tavern Hall he went so far as to identify Shakespeare clearly as 'that mute but eloquent teacher of mine' and referred to his English as 'your language I learnt from him'.[28]

When Kossuth arrived in England in late 1851, there were 182 Hungarian exiles in London.[29] The group was much divided along social, economic and political lines. Some of its members lived in aristocratic seclusion and kept their social circles tightly closed against the bulk of the Hungarian group. They included luminaries such as Count Gyula Andrássy, Generals György Klapka, János Czetz and Antal Vetter, Kossuth's British diplomatic agent Ferenc Pulszky, Colonel Imre Szabó, Ödön Beöthy, Count Karacsay and some others. Other aristocratic Hungarians, such as Counts Pál Esterházy, László Vay and Sándor Teleki, were much more favoured by the rank-and-file members of the Hungarian émigré group because they shared their wealth with the poor.[30] Political loyalty also notoriously caused division: some Hungarians felt that they had no choice but to support their internationally recognised and celebrated leader, Kossuth. This group included Ferenc Pulszky and his circle, former officers such as Dániel Ihász, Fülöp Figyelmessy, Richárd Gelics, Adolf Mogyoródy and several others.[31] Others turned against Kossuth soon after he left for the USA.[32]

Kossuth, however, also had a number of enemies, including General Mór Perczel, 1849 Hungarian Foreign Minister Count Kázmér Batthyány and Speaker of the House Pál Almásy. Most notable among them was Bertalan Szemere, Prime Minister in 1849, who had become a bitter opponent of Kossuth and the former governor's angriest critic, one who shrank from no course of action that might demean Kossuth in the eyes of the Hungarian émigrés and of international public opinion.[33] He therefore established closer links with all those who could assist him in achieving his goal.

> Szemere has so few friends... [wrote Jácint Rónay concerning the former prime minister's position in Paris], the main reason for which, I would venture, is the bitter battle he has been waging against Kossuth, of which here on foreign soil even Kossuth's opponents don't approve; at home, however, people can't forgive it, because it's the action of an enemy. He avoids and easily suspects those who have been Kossuth's friends or adherents; with those who parted company with him he has shaken hands, even when he didn't otherwise respect them. He for his part has been collecting information against the regent, and those who could provide this have been if not his welcome then his honored guests.[34]

In the summer of 1851 Sebœ Vukovics 'found conspicuous the general alienation from Szemere everywhere our fellow-countrymen come together.' Szemere was also voted off the émigré committee in Paris: 'of the twenty-four voters only two cast their ballots for him. I was one of them' – the one-time justice minister wrote to Kossuth.[35] In a letter written to his crony János Bangya, the Austrian spy Gustav Zerffi aptly described their mutual 'friend': 'With this amicable fox one can't get far. He would like to see the whole world serving him, and for free at that. He would not make the slightest, most necessary, sacrifice either for himself or for the party. This is why he is so much without a party.'[36] Of the leaders of the war of independence only those who regarded Kossuth – at least at this time – as their opponent maintained contact with Szemere; these included, for example, Pál Almásy, Count Kázmér Batthyány and General Mór Perczel. The surviving items of Szemere's correspondence are imbued with blind hatred of Kossuth, of jealous and furious passion against the 'triumphator'.[37]

In his first years in Paris Szemere planned and put into effect numerous well-considered moves against Kossuth, partly with the co-operation of the former governor's declared political enemies and partly with that of underworld elements with links to Vienna.

The first anti-Kossuth move to produce major reverberations was made by Szemere along with Count Kázmér Batthyány. Having moved to Paris after his exile in Turkey, the Hungarian Foreign Minister of 1849 came under Szemere's direct influence and, in the unanimous view of contemporaries, acted as his mouthpiece. In open letters published in *The Times* on 30 December 1851 and 2 February 1852 (and drafted with the help of J. A. Blackwell, a British agent in Pest during the Reform Age and the revolution), he fiercely attacked Kossuth.[38] The letters were read with horror in émigré circles.

According to a letter from Gyula [Andrássy], K[ázmér] B[atthyány] has fallen into Szemere's hands entirely, and this action is Szemere's work – believe me, the man's labyrinthine – and for all his great intellect has with the last deed done K[ossuth] more service than harm – and has cut even more at the branch on which he's sitting,

wrote Sándor Karacsay to Klapka after publication of the first letter.[39] Even Pál Almásy, who zealously continued to send his sharply anti-Kossuth letters to Szemere for months after the appearance of the piece in *The Times*, repeatedly poured out his spleen against Szemere. 'That letter is not Batthyány's doing. That scoundrel Szemere is at the bottom of it. Batthyány let himself be used, and was deceived by him.' Then again to Sebœ Vukovics:

the entire masterpiece, this we Parisians know only too well, was written by Szemere. This is S[zemere]'s trick exactly, that he himself never stands up against K[ossuth], lest the possibility for any approach be cut in case events take a turn. And this is why I now regard Szemere as a wretched intriguer who pours his poison in the cups of others – keeping himself distant from his passion and his jealousy in front of the public. He's a sinister character, believe me. But in his case, too, the adage will apply: the higher up the tree the monkey climbs, the more it shows its ugly backside.[40]

Influenced by the letters in *The Times*, the Paris émigrés worded a statement in which they protested against the pieces by Batthyány and by Szemere, who had in the meantime declared his position.

The Paris émigrés were not only scandalized at these actions, but also thought it necessary to declare ... in a statement that they condemn the actions of the above-mentioned ministers as jeopardizing Hungary's interests and relations between the émigrés alike, and as uniformly injurious to Hungary's case, and that they emphatically reject as lack of patriotism the principles expressed in the Szemere article against the integrity of the country...

The declaration was endorsed by seventeen of the twenty-one registered émigrés in Paris; 'Szemere, Batthyány, Bogdány, and Zerffy were the four who did not sign it' – General Czetz reported to Kossuth by way of Miklós Kiss.[41] Thus Zerffi sided openly with Szemere and Batthyány, and by doing so blatantly professed his opposition to Kossuth, although for political reasons the Paris declaration – and therefore the list of its signatories – was never made public. However, Vienna's agents took an even more active role in Szemere's anti-Kossuth policy when they assisted in publishing the German edition of Szemere's violently anti-Kossuth 'character sketches.'[42]

Legacy

Nineteenth-century Hungarian history has few more intricate questions than the political function of the 1849 exiles.[43] Did they serve the legacy of the revolution of 1848 and uphold the political ideals of Lajos Kossuth: independence from Austria and sovereign nationhood? Or did they realise that Hungary should contribute to the restructuring of the Habsburg Empire and take its new position as an integral part of the Austro-Hungarian Monarchy soon to be established? The long years between revolution and compromise gave those in exile much food for thought. Most decided to return to Hungary: some returned in the 1850s, the rest took the opportunity offered by the Austro-Hungarian Compromise of 1867. Some of the returnees succeeded in establishing themselves in the new political structure, such as Count Gyula Andrássy, who became Prime Minister of Hungary (1867–71) and, later, Foreign Minister of the Monarchy (1871–9). Most, however, could find a new niche only in the revitalised economy, not in government. They joined the new banks, railway companies and river regulatory bodies, using their international experience and connections.

There were few, who, like their leader Lajos Kossuth, chose to stay away from their homeland for the rest of their lives. Fiercely opposing the compromise with Austria, Kossuth became a legend during his own lifetime, a symbol of intransigence, willpower and political determination. His name gave birth to a cult that was to be built around the myth of 1848 and 1849 though it was often used (and misused) for the political purposes of the day. To the present day the political watershed of the exile period serves as an allegory or a metaphor – a national example of how to choose between unwavering struggle for an immutable political programme, and yielding to the ever-changing realities of the day.[44]

Notes

1 Arthur Lehning, 'The International Association (1855–1859)', in idem., *From Buonarotti to Bakunin. Studies in International Socialism* (Leiden, 1970), p. 169.

2 Eugen Oswald, *Reminiscences of a Busy Life* (London, 1911), p. 245.

3 Johanna Kinkel, *Hans Ibeles in London. Ein Familienbild aus dem Flüchtlingsleben*, 2 vols (Stuttgart, 1860), II, pp. 122–3.

4 A.I. Herzen, *Byloje i dumy, 1852–1868*. Sobrannye sochinenia VIII–XI. (Moscow, 1956–7), XI, pp. 32–4, 40; A.I. Herzen, *Erlebtes und Gedachtes* (Weimar, 1953), p. 203. Many other London refugees among

the revolutionaries also give accounts of levitation and the conjuring of spirits: Kinkel, *Hans Ibeles*, II, pp. 194–5, 202–28, 260; Dániel Kászonyi, *Ungarn's vier Zeitalter. Erlebnisse und Lebensansichten eines Mitspielers vor, während und nach der ungarischen Revolution in Ungarn und im Auslande* (Leipzig, 1868), III, pp. 176–89; Lipót Fülepp to Vukovics, Jersey, 13 October 1853, MOL: R 216. For the fashion for the occult on the Continent at this time see Josef Karl Mayr (ed.), *Das Tagebuch des Polizeiministers Kempen von 1848 bis 1859* (Vienna, Leipzig 1931), p. 280, note 8. Indicative of the influence of spiritism in Hungary is the fact that even János Arany and his circle engaged in 'table tipping' in the early 1850s; see Albert Berzeviczy, *Az absolutismus kora Magyarországon 1849–1865* [The Age of Absolutism in Hungary 1849–1865], 3 vols (Budapest, 1921, 1926, 1932), II, pp. 402–3.

5 Herzen, *Erlebtes*, pp. 202–3; Kászonyi, *Ungarn's vier Zeitalter*, III, pp. 78–83; E. H. Carr, *The Romantic Exiles: A Nineteenth-Century Portrait Gallery* (London, 1933, Penguin Books-Peregrine Books, reprinted 1968), p. 123.

6 Colloredo to Buol, London, 4, 5, 10 March 1853; Haus-, Hof- und Staatsarchiv, Vienna MÄ PA, England, Berichte. Copies: OSZK–Kt: Fond 27: 56: 683–90. Quotation: Jácint Rónay, *Napló-töredék. Hetven év reményei és csalódásai* [Fragments of a Diary. Hopes and Disappointments of Seventy Years] (MS, n.p., n.d.), I, pp. 329–30.

7 Colloredo to Schwarzenberg, London, 8 June 1850, Haus-, Hof- und Staatsarchiv, Vienna: MÄ IB, Kt 5 (1850), 2293/A; Bach to Schwarzenberg, 10 September 1851, Haus-, Hof- und Staatsarchiv, Vienna: MÄ IB, AHP, Kt 14 (1851), Interna, 1074/g; Report by the London ambassador, 13 March 1879, Haus-, Hof- und Staatsarchiv, Vienna: MÄ IB, Kt 386 (1878), 512/IB: Heider to Kálnoky, London, 11 October 1888, Haus-, Hof- und Staatsarchiv, Vienna: MÄ IB, Kt 524 (1888), Konvolut 87, 3204/4/IB.

8 Colloredo to Schwarzenberg, London, 8 June 1850, Haus-, Hof- und Staatsarchiv, Vienna: MÄ IB, Kt 5 (1850), 2293/A.

9 Bach to Schwarzenberg, Vienna, 25 October 1851, Haus-, Hof- und Staatsarchiv, Vienna: MÄ IB, AHP Türkey 1851. AK–MS Collection. Hajnal papers, Ms 5405/11/113.

10 Buol to Kempen, Vienna, 10 June 1852, Haus-, Hof- und Staatsarchiv, Vienna: MÄ IB, Fasz. 24 (1852), 29/BM, 350/g.

11 Konfidentenwesen in genera, Vienna, 5 April 1853, Haus-, Hof- und Staatsarchiv, Vienna: MÄ IB, AHP, 1853, Interna, Fasz. 24, 207/g. Copy: NSL–MS Collection: Fond 27: 109, 173.

12 Colloredo to Buol, London, 2 May 1853, original: Haus-, Hof- und Staatsarchiv, Vienna: MÄ IB, AHP, copy: NSL–MS Collection: Fond 27: 57: 725.

13 Mednyánszky to Klapka, 20 November 1851, MOL: R 295 (Klapka: Mednyánszky.)

14 Kászonyi, *Ungarn's vier Zeitalter,* pp. 176–7.

15 Dániel Kászonyi, *Die Lorette. Bilder aus dem ungarischen Emigranten-Leben in London. Von einem Mitglied der Emigration,* vols. I–IV (Berlin, 1864), III, p. 270–9.

16 Kinkel, *Hans Ibeles,* II, p. 278. Cf. Malwida von Meysenbug, *Memoiren einer Idealistin* (Berlin and Leipzig, n.d.), II, pp. 74–5; Gercen, *Byloje i dumy,* XI, pp. 197–204.

17 Kászonyi, *Ungarn's vier Zeitalter,* pp. 214–15; Gercen, *Byloje i dumy,* XI, p. 199.

18 Oswald, *Reminiscences,* pp. 270, 299, 303–4, 347–52; Meysenbug, *Memoiren,* II, pp. 12–13, 35–6, 108–27, 148–50, 190–5; Ruge to person unknown, Brighton, 14 June 1853, CPA IML: f. 172, d. 82.

19 Herzen, *Byloje i dumy,* XI, p. 179, 186.

20 Kinkel, *Hans Ibele,* I, pp. 329, 339, 354, 377–8, and 353–83 *passim*; Kászonyi, *Ungarn's vier Zeitalter,* III, pp. 33–4.

21 A. H. Johnson, The Letters of Charles Greville and Henry Reeve (London, 1924), p.203. Quoted by Dénes A. Jánossy, *Great Britain and Kossuth* (Budapest, 1937), p. 112.

22 Ibid., On the history of the 1851 subscription initiated in the *Daily News* by Douglas Jerrold see É. H. Haraszti, *Kossuth: Hungarian Patriot in Britain. A Book to Commemorate the Centenary of his Death 1894–1994* (London-Budapest, 1994), pp. 29–31. For a recent, excellent treatment of the Shakespeare presentation see Ágnes Deák, 'Két ismeretlen Kossuth-dokumentum' [Two unpublished documents by Kossuth], *Holmi,* 6 (1994), pp. 832–48.

23 Harriet Beecher Stowe, *Sunny Memories of Foreign Lands* (London, 1854), p. 182.

24 Harper's *New Monthly Magazine,* 6 (1852), p. 277. Copied by István Gál, courtesy of Gál's family.

25 Kossuth to Charles Gilpin, Esq., 21 Alpha Road, Regents Park, 3 May 1853. The Folger Shakespeare Library, Washington. I am greatly indebted to Dr. Péter Dávidházi for drawing my attention to, and allowing me to use, this document which he found in Washington, D.C. Unfortunately, Gilpin's answer is not available in the Hungarian National Archives where most of his correspondence with Kossuth is preserved.

26 Kossuth's speech was found and recently published in Hungarian translation by Deák, 'Két ismeretlen Kossuth-dokumentum', pp. 832–48. I am indebted to Dr Deák for generously allowing me to quote from Kossuth's original version which she found in the British Library in London.

27 Ibid.

28 Ibid.

29 Kászonyi, *Ungarn's vier Zeitalter*, III, p. 50.

30 Ibid., III, pp. 50–3.

31 Ibid., III, pp. 119–20.

32 Ibid., III, pp. 71–7.

33 Maller Sándor, 'Marx és Szemere [Marx and Szemere],' *Századok* 90 (1956), pp. 668–9; Klára Málek, *Szemere Bertalan az emigrációban* [Bertalan Szemere in Exile] (Pécs-Balatonfüred, 1940), pp. 20–2; István Hajnal, *A Kossuth-emigráció Törökországban* [The Kossuth Emigration in Turkey], 2 vols (Budapest: Magyar Történelmi Társulat, 1927), I, p. 384.

34 Rónay, *Napló-töredék*, II, p. 106.

35 Ibid., *Napló-töredék*, II, p. 106. Vukovics to Kossuth, MOL: R 90, I. 1288, Paris, 12 July 1851.

36 Zerffi to Bangya, Paris, 27 August 1852, CPA IML: f. 458, op. 1, d. I. 11289.

37 See, for example, Almásy to Szemere, Zürich, 1851, EK–MS Collection: Litt. Orig. 582: 16; also other letters preserved in the Szemere papers at the UL–MS Collection.

38 Dénes Jánossy, *A Kossuth-emigráció Angliában és Amerikában 1851–1852* (Budapest, 1940-44–48), Vol. I: 347–52; II: 1: 158–71; Blackwell: Memoir for Count Emanuel Zichy-Ferraris, 10 July 1868, AK–MS Collection: Blackwell papers, Ms 10.008, fol. 11–16. For similar press attacks by Szemere see Jánossy, *A Kossuth-emigráció*, II, 1: pp. 290–4, 463–76.

39 Karacsay to Klapka, London, 5 January 1852, MOL: R 295, Bundle 7.

40 Almásy to Vukovics, Jersey,27 January 1852, MOL: R 216.

41 János Czetz to Miklós Kiss, Paris, 26 February 1852 (copy); Miklós Kiss to Kossuth, London, 5 March 1852 (copy), MOL: R 279. Cf. Jánossy, *A Kossuth-emigráció*, I, p. 352, II, 2: pp. 578–9.

42 Bartholomäus Szemere, *Graf Ludwig Batthyány, Arthur Görgei, Ludwig Kossuth. Politische Charakterskizzen aus dem Ungarischen Freiheitskriege* (Hamburg, 1853).

43 Lukács Lajos, *Magyar politikai emigráció 1849–1867* [Hungarian Political Exile 1849–1867] (Budapest, 1984), pp. 359–63.

44 I have drawn on my book *From Habsburg Agent to Victorian Scholar: G. G. Zerffi (1820–1892)* (Boulder, Colorado, 2000), and my article '"Give Me Shakespeare": Lajos Kossuth's English as an Instrument of International Politics', in Holger Klein and Péter Dávidházi (eds.), Shakespeare and Hungary, *Shakespeare Yearbook*, 7 (1996), pp. 47–73.

9

The Politics of Czech Liberation in Britain after 1849*

Ivan Pfaff

Around 125 Czech radicals who had taken part in the revolutionary upheavals in Saxony and Baden in May 1849 fled to, or settled in, the West after they were amnestied in 1849 and 1850. Most of them were second- or third-rate revolutionaries who lacked not only the material means, but also the ability and the courage to commit themselves to a new revolutionary struggle. They were unable to integrate, politically and culturally, into new surroundings, and had no idea how to continue their political struggle from exile. Many of these revolutionaries therefore disappeared without trace, and we know the names of only a few. Among these are Josef Václav Frič, Karel Maux, Jan Mráček, Jirří Nedvídek, Karel Korbel, and, in particular, Karel Jonáš and Adolf Straka.

Straka was Bakunin's closest collaborator in preparing the May conspiracy. After the military defeat of the revolutionary upheavals of May 1849, he fled to Britain and worked with a number of Germans who had previously shared his opinions, including Gottfried Kinkel, Arnold Ruge, Karl Vogt, Eduard Juch and Karl Blind. Straka was one of the few Czechs who we know was politically active in London. Most of the other Czech exiles were completely occupied with their own survival. Other exceptions were Jan Heidl, František Rieger, and Václav Frič, already mentioned above. Heidl was a socialist and an enthusiastic Marxist. Unlike Frič, he had doubts about the legitimacy of an independent Czech state, and firmly rejected any attempt to strengthen Czech nationalism.[1]

The real political leader of the Czech liberals in 1948–9 was Dr František Ladislav Rieger (1818–1903). He travelled from Paris to London on 28 April 1850, and spent two years in British exile. There he joined his friend Antonín Springer,[2] who had gone to London

---

* Translated by Angela Davies, GHIL.

from Belgium before Rieger. In Britain, Rieger witnessed the birth of the trade union movement out of a declining Chartism after 1848. His interest in the British trade union movement gave rise to an interest in the British economy in general. Attending debates in the House of Commons, he witnessed the rhetorical duel between Gladstone and Disraeli on the issue of free trade and the abolition of protective tariffs. He also followed with interest Cobden's and Bright's agitation for the introduction of universal suffrage, a decrease in military expenditure, and the consistent application of free trade and a free market.

On the recommendation of the Bohemian Count Moritz Deyne, whom he had met by chance in London, Rieger was invited by Lady Lovelace to a party where he made the acquaintance of a number of interesting and important people in British society, including Lord Palmerston.[3] It is difficult to say whether Rieger's audience in the Foreign Office was arranged on this occasion. Rieger himself described the evening as extraordinarily instructive.

Even before his arrival in London, Rieger had written from Paris to his friend Karel Havlíček, reporting his experiences of Western Europe, which had been totally unfamiliar to him:

> In Rome and Naples I assisted in overturning a rotten government, and in Paris, in proclaiming the new constitution in June 1848. Everywhere I saw political parties acting, heard tribunes giving speeches, saw the parliaments of so many peoples in action … I was involved in so many important matters, experienced and tried out so much – what wonderful opportunities I was offered to get to know the various nations, and powerful political parties, as well as excellent men, and statesmen in particular.[4]

During his stay in Britain, Rieger undertook a systematic analysis of the British nobility, and out of this work grew an essay which was published on 19 June 1850 in the Bohemian journal, *Slovan*.[5] In this essay, Rieger defined the House of Commons as 'the most competent political body in the world', and claimed that 'at home [in Bohemia], more than in any other country, are to be found the elements natural to a constitution of the British type'. He arrived at this conclusion by comparing the English with the Bohemian nobility. However, he uncritically idealised the English nobility to such an extent that doubts must arise as to the adequacy of his analysis of his experiences in Britain. By comparison with the uncultivated Bohemian nobility, he suggested, the qualities of the English nobility shone all the more brightly. Above all, the English nobility seemed to him to be 'national'. According to Rieger, it was at the peak of everything 'sublime, noble, educated, and beautiful', 'everything proceeded from it, everything tended towards it, everything thrived under its generous protection'. It promoted charity, he argued, and 'all progressive movements among the people'. The caste system was alien to it, he wrote, as it 'formed merely the next level in a compact national body'. Its influence in society did not derive from privilege, he continued, but was the outcome of many natural factors. The qualities of the English nobility that Rieger valued most highly were its 'eloquence, impartiality, independence, discretion, political experience, personal honesty', and its 'social connections'. Rieger's Anglophilia and his deep admiration for British political and social institutions undoubtedly contributed to the distortions and one-sidedness of his image of the English nobility. In his homeland, this was met with a lack of understanding, especially as he had left out all the negative aspects of this class–aspects which Dickens had begun to depict clearly at about the same time.

Rieger was still in England in mid-July 1850 when his friend Karel Havlíček, the founder of modern Czech journalism, began to publish a series of commentaries on English works in *Revne Slovan* (The Slav), which appeared in Kutenberg (Kutná Hora). After reading Macaulay's *History of England from the Accession of James the Second,* Havlíček reflected on the work of the historian and England's political development. Havlíček valued Macaulay as a 'highly honourable English statesman and one of the most eloquent members of the House of Commons'. Especially important to Havlíček was Macaulay's account of the Glorious Revolution of 1688, which made it possible for England to 'develop peacefully' without 'any sort of intervention by the government'.[6] Havlíček, convinced of the 'sublime and wonderful qualities' of the English constitution,[7] was a passionate supporter of Palmerston's Liberal domestic and foreign policy. He therefore fiercely denied the rumours circulating in the Viennese press that Palmerston would soon lose his position as Foreign Secretary. On the contrary, Havlíček was convinced that the British Foreign Secretary would 'achieve even greater power in the future cabinet than he already enjoys under the Prime Ministership of Lord Russell!' It was even possible, he suggested, that 'Palmerston might be called by the Queen to form the new government'.[8] This was an expression of Havlíček's wishful thinking. He expected too much from Palmerston in respect of his own political interests, and forgot that it was Palmerston who had pushed British imperialism in the overseas colonies. Havlíček's comment on the crisis in the British government was correct, however. He argued that 'all that was required for the complete victory of the forces of reaction in Europe was the fall of the Liberal government in England, and the installation of a Conservative government which, unlike the Liberal Palmerston, would support the European governments introducing reactionary measures'. For this reason alone, Havlíček's one-sided idealisation of Palmerston is understandable:

> God grant Palmerston a long period in power, for he is the first Secretary of State ... to make some rulers quake. ... Lord Palmerston has been the concience of a number of cabinets, especially of those which do not like to keep their word. As long as Lord Palmerston is the British Foreign Secretary, a number of constitutions ... will survive, at least on paper.[9]

Havlíček overestimated Palmerston's real opportunities, and did not take account of his personal ambitions, as Palmerston's Italian policy after 1859 demonstrated.

Like Rieger, Havlíček also dealt with economic questions. In April 1851 he reflected on the abolition of duties on imported corn, which, he argued, would lead to lower food prices, a pressing need for the people, and to a loss of the high profits made by the British gentry.[10] He thus demonstrated a mature understanding of complicated economic matters. 'It is our task', Havlíček wrote, 'to value the English nation, the first and most cultivated in the world, to learn from its example, and to strive to achieve the same happiness.' He expressly praised 'all the excellent aspects of Britain's government and the community of freedom and law', and recommended it as a basis by which to orientate Czech politics and cultural developments in future.[11] In the last issue before *Slovan* was officially closed down in August 1851, Havlíček discussed the models of passive resistance which he had found in works by Daniel O'Connell and John Hampden, the Renaissance statesman and scholar.[12] The fact that Havlíček planned to flee to London should he be expelled from Austria was indicative of his enthusiasm for England.[13]

Frantisek Ladislav Rieger was received by the British Foreign Secretary, Palmerston, on 7 July 1850. It is not known who arranged this audience for Rieger. What did Rieger expect of Palmerston? He knew that Palmerston had contrived weapons deliveries for Sicilian rebels. As a politician he continued his public demonstrations against authoritarian regimes. Reiger was aware that Peel had accused Palmerston of judging foreign governments. Yet in this way, Rieger at least believed, Palmerston kept Russia and Austria in check. Palmerston had only recently refused to apologise to the Austrian envoy for the demonstrations staged by the people of London against the 'bloody' Austrian general, Haynau, who had so brutally put down the Hungarian rising of 1849.[14] It can come as no surprise that Rieger's expectations were high when he finally met the British Foreign Secretary in person. Yet his hopes were dashed. Rieger discussed the Balkan question with Palmerston, revealed to him the situation of the Balkan peoples, and explained that British support for Turkey was misplaced. The best course for British foreign policy, he suggested, was to expel the Turks from Europe and thus to liberate the people of the Balkans. Rieger explained to Palmerston why this policy would be to Britain's long-term advantage, even if it must appear absurd to Palmerston at present. Rieger, who alienated Palmerston on this point, did not understand that for Britain 'the sick man on the Bosporus' provided an effective barrier to Russia's expansionist ambitions in the Mediterranean, where, after the dismemberment of Turkey, Russia would pose a threat to British interests. Rieger therefore switched quickly to the Austrian and Bohemian question. Here he was more likely to attract Palmerston's attention. Palmerston saw the only solution as the establishment of a confederation in central Europe, in which the various nationalities would have equal rights. However, he considered that the chances of such a confederation being set up were small, first because of the resistance to be expected from the Austrian government, and secondly because of the heterogeneous interests of its potential members. In the end, Palmerston suggested that the Czechs should turn to Russia if they wanted to preserve their national identity.[15]

On this, Palmerston was of the same opinion as Thomas Carlyle, an internationally recognised authority, to whom the Czechs had turned for advice in June 1850. Carlyle recommended to Antonín Springer that the Czechs should Russify in order to avoid being Germanised. 'What do you want to achieve with this preservation of your nationality?' Carlyle remarked to Springer. 'All such ideas are obsolete, not appropriate for times calling for simplification of the current multiple powers. You say that the Germanization of your nation is unacceptable, allright then, let it become Russian.'[16] Carlyle was not a particularly happy choice because of his Germanophile and imperialist inclinations. In this respect he personified a type of

Western intellectual with a broad perspective and international reputation who, nevertheless, only disorientated the thinking of Czech
exiles. How much bitter truth was in Springer's reply to a British
author, in which he commented on Carlyle's ideas: 'They want us
to be liberal, but never free; they accuse western Slavs of loving the
Russians, but deprive us of any means to remain Slavs in any form
other than Russian ... Make it so that Russia is not their only helper,
and it will not be the only master, in fact it will be no master at all
in the East.'[17] Carlyle's absurd opinion was also shared by Lord
Clarendon, Palmerston's successor in the Foreign Office in Gladstone's first cabinet. As late as October 1868, in a style clearly
reminiscent of Chamberlain, Clarendon dismissed with contempt the
'ludicrous demands of a nation of whose existence Europe does not
know'.[18]

In July 1850 Rieger had sent Havlíček in Bohemia, via Springer,
a number of British weeklies to serve as models for his own planned
journal project.[19] Even before his audience with Palmerston, Rieger
had planned to visit a number of English and Scottish industrial
areas with Antonín Springer in order to gain a first-hand impression
of social and economic conditions there. Their observations could
also be 'highly significant' for their own homeland because it seemed
to Rieger that Bohemia must 'take the same path'.[20] After returning
from a private trip to Scotland, Rieger met Springer in Manchester,
where they visited the big factories together. Then they went on to
Liverpool and Birmingham. Rieger noted that in these advanced
industrial regions it was possible to 'observe phenomena which will
also characterise our own industrial age, and to see social conditions
which we will also arrive at through the development of industry,
for our country will proceed along the same path'.[21] Astonishingly,
his visit to Manchester, Birmingham and Liverpool did not provoke
indignation in Rieger about the social conditions of exploited
workers, as could have been expected. Instead, he became a
supporter of unrestrained Manchester liberalism.

In 1852, when Springer published his experiences of the journey
they had undertaken together, Rieger was already back in Bohemia.
The essay, written in Czech, was devoted to social life in England.
In it, Springer looked at the poverty in England from the point of
view of classical liberalism, and concluded that the best solution
would be to combine freedom of trade with freedom of assembly.
However, England remained the model for the economic development of a future, emancipated Czech society:

Knowledge of economic conditions in England touches our own economic interest, because in Britain all politics grows out of the same confident and complete character of the country. Britain constantly weighs up whether this or that political direction will bring the country material wealth and thus hold out to society the promise of success. Britain has long since abandoned dynastic politics. The main motive behind the entire life of the state is the consideration of material prosperity.[22]

At the beginning of 1852, another Czech revolutionary, the Liberal politician and friend of Havlíček, Antonín Maria Pinkas,[23] was also pleased that Britain was the only country not to have fallen victim to absolutism. He considered it an 'empire of humanity', and thus as a suitable model for Czech conditions.[24]

Rieger's Czech opposite in London was Josef Václav Frič (1829–90), a Czech student leader of 1848 and head of Czech political radicalism. On 30 April 1859 Frič, who had been amnestied by Austria, went to London, where he stayed until the beginning of 1861 before moving to Paris. Frič, a politically suspect revolutionary in Austria, was soon kept under surveillance by Austrian police spies in London. Thus in a letter to the chief of police in Prague, dated 26 July 1859, the Prague governor wrote: 'I lay special emphasis on the connection between this matter [Frič's departure for Britain and his revolutionary activities in Western Europe in support of Czech independence] and the aspirations of … Joseph Fritsch, at present living among political refugees in Britain.'[25] In London, Frič co-operated with the German democratic exile, Gottfried Kinkel, and published a number of commentaries in Kinkel's journal *Hermann*. Frič later explained: 'It is our aim, modelled on peoples such as the Italians, the Poles, and other aspirants for freedom, to struggle hard to achieve independence within the family of fraternally thinking nations of Europe.'[26]

Frič's diary allows us to reconstruct the emotional turmoil which an emigrant in London went through. On 1 May 1859 Frič was convinced that London held out great opportunities for anyone who wanted to be successful.[27] On 9 May 1859 he was greatly impressed by a visit to St Paul's Cathedral.[28] On 4 July of the same year he visited the National Gallery.[29] On 20 December 1859 he was plagued by doubts as to whether he would ever get used to England.[30] Although Frič had some English contacts, he mostly worked with other European emigrants. In addition to Kinkel, Frič valued contact with Straka. On 30 May 1859 he negotiated with Ledru-Rollin. Between 18 and 20 January 1860 Frič's diary entries provide information about his correspondence, published in *The Times*. It all dealt with the suppression of the Czech national movement in Austria and the necessity for the multinational Austrian state to form a confederation.[31] On 17 February 1860 another article in *The Times* is mentioned.[32] Between 20 and 24 October, Frič noted that he had met the British journalists Bolton, Griffin and Wylde, and that he and Straka had discussed the political future of the Czech people with them.[33] Between 13 and 16 December 1860, he again wrote articles for *The Times* of London.[34]

Rieger himself informed Frič about his second audience with Palmerston on 21 July 1862. We have less information about this meeting than about the first one in 1850. Rieger reminded Palmerston of the advice he had given at that time, namely, that the Czechs should turn to Russia if they wanted to preserve their national identity. He informed Palmerston that, in his experience, this would be tantamount to committing national and political suicide. Rieger told Palmerston about a meeting of Europe's revolutionary parties which he had attended in Southampton Street, at which Herzen and Bakunin had arrogantly declared that the future liberal and revolutionary Russia would simply 'swallow' small Slavic peoples. Rieger asked Palmerston for his advice on how to make it possible for small Slavic peoples like the Czechs, but also others which were at present part of the Habsburg monarchy, to be integrated into a Western European system of states as independent entities. Unfortunately, we do not know what Palmerston replied.[35]

Frič sought out the London leader of Russian revolutionary democrats, Alexander Herzen, and established contact with him. Frič hoped that cooperating with Herzen would give him opportunities for his own work with Czech exiles. On 19 July 1859 Frič met Herzen for the first time. A number of further meetings ensued. On 8 May 1860 Herzen promised Frič that he would support Czech propaganda, but the connection was of no advantage to Frič because the promised support never materialised. On 20 May 1860, Frič noted: 'It is a bad situation; he [Herzen] does not want to compromise himself with us, he does not know or trust us. He does not need our help.'[36] It is true that Herzen regarded the Czechs as politically immature and incapable of having a revolution. Disappointed, Frič withdrew, and, soon after, he moved to Paris. He returned to London on 27 April 1862 for the World Exhibition, and stayed until 9 May. At Bakunin's request, Frič returned to London from Paris on 16 June 1862, in order to discuss with him the publication of a journal, *Svoboda všeslovanská* (Pan-Slavic Freedom), which was to be produced in Geneva. Frič stayed at his previous accommodation, at 10 Norfolk Road, and at Rieger's home, whose address we do not know. Frič met his friend, the Prague radical Vojta Náprstek, at Evan's Music and Supper Room, Covent Garden, and at the Eldorado Music Hall.[37] Both agreed that Bohemia should take Britain as a model.

During the World Exhibition, Rieger also met Frič and Bakunin to discuss the journal project.[38] At the same time, Frič's brother Václav Frič was in London for two months. He was a member of the radical Prague group which Karel Jonáš and Adolf Straka had worked with. In London, Václav Frič met numerous leaders of the European emigration. As mentioned above, he negotiated with Bakunin the planned publication of the revolutionary, anti-Austrian journal *Svoboda všeslovanská* in Geneva.[39]

English influences can even be traced inside Bohemia. Thus, for example, the future leader of the Young Czechs, Karel Sladkovský, a 'renegade' from 1848 radicalism and a political friend of Frič's, was inspired by British Chartism. In the early 1860s, Sladkovský attempted to force the Austrian government to implement social reforms by staging large public gatherings and workers' demonstrations.[40] In a speech which Sladkovský gave at an outdoor rally on 12 March, he held up Britain as a model. He pointed to the relationship between Belgium and Holland as a confederal community of two independent states, and compared the position of Bohemia in relation to Hungary. Yet he was convinced that Bohemia should not be brought into a similar relationship. Instead, following Britain's example, he urged, Bohemia should step by step work towards a Reform Bill.[41]

The Austrian authorities were uneasy about the clear reference to Liberal Britain as a model for Czech politics. Their unease increased when, in the summer of 1863, they were informed that the British consul, George Mitchell, was on his way from St Petersburg to Prague. As the Austrian Interior Minister reported to the Prague governor on 13 June 1863, Mitchell seemed to have been instructed by London to exchange information about the current situation with former Czech politicians. Whether this meeting actually took place or not, however, we unfortunately do not know.

Czech exile politics in Britain after 1849 had its limits. It is hardly more than an interesting, but hitherto unknown episode in nineteenth-century Czech history. Yet it also marks a new quality in Czech politics, which, for the first time, opened itself to Western Europe. Until 1849–50, the Czech national movement had related primarily to the Habsburg monarchy. At most, adopting a backwards-looking pan-Slavism, it had looked towards Russia. Rieger's and

Frič's approach to Britain was the first time that Czech political representatives had ever turned towards Western Europe. This unique and completely new orientation brought fruitful new themes and contents into the discussion, thus signalling a new quality in Czech politics. The episode seems characteristic of the postrevolutionary situation in Central Europe, which was marked by political reaction. Seen in this light, it is a revealing testimony to the Czech striving for freedom in a pan-European context around the middle of the century. As such, it is of lasting value.

Notes

1 Heindl to Frič, London 24 March and 3 April 1863. Literární archiv Pamaátníku národního písemnictví, Prague (hereafter cited as: LA PNP), Sign. Fa 44.

2 Antonín Springer, doctor of law (1825–91), German–Bohemian art historian, historian and politician. In 1848 and 1849 he taught a course of lectures on 'The History of the Revolutionary Age (1789–1848)' at the University of Prague, and in 1849 his book of the same title was published there; appointed Professor of Art History at the University of Bonn in 1860, prominent political and intellectual figure of European stature for the Czech national movement.

3 Karel Kazbunda, 'Pobyt Dr. F. L. Riegra v cizině r. 1849–1850' (Rieger's Sojourn Abroad), *Zahraniční politika*, 8 (1929), pp. 1026–9; 'Z vlastnich pamětí Dr. F. L. Riegera I. Pobyt za hranicemi 1849–1850' (From Rieger's Memoires, i: Sojourn Abroad), in Bohuš Rieger, *Spisy drobné*, ii (Prague, 1905), pp. 640–3.

4 Rieger to Havlíček, Paris, 12 December 1849, printed in Jan Heidler (ed.), *Příspěvky k listáři Dr. F. L. Riegra* (Contributions to Rieger's Correspondence), i (Prague, 1926), nos. 124, 73.

5 F. L. Rieger, 'Aristokratie a ústavni svoboda' (Aristocracy and Constitutional Freedom), *Slovan*, 19 June 1850, pp. 307–11.

6 Karel Havlíček, 'Macaulay o revolucích', *Slovan*, 13 July 1850, reprinted in Zdeněk Tobolka (ed.), *Politické spisy K. Havlícka* (The Political Writings of K. H.), iii/1 (Prague, 1902), p. 152.

7 Havlíček, 'Pozorovatel politický' (The Political Observer), *Slovan*, 1 March 1851, p. 1,293.

8 Havlíček, 'Pozorovatel politický', *Slovan*, 5 March 1851, pp. 1,299–1,300.

9 Havlíček, 'Pozorovatel politický', *Slovan*, 8 March 1851, pp. 1,300–1,306.

10 Havlíček, 'Svobodný vyrob a a svobodný obchod' (Free Production and Free Trade), ii, *Slovan*, 12 April 1851, pp. 696–8.

11 Havlíček, 'Pozorovatel politický', *Slovan*, 2 July 1851, pp. 1,415–17.

12 Havlíček, 'Něco o zakoním odporu' (Concerning Lawful Resistance), *Slovan*, 10 August 1851, pp. 800–4. As early as the 8 January 1851 issue of *Slovan* Havlíček had published the translation of the entry for John Hampden *Rottecks Staats-Lexikon* of 1847under the title 'Příklad zakonního odporu' (Example of Lawful Resistance). On 15 August 1851 he reprinted Jakob Venedy's essay 'Daniel O'Connell' in *Slovan*.

13 Havlíček to Palacký, Brixen, 17 August 1853, in Ladislav Quis (ed.), *Korrespondence K. Havlicka* (Prague, 1903), p. 669.

14 Benedetto Croce, *Geschichte Europas im 19. Jahrhundert* (Zurich, 1935), p. 185.

15 Notes by Marie Červinková-Riegrová, dated 6 February and 13 May 1886, manuscript, Archive of the National Museum, Prague. Rieger does not mention his meeting with Palmerston in his memoires.

16 Springer on his visit to Carlyle in Chelsea, London in June 1850, reprinted in Jan Heidler, *Antonín Springer a česká politika v letech 1848–1850* (Antonín Springer and Czech Politics 1848–1850) (Prague, 1914), p. 174.

17 Ibid. 'We know that we must give a shadow of power in the West priority over real influence in the East', Springer's commentary on Carlyle continued. 'Thus all that is left is Britain–the only Great Power which is capable of paralysing Russia's might. This is its interest and endeavour. Britain's true task on the Eastern question should be to support the efforts which the oppressed peoples are making towards emancipation, so that they do not have to be dependent on Russia.'

18 '… de mettre fin à ces troubles et de ne pas trop tenir compte des ces, ridicules pretentions d'une Nationalitè dont l' Europe ignorait l'existence … si des encouragements impolitiques.' Vitzhum to Beust, Paris, 11 October 1868, no 28/C , très reservé/G.P.–BM 68, IBAM, HHSA – ÖSA Vienna.

19 Rieger to Havlíček , London, 9 August 1850, in Heidler, *Příispěvky k listáři Dr. F. L. Riegra*, i., nos. 128, 77.

20 Rieger to Palacký, London, 5 July 1850, ibid. nos. 127, 75–6. Rieger had already informed his brother-in-law of this intention on 22 June 1850; ibid. nos. 126, 75.

21 From Rieger's Memoires (cf. note 3), p. 643.

22 Antonín Springer, *Studie socialniho zivota v Anglicku* (A Study of Social Life in England), Časopis Ceskeho Musea 1852, quoted from Heidler, *Antonín Springer a česká politika v letech 1848–1850*, pp. 190–1.

23 Antonín Maria Pinkas, doctor of law (1800–65), important Czech Liberal politician. Took part in the revolution of 1848, was a friend of Havlíček and Palacký, and in 1848–9 he was a minister and deputy at the Vienna and Krems Imperial Diets. A lawyer in Prague, in 1861 Pinkas was a member of the Vienna *Reichsrat* (the first parliament after the reintroduction of constitutional life in Austria).

24 Pinkas to H. W. Dimmer in Prague, Bonn, 21 January 1855, in František Kutnar, 'Názory A. M. Pinkase na Rusko a slovanskou otázku za Krymské války' (A. M. P.'s Views of Russia and the Slavic question during the Crimean War), in *Kapitolky z děin vzájemných vztahů národu ČSR a SSSR*, i (Prague, 1858), p. 190.

25 Mescery to Päumann, Prague, 26 July 1859, no. 7617, 8100, 8501/ P.M PM 1855–59 fasc. 8/22/94, SÚA Prague.

26 Josef Václav Frič (ed.), *Čech* (Geneva, 1861), Afterword, p. 98.

27 Frič's diary entry for 1 May 1859, X I, FA, LA PNP Prague.

28 Ibid. 9 May 1859.

29 Ibid. 4 July 1859.

30 Ibid. 20 December 1859.

31 Ibid. 18 and 20 January 1860.

32 Ibid. 17 February 1860.

33 Ibid. 15, 20 and 22 October 1860.

34 Ibid. 13 and 16 December 1860.

35 Václav Frič to J.V. Frič at Paris, London, 23 July 1862, FA – LA PNP; Marie Červinková-Riegrová diary notes of 8 September 1884, ibid; Rieger to his wife, London, 25 July 1862, Ms. ANM Prague.

36 Frič's diary entry for 20 May 1860.

37 Náprstek's diary entries of 16, 28 and 29 June 1862 / AR III/, Náprstek's Museum in Prague.

38 Anna Fricová's diary notes of 11 and 14 August 1862: Frič's diary of 1862, vol. II, FA – LA PNP; J.V. Frič to Josef Frič, London, 26 August 1862, ibid; see also Bakunin to Václav Frič, 12 May 1862 (printed in Vaclav Zacek, Ohlas polskéno porstání 1863, (Prague 1935), pp. 202–4; J.V. Frič's diary entries of 10 July 1862, FA – LAPNP-

39 Václav Frič to J.V. Frič at Paris, London, 25 July 1862, ANM Prague; Marie Červinková-Riegrová's notes of 8 September 1884, ibid.

40 Josef Matoušek, Karel Sladkovský a český radikalismus za revoluce a reakce (Karel Sladkovský and the Bohemian Radicalism in the Age of Revolution and Reaction), (Prague, 1929), p. 19.

41 Rieger to his wife, London, 18 June 1862, ANM Prague; and Marie Červinková-Riegrová's notes of 30 March and 2 May 1886, ibid.

III

Emigré Politics

10

Voices of Exile:
French Newspapers in England

Sylvie Aprile

Exile imposes the need to earn one's living, and to think and act politically. French refugees in England used meetings, conspiracies, their pens and the gift of speech for this purpose. Howard C. Payne and Henry Grosshans have already studied in depth the exiled revolutionaries' lack of influence in France.[1] Like other means of resistance, newspapers became increasingly marginal and were finally buried in the reports of police officials. But this downfall needs to be reexamined. The German writer Franck Tramler has written about the literature of exile during the Nazi period: 'the fact that this literature has only a small impact in the fight against National Socialism is not an end result but an opening for reflection'.[2] The influence of newspapers was widely exaggerated by the French police and at the same time underestimated by the Republicans, especially at the end of the Second Empire and later. This paper proposes a rereading of these newspapers in terms of links between the French refugees, and also between the French, British and others exiled in England, in order to analyse the networks and the human and ideological conflicts of these exiled voices.

The essay will explore three principal aspects. It begins by presenting these newspapers, and, in particular, the most important one, *L'Homme*, as a link between the French community and the newspaper's exile organisation. This is to be followed by an examination of the role played by these newspapers in England as a reflection of brotherhood and hospitality. Finally, it analyses in depth the importance and limits of newspapers as the voice of a universal democracy, the subtitle of *L'Homme*. This newspaper grew in importance during 1856, a few months before it ceased publication, marking the end of the French press in exile.[3]

Community Newspapers

The first French exiles arrived in England in May 1848. They were followed by further waves in June 1848, June 1849, and from December 1851 onwards, after Napoleon III's *coup d'état*. As soon as Alexandre Ledru-Rollin arrived in England, after the failure of the last left-wing insurrection in June 1849, he decided to maintain his audience by continuing to publish a newspaper in France and then in England. In July 1850 he created *Le Proscrit*, which was suppressed by the French authorities after only its second issue. However, this misfortune was soon remedied when, on 27 October, the first issue of *La Voix du proscrit* appeared. It was edited by Ledru Rollin and Charles Delescluze and printed in Saint Amand, in the north of France. This location was chosen because of the difference in the deposits requested. While Paris required the high sum of 18,000 francs, the country printer asked for only 1,800 francs. A further obstacle that needed to be overcome was to find a publisher who lived in the country, as the law of 1828 decreed. *La Voix du proscrit* was Ledru-Rollin's platform. In it he published manifestos and articles written by his close acquaintances, Delescluze, Ribeyrolles and Karcher. But even before the *coup d'état* of 2 December 1851, censorship had halted the publication in autumn 1851.

The newspaper *L'Homme*, published from 1853 to 1856 in Jersey and afterwards in London, was less ephemeral. Containing four pages, it came out every Wednesday, and was printed in St Helier on the printing press belonging to the Polish editor Zeno Swietosławski, who had lived in Jersey since 1835.[4]

Similarities and differences of ideology and form can be seen in these newspapers. Both found it difficult to fill their columns with articles and therefore published a multitude of manifestos, pamphlets, book abstracts (such as the *Bonapartist Biographies* by Philippe Berjeau or the poems of *Les Châtiments* by Victor Hugo), speeches, funeral orations and even toasts. However, the chief editor of *L'Homme*, Charles Ribeyrolles, was more than a simple political activist. He was actually a journalist who, in 1848, replaced the famous critic Ferdinand Flocon as chief editor of the famous left-wing newspaper *La Réforme*. Ribeyrolles was sentenced to death in his absence and went to London after leaving Jersey. His notorious articles, combined with all the other contributions, created a true newspaper. Ribeyrolles is well known thanks to Charles Hugo, the elder son of Victor Hugo, who wrote a book called *Les hommes de l'exil*, in which he dedicated a whole chapter to the journalist and his work. He draws a contradictory but enthusiastic portrait of the only man capable of creating a real platform for the fugitives, a space of freedom. According to Hugo, thanks to Ribeyrolles and his 'special popularity' *L'Homme* was the only collective work of the French exile.[5]

Ribeyrolles wrote in every issue, took the main responsibility for the leading articles and gave his opinion underneath or in articles by others as well. *L'Homme* had regular and episodic collaborators. Ribeyrolles's acquaintances played a large part, and the arrival and departure of refugees was heavily featured. The most regular collaborators were Prosper Bonnet-Duverdier, Philippe Faure and Philippe Berjeau. Amongst the episodic collaborators were Martin Bernard, Edgar Quinet, Jeanne Deroin[6], Octave Vauthier, Pierre-Alfred Talandier, a barrister and a member of the *Commune révolutionnaire* of Felix Pyat, Alphose-Alexandre Bianchi, and a man called Cholat writing from Bruges, Xavier Durrieu from Spain, Hyppolite Magen, Victor Meunier, and Victor Schoelcher who focused on the tragic situation of workers in the French West Indies after the abolition of slavery. Like *La Voix du proscrit*, *L'Homme* did not set out to inform refugees of what was happening in France. This might seem strange, but was clearly explained by both papers: they were unable to comment on French events. In *La Voix du proscrit* there was indeed a regular section entitled *Chronique de l'intérieur*, but the first issue stated that 'politics without action is the affair of speculation: like paintings this needs perspective.' Published first in Jersey and later in London, *L'Homme* could not report on France. Equally, the section entitled *Correspondance parisienne* never became a regular feature. Its first author was Philippe Faure, who had settled in Brussels, but after his arrival in England the articles from Paris were published anonymously.

The contents were disappointing. The writers did not attempt to provide information about imperial politics or the French opposition for two main reasons: the police and censorship. The journalists denounced the 'crime of December' in the same way as the exiled writers Hugo or Schoelcher. The information served purely to reinforce the representation of France as a land 'frozen' in dishonour and misfortune since 1851. For example, on 15 February 1854, an article stated: 'News about France falls on us, sad and icy like the dead December leaves' and in another issue 'we prophesy rebellions and people are talking about angry peasants.' However, certain exceptions can be found, for example, in articles about strikes such as that by the slate-quarry workers (ardoisiers) of Angers at the end of August 1855.

Information was difficult to collect and did not always accord with the ideas of the refugees. For example, we find only a 'reference' to the support given by the *faubourgs* of Paris and Lyon to the Crimean War.[7] Some exiles criticised the lack of information. Victor Schoelcher, for instance, wrote to Victor Hugo in January 1855: 'It is deplorable that *L'Homme* neglects all these current issues. This devil of a newspaper seems to be written in a faraway land and for faraway democrats, the paper does not like controversy.' Schoelcher, unlike Hugo, did not support Ribeyrolles and his friends and resigned from the new *Commission de secours*, which had been created in 1854 to assist all French exiles.[8] On 17 November 1855 the editorial staff, acknowledging this problem, promised their readers that improvements – such as a section of detailed correspondence from France – would be made to the newspaper.

The newspaper was better informed about and more concerned by the tragedies in jails and the deaths of exiles. Charles Ribeyrolles wrote a book entitled *Bagnes d'Afrique* in 1853. The newspaper also published a list of those who had been transported, and the testimonies of former prisoners. In fact, the main role of the newspaper was to preserve and tighten links between the exiles. It paid great attention to funerals, which were great meetings for displaying brotherhood or conflicts. Speeches given on these occasions were printed immediately. Many refugees died, not by committing suicide, but as the result of widespread material and psychological difficulties.

L'Homme provided a structure for socialising and a forum for political debates. It tried to help all exiles and to keep them informed of any assistance that might be available. The newspaper provided work for exiles. In letters sent by the exile Bergounioux to his wife, he explained that *L'Homme* paid four shillings for a work which had taken him one day and one night. He had previously been a vet, but could not find work in his profession in Jersey. Pierre Leroux, his brother and his son-in-law worked for *The Universal Library* which published *L'homme* and also books written by the exiles.[9] The last pages of the newspaper were filled with classified advertisements for work wanted, testifying to everyday difficulties. In order to obtain a job, the refugees advertised their skills which were most often intellectual ones. If, for example, French or English lessons were not required, some of them could offer riding lessons instead. Similarly, they advertised their skills as craftsmen, such as moulders or bootmakers. The newspaper also ran advertisements promoting works written by refugees.

The newspaper's aim was also to maintain relationships within a community scattered over Britain, Europe and all over the world. Isolation needed to be overcome everywhere. *L'Homme* informed its readers about meetings such as festivals commemorating the February Revolution and refugee funerals. The newspaper featured a French meeting in Birmingham as prominently as a French meeting in Mexico. *L'Homme* also announced acts of solidarity, such as those by Doctor Philippe who gave free consultations every evening in Soho Square in the French pharmacy, or by Jules Allix, who gave French lessons free of charge to the citizens of Jersey.

The newspapers were also a forum for debating the different political leanings among the republicans. *L'Homme* bears witness to divisions and rivalries. The tensions between the *Commune révolutionnaire* and the *Comité international* was one of the most important conflicts.[10]

Indeed, political friendship, as John Le Senne's aphorism says, is only a dislike in common. Nevertheless the newspaper attempted to transcend this problem. Charles Ribeyrolles declared in the first issue of *L'Homme*: 'We bear in us, …, exiles of the nations, a whole past of controversy, of divisions, of systems of enemies, of rancour perhaps, well one must learn to forget (all that) in the name of our homeland, captive and dishonoured.'[11] The newspaper wanted to be tolerant and open to all convictions, although this aspect remains largely unknown. Thus it published violent articles by Ernest Coeurderoy condemning all the exiles, Pyat's manifesto, Louis Blanc's attacks on the manifesto of Ledru-Rollin, Mazzini and Kossuth, as well as poems by Victor Hugo. In many issues, Charles Ribeyrolles had to explain his opinions, and received much criticism. Some editors, such as Luigi Piancini, even resigned.[12]

It would be interesting to reread all these articles, entitled 'the politics of exile', as they provide deep insights into what we generally imagine about the past and the future of the socialist movement. In a highly interesting paper, Bonnet-Duverdier explained the subtitle of the newspaper, '*Science and Solidarity*': 'Man is the object, solidarity is the goal, science is the means of socialism, socialism is the science of brotherhood.'[13] This offers a reflection on the thoughts and actions of the people and their leaders, and on equality between men and women. Of course, Ribeyrolles did not wish to take sides, but he enjoyed finding new contributors. He wrote about Pierre-Alfred Talandier's collaboration: 'It is with great pleasure that we welcome the contribution of citizen Talandier. We are certain that he will not engage in futile controversial debate, in those about persons, or about ideas, but if this should happen, a discussion must be held.'[14]

Ribeyrolles did not despise the older leaders. On 15 August 1855 he commented on an article by Louis Blanc: 'Louis Blanc shares the same point of view, of that we are convinced, and if, however, during the trial, on the eve of the combat, he finds it useful to send us a few studies on the question of the day after, we will be happy to publish his thoughts, as this will be once again the Revolution. Ideas are as gunfire!'[15]

This refusal to belong to a 'clan' is constantly declared after a new debate. Ribeyrolles stated in 1856 that 'the newspaper (*L'Homme*) belongs to general matters'. This democratic attitude concurred with the wishes of Louis Blanc, who condemned Ledru-Rollin, Kossuth and Mazzini for not having followed the consultation procedure for obtaining general approval for their brochure. But some of the leaders remained silent. Ledru-Rollin and Delescluze never published in *L'Homme*. At this time the leader of the far left wing abandoned journalism altogether, but nevertheless provided contributions to Belgian journals such as *Le Drapeau*. *L'Homme* published only one article by Ledru-Rollin, from *La Nation* in March 1856.

Even though *L'Homme* could not be a platform for the whole of the French community, this raft of shipwrecked men fulfilled its aims – continuity and reflection about a future revolution – more successfully than we believe.

It is almost impossible to establish how many readers the newspaper had. When the exiles were expelled from Jersey, *L'Homme* ironically placed great importance on a story which was read by only 400 people in the Channel Islands. Of course the newspaper was banned in France and also in Belgium. Nevertheless, it managed to come into France via several networks of smugglers. Visitors and tourists returned from journeys to the Channel Islands with copies of the papers, and copies of the bestsellers of exile propaganda, such as *Napoléon le petit* by Victor Hugo. Records of arrests reveal the different ways in which these publications entered the country. Police archives are full of examples of the cleverness of the traffickers using boats, networks of tobacco smugglers, and even hollow statues of Queen Victoria.

Howard C. Payne and Henry Grosshans have already explained the role of the exaggerated fears of French officials. The authorities made public use of the 'red spectre' to justify the *coup d'état* and censorship. However, one official pleaded that the newspapers were only read by republicans, had no role in creating a latent organisation and did not prove the existence of a link between refugees and domestic revolutionaries. If the main difficulty of *L'Homme* was censorship, it also faced problems in Britain – material problems such as the increase in the price of stamps. A report in the issue of 28 July 1855 highlights the lack of subscriptions, which in turn meant that the price of *L'Homme* had to rise. Nevertheless, rivalries and especially the return of many exiles to France after the first amnesties were the real reasons for the newspaper's loss of popularity.

The Refugees and Britain

One of the greatest difficulties that arose from the 1855 crisis was the expulsion of French refugees from Jersey and the relocation of the newspaper to London. How did *L'Homme* deal with its new political and social surroundings? The attitude of the French exiles towards England was somewhat ambiguous.

Articles in the newspapers provide evidence of difficult relationships. In his initial editorial Ribeyrolles asked his readers and his journalists to reserve judgement: 'We are seated in the stranger's hallway, and the hospitality that covers entails a serious duty: to keep in the internal wars of the refuge country, the neutrality of hardship.'[16] It is interesting that there were no articles on Ireland in the paper, and no issue was devoted to the recent past of the island and the great famine. This could not have been an oversight. On the contrary, in his book Charles Hugo mentioned some articles on Ireland.

This cautious attitude is easily explained. *L'Homme* was published after the scandal of Ledru-Rollin's book *De la décadence de l'Angleterre*. Ledru-Rollin claimed that his book was a reply to English insults to French refugees. At the end of 1853 Victor Schoelcher also decided to respond, not in a book but in a letter in an English newspaper. *L'Homme*, wishing to be careful, reprinted only articles which had already been published in the *Morning Advertiser*, but these articles constituted the main part of the paper. In January 1854 Schoelcher attacked the remarks made by Alfred Richards, known as esquire 'gallophobe'. More important were the accusations deal with by Schoelcher, as they touched the heart of the problems between the French and the British. The English journalist presented Ledru-Rollin's book as evidence of a French plan to invade England, this old subject of mistrust. Another cause of tension was the alleged French taste for violence. Schoelcher discredited the claim by referring to the abolition of the death penalty, ratified by the Second Republic and upheld by great exiles such as Victor Hugo. In 1854, despite his will to respect English political life, Victor Hugo sent a public letter to Lord Palmerston to plead for the life of a prisoner called Tapner, who had been sentenced to death. Tapner was later executed, in spite of Hugo's intervention.

Schoelcher and others also replied to very precise accusations, such as Richards's claim that in 1848 the French Republic had expelled English workers and refused naturalisations. Schoelcher answered in *Franglais*: 'Son Statement est d'un bout à l'autre une misrepresentation difficile à excuser' which can be translated as 'His statement is from start to finish a misrepresentation difficult to pardon'.[17] He added a declaration made by Louis Blanc on 8 April 1848 and a decree of 28 March 1848 concerning naturalisation, both proving to him that the French government on the contrary intended to assimilate foreigners.[18]

Apart from this dispute, *L'Homme* did not express the Anglophobia widespread among French refugees. We can note only a series of articles entitled 'Jean Raisin', in which prejudices about England and English society can be found. They tell the story of a young Frenchman who meets a rich Englishman in the Pyrenées. The Englishman offers the Frenchman some money to go to London, and in exchange he must send a letter every week describing what he has seen. Of course, after three or four enthusiastic letters about consumption and industrialisation, the Frenchman discovers the reality of the misery of the working class and wants to return home.

Compared with the news about France, the London correspondence section in *L'Homme* was more detailed. The editor of *Les chroniques londoniennes*, Philippe Berjeau, knew British politicians fairly well and attempted to analyse British politics. If we compare this to the attitude of French papers in the USA, the tone in which political life was discussed was more enthusiastic across the Atlantic. Most of the time the journalists criticised *The Times* but they attacked neither 'le peuple anglais' nor the British government. Without a clear knowledge of English law, they feared a lack hospitality in Britain. French journalists unanimously appeared to mistrust English hospitality. They seemed to be unable to understand the profound spirit of independence of the English people, and worried about rumours of expulsions or restrictions and of administrative procedures. This reaction originated in a misunderstanding of the freedom of the press in England, where censorship did not exist. When Victor Hugo arrived in Jersey he was astonished and wrote, in an article for the local newspaper, *L'Archipel de la Manche*: 'Imagine a desert island: the day after his arrival, Robinson Crusoe starts a paper and man Friday subscribes to it. ... You speak in the streets of Saint Helier or Saint Peter Port to an irreproachable passer-by dressed in black, severely buttoned, his linen very white and he tells you about Garibaldi. Is he a clergyman? No a cowman.'[19]

The relationship between the Queen and the former Special Constable of Pall Mall (the nickname of Napoleon III), was criticised in principle in the columns of the paper, especially during the Crimean War. Napoleon III's journey to London in April 1855 was severely commented upon as a sort of provocation. *L'Homme* published an article by Victor Hugo entitled 'Que venez vous faire ici?' The result of this trip was to bring together French exiles and Chartists. On 22 November 1854 the newspaper published a manifesto called 'Qu'est ce que Napoleon?' For the authors the answer was 'this man is a perjurer, a murderer'. The manifesto was signed by sixty workers and Chartists, including George Harrison and Ernest Jones. It announced meetings to celebrate the imminent coming not of Napoleon III, but of an old veteran of republican battles, Armand Barbès. The columns of *L'Homme* also reported that Chartists were arrested when selling Victor Hugo's book, and that the bookshop of his publisher, Truelove, had also been smashed up.[20] But it was the Queen's visit to France several weeks later which created real brotherhood, and became a symbol of solidarity.

The threat of an *Alien Bill* was constantly brandished, naturally more by the French than by the English papers and authorities.[21] The crisis of 1855, called 'le coup d'état de Jersey' by Charles Hugo, came as almost a relief to the French revolutionaries. English or Channel Island authorities were like all others.[22] The radical Félix Pyat read his letter to the Queen at the meeting of the *Comité international* and the *Commune révolutionnaire* on 22 September, without evoking a reaction. This letter was published in *L'Homme* on 10 October, and it was this publication which was judged defamatory to the Queen, causing the expulsion of the chief editors of *L'Homme*. According to Victor Hugo and Victor Schoelcher, this letter was a mistake, even though they understood it to be a pretext. The following year, Pyat, Rougée and Jourdain signed another manifesto, published on 8 March 1856. Called *Lettre à Marianne*, it was also highly provocative: 'Marianne, you are our Queen'. This manifesto evoked no reaction.

The English radicals supported the French by organising meetings and protesting against their expulsion. The main English newspapers also criticised this action and *L'Homme* thanked the *Daily News*, the *Morning Advertiser* (Reynold's papers), the *Daily Telegraph* and the *Mercury* of Liverpool for their support. Do the columns provide evidence of a political link between the French and the Chartists? The answer is: not really. One of the reasons was the distance between London radicals and Jersey refugees. Philippe Faure seemed to be an exception. He was a close friend of Julian Harney, spent time in London, translated English articles, and was a Freemason, which was a major link between foreign refugees. But the majority of refugees had no radical networks in England.[23] We can only conclude that they knew each other, but *L'Homme* never attempted to be a platform for Chartist ideas or a forum for a debate between French and English socialists. We will mention only the last, bitter article by Linton, when he decided to stop publishing his newspaper, the *English Republic*.[24]

More important than the relationship between French exiles and Chartists were the links between French and other exiles. The fact that most exiles from Central Europe were not republican and would accept a king or an emperor with the recognition of their nation was a way to counter one of the most dangerous accusations by English liberal journalists. The context of the Crimean War emphasises this underground debate between French revolutionaries and other exiles.

French and European exiles

French exiles were not the first to arrive, and they followed with interest the experience of the Poles, known as the 'veterans'. The French, not being the first, benefited from others' experiences of the practices of European proscription, especially those of the Polish exiles. We know that after Schoelcher established his press in Jersey, he soon sold it to Zeno Swietosławski, the rich Polish exile who started printing a series of political pamphlets in French, English and Polish. Like the editorial structure, the meetings celebrating the anniversaries of the Polish Revolution served as models for the French anniversaries of the February revolution of 1848. French proscription was numerically inferior to Italians and Hungarians.

In the context of the Crimean War, *L'Homme* had three essential missions. The first was to celebrate the union between European exiles by reproducing the toasts given at the meetings that largely occupied the columns of the paper. Solidarity among the refugees was also experienced through funerals. We can quote the example of the funeral of Georges Gaffney, who died in Jersey, a former journalist from Le Havre. Four exiles carried his coffin: a Hungarian, a Pole, an Italian and a Frenchman. Fraternity was equally apparent at the time of the 'coup d'état in Jersey'. Exiles from the whole of Europe joined the French and left the island with them. Swietosɫawski settled in London.

The second goal was to provide information on Europe: for example, through historical reminders of European revolutions, as in the articles by Théodore Karcher, through articles on European diplomacy and through the publication or reproduction of editorials written by important European exiles such as Mazzini or Kossuth. Ten articles by Kossuth, translated by Philippe Faure, filled half of the issues published in 1855 and 1856.

The third aim of the paper was to reject patriotism and claim what can be called a French universalism. They feared that Poles, Hungarians or Italians would help Bonaparte or Nicholas II in order to obtain advantages. The attitude of Prince Czartoryski was condemned.[25] Daniel Manin was also criticised in May 1856 when he accepted the ideas of Camille Cavour.[26] The French exiles became more and more suspicious of those who defended their nation. In the issue of 6 December 1854 Ribeyrolles criticised the attitude of the *Comité de Londres* which had organised a meeting for Poland, on the grounds that this meeting had been called for only one nation.

The final mission concerned the propaganda of the newspaper's subtitle, 'la démocratie universelle'. *Republique universelle* began publication in France with the Peace Congress of 1849 in Paris, where French republicans and socialists, but mainly Anglo-Saxon liberal Christian thinkers, gathered together. For people like Victor Hugo it offered a way of defining a moderate republic, model for a further 'Etats-Unis d'Europe'.[27] The congress ended in a complete failure. In exile, at the end of each meeting or funeral Hugo concluded with the cry: 'Vive la Republique universelle!' But every time the newspaper quoted this, more radical exiles such as Joseph Déjacque or Alphonse Bianchi went further, screaming: 'Vive la Republique universelle et sociale'. Once again, this turned into an internal debate, a French reference.

L'Homme, however, had a number of difficulties in becoming a European paper and its universal vocation was often hindered by the

French claim to universality. A certain bitterness can be detected, and a feeling of injustice when contemplating Kossuth's success, even though the French always pretended to admire the great Hungarian orator. This bitterness was sometimes expressed quite clearly. Charles Ribeyrolles, for example, deplored the fact that during the last gathering to mark the anniversary of the Polish Revolution nobody had mentioned the French Revolution: 'Ah! l'on bannit l'ayeule, la Révolution française de son foyer de famille, le meeting! On ne veut ni son drapeau, ni de ses devises, ni de ses divines formules, ni de ses haines qui sont trois fois saintes et légitimes.'[28]

The tensions were, of course, linked to the French republican claims and their rejection of all forms of constitutional monarchy, which were not necessarily rejected by all of the European exiles. In the first issue, *Proscrit* published a statement of principles to which the *Comité central démocratique européen* subscribed. They declared that democracy had only one logical form, the republic, and that this republican form of government must entail universal suffrage, the right of association, free and compulsory education, a single progressive tax, and abolition of all indirect taxes. Even *L'Homme* was less narrow-minded. The Germans, the Poles and the Hungarians preferred to write in English newspapers and spent less money and time creating their own newspapers.

The reality of the exchanges is also difficult to understand, but certain republicans clearly felt that a regular publication addressed to all was necessary. Charles Ribeyrolles had the idea of founding a bilingual newspaper in 1855:

> We wish to establish in London a daily paper published in two languages which would make of this metropolis of commerce a metropolis of ideas. The word is not too ambitious and of this I will convince you when I tell you that Victor Hugo whose light has a universal diffusion, will write for it, as also Mazzini, Ledru-Rollin, Kossuth.[29]

However, this plan was never realised. French exiles hardly understood that exiles from other countries often adapted more easily to the English language and therefore preferred to publish in English newspapers.

Charles Ribeyrolles seemed to be fascinated by Alexander Herzen, the Russian refugee who, in February 1854, contributed to *L'Homme* three letters which had not been published in his book *Letters about Italy and France*. These letters revealed the point of view of a Russian in Europe. Herzen underlined the main problem of these years, sometimes ironically called 'cossackism'. Herzen revealed other ways of thinking about revolution, people and power. On 12 April 1854 he wrote: 'This war will be l'introduzione maestosa e marziale du monde slave dans l'histoire universelle et une marcia funebre du Vieux Monde.' At the end of Herzen's first article published in *L'Homme* on 22 February 1854 Ribeyrolles commented: 'We like all those who dare, either in thought, or in combat'.[30] But he preferred to be cautious. Herzen's letters were mostly addressed to Linton, who published them in the *English Republic,* printed in Newcastle.

In conclusion, it would be absurd to argue in terms of failure, breaks or continuity, as these are false debates and issues. The richness of this press, and the diversity of the collaborators and the subjects broached upon should be noted. In this essay, I have not dealt with scientific articles, religious debates or social utopias, which should not be neglected. This press seems to have had little impact, and hardly provided any leverage for the internal opposition.

It was none the less taken extremely seriously as a 'danger' by the French government, because of the fear of an external conspiracy, especially during the war, and it justified the need for repression and surveillance. The government chose to see the paper as evidence of plots and a conspiracy on a European scale. This equation can also be found in the Belgian archives: conspirator equals collaborator or a reader of *L'Homme.*

It would be just as illusory to consider *L'Homme* – even though it was not a particularly radical paper and its columns were open to all – as a milestone in the creation of an international paper. In foreseeing 'the blessed dawn of the United States of Europe' the newspaper was close to the peace congresses that took place in Switzerland in 1867 and 1868. These European and pacifist networks are not well known and should be reexamined. This press created during the proscription a link between '*The springtime of nations*', the exiles of the 1840s and 1850s and the organisations of the 1860s: The International Workingmen's Association and peace congresses.[31] But the European context of the construction of nationalities and nationalism largely blurred a Republican universalism whose complexity I have tried to show here.

Notes

1 Howard C. Payne and Henry Grosshans, 'The Exiled Revolutionaries and the French Political Police in the 1850's', *American Historical Review,* 68/2 (1963), pp. 954–73.

2 Franck Trommler, Emigration und Nachkriegsliteratur in Exil und Innerer Emigration, Third Wisconsin Workshop, ed. by J. Hermand (Frankfurt, 1973); quoted in Jean-Michel Palmier, Weimar en exil (Paris, 1988), p. 947.

3 If we except the short-lived paper of Bonin, La république exilée and Pierre Leroux's L'espérance.

4 Peter Brock, 'The Polish Revolutionary Commune in London', Slavonic and East European Review, 35 (1956), pp. 116–126.

5 Charles Hugo, Les hommes de l'exil (Brussels, 1895), Ch. IV.

6 See Pamela Pilbeam's contribution on Jeanne Deroin in this volume, Chapter 16.

7 L'Homme, 18 October 1854. 'Les faubourgs de Paris et de Lyon, ont à l'endroit de la guerre, une opinion qui n'est pas tout à fait la nôtre . Ils voudraient pour les armées alliées ,une légion de victoires'.

8 Nelly Schmidt (ed.), Correspondance de Victor Schoelcher (Maisonneuve/Larose, 1995).

9 For example in 1855: L'Almanach de l'exil pour 1855; Charles Ribeyrolles, Les bagnes d'afrique; Aux républicains, appel de Kossuth, Ledru-Rollin et Mazzini.

10 Iouda Tchernoff, Le parti républicain au coup d'Etat et sous le second Empire (Pedone, 1906).

11 L'Homme, 30 November 1853.

12 L'Homme, 28 June 1856.

13 L'Homme, 18 January 1854.

14 L'Homme, 15 August 1855.

15 L'Homme, ibid.

16 L'Homme, 30 November 1853.

17 L'Homme, 25 January 1854.

18 Schoelcher ends his letter: 'Je crois avoir répondu à tous les points de son acte d'accusation. Puissé-je avoir convaincu lui et ceux de ses compatriotes auxquels je m'adresse. Je voudrais ardemment que les libéraux anglais nous voient tels que nous sommes et non tels que l'absolutisme nous a dépeints, cela servirait à détruire des antipathies nationales funestes à la sainte cause de la liberté défendue par nous comme par eux avec sincérité.'

19 L'Archipel de la Manche, September 1852.

20 L'Homme, 2 May 1855: 'Il est vrai que c'est parfois une étrange liberté que celle de l'Angleterre. ainsi non seulement on pille, on dévaste la boutique d'un libraire qui paie comme tous ses confères ses impositions et ses taxes mais on refuse des timbres à M. Ernest Jones le courageux éditeur et on le poursuit.'

21 Bernard Porter, *The Refugee Question in Mid-Victorian Politics* (Cambridge, 1979).

22 Charles Hugo writes: 'Il (L'Homme) mourut dictorialement exécuté, pour être agréable à l'alliance française par le gouvernement anglais, qui sait quand il veut introduire dans cette fameuse liberté de la presse si haut vantée, des parenthèses d'arbitraires dignes à la fois des gouvernements absolus et des gouvernements serviles.' Hugo, *Les hommes de l'exil*, pp. 63–4.

23 Margot C. Finn, *After Chartism: Class and Nation in English Radical Politics, 1848–1874* (Cambridge, 1993.)

24 *L'Homme*, 23 May 1855; Linton wrote: 'Les meilleurs actes de la génération présente ne sont après tout que des paroles.'

25 *L'Homme* , 13 September 1854.

26 *L'Homme*, 31 May 1856.

27 See Evelyne Lejeune-Resnick, 'L'idée d'Etats-Unis d'Europe au Congrès de la paix de 1849', *Revue d'histoire du XIXeme siècle*, 7 (1991), pp. 65–73.

28 *L'Homme*, 6 December 1854.

29 Letter from Ribeyrolles to Sanders, Felecky Papers, quoted in Alvin R. Calman, *Ledru-Rollin après 1848 et les proscrits français,* Rider et cie éditeurs (Paris, 1921), p. 122.

30 *L'Homme*, 22 February 1854.

31 Remi Gossez, 'La proscription et les origines de l'Internationale', *1848. Revue des révolutions contemporaines*, 12 (1951), pp. 97–115.

11

'The Begging Bowl of Revolution': the Fund-raising Tours of German and Hungarian Exiles to North America, 1851–1852

Sabine Freitag

For many political exiles of the continental revolutionary upheavals in 1848–9 Great Britain was just a stepping-stone to the United States. But the reverse was also true: some of the London refugees visited the United States only to return voluntarily to Great Britain after a few months. This essay tells their story. It is about the very first years of their exile in England, when most political refugees were still excited but paralysed by the revolutionary events which lay behind them, and expected further major European revolutions to break out soon, perhaps in just a few months' time. This vague hope was connected with events in France. After the differences and tensions between Napoleon III and the National Assembly in Paris, many revolutionaries came to regard France as a potential source of new revolutionary upheavals. For once the revolutionary victory had only been postponed. In their imagination the coming year, '1852', acquired an almost mythical character. In several articles and pamphlets 1852 was celebrated and talked of as the crucial year of definite changes. It was the 'magical year', the 'battle year', a 'rendezvous with destiny'.[1] So the exiles had to be prepared. What was needed most was, of course, money: money to furnish troops as well as money to build up an efficient propaganda machine.

Since the German exile community in London in 1850–1 was far from united it was not surprising that even when the idea of a fund-raising tour to America was raised, only a part of the German exile community was united behind Gottfried Kinkel.[2] Moreover, the London quarrels were to follow him on his journey to the USA. Kinkel was the only one among the German exiles whose fame had preceded him to England. He had been a handsome young professor of church history at the University of Bonn in the early 1840s but became an atheist on reading Hegel and Feuerbach and therefore switched subsequently from church history to art history. His rhetorical skills were unquestioned. His editorship of a radical local Bonn newspaper, and his sympathy with his radical students attracted the attention of the Prussian authorities. Disappointed by the proceedings and finally by the dissolution of the Frankfurt parliament in 1849, he joined the Baden uprisings in the summer of 1849, and was wounded and arrested on charges of treason. Though he was given the death penalty, his sentence was commuted to life imprisonment in the fortress of Spandau, where he was doomed to spin wool for the rest of his life. Eventually he managed to escape, thanks to the help of an admiring student called Carl Schurz. Kinkel and Schurz set off for England. Well equipped with money and letters of introduction, Kinkel settled in London in January 1851.

At first he tried to stay on friendly terms with all groups, except that of 'Doctor great Mogul Marx'. And indeed, Marx, who envied Kinkel's success but also hated his moderate attitude towards politics, became his fiercest enemy. While Arnold Ruge tried to win Kinkel for Mazzini's European Democracy movement, August Willich, another German émigré, unaware of the tensions between Kinkel and Marx, tried to gain the professor as an ally in the battle for the communists' and workers' cause. It seems quite natural that Kinkel should become the favourite candidate of the more moderate group of German exiles in London for the fund-raising tour to North America. The original plan came from the Italian revolutionary, Giuseppe Mazzini, who had launched an Italian national loan in 1849 and was pretty successful in using it to raise money. But it was Carl Schurz who insisted that Kinkel had a duty to capitalise on his fame by undertaking a begging tour of America to raise money for a German national loan.[3]

There had been difficulties right from the start. At one of the first official meetings of the German émigrés in London, differences on the question of how to organise and what to plan became obvious. Men such as Arnold Ruge, Josef Fickler, Amand Goegg and Franz Sigel stressed the need to form an official committee as a representative organ of the London émigrés. They pleaded for efficient propaganda against reactionary European governments and wanted 'action' in every case. Gottfried Kinkel, Carl Schurz, August Willich, Gustav Adolf Techow, Eduard Meyen and Graf Oskar von Reichenbach, on the other hand, were against anything along the lines of

an official émigré committee. They did not want to arouse the suspicion of the British authorities and were sceptical about any kind of
'agitation' such as the publication of a radical newspaper, magazine
or journal (which would also be expensive in London). When Kinkel
announced that he had received £160 from a political friend called
Fischer, editor of the *Deutsche Zeitung* in New Orleans, for revolutionary purposes, the discussion about how to spend it precipitated
the final split between the two factions. The radical leftists founded
the so-called *Agitationsverein* (agitation society), stressing that this
was not a forum for discussion, but a working committee, intended
to produce 'works', not 'words'.

Meanwhile Kinkel was already on his way to North America, where
he set about circulating the German national loan bonds among the
German population. For many reasons America was an obvious place
to collect money. Over 2.5 million Germans had emigrated to the
United States by the middle of the nineteenth century, but the biggest
influx was yet to come. The peak was reached in 1854 when almost
240,000 Germans migrated to the USA. Although many were still
struggling to making a living in the New World they were also
believed still to have a lively interest in the ongoing political process
in the fatherland, where they had left many relatives behind. America
was seen as the naturally ally of all German democrats who had been
forced into exile. All public sympathies were with the revolutionaries
and their cause because their political goals, which were considered
'criminal' in Germany, were held to be legal, indeed, even laudable,
in the United States. The USA had been one of the first nations to
recognise the Frankfurt parliament in 1848 as the legal representative
of a new constitutional Germany. Later, when doubt was cast on the
idea of a new revolution and the scope of political action was therefore limited, some of those who initially went to England travelled
on further to the United States.

When Gottfried Kinkel arrived in New York on 14 September 1851
he was confronted with unexpected rivalry and harsh critics, so he
left for Philadelphia only four days later.[4] The cold New York
welcome had been the result of critical and cynical articles published
in the *New Yorker Deutsche Zeitung*, which was edited by the ultra-
radical Karl Heinzen who was a close friend of Arnold Ruge, Karl
Tausenau, Franz Sigel and Amand Goegg.[5] Heinzen supported their
cause and asserted that Kinkel was travelling in secret, had only a
few supporters and was therefore not authorised by the whole of the
exile community in London: 'Mr. Kinkel might be uplifted over our

unfriendly greeting', he wrote. 'We are even less uplifted over his speculations and believe it harmful to support him.'[6] Perhaps Kinkel thought New York was hostile terrain for him, even though Heinzen's newspaper collapsed shortly thereafter, in early December 1851, lacking readers and therefore money.[7] But while other New York German newspapers, such as the *Staatszeitung* and the *Abendzeitung*, welcomed Kinkel and his cause, the *New York Times* and the city's biggest papers, the *Tribune* and the *Herald*, remained critical. In the latter case this was not surprising because one of its contributors was Marx himself, Kinkel's arch-enemy.[8]

There were more difficulties to come for the German professor. His first mass meeting was held in Philadephia, supported and organised by Heinrich Tiedemann, a brother-in-law of Friedrich Hecker, another famous revolutionary hero from southwest Germany, who had settled in southern Illinois as a farmer in 1849. Influenced by rumours of a dissenting revolutionary community in London, the financial committee which was appointed after the mass meeting in support of Kinkel's national loan decided to collect the money and administer it, but not to send it to London immediately. The committee declared that it would keep the money until the internal struggles in London had been resolved and the political émigrés were united. Kinkel agreed and travelled on to Baltimore. Here he found a more trusting audience and it was agreed that as soon as $100 had been collected the money would be sent to London directly. The so-called 'Philadelphia platform' was the subject of considerable criticism by the German-American communities Kinkel visited subsequently. Here he received unanimous support and was honoured by parades, serenades, fairs and bazaars.

Nevertheless the incident had made clear – and Kinkel himself was aware of the problem – that his mission lacked authority. People had a right to know where their money would be sent, who was responsible for it, and how it would be used. A solution was found in the creation of a 'guarantors' committee' of well-known and proven 'Forty-Eighters' from both sides of the Atlantic. In addition to Kinkel's friends in London (Schurz, Meyen, Reichenbach), Richard Wagner from Dresden, for instance, was one of these appointed guarantors who pledged themselves to make all possible efforts to have the loan acknowledged after a successful revolution in the Republican legislation then to be passed.[9] The *New York Times* criticised the fact that 'the present chase after funds was without any better authority than that of a few of the illustrious obscure men in London

... who placed themselves in the nominative case at the foot of the loan certificates'.[10] In other words, the *New York Times* thought the scruples of the Philadelphia committee justified. A second critical objection with which Kinkel was confronted was that he had not said anything about a real plan or even a programme of the projected revolution. Indeed, no plans had been formulated so far because Kinkel and his friends could not know how things would develop and how they would be able to react. But Kinkel felt obliged to clear up confusion. In Cincinnati, at a meeting of the American guarantors' committee attended by only eight delegates,[11] he launched the *Denkschrift über das deutsche National-Anlehen zur Förderung der Revolution* (Memorandum on the German National Loan to Promote Revolution), explaining the original thoughts behind his mission.[12] This was subsequently reprinted in many German-American newspapers. In this memo, Kinkel explained that naturally nobody had thought of initiating a German revolution from exile, because nobody doubted that a new outbreak within Germany was imminent. Money from outside could be a decisive. No pure revolutionary would want to collect uncounted and 'uncontrolled' money, which would make him look suspicious. That was why the national loan had been launched as a system that was fully accountable. The issue of shares meant that everyone knew how much they were paying, and how much they could expect to receive after a successful revolution. Another advantage of a national loan was that it generated paper money immediately. After the establishment of a new political order in Germany this 'loan money' would have its full value as 'real money' and could replace the old monarchical money at once. The argument was that all former aristocratic estates which would then become public estates, together with the property of revolutionaries in Germany confiscated in 1848-9, guaranteed enough value for the repayment of the bonds. Kinkel once again emphasised that it would not be wise to draft a precise platform. The German situation was far more complicated than that in Hungary, Poland or even Italy, which were straightforward struggles for national independence from foreign occupation. But in Germany discussions about the final form of political organisation, the social and economic issues raised and discussed by different factions and different 'schools', would have to be postponed until the German republic had been established, Kinkel suggested, otherwise all revolutionary power and energy would be dissipated in these struggles. Kinkel admitted that his success in America would certainly have been even greater 'if the old German squabbling for principles and lack of unity had not crossed me at every step and made people suspicious of my mission.'[13]

Despite the various critical voices, however, Kinkel's tour went reasonably well. He travelled further south and then to the west, visiting many counties with a significant German-speaking population. Cincinnati, a community with over 50,000 Germans, was the most supportive city and Kinkel therefore visited it twice. German women in particular were keen to support the professor's cause by organising fairs, and they succeeded in engaging music associations for concerts, the proceeds of which were to go towards the loan.[14] It is almost impossible to arrive at even a rough estimate of how much money Kinkel collected, as there was a difference between donating money and subscribing to a list to receive shares in the loan. Quite substantial subscriptions were obtained in Baltimore, Pittsburgh and Cincinnati. The various fairs that were organised sometimes raised between one and two hundred dollars.

On 2 March 1852 Kinkel left New York for London, while political friends such as Gustav Struve in New York and Adolph Bauer in Cincinnati stayed on to promote the national loan project. Even the women's fairs went on for a while. It was the general idea of all three European fund-raisers that the campaign should continue with the support of the committees that had been set up in all the major cities, so that their presence in the USA would no longer be necessary. After Kinkel's departure, however, interest and energy declined rapidly. In fact, there was a presidential campaign coming up on an issue which concerned the German émigrés in America as much as revolutions in their old fatherland – the issue of slavery and its aftermath.

It was certainly to Kinkel's advantage that he had set out for North America two months before another well-known and celebrated revolutionary hero reached American shores: Lajos Kossuth. Compared to the attention Kossuth received from American as well as German-American newspapers, Kinkel was a minor celebrity.[15] While Kossuth was a front-page hero, Kinkel was usually mentioned on page 2 or 3 and Amand Goegg was mentioned only occasionally. Events in Hungary had captured the nation's interest since August 1849, for it was there and then that the last act of the mid-century revolutions was unfolding. 'The question whether continental Europe shall be under Cossack or republican rule hereafter will, in all probability, be definitely decided on the plains and the passes of Hungary', wrote Dudley Mann, special emissary to Europe, to the American Secretary of State, Daniel Webster, in August 1849, reflecting the main American attitude towards events in Hungary.[16] Long before the Hungarian patriot set foot in America, the story of how he had declared Hungary's independence from the Austrian Habsburgs had been published in the American press. When the Hungarian republic collapsed under the Austrian assault, Kossuth fled to Turkey, where he was interned as a result of Russian and Austrian pressure on the Ottoman Sultan, but regained his liberty because of American and British intervention. The USA sent one of its vessels, the U.S.S. *Mississippi*, to the Porte in order to escort Kossuth and his friends to the New World, where most Americans assumed he would take up land in the West and, as one newspaper put it, 'end his days in philosophical retirement.'[17] But Kossuth wanted to visit England first. This he did before setting out for America on the ship *Humboldt* after three weeks of continuous celebrations in England.[18]

On board the *Humboldt* was another celebrity as much in need of American money as Kossuth: the notorious dancer Lola Montez. The countess was, as her biographer put it, 'not pleased to be sharing the ship with another celebrity, particularly one who seemed to have an ego as healthy as hers. Fortunately for Lola, Kossuth's seasickness was far worse than her own, and the hero spent most of the voyage in his cabin, leaving her alone to fascinate and amuse the passengers and crew.' But when the ship slipped into pier 4 at Staten Island in New York harbour on 5 December 1851, the huge welcome and the thunder of saluting canon were not for Lola but for the Hungarian hero.[19]

Kossuth's *Address to the People of the United States of North America*, written at his place of banishment in Broussa in Turkey in March 1850 but withheld because of diplomatic proceedings between the USA and the Turkish government, was published in almost every single newspaper shortly before his arrival.[20] In this address Kossuth told the story of the Hungarians' battle and their defeat, his own position and recent treatment, praising and flattering the American people. It was here that Kossuth for the first time emphasised his central message that the USA had a moral obligation to fight for Hungarian freedom – in other words, that the USA must intervene in European politics: 'May your great example, noble Americans, be to other nations the source of social virtue. Your power may be the terror of all tyrants – the protector of the distressed and your free country ever continue to be the asylum for the oppressed of all nations.'[21]

It seems that the idea of 'humanitarian intervention' which has become so prominent in late twentieth-century politics, was born in 1852. Kossuth had come to challenge the Americans to accept their destined role as a world power. The American nation, on the other hand, was so convinced of Kossuth's virtue that it became hazardous to attack him publicly or to question his dedication to those principles Americans claimed as their own.[22] For weeks the American nation had been waiting for Kossuth's arrival in a state of paralysed anticipation. Now his reception was beyond measure. Banquets, escorts of honour, serenades and deputations vied with one another. What became clear during the almost hysterical welcome proceedings in the days after 6 December was that the celebrations served different purposes: some just wanted to celebrate a new citizen, others were making a serious political demonstration of the continuing hope for republicanism in the Old World.

Kossuth's speeches were printed at full length in the newspapers, and that is why, although the American Congress had been responsible for Kossuth travelling to the USA, Senators and Representatives now felt uneasy about welcoming him in Congress when he arrived in Washington early in January 1852. To support Kossuth marked a clear departure from traditional American foreign policy, which meant, first of all, from the classic notion of 'isolation'. Since his arrival Kossuth had stressed that he had no wish to become an American, even less a farmer. He wanted American help in renewing his quest for independence. He emphasised constantly the USA's duty to protect the law of nations and to move against Russian aggression which was preventing Hungary's peaceful progress towards national autonomy, a right even the smallest nation must have. The USA, as a leading power, he repeated everywhere, could not isolate itself from Europe; it must function as the guarantor of the nonintervention principle. He argued that just as American independence had been won by European weapons and soldiers, so now the time had come for America to repay its debts. But Congress did not share this view. The Whigs were openly hostile to it and only a few Democrats who were influenced by the Jacksonian notion of a 'manifest destiny' demanded that the USA should issue a proclamation officially condemning Russian intervention in Hungary. Kossuth was disappointed, and some Americans considered him ungrateful for their hospitality. This last impression was conveyed by Captain John C. Long's reports on Kossuth's behaviour as a guest on board the US vessel *Mississippi*. Kossuth had accused the Americans of operating a prison ship because he had not been allowed to leave the ship in Marseilles to cross French territory on his way to England. Kossuth, eager to grasp every opportunity to harangue the local population in every port about his revolutionary cause, had done so at the expense of American neutrality. In order to protect the reputation of the American flag in friendly ports, the crew had orders to touch as few ports as possible and to remain in them for as short a period as possible. Kossuth was furious when he learned about this limitation, and in expressing his anger he offended every American on board. When he left the ship at Gibraltar to depart on another ship for England he had felt no need to utter one word of thanks.[23]

Because Kossuth appealed to all Americans, while Kinkel and later Goegg concentrated their efforts only on the German-American population, Kossuth was unable to prevent American political parties and movements exploiting him for their own purposes. Aware that any involvement in internal American politics would jeopardise his mission, Kossuth, while still in England, had declared that he would not take any stand on the slavery question. However, wishing to flatter the British he had made the mistake of congratulating them on repealing the slave laws in the West Indies. Abolitionists in America could therefore entertain some hope that Kossuth would speak out on their behalf after his arrival in the USA. For them it was easy to consider Kossuth a victim of oppression and to transform his war of ethnic independence into a proud crusade for liberty and the rights of man. However, their idea of a common interest was an illusion. For weeks Kossuth tried hard to divorce himself from domestic questions, and especially from a public attack on the institution of slavery. When a delegation of more than a dozen black men awaited him in his New York hotel lounge to deliver a memorandum, the famous Magyar could not think of an appropriate response and consequently gave none. He was so annoyed by this incident that he drafted a public note stressing that his clear intention was not to be mixed up with any aspect of the sectional struggle.[24] The abolitionists' frustration with Kossuth was obvious in the changing tone of newspaper reports about him. Now Kossuth was accused of being a hypocrite who had come to the USA just for guns, money and men, but not to further the universal struggle for human rights. As he had initially travelled with a court of fifty-six people and had sent his companion, Ferenc Pulszky, ahead to prepare for his arrival, the anti-slavery newspapers now ridiculed Kossuth's monarchical attitudes, his pompousness and self-promotion. They became aware of what Karl Heinzen's *New Yorker Deutsche Zeitung* had already stated before Kossuth's arrival in the USA: that he was 'basically a nationalist' and 'a republican at the most (at best) in an aristocratic-oligarchic sense'.[25] Criticism also came from his own former ranks. When on 30 December 1851 Kázmér Batthyány, Foreign Minister of the short-lived

Hungarian republic, writing in *The Times* of London, accused his former chief of 'hankering after notoriety' and pursuing an inconsistent policy defined by 'self-willed and arbitrary measures', American newspapers reprinted the open letter in the early months of the New Year.[26] One week after Batthyány's accusation, Bertalan Szemere, former president of the Hungarian Ministerial Council, added further details from Paris. He called Kossuth a coward, who had fled his homeland prematurely because he had been thinking only of himself and not of his friends, the party, the army or the nation.[27]

Unfortunately, not being an outspoken abolitionist and demonstrating aristocratic attitudes did not help Kossuth to gain favour in the Southern States. Even though Kossuth tried to please by stressing the issues of local self-government and state rights, Southerners stayed away for different reasons. Kossuth's urge for intervention against Russian aggression in Hungary – in short 'intervention for nonintervention' – meant a departure from traditional US foreign policy, and was based on an idea totally alien to the American character. Moreover, interventionism represented a dangerous abstraction that could be applied, at some future time, against the Southern States. Therefore they feared the consequences which could result from supporting Kossuth's appeal.

Although Kossuth's star started to decline rapidly in US political circles in the following months, he continued to attract the support of thousands of private citizens. At meetings he pleaded for funds to continue his struggle. He offered to accept loans, he said, but preferred 'free subscriptions', and suggested helpfully that committees be organised to solicit gifts.[28] Of significance at national level was the creation of the Central Hungarian Committee, which immediately became the vehicle for Kossuth's national fund-raising drive. Hungarian bonds bearing Kossuth's portrait and his personal autograph if they were $50 or $100 certificates formed the basis of the Committee's efforts. These certificates issued in denominations of one, five, ten, fifty and one hundred dollars promised repayment when (not 'if') Kossuth was safely returned to the governorship of an independent Hungary.[29] More than once Kossuth's scheduled lectures were closed to all those who could not show a Hungarian bond at the door. Kossuth's refusal to detail how he was spending these contributions evoked some criticism, but his standard explanation: 'I cannot tell the public (which is to tell my country's enemy), how I dispose of the sums which I receive', seemed to satisfy most of his supporters.[30]

But as time went by not only American politicians but also private citizens became weary of Kossuth's endlessly repetitive speeches on Hungarian independence and American duty. Eager to see and hear the Hungarian hero for herself, Anne Emily Lane, 22–year-old daughter of St Louis's mayor, William Carr Lane, managed to attend Kossuth's meetings in Philadelphia and Allegheny. She is an example of how attitudes towards Kossuth changed when the national hysteria cooled down and the general interest declined. To her friend Sarah in St. Louis she confessed:

> How tired I am of hearing of him [Kossuth] and his bleeding country. I manufactured a decent amount of enthusiasm in Philadelphia but it is all used up. I am sorry for Kossuth but I think the most *sublime* thing about him is his assurance in wanting us to engage in a war for the benefit of his country. If he would accept that we are willing to give him an asylum it would be well enough but I am against fighting any but our own battles.[31]

In celebrating Kossuth, Americans had celebrated themselves and their nation as one of the leading democracies on earth. But now they were becoming impatient with their guest, just as he was frustrated by them. Kossuth therefore began to concentrate his efforts more and more on the German-American population during his trip to the West. Since at that time there were only a few Hungarians in the USA who could support his cause,[32] Kossuth sought a coalition with the German-Americans who still identified with the fate of Central Europe. He therefore changed the subject of his speeches in order to win the Germans over. This turned out to be no difficult task, since Kossuth knew that Germans, especially those from southern regions, had had some experience of Prussian and Austrian interventions and therefore entertained strong sympathy for the principle of 'intervention for non-intervention'. Even before his arrival in the United States, the German-language press had celebrated Kossuth as 'the political saviour of the century', 'martyr of European democracy', and the 'Messiah of European republicanism'.[33] German-American newspapers in America, edited by many German Forty-Eighters sharing the fate of political exile with Kossuth, stressed the common cultural background of Hungarians and Germans, and claimed Kossuth's endeavours for the sake of the whole of Europe. When Kossuth and Kinkel addressed a German-American audience together in Cincinnati, they emphasised their common cause and declared that solidarity between Hungarians and Germans would help both movements. Consequently Germans were as eager to buy Kossuth's bonds as they were to organise the German national loan.

In Buffalo and later in New York, Kossuth and Amand Goegg spoke at the same events and Kossuth suggested that part of the money collected for his cause by German Americans should be shared with the German revolutionaries. He wanted to make sure that after his departure the Germans would continue to act as his agents because he knew very well that there was nobody else left he could count on, since Anglo-American interest had vanished completely.

The financial structure Kossuth had built over the preceding months was so confused and so informal that it is impossible to ascertain how much money he received or where it went. During Kossuth's last days in the United States, the full burden of his fiscal incompetence became apparent: the Philadelphia printer who had supplied the entire stock of 'Kossuth Bonds' had not yet been paid; weapons bought on credit for $2 apiece were pawned for half that amount, etc. Such practices, along with the discrepancies between newspaper reports of donations and Kossuth's announced receipts, cast doubt on the accuracy of the Hungarian's official figures. On 10 June 1852 these were $85,000 in contributions, with only $1,132.34 remaining after expenses.[34] On 14 July 1852 Kossuth and his wife slipped aboard the Cunard Liner Africa under the aliases of Mr and Mrs Alexander Smith without any official or public attention and accompanied only by Amand Goegg, who was also on his way back to London. The forthcoming presidential election had absorbed all public attention and – as Kossuth put it – 'lowered every high aspiration into the narrow scope of party spirit.'[35]

Kossuth's farewell speech during a German mass meeting at the Broadway Tabernacle in Manhattan on 23 June revealed his disillusionment and bitter disappointment.[36] He showed little hope in the American element and asked his audience whether everything was going to fail because of idleness and lack of enthusiasm in a materialistically orientated nation that did not care about others. He warned them that unless the USA took seriously its role as a leading democratic power, it would soon lose all political influence on world politics. Kossuth appealed to his German audience to persuade the American government to abandon its policy of isolation. 'Not to fulfil one's duty', he declared bluntly, 'is guilt'.[37] On the other hand, aware of how much he depended on the goodwill of the Germans, Kossuth flattered them enormously by talking about their role in future world history and how his tour had to be praised for at least one result: it had brought Germans and Hungarians closer together and had created a sense of brotherhood and solidarity. He pleaded for a joint effort to establish democracy in their respective countries, but while he stressed the need to strengthen their efforts by coordinating their work, he made it unmistakably clear that only two completely separate, independent nations could be the outcome. In his speech, and in a letter secretly circulated to various German societies and local political leaders shortly before his departure, Kossuth, overestimating the importance of the German vote in the political campaign of 1852, urged the German population to influence the US government to assume a larger role in world affairs, to repeal the Neutrality Act of 1818 and to vote only for the party that gave Kossuth an assurance that it was determined to proceed upon the basis of the fundamental principles Kossuth had laid down in his address of 23 June. When this secret letter, which 'should not be publicized, but can be used for private communications only'[38], was published in the *New York Herald* (Karl Marx had prepared the translation[39]), American readers were surprised to see how close the Hungarian hero had become to the Germans while fund-raising in the USA.

Since their differences had still not been settled, and fearing that Kinkel did not intend to share the American funds with them in London, the eight members of the *Agitationsverein* decided to send their own agent to make an appearance in the New World. Amand Goegg, accompanied by Josef Fickler, arrived in Boston in the last week of 1851.[40] Amand Goegg had studied *Kameralwissenschaften* (administrative law) in Heidelberg and worked as a freelance journalist for the democratic cause. In the Baden revolution he had belonged to the republican wing and had been the leading organiser of popular associations (*Volksvereine*) set up throughout Baden to strengthen the democratic feeling of its people. He had served as finance minister in Brentano's provisional government before he had to flee to Switzerland. Via Paris he had gone to London, where he was active as a leading figure in his revolutionary society, the *Agitationsverein*.

Josef Fickler had been the publisher of the radical *Seeblätter* in Constance, which at an early stage had demanded that the Grand Duchy of Baden should be made a republic, if necessary, by means of an armed rising. He was a fierce opponent of Lorenz Brentano and his provisional government, established in the summer of 1849, because he did not consider it sufficiently radical. He was arrested, but managed to escape from prison and went to London. Unlike Goegg, he did not return to London after his fund-raising trip but stayed in the USA until he was able to return to Germany in the mid-1860s, after a general amnesty had been proclaimed. Shortly thereafter, in 1865, he died there, in his home town of Constance.

Both men represented the extreme left wing of the German émigré colony in London. Goegg advocated the distribution of revolutionary pamphlets intended to educate and enlighten the German population. He insisted that the only efficient way to overthrow the German princes was by secret propaganda. He also wanted to gain support for the US policy of cooperating with the revolutionary elements in Europe, and in this respect Goegg's programme had some similarities with Kossuth's idea of humanitarian intervention for democratic purposes.[41] However, in addressing the problem of money, he had developed another idea. He tried to collect money by subscription, not by selling shares in a national loan. The idea was that if every German in America (they estimated that there were about 3 million) paid only one cent per week, they would collect 3 millions cents each week, which is the equivalent of $30,000 a week or $1,560, 000 a year. This was considered enough to build up an efficient organisation to agitate and overthrow German princes and monarchs.[42] But there was one problem: although Goegg was one of the most sympathetic figures among the Baden revolutionaries and served the republican cause with unselfish integrity, he was not a gifted speaker. He simply lacked the rhetorical skills to win his audience over.[43] His theoretically overloaded speeches were seen not only as dry, but also as marred by a heavy Baden accent. 'People always simply laugh at him when he [Goegg] proves the necessity of revolution by reference to the history of antiquity', reported one of Marx's friends from Washington.[44] In fact, Goegg's tour was not as successful as Kinkel's, although he gained more support in New York, and as Philadelphia saw him as the official, authorised agent of the London political refugee's society in general, he was given considerable backing there. Goegg and his cause were not only supported by the radical prose of Karl Heinzen, but also by small *Revolutionsvereine* (revolutionary societies) which had been founded by German Forty-Eighters in many localities on the East Coast and in the Mid-West. Non-refugees and anybody who took an interest in Europe's revolutions were also welcomed as members.[45] Their central headquarters would be in Philadelphia. Hoping to end the controversy between Kinkel and Goegg, a number of German organisations, some of the revolutionary societies as well as the Turner associations, called for a congress to be held in Philadelphia in late January 1852.[46] With the intention of settling the conflict, the congress's aim was to form a coalition of all German democratic forces in connection with Europe. Thus the *Amerikanischer Revolutionsbund für Europa* (American Revolutionary League for Europe) was founded, and Goegg solemnly declared the London agitation society dissolved.[47] The 'real and effective liberation of the European continent' was announced as the purpose of the new League by (1) overthrowing any monarchy and establishing a republic; (2) introducing universal (male) suffrage; (3) dissolving all standing armies and establishing the principle of the inviolability of a people's army (*Volksbewaffnung*); and (4) destroying all oppressors of the people. The means were to be agitation in Europe and America, setting up revolutionary funds and forming military bodies.

Kinkel had not taken part in the congress's proceedings; nor had any delegates from New York, the South or the Mid-West. It seems that the radical language and programme kept them away. For Goegg, who was still travelling, Kinkel's absence created a serious problem. Since he was going to most of the cities Kinkel had already visited, Goegg was more than once forced to explain his relationship with Kinkel. After all, he emphasised, they were supposed to be fighting for the same cause. He demonstrated his goodwill by stressing the need to create a universal organisation which brought together the leaders and factions of the different movements.[48] Goegg and Fickler were among those who tried hard to reach an understanding and to stop the competitive agitation.[49] Financially, Goegg's mission was less successful than Kinkel's.[50] On 14 July 52 he left New York for London, accompanying Kossuth and his wife.

Goegg was expected to return to the USA to chair the second congress of the *Amerikanischer Revolutionsbund für Europa* held in Wheeling from 19 to 22 September 1852. The congress had been called by the Philadelphia group, Goegg's ardent supporters. But in a letter addressed to the committee he admitted that he was unable to attend for financial reasons. The Wheeling congress marked the final chapter in the history of transatlantic cooperation in order to establish republican governments in Europe and its political programme represented a strange amalgam of Kinkel's, Kossuth's and Goegg's intentions. The sixteen delegates testified to the sincerity of both Kinkel and Goegg, and also endorsed Kossuth's loan. Letters from the London exiles were read, in which Goegg advised supporting Kinkel, Kossuth reminded his readers of the need to cooperate with German, Hungarian and Italian revolutionaries, and promised, 'in the spirit of brotherhood', to put some of the money collected by Germans for his own crusade at the disposal of the German cause,[51] and Giuseppe Mazzini, Alexandre Ledru-Rollin and Arnold Ruge, all members of the Central European Democratic Committee, appealed for financial assistance for further political activities. But the major concern of the congress was the question of how to encourage the USA to fulfil its destiny to build a world republic under its leadership. The delegates prepared a manifesto in which they stressed the historical necessity of the American Union to expand until it included all the states of Europe. As Rome had absorbed the ancient world, the nation-states of Europe, they argued, must be dissolved in the 'universality of the American character.'[52] After the absorption of Cuba, Canada and Mexico the American republic should use its overwhelming power to build 'one universal federal state of the civilized world'. In Europe the conflict of competing sovereignties would come to an end when every nation joined the universal republic. Believing in America's global mission as the nucleus of a future world state, the congress changed its name to *Volksbund für die Alte und Neue Welt* (People's League for the Old and New World) and sent an enquiry to President Franklin Pierce to find out his opinion on American intervention in Europe. The fact that they never received a reply was a clear indication of the President's views. Not only the President but also most Forty-Eighters were critical of, even cynical about, these ideas, which they rejected as fantastic, absurd and impractical. But such radical resolutions represented the desires of some parts of the refugee community who would have liked to use the USA to change the political landscape of Europe.[53] The League itself died 'a peaceful death' shortly thereafter, in 1853.[54]

For many German-American Forty-Eighters who had actively supported the fund-raising tours of Kinkel, Kossuth and Goegg, it was the last time that their political commitment was orientated towards Europe. As the three money-collectors themselves were, in a way, disappointed with the results of their efforts, more and more German-American political refugees became aware that revolutions in Europe were not just around the corner. Napoleon's coup in France in early December 1851 had destroyed hopes of an immediate revolution anywhere in Europe. Former London exiles such as Carl Schurz, Franz Sigel, August Willich, Alexander Schimmelpfennig and Oskar von Reichenbach set out for the USA shortly after Kinkel's return to London and decided to concentrate their future political efforts on reforming US institutions which were, after all, far from perfect. The *New Yorker Staatszeitung* pointed out to its German compatriots that 'the United States of America are not born simply as Europe's milk cow' and reminded them 'that American citizens do have other and higher duties to fulfil than to think of Europe's liberation alone.'[55] Unlike Kossuth, Carl Schurz blamed not

Americans, but the German-American political community for the exhausted revolutionary *élan*. To his former teacher and mentor he wrote from Philadelphia:

> Your agitation and Kossuth's and the Revolutionary Confederation have so used up the enthusiasm for transatlantic affairs, and the European events since 1851 have made the Americans so distrustful that the people must be given rest and quiet to recover from their chagrin and disappointment ... If the Americans have hitherto had not much use for the German revolution, no one is to blame for that but the Germans here.[56]

For American observers it was always clear that although the money-collectors had attracted considerable attention in the German-language press, their real influence had been negligible as far as the course of American politics was concerned.

The *Agitationsverein* dissolved, and the exile community reduced in numbers by those who emigrated further to the USA, Amand Goegg and Gottfried Kinkel followed a policy of rapprochement over the question of what should become of the collected money, an amount, the *Cincinnati Volksblatt* stated, 'not large enough to be called amazing, but enough to cover the current costs of the most urgent and still possible revolutionary tasks.'[57] As early as August 1852 Goegg, Kinkel and August Willich drafted a 'Union Contract' between the *American Revolutionary League for Europe*, which was still in existence, and the contributors to and guarantors of the German national loan, in the hope of overcoming their rivalries. But the variety of conflicting proposals made it difficult. Goegg still wanted to set up a revolutionary newspaper and print propaganda for circulation in Europe, while Kinkel, scrupulously honest in administering the fund and still believing in a new military conflict between republicans and reactionaries, insisted on saving the money for the next revolutionary outbreak. He also refused to use the money for needy exile literati in London and questioned how useful a German newspaper in London would be for influencing the political situation in Germany itself. To make this point clear he wrote a letter to German-American newspapers assuring them that no member of the administrative committee would be paid for his work out of the loan.[58] Although donors from Detroit wanted their money back to invest in a German school, and in Pittsburgh they pleaded for it to be returned to the original donors,[59] the funds were finally deposited in the Bank of England. Kinkel gave Amand Goegg access to the account when he left to take up a professorship in Zurich in 1866. Some of the money was used to set up August Bebel's Social Democratic Party and its journal, which meant, ironically, that in a way Kinkel had collected money for his fiercest adversary: Karl Marx.[60]

Amand Goegg was the only one who returned to the USA. Twenty years after his first appearance on American soil he lectured throughout the USA on socialism and his latest plans to save the world. Still an ardent propagandist and a pacifist at heart, he advocated a *League of Freedom and Peace* for the disarmament and the republicanisation of Europe.[61] His lectures on international socialism were popular in cities with a large working-class population, such as Chicago, Detroit and Pittsburgh.[62] After the Baden government granted a general amnesty, Goegg was able to return home. He died there in 1897.

Lajos Kossuth never felt the desire to visit the USA again, although in many cities monuments were erected commemorating his visit and his cause. When in 1881 the leader of the small Hungarian community in St Louis, R.J. Rombauer, invited Kossuth to a memorial celebration of another revolutionary hero, Friedrich Hecker, the famous Magyar could not remember that he had once proclaimed a close coalition between Germans and Hungarians. In his letter to Rombauer, who had enthusiastically supported Kossuth's visit to St Louis in 1852, he admitted: 'Since better than thirty years I have not been engaged with German history, neither did I have any contact with Germans.' And he confessed: 'For lack of necessary familiarity with the facts … I am entirely incompetent and inept to participate in the planned commemoration even in the most remote manner.' Kossuth felt unable to attend a memorial service for a man whose merits he could not remember.[63] Strangely enough twenty-nine years previously Kossuth, in his attempt to win over the Germans to his cause, had recommended the very same man, Friedrich Hecker, as the leader of the German-American community in supporting the European revolutions.[64] But in the end, what Kossuth declared to Rombauer had come true: 'Time has taken its toll on my overburdened recollection as to the degree of personal participation of individuals and the special events of that stormy period.'[65]

Notes

1 E.g., the European correspondence in German-American newspapers: *Cincinnati Volksblatt*, 24 September 1851 (London correspondence by Carl Schurz); 18 October 1851; 6 November 1851 (London correspondence by Eduard Meyen); 26 November 1851 (London correspondence by Gustav Techow); *New Yorker Deutsche Zeitung*, 1 December 1851.

2 On Gottfried Kinkel and Arnold Ruge see Rosemary Ashton, *Little Germany: Exile & Asylum in Victorian England* (Oxford and New York, 1986), 139–67.

3 See Ashton, *Little Germany*, 159.

4 Gottfried Kinkel's itinerary: New York (arrival: 14 September 1851; departure to 'The West': 18 September 1851) ⇒ Philadelphia (mass meeting, 27 September 1851) ⇒ Baltimore (4 – c. 16 October 1851) ⇒ Washington ⇒ Pittsburgh (21/22 October 1851) ⇒ Alleghany ⇒ Wheeling ⇒ Cincinnati (1 – 6 November 1851) ⇒ Cleveland ⇒ Buffalo ⇒ Niagara Falls ⇒ Detroit ⇒ Ann Arbor ⇒ Chicago (29 November 1851) ⇒ Milwaukee (29./30 November 1851) ⇒ Chicago (11 December 1851) ⇒ Peoria ⇒ St. Louis (arrival: 17 December 1851; 20 December 1852: mass meeting) ⇒ Belleville (31 December 1851: mass meeting with Friedrich Hecker) ⇒ Natchez ⇒ Lafayette ⇒ New Orleans (January 1852) ⇒ Cincinnati (3 – 8 February 1852: guarantee's meeting; 5 February 1852: 'Denkschrift über das deutsche National-Anlehen zur Förderung der Revolution'; 11 February 1852: private meeting with Kossuth; 15 February 1852: German mass meeting with Kinkel and Kossuth) ⇒ Louisville (18 February 1852) ⇒ Dayton ⇒ Columbus ⇒ Elmira, NY (22 February 1852) ⇒ New York (meeting with Josef Fickler; 24 February 1852: German mass meeting; departure for London 2 March 1852)

5 See letters from Sigel, Ruge, Tausenau and Goegg in *New Yorker Deutsche Zeitung*, 9, 10, 11, 12, 16, 17, 18, 20, 25, 26 September 1851.

6 *New Yorker Deutsche Zeitung*, 16 September 1851; see also the bitter commentary on Gottfried Kinkel in America in Karl Heinzen, *Teutscher Radikalismus in Amerika: Ausgewählte Abhandlungen, Kritiken und Aphorismen aus den Jahren 1854–1879* (Milwaukee, 1898, 3 vols), I, pp. 63–7.

7 Abschiedsworte, *New Yorker Deutsche Zeitung* (last edition), 4 December 1851.

8 For Marx's contribution to the New York Herald see Adolf Cluß to Karl Marx, Washington, 5 August 1852, see *Marx-Engels Gesamt-Ausgabe (MEGA)* III/5, p. 458; Ashton, *Little Germany*, p. 9.

9 Karl Marx to Hermann Ebner, London, 2 December 1851, *MEGA* III/5, p. 255.

10 *The New York Daily Times*, 19 January 1852.

11 'Bericht über die Berathungen und Beschlüsse des Kongresses der Garanten der deutschen Revolutionsanleihe, gehalten in Cincinnati am 3., 4., 6., 7. und 8. Februar 1852', *Cincinnati Volksblatt*, 10 February 1852; Carl Wittke, *Refugees of Revolution: The German Forty-Eighters in America* (Philadelphia, 1952), p. 102.

12 Gottfried Kinkel, 'Denkschrift über das deutsche National-Anlehen zur Förderung der Revolution, Elmira im Staate New York, 22 February 1852', *Cincinnati Volksblatt* 10 March 1852 (Part I), 11 March 1852 (Part II), 12 March 1852 (Part III), 13 March 1852 (Part IV), 14 March (Part V), 16 March 1852 (Part VI), 17 March 1852 (Part VII); *New Yorker Staatszeitung*, 6 March 1852 (here the official date is Cincinnati, 5 February 1852).

13 *Denkschrift*, 13 March 1852.

14 *Cincinnati Volksblatt*, 11 November 1851, 4 December 1851, 2 April 1852, 6 April 1852, 11 July 1852.

15 See, e.g., the huge front-page articles on Kossuth in *The New York Daily Times*, 24 November 1851; 27 November 1851; 8 January 1852; 9 January 1852.

16 Donald S. Spencer, *Louis Kossuth and Young America. A Study of Sectionalism and Foreign Policy, 1848–1852* (Columbia and London, 1977), pp. 22, 26; this study contains an excellent bibliography; for a general account of Kossuth's visit to the United States see John H. Komlos, *Louis Kossuth in America, 1851–1852* (Buffalo and New York, 1973).

17 Spencer, *Kossuth*, p. 49.

18 Lajos Kossuth's itinerary: New York (arrival: 5 December 1851; 11 December 1851: speech City Council of New York; 18 December 1851: Brooklyn) ⇒ Philadelphia ⇒ Baltimore (2 January 1852) ⇒ Washington (5 January 1852: reception (US Senate); 7 January 1852: Congressional Banquet; reception (House of Representatives); dinner with President Fillmore; speech and reception (Jackson Association); talk to Henry Clay) ⇒ Annapolis (13 January 1852: reception, Legislation of Maryland) ⇒ Harrisburgh (14 January 1852: reception, Legislation of Pennsylvania) ⇒ Pittsburgh (22 January 1852) ⇒ Salem & Ravenna (short speeches) ⇒ Cleveland (arrival: 31 January 1852; 2 February 1852: speech) ⇒ Columbus/Ohio (4 February 1852) ⇒ Cedarville ⇒ Xenia ⇒ Springfield ⇒ Dayton ⇒ Hamilton ⇒ Cincinnati (two-week visit; arrival: 9 February 1852; 11 February 1852: private meeting with Gottfried Kinkel; 13 February 1852: city's official reception; 15 February 1852: mass meeting with Kinkel und Kossuth; visits to Newport and Covington) ⇒ Louisville (22 February 1852) ⇒ Indianapolis (28 February 1852) ⇒ St Louis (9 –16 March 1852) ⇒ Memphis ⇒ Jackson ⇒ Natchez ⇒ Baton Rouge ⇒ New Orleans (arrival: 27 March; 31 March 1852: speech; departure: 1 April 1852) ⇒ Mobile (2 – 3 April 1852) ⇒ Montgomery ⇒ Augusta ⇒ Charleston ⇒ Wilmington ⇒ Washington (13 April 1852) ⇒ New Jersey (c. 24 April 1852) ⇒ Boston (24 April 1852) several other Eastern cities ⇒ New Haven ⇒

Springfield/Mass (27 April 1852) ⇒ Brookfield (April/May 1852) ⇒ Lexington (10 May 1852) ⇒ Albany (May 1852) ⇒ Buffalo (June 1852: German mass meeting with Goegg and Kossuth) ⇒ New York (arrival: *c.* 20 June 1852 accompanied by Amand Goegg; last public speech: 21 June 1852; 23 June 1852: German mass meeting with Goegg at the Broadway Tabernacle in Manhattan, Kossuth's farewell speech to the Germans in America; 4 July 1852 'Sängerfest'; departure for London: 14 July 1852 accompanied by Goegg).

19 Bruce Seymour, *Lola Montez: A Life* (New Haven , CT / London, 1996), pp. 281–2.
20 Lajos Kossuth, 'Address to the People of the United States of North America,' *The New York Daily Times*, 20 October 1851; in German: *New Yorker Deutsche Zeitung*, 20, 21, 22, 23, 27 October 1851.
21 Kossuth, *Address*, see footnote 20.
22 See Spencer, *Kossuth*, p. 43.
23 'Captain Long', *New York Daily Times*, 8 January 1852; 'Captain Long and Kossuth', *Cincinnati Volksblatt*, 17 January 1851; *Morning Courier and New York Enquirer*, 15 February 1852.
24 Spencer, *Kossuth*, p. 77.
25 *New Yorker Deutsche Zeitung*, 29 November 1851.
26 *The London Times*, 30 December 1851; *The New York Daily Times*, 10 January 1852; *The North American Review* 75 (September 1852), pp. 458 – 9; see also Spencer, *Kossuth*, pp. 146–7.
27 *The New York Daily Times*, 2 February 1852; *Morning Courier and New York Enquirer*, 9 February 1852.
28 Spencer, *Kossuth*, p. 53.
29 Ibid., *Kossuth*, p. 58.
30 Ibid., *Kossuth*, p. 155.
31 Anne Emily Lane to Sarah Glasgow, Alleghany, 19 January 1852, *Lane Collection WCL*, Missouri Historical Society, St Louis/MO, USA.
32 In 1870 the whole state of Missouri counted only 599 citizens of Hungarian origin; *c.* 4,000 Hungarians had sought refuge in the United States after the upheavals of the years 1848 – 50, 'Kossuth in St Louis', *Bulletin of the Missouri Historical Society*, 1/IX (October 1952), p. 101.
33 *Cincinnati Volksblatt*, 20, 26 December 1851; *Cincinnati Volksfreund*, 27 December 1851; also 'Kossuths deutschfreundliche Rede in Boston', *Cincinnati Volksblatt*, 23 May 1852.
34 Spencer, *Kossuth*, p. 166.
35 Quoted in ibid., *Kossuth*, p. 168.
36 'Kossuth's Abschiedsrede', *New Yorker Staatszeitung*, 26 June 1852; 'Deutsche Kossuth Versammlung', *Cincinnati Volksblatt*, 27 June 1852.

37 'Kossuth's Abschiedsrede', *New Yorker Staatszeitung*, 26 June 1852.

38 Lajos Kossuth to Wilhelm Stängel, New York, 52 E. 16th Street, 28 June 1852, *Staengel Collection*, Missouri Historical Society, St. Louis/MO, USA; English translation in Leslie Konnyu, 'Two Kossuth Letters in the Archives of the Missouri Historical Society', *Bulletin of the Missouri Historical Society*, 1/XVIII (October 1961), pp. 50–2.

39 Karl Marx's translation in *New York Tribune*, *MEGA* III/5, p. 480.

40 Amand Goegg's itinerary (accompanied by Josef Fickler): Boston (late December 1851) ⇒ New York (19 January 1852: mass meeting) ⇒ Philadelphia (29 – 30 January 1852: Refugee's congress, foundation of 'Amerikanischer Revolutionsbund für Europa'; Fickler returns to New York and stays there) ⇒ Baltimore (14 – 18 February 1852) ⇒ Washington ⇒ Reading ⇒ Harrisburgh ⇒ Pittsburgh ⇒ Alleghany ⇒ Wheeling ⇒ Columbus ⇒ Dayton ⇒ Cincinnati (4 April 1852) ⇒ Louisville ⇒ St. Louis (arrival 6 April 1852) ⇒ Belleville/Summerfield (10 April 1852: private meeting with Friedrich Hecker) ⇒ St Louis (arrival: 7 April 1852; 12 April 1852: mass meeting with Heinrich Börnstein, editor of the *Anzeiger des Westens*) ⇒ Pekin/Ill. (May 1852) ⇒ Peoria/Ill. (May 1852) ⇒ Chicago (May 1852) ⇒ Milwaukee (May 1852) ⇒ Chicago ⇒ Detroit ⇒ Sandusky (May 1852) ⇒ Cleveland ⇒ Erie ⇒ Buffalo (June 1852: German mass meeting with Goegg and Kossuth) ⇒ Albany ⇒ New York (arrival *c.* 20 June 1852 accompanied by Kossuth; 26 June 1852: German mass meeting with Kossuth, 14 July 1852: departure for London accompanied by Kossuth).

41 See Wittke, *Refugees*, p. 101.

42 Friedrich Hassaurek, 'Die "Achtundvierziger" in Amerika. Rede gehalten beim Stiftungsfeste der deutschen Pioniere in Cincinnati am 25. Mai 1875', *Tägliche Illinois Staatszeitung*, 28 May 1875, p. 3.

43 Marx on Goegg, *MEGA* 5/III, pp. 320ff. 'Massenversammlung im Shakespeare' (19 January 1852), *Cincinnati Volksblatt*, 28 January 1852: 'In his speech Mister Goegg gave a historical survey of all revolutions which took place in the last 50 years.'; Amand Goegg, 'Ein Blick in die sociale Geschichte der Völker', *New Yorker Deutsche Zeitung*, 5, 8, 12, 20 November 1851.

44 Adolf Cluß to Karl Marx, Washington, 15 April 1852, *MEGA* 5/III, 320.

45 *Cincinnati Volksblatt*, 1 December 1851; *New Yorker Deutsche Zeitung*, 13 November 1851; Wittke, *Refugees*, p. 99.

46 First proposals for a joint congress of all democratic societies in Philadelphia, *New Yorker Staatszeitung*, 27 November 1851; 'Platform', *Cincinnati Volksblatt*, 7 February 1852; *New Yorker Staatszeitung*, 7 February 1852; Eitel W. Dobert, 'The Radicals', in Adolf Zucker (ed.),

The Forty-Eighters: Political Refugees of the German Revolution of 1848 (New York, 1950), pp. 157–81.

47 *New Yorker Staatszeitung*, 7 February 1852.

48 *Cincinnati Volksblatt*, 21 March 1852.

49 Ibid., 27 March 1852; 22 April 1852.

50 His rival organisation had raised exactly $ 36.07 in the five months following the adjournment of the Wheeling Congress, Wittke, *Refugees*, p. 107.

51 Lajos Kossuth, 'Brief an den Congress des Amerikanischen Revolutionsbundes für Europa, London, den 31. August 1852', *New Yorker Staatszeitung*, 16 October 1852.

52 'Manifest des Völkerbundes für die alte und neue Welt an die europäische Demokratie', *New Yorker Staatszeitung*, 2 October 1852.

53 Wittke, *Refugees*, p. 105.

54 Dobert, *'Radicals'*, pp. 157–81.

55 *New Yorker Staatszeitung*, 21 August 1852.

56 Carl Schurz to Gottfried Kinkel, Philadelphia, 12 April 1853, in Joseph Schafer (ed.), *Intimate Letters of Carl Schurz, 1841 – 1869* (Madison, 1928), pp. 119–20; also quoted in Wittke, *Refugees*, p. 197.

57 'Kinkels Bericht auf dem Garanten-Treffen, 19. März 1852', *Cincinnati Volksblatt*, 13 April 1852.

58 'Brief von Gottfried Kinkel, London, den 2. September 1852', *New Yorker Staatszeitung*, 29 September 1852, p. 4.

59 Wittke, *Refugees*, pp. 106– 7.

60 See Ashton, *Little Germany*, p. 160.

61 *Wächter am Erie*, 14 February 1872, 11 May 1872; *Tägliche Illinois Staatszeitung*, 25 April 1872, 29 April 1872, 9 May 1872.

62 See Bruce Levine's contribution in this volume, Chapter 14.

63 Lajos Kossuth to Colonel R. J. Rombauer, Collegno / Banuone, Italy, 3 September 1881, *Rombauer Collection*, Missouri Historical Society, St. Louis/MO, USA; English translation in Leslie Konnyu, 'Two Kossuth Letters in the Archives of the Missouri Historical Society', *Bulletin of the Missouri Historical Society*, 1/XVIII (October 1961), p. 53.

64 'Brief Lajos Kossuths an den Congreß des amerikanischen Revolutionsbundes für Europa, London, 31 August 1852', *New Yorker Staatszeitung*, 16 October 1852.

65 Kossuth to Rombauer, see footnote 63.

12

German Socialism in London after 1849:
The Communist League of August Willich and Karl Schapper

Christine Lattek

The Communist League in London

German socialists arriving in London from 1849 on could rely on a well-established network of assistance. In 1840 a continental artisans' secret society had established a London branch and a public workers' educational society, the *Communistischer Arbeiter-Bildungsverein,* or CABV, which was to survive the various stages of London exile politics until the First World War. Originally inspired by the writings of Wilhelm Weitling, a utopian communist, the CABV had, under the influence of its British surroundings, developed a unique form of socialism throughout the 1840s.

Its most significant exponent was Karl Schapper, who had become involved in revolutionary nationalist agitation and Giuseppe Mazzini's expedition to Savoy in the 1830s. By 1838 he was advocating 'community of goods [as] the first and essential condition of a free democratic republic.'[1] He joined the 1839 Blanquist uprising in Paris and was forced to flee to England. Within a few years, the CABV members around Schapper had distanced themselves from Weitling and begun to develop their own distinctive brand of communism: they saw 'human nature' as the basis for communism, and acknowledged historical development without linking it to production or to classes. Crucially, they also developed connections with French and other refugees as well as with British Chartists. Soon, however, contacts with Marx and Engels in Brussels made the Londoners set aside their distrust of 'arrogant intellectuals' with their one-sided emphasis on political economy, but they continued to regard themselves as 'the proletarians' *vis-à-vis* Marx and his followers. In 1847 a rapprochement was reached, and the Londoners entrusted Marx with the task of formulating their joint 'Communist Manifesto' for the newly reconstructed Communist League, which boasted a more open and democratic structure and aimed principally at extending socialist propaganda.[2]

Any remaining friction between the Londoners and Marx was drowned in the outbreak of revolution on the Continent, which sent many emigrants straight back to Germany and into the fray. Marx and some of the Londoners disagreed about the role of the Communist League during the revolution; for practical purposes most members concentrated their efforts on the Rhineland Club movement, agitation in the press, and the Baden-Palatinate uprising, while attempting to keep the workers' movement an independent affair. In London, in the meantime, the much reduced Club supported the Chartist demonstration on Kennington Common and formed a new secret Central Authority in late 1848, in open defiance of the policy advocated by Marx, who still favoured public and legal activities.[3] These organisational fragments which survived in London would be built upon when the defeated revolutionaries returned to exile.

Around 1,500 German 'Forty-Eighters' arrived in England after the revolution (with more passing through), often destitute and in need of relief.[4] The CABV expanded to three branches and ran a 'social democratic refugee committee' headed by Marx and Engels, now exiled in London themselves. The club also provided Marx with a basis for rebuilding the Communist League, whose remnants he was now happy to utilise. Yet the relationship between Marx and the German workers was neither easy nor straightforward.

The question of reorganising the League itself was closely related to the communists' position *vis-à-vis* other émigré groups. By November 1849 Karl Heinzen (an admirer of Mazzini and Arnold Ruge) and Gustav Struve had established a democratic society, and interaction and competition between the two camps of democratic and socialist exiles played a crucial role for both sides. The League twice stated its policy in this regard, in 'Circulars' issued in March and June 1850. These clearly reveal the more important points of friction between Marx and various CABV members, amongst which alliance strategies were particularly prominent.

In March 1850, Marx still expected a revolution to break out soon on the Continent. But since he was sure that this revolution would first bring democrats into power, he thought it necessary to arouse the socialists' suspicions of the democrats' social and political intentions, and to prepare them for a struggle with the new democratic state. The main lesson drawn from the revolution was the need for a separate workers' party organised independently of democrats, and the League was to focus chiefly on limiting the extent of possible cooperation, and on devising plans to push the democrats as far as possible. Hence there were emphatic warnings against the democrats as 'the party that wishes to exploit the common victory for itself alone' and the repeated call for 'the Revolution in Permanence'.[5]

This was especially necessary in London itself, where democratic exiles made several efforts to unify, literally from around the corner of Marx's club. This context of day-to-day émigré politics explains the urgency with which Marx opposed attempts at alliances, as it was here that unification seemed most likely to occur. On the whole, the March Circular was less a concession Marx had to make to the radicals and artisans in the Communist League than an attempt to keep League members from conceding too much to the democrats. A few months later, in June 1850, the League reiterated that 'a specious unity' could only fragment or misuse the League: 'The workers' party can use other parties and party factions for its own purposes on occasion but must never subordinate itself to any other party.'[6] But it was exactly this ambiguity which again brought several groups within the League into contact with democrats, such as the Swiss 'Centralisation'.

This willingness inside the League to compromise with some democrats may have induced Marx to join an organisation with the Chartist G. J. Harney and French Blanquists, which was quite definitely orientated against nonsocialist revolutionaries and which could accommodate the more radical wing of the Communist League. This much-discussed 'Universal Society of Revolutionary Communists' declared as its aim 'the downfall of all privileged classes [and] the submission of those classes to the dictatorship of the proletarians by keeping the revolution in continual progress until the achievement of communism'.[7] Although this group was tiny and short-lived, it has great theoretical significance because it places Marx close to Blanquist concepts. 'Revolution in permanence' and 'dictatorship of the proletarians' echoes the language used by the much-admired French revolutionary Auguste Blanqui, in one of whose putsches Schapper had participated in 1839. His conspiratorial practices and advocacy of a minority insurrection and of a dictatorship by a revolutionary vanguard exercised a constant attraction for the impatient exiles. Undoubtedly the Universal Society contributed to a closer understanding between German communists and the London Blanquists.

August Willich and the split of the League

In the next few months, however, Marx and Engels moved away from expectations of an imminent revolution, and began to concentrate on economic preconditions for upheavals and to emphasise the need for economic study. This irritated many in the CABV, who wanted communism to be introduced immediately after the next revolution.

The main person to voice the workers' discontent with this view was August von Willich, who together with Schapper led the faction which broke with Marx's Communist League in September 1850. The colourful Prussian – a persistent rumour held him to be an illegitimate offspring of the Hohenzollerns – had commanded a company in the Rhineland, where feelings against the Prussian military ran high. By 1847 he had become a 'true socialist' who viewed 'humanity' and 'human rights' as the highest principles which ought to, but did not, govern the military.[8] He became a carpenter – which later greatly amused Marx, who referred to him as 'Jesus Willich' – and 'each morning took special delight in marching by the officers assembled on the parade ground, wearing his leather apron and carrying an axe on his shoulder'.[9] Willich joined the Communist League, and in 1848 assumed command of a republican army unit under Friedrich Hecker. After their defeat, Willich reorganised his troops in Besançon as the 'Workers' League', finding faithful adherents among the 320 volunteers whose poverty and hard labour he shared. In the Baden-Palatinate uprising of the following spring these men were to form the nucleus of a corps of volunteers whom Willich commanded. Just after their defeat Willich's adjutant Friedrich Engels praised him as 'the only officer who was any good ... Willich is brave, cold-blooded, skilful, and surveys things quickly and correctly in battle, but out of battle he is plus ou moins a boring ideologist and True Socialist.'[10] Starting from the premiss that all men were brethren with the same basic needs and rights, Willich at this time drew up a list of demands whose aim was to create equality. A committee of public welfare in each local community was to arrange production and housing communally, while large-scale heavy industry would become the responsibility of the nation-state.[11]

Willich was extremely popular in the CABV, and overshadowed Marx as its unrivalled leader. He shared the refugees' life in their communal house – appropriately called the fugitives' 'barracks' – and as a bachelor enjoyed its soldierly atmosphere and male camaraderie as well as the heavy drinking and conviviality of refugee taverns. He joined the cooperative broom-making venture of the 'barracks', and won adherents through his pub oratory and his plans for liberating Germany, which kept up their hopes in exile. In retrospect, thus, Engels saw Willich as

> one of those sentimental communists so common in western Germany since 1845, who on that account alone was instinctively, furtively antagonistic to our critical tendency. More than that, he was entirely the prophet, convinced of his personal mission as the predestined liberator of the German proletariat and as such a direct claimant as much to political as to military dictatorship. Thus, to the primitive Christian communism previously preached by Weitling, was added a kind of communist Islam.[12]

With this 'communist Islam' came another crucial disagreement which centred on the difference between the 'men of action' and the 'literary characters'. Willich was unwilling to forsake his schemes for a seizure of power, so much admired among the London refugees, merely to sit back and read. He had experienced the revolution not as a journalist but as the leader of an enthusiastic group of volunteers. Willich's own literary products were not concerned with analysis but were calls to action, always his primary interest. He recoiled from the idea of a long wait before the proletariat could take power, and, refusing to admit the possibility of a nonsocialist revolution, devised plans for seizing power, above all through military schemes. This emphasis on 'action' was, of course, welcomed by all those workers in the CABV who still distrusted 'the intellectuals' and longed for prompt revolutionary activity.

As the two sides grew further apart, violent quarrels occurred in the CABV, even resulting in a duel between Willich and one of Marx's followers, in which Willich was seconded by the Blanquist Barthélemy and a former fellow-Prussian officer, Gustav Adolf Techow. By now all paths to reconciliation were barred. The quarrel culminated in a session of the Central Authority on 15 September 1850, at which the League split.[13] Willich and Schapper set up their own Central Authority in London immediately afterwards, and each group expelled their most prominent opponents from their respective Leagues. For Marx, this marked the end of the only phase in his political career in which he had actually headed an organisation of the German workers' movement. He transferred his Central Authority to Cologne. In London, his League survived only until the following January, and was revived with the sole purpose of helping the defendants in the notorious Cologne Communist Trial of 1852.

The reasons for the break-up have remained controversial. Willich initially presented the differences in terms of 'mere personalities', as if the quarrels simply resulted from incompatible styles and personal rivalry.[14] But the old mistrust between the barracks group, eager for an armed campaign, and the intellectuals of the League had been festering underground and was easily revived when theoretical differences cropped up.

Marx was convinced from early June that the economic and political situation had stabilised. He now described growing economic prosperity and subsequent political stability as 'realities', and stated explicitly that 'there can be no talk of a real revolution' in the near future.[15] Partly because of their different time frames, the two factions thus, secondly, went on to advocate different ways for the League to prepare for the next revolution. Willich emphasised the need for military training to harden his cadres for the inevitable battles, and the need for a 'firm organisation of the League as soon as possible'; 'unity' and 'action' became his catchwords. Marx, on the other hand, held that education and propaganda alone would allow the proletariat to develop its class consciousness and an organisation strong enough to survive the years of struggle which lay ahead.

The third point of contention, however, was decisive for all participants. This was the problem of the anticipated role of the proletariat in the revolution. The League's March Circular, while still describing revolution as imminent, had been adamant that this would bring the 'petty bourgeois' democrats to power, against whom the proletariat then would have to conduct a long struggle. Willich and his supporters now maintained that there was little point in fighting unless it gave power directly and immediately to the workers. Schapper did not give 'a brass farthing for the whole affair' unless a proletarian government was the immediate goal.[16]

Schapper also indicated how the proletariat should guarantee its rule: through the guillotine. Paralleling Blanqui's hopes that a dictatorship of a proletarian vanguard would exercise terrorism, Schapper flatly reiterated that 'the question is whether we ourselves are going to be beheaded at the beginning or whether we behead others'.[17] Willich echoed these views on revolutionary terror by a minority. He insisted that communism had to be introduced by the next revolution, 'even if only through the power of the guillotine' and 'even against the will of Germany as a whole'.[18]

A fifth point, later often repeated, was that Willich and Schapper had fallen for the 'bourgeois-democratic artificers of revolution', when

'Ruge, Kinkel, Goegg and the rest of them crowded in London to form provisional governments of the future ... and when the only thing still necessary was to obtain the requisite money from America'.[19] This, however, holds events of early 1851 responsible for the split of the previous September. After the split, alliances with non-socialist exile groups became a major dividing line between the two factions, but they contributed only marginally to differences within the League beforehand. In fact, Willich's supporters in both the League and the CABV always emphasised the purely proletarian basis and aims of their organisation, and accused the faction around Marx of not being radical enough to demand a wholly proletarian revolution.

As much as theory, it was Marx's personal politics which earned him enemies. A recurrent theme in the workers' complaints against Marx was that he treated them like 'zeros'. Marx differentiated between real German artisans – the men he was actually dealing with in the League, and whom he regarded as undeveloped economically, politically and socially by comparison with their Western European contemporaries – and the abstract proletariat for whose eventual emancipation he worked and who would have to evolve from the existing artisans through decades of struggle in order to be able to rule. For the purposes of day-to-day politics, however, this distinction certainly came across as hypocritical, or at best as patronising. The Willich-Schapper faction thus repeatedly accused Marx of seeking personal power through intrigues, and of creating a small élitist circle of devoted personal admirers, which explains their obsession with 'scandals' and 'incidents', minutely described in their proclamations. Consequently they insisted that the proletariat take its affairs into its own hands, both in the present organisation and the coming revolution, so that the 'party of the intellectuals' could no longer 'lead the people by a string'.[20] They saw the breach in the League as a sign of the proletariat's split from 'the press', while maintaining that the communist 'principle' of both factions remained identical.

Thus the first year of exile clarified several kinds of disagreements. Aware that most refugees were, broadly speaking, 'democrats', the Communist League regarded it as necessary to separate its own views clearly from those of mere political reformers, since democratic groups had begun to threaten the organisational advantages the communists had held through the remnants of their League and the CABV. This need for juxtaposition and boundaries dominated the League's activities in the first half of 1850, and resulted not only in the Circulars of March and June, but also in the desire to form an 'anti-democratic' bloc. This led to cooperation with French Blanquists in the Universal Society and – ironically, since these would ultimately help break up the organisation – increased Blanquist sympathies within the League itself. The resulting tensions combined with older currents and anti-Marx sentiments until the League gave way under the pressure. While the break-away faction had not flirted with an alliance with democrats, this became a major issue after the split, when democrats succeeded in attracting large numbers of communists in the name of a common cause.

The Willich-Schapper League

After September 1850, the history of the Communist League in London is virtually identical with that of the group around Willich and Schapper. Sixteen to eighteen socialists regularly participated in the 'Society of Dr Marx', but their opponents could muster over three times as many adherents.[21] The three branches of the CABV and Willich's 'barracks' provided a base for Willich's League, as did the popular emigrants' tavern at 27 Long Acre, run by the cooper August Schärttner, who had led a *Turner* group in the Baden uprising and now joined the Central Authority. Willich, not Marx, was the best-known communist among democratic exiles in London, even appearing as 'Wildemann' in Johanna Kinkel's semi-autobiographical novel.[22] None the less, historians have strangely neglected the Willich-Schapper group, partly because of Marx's biases, and partly because of its increasingly unrealistic schemes for revolution. While in the long term, and especially after the First International, Marx and his followers eclipsed rival forms of socialism, Willich's League left its mark on German socialism in London. The revival of clubland activities in the mid-1850s was due to former members of Willich's League, as well as the CABV's involvement in the International Association alongside Blanquists. Indeed, in the 1850s, the idea of revolution held by Willich and his adherents, and their attempts to achieve a 'united front' of all revolutionaries against the old regimes, epitomised the *Zeitgeist* of the exiled 'red' Forty-Eighters much better than did Marx and Engels.

Outside London, the Willich-Schapper group consisted largely but not exclusively of adherents of Weitling, with close links to communist groups around Moses Heß in Switzerland, millenarians in Belgium and around the tailor Andreas Scherzer in Paris, and Weitling in the USA. Although neither communitarian nor Christian socialist ideas had played a part in the League's break-up, they reappeared here. This allowed for a very broad definition of 'party' without ever seriously questioning allegiance to the London Central Authority. Connected by anti-intellectualism and a desire to act, these groups contained very disparate elements. In Germany itself, the Rhineland communists remained largely on Marx's side, while Willich's League managed to establish only a few outposts in northern Germany, mostly through the *Arbeiterverbrüderung* in Hanover. Some individual support came from Wiesbaden, Mainz and Heilbronn.

Back in London, members of the League founds themselves in the same Soho haunts as refugees from France, Italy, Poland and Hungary. This naturally intensified their internationalist inclination. They were closest to the Chartists around Harney, who had cooperated with Schapper since 1846, and to exiled Blanquists, in particular the violent Emmanuel Barthélemy, who, with Willich, constituted the core of an 'International Social Democratic Committee'. This relationship became clearest in February 1851, when French socialists organised a large-scale 'Banquet of the Equals', with Schapper and Willich in prominent roles.[23] From prison, Auguste Blanqui had sent one of the customary addresses to the Banquet, stressing the need for a military organisation of the workers above any preoccupation with social theories. It concluded with eloquent praise of revolutionary power remarkably similar to Willich's exhortations. But as the letter also criticised other participants at the Banquet, Barthélemy (unsuccessfully) attempted to suppress it, and the subsequent scandal of an avowed leading Blanquist censoring Blanqui's opinions was enormous. Chiefly to discredit Willich and Schapper, Barthélemy's allies, Marx and Engels, translated Blanqui's 'Toast' into German and had the astonishing number of 30,000 copies distributed.[24] In the uproar, some groups in Switzerland seceded, and the 'International Social Democratic Committee' collapsed. This was a severe blow to the League's image as the 'true' proletarian organisation of the German émigrés. They regarded their alliance with Blanqui, whose integrity and revolutionary credentials were undisputed, and with the French Blanquists in London, as irrefutable proof that they were siding with the most uncompromising revolutionary workers' party of France.

Like Blanqui, Willich saw 'revolutionary deed' as more important than economic development or theoretical debate. Revolutions were military enterprises, their failure or success being determined by military preparation, strategy and strength. One of Willich's first statements after the split began by summarising continental political events, which were quickly reduced to the single fact of the massive build-up of troops on the side of 'the despots'.[25] A similar proclamation of the following spring reiterated this view of revolution. 'Perhaps already this year', it announced, 'either the general world war ... or the social revolution' would break out, but as there was little prospect of a popular uprising in Germany, the Londoners assumed that a revolution could be instigated there 'only through a military uprising'. This, however, 'could scarcely bring the proletarian party to power at once ... League members would have to form revolutionary committees to force the provisional authorities installed by the army to take the most energetic measures against the external and internal enemy.'[26] Willich hoped that the 'revolutionary army proper' would emerge from a general military movement in Germany, seeing this as 'the luckiest form of revolution'.[27] The address proposed no social or economic changes beyond vaguely promising to 'care for the families of the fighters'.

Willich even detailed plans a military insurrection in Germany, arguing that the militia (*Landwehr*) predominated in the Prussian army, and since it was composed mostly of 'workers, peasants, day labourers, petty bourgeois', it could fairly easily be incited. Once the militia chose 'to look after things' themselves, they would 'transfer executive power from the hands of the government into those of the revolutionary authorities'. Thereafter all power was to be concentrated in a revolutionary government which would also have military authority, and all resistance treated as treason.[28]

But this increasing concentration on armed revolt led the Willich-Schapper League to explore further the relation between class and power, for they faced the dilemma of needing troops while rejecting the 'petty bourgeoisie'. In its Circular of spring 1851, the League continued to focus intensively on the problem of the democratic revolutionaries, and rejected a possible tactical alliance with democratic or republican groups before the revolution.[29] Taking part as an independent force in the revolution, indeed as its main force, would give the proletarian party the right and the might to decide which institutions should be the first to be installed.[30] But the effort of avoiding purely putschist tactics inevitably led the League into an alliance with democratic groups. This was in itself not sufficient to change their proletarian orientation, but such strategic considerations combined with ideological haziness and a rejection of revolutionary theory also resulted in a theoretical rapprochement. This was mostly Willich's doing, and remained hampered by various provisos.

From military to political cooperation:
Support for the democrats' 'Revolutionary Loan'

It is perplexing that a group regarding itself as the true proletarian core of the Communist Party could so quickly – and apparently unquestioningly, after long fulminating at any such strategy – join forces with its erstwhile enemies around Kinkel, as the Willich-Schapper group did in the course of 1851.

This process appears to have begun with Willich and Alexander Schimmelpfennig (another lieutenant turned republican), who in early 1851 jointly addressed the Prussian officer corps, still in the hope of inciting a rising.[31] But it was also indicative of a new shift in strategy. This call clearly abandoned the appeal to 'the people' and demanded redress for the social injustices which had permeated Willich's earlier overtures to the Cologne militia. Designs for the future society were left vague, and the audience was exclusively the military 'estate'. Willich here wrote not as a communist but purely as a former officer turned guerrilla leader. With Schimmelpfennig he now constituted the core of a 'military clique' (which also included Techow and Franz Sigel) linked by democratic revolutionary convictions as well as aristocratic background and military manners, which formed a very distinct subgroup in exile. Here Willich represented 'the communist element', and Engels suspected that 'this pack of soldiery' saw the CABV as 'a battalion, ready, willing and eager to march'.[32]

This social and cultural affinity drew Willich tentatively towards alliances with other democrats as well, and hints about a rapprochement between Willich and Kinkel surfaced in the German press. The flamboyant theologian and art historian Gottfried Kinkel had become a national hero to many Forty-Eighters and enjoyed a reputation as a socialist among republicans. After a spectacular escape from imprisonment in Spandau fortress, he had arrived in London some months after the split of the Communist League. In February 1851 Willich, under whose command he had served in the Baden-Palatinate uprising, demanded that Kinkel throw his 'capital of popularity

... which I regard as property of the people, especially of its suffering part', into the scales to support refugees.[33]

In March, both Kinkel and Willich signed the first hurried application for a National Loan, which announced that 'we have asked the social democratic workers to send a representative into our midst'.[34] The workers in question, that is, the CABV, rejected this proposition as put to them by Arnold Ruge, an admirer of Mazzini and advocate of democratic internationalism, whose anti-communist stance was well-known.[35] Willich, for his part, noted regretfully that the workers in the CABV, most vociferously the East End furrier Salomon Fränkel, exhibited 'an almost insurmountable antipathy to any alliance with Kinkel, Ruge, etc.',[36] so that in May 1851 the League simply refused to collaborate 'with any other party which does not have as its first and foremost principle the complete liberation of the proletariat.' Willich, however, maintained that he still thought it worthwhile to join a commission with 'no specific principles but only financial purposes'.[37]

In the spring of 1851, Kinkel embarked upon refugee politics as the figurehead for a new modified loan project, now without Ruge (who instead led a rival exile organisation which rejected 'the social doctrines'). This scheme was the 'German National Loan', which was to dominate exile politics and the minds of the German governments to the point of obsession for nearly two years. This project aimed to collect money from sympathetic democrats in Europe and America,[38] with the intention that the loans were to be repaid by a future republican government. Trying to avoid any association with Kinkel's politics while at the same time cashing in on his fame, Willich became a guarantor of the loan. For the rest of his days in London, Willich remained closely linked to Kinkel's project.[39] While Marx remained scathing about the enterprise, other socialists such as Weitling in New York followed Willich's example (with the notable exception of Schapper). Besides Kinkel's enormous prestige among German democrats, it was this precarious alliance with the communists around Willich that permitted the National Loan to receive the publicity and support needed to survive the initial stages.

Willich's willingness to cooperate with non-socialist revolutionaries was based upon a differentiation between 'national' and 'principled' approaches. The demand for practical 'action' permitted joining forces with, for example, Mazzini, and 'the principle [was] irrelevant for the time being, if only mutual help could assure the victory of the revolution'. There was, however, nothing in common between mere republican principles and the views of Willich, who was 'fighting mainly with the proletarians and *only* for them ... In the next revolution the workshops are going to be the legislators proper.'[40] In the CABV (over whose Whitechapel section he presided), indeed, Willich was much more critical of Kinkel, accusing him of envisioning 'intellectuals' instead of workers as future rulers.[41]

Communist agitation

In internal documents, too, Willich's League clearly reiterated its communist principles. Its first statutes after the split declared: 'The League aims to bring the proletariat to power, to abolish the old bourgeois society which rests on class antagonisms, and to found a new society without classes and without bourgeois property relations; i.e., the social democratic republic.'[42] Similarly, in June 1851 Willich argued in almost Marxist language that

> in the rule of private capital over the relations of production, i.e., in the basis of its own existence, also lies its own destruction. [The bourgeoisie] does not understand that the nature of capital to concentrate more and more cannot come to a halt until the entire capital has become concentrated, and that only then the fourth estate, the proletariat, will cease to be revolutionary, because concentrated capital can only be social capital.

Hence the League's tasks were 'to help prepare and expedite the revolution' and 'during the revolution itself to bring power into the hands of the fourth estate'.[43] This was combined with a distinctly gleeful anticipation of revolutionary terror. For instance, special 'commissars' were to punish traitors, produce lists of 'enemies of the people who have to be handed over to the people's justice' and to prevent their emigration – the authors seemingly oblivious to the irony of writing as emigrants themselves.[44]

Yet the anticipated dictatorship was to combine centralised political power – in effect, Willich's military order extended to the civil administration – with democratic control, partly to ensure that control over the army by the working classes was not lost. (Possibly this was influenced by the Blanquists around Barthélemy, whose ideas had coloured their common manifesto of the previous December.) The militia and the armed workers' organisation were to complement one another. Elected local committees were to form the basis of the political and administrative structure, headed by a government 'by those who brought about the revolution'. Since only 'the armed fourth estate' would vote and form a central committee with dictatorial powers – in which they optimistically assumed their own influence would predominate – the League apparently did not contemplate the possibility of any considerable conflict between itself and the 'fourth estate'.

After the revolution some of the apparatus of dictatorship would be dismantled. The people's army would gradually 'merge into the organisation of labour', which would then 'form the only armed force of the state'. The commissars would relinquish their powers to a central committee formed of elected deputies from labour organisations and regions of the country. The 'fundamental condition of the social state' was to be 'on the one hand, centralisation of all economic means of production and of political power. On the other hand, free self-administration, from which this centralisation has to emanate.'[45] This ideal of 'free self-administration' appeared, however, as an afterthought and was not integrated into the overall plan with its extremely regimented vision of a centralised state.

A flysheet published in the summer of 1851 gave much more weight to economic and social developments, with international politics and armed struggle coming a distinct second.[46] It proposed that the 'armed people' elect 'revolutionary committees' which would become the main sovereign power. The state was to guarantee the subsistence of all revolutionaries and their families by giving work 'for a good wage, to be decided by workers' committees', and would also finance public services. This would be paid for by confiscations from princes and banks, 'mandatory loans from all capitalists', and newly created paper money. Besides palaces and all means of communication, 'all factories and workshops which do not have full employment and which [the State] needs for the employment of the workers' would be confiscated. The League here aimed above all to give practical, concrete goals in possible new upheavals, for which its members could start preparing immediately.

After Napoleon's *coup d'état* of December 1851, Willich put more stress on the socialist aims of the League. He claimed that 'creating new political institutions was impossible unless capital relations had been overthrown ... No revolutionary form of state is tenable unless it is founded on an equally revolutionary organisation of economic conditions'.[47] A republic, even with free associations supported by a state bank, was not sufficient to alter the fundamental economic situation: 'The only remedy is for the entire society to seize and to organise these means of production.' Despite the use of Marx's language here, Willich in fact came very close to Weitling's visions of structuring communist society around individual branches of industry. 'Abstract' government in a 'political state' could be superseded by the 'economic state' or 'social republic', where each branch of industry would be a basic organisational unit and the central administration of the different trades would form a central committee. This 'economic administrative council of potent productive forces, forming an entity whose elements interlock organically and naturally', would then replace political government. Politics would no longer be remote, and people would 'be able to understand their own affairs and cease being objects of manipulation for the intellectual aristocracy.'[48] In the communist state all class differences would of course be abolished and the proletariat would cease to exist.

Once the shock of the catastrophe in Paris began to wear off, the remnants of the groups in London resumed their customary propaganda in Germany through correspondence and emissaries, and pursued contacts with other political organisations. Although separate groups of the League continued to exist, all such activity was now concentrated in the Central Authority. Its twenty-odd members[49] continued their regular procedure of vetting prospective new members, rooting out police informers, dealing with finances (which amounted to about £144) and supporting jailed comrades.[50] They still expected an imminent revolution but most hopes were pinned on movements outside Germany. Willich still distributed leaflets among the German armies, and compiled lists of arms and ammunition stocks.[51] At least twenty-four different towns in Germany sent money to the *Sonderbund* in London between January and May 1852. The largest sums came from Hamburg, Hanover, Hildesheim, Bremen, Ulm and Wiesbaden.[52] The League continued to send emissaries to the Continent. The most successful journey was undertaken by August Gebert of the Central Authority, who assembled nearly thirty sympathisers in Magdeburg for three days of discussions.[53]

In London, Willich's former corps, about 160 men, met three times weekly for exercise and shooting practice.[54] Between January and August 1852, the CABV debated topics such as the relation of communism to religion, education and individual liberty, demonstrating a very uneven understanding of economic doctrines and political theory, but a continued commitment to communism on a range of economic, social and ethical issues, and the clear reception and adaptation of both Marx's teaching and Blanqui's influence. This 'business as usual' attitude combated the spreading demoralisation among the dwindling group, and showed that Willich's League was definitely not 'virtually inactive' after its congress of 1851.[55]

After Kinkel's return from the USA in March 1852, Willich was also involved in all the stages of the winding up of the national loan. Some of the money financed trips by League emissaries, and in April 1852 the League formally approved of a secret contract between Willich and Kinkel.[56] The Loan thereby became the League's business as well, although they were not concerned with its administration or propaganda but merely hoped for some funds.[57] Eventually the money was deposited, pending future revolutionary use, in a London bank under the supervision of Kinkel, Willich and Reichenbach.

Spies and emigration

After Napoleon's *coup d'état* in December 1851 many realised that a revolution was not imminent. Financial worries increased, and many decided to emigrate to the USA. In March 1852 the tailor Albert Lehmann, a Central Authority member, left with thirty from the CABV, and the *Republik der Arbeiter* reported shortly afterwards from New York that 'all those German refugees, who are able to prove their identity through credentials signed by well-known refugees in London, receive from the English government free passage to America and £2 on arrival. The whole of the London workers' society seems to want to make use of this offer.'[58]

Already in decline, the CABV at this point suffered an almost fatal blow as a result of police activity. That spies always had the capacity to cripple the League is undoubted, as is the fact that their activities were based on a plan conceived in Berlin. Edgar Bauer, a police informer himself, explained with amazing openness that 'the history of the emigration in London is not described completely if one does not add a history of the secret police. Emigration and political police are two branches growing on the same revolutionary tree.'[59] In the background was the expressed and (in his own words) 'not quite honourable' wish of the king, Friedrich Wilhelm (Frederick William) IV, to have the Prussian police discover a conspiracy so that 'the desired spectacle of an exposed and (above all) punished plot can be performed'.[60]

To this end the Prussian police director Wilhelm Stieber managed to procure some fifty original documents from the CABV's archives, though this had to be kept strictly secret for fear that 'it would be called theft in London'.[61] Returning to Germany in the summer of 1851, Stieber passed through Paris, where letters found on the prominent League member Cherval led to the arrests of 200 Germans and the conviction of the ten most prominent socialists. This almost completely dismantled the League in France.[62] Soon, however, it was disclosed that Cherval had been paid by the Prussian police and had been responsible for the arrests.[63] Willich sounded genuinely distraught 'that a member of our party can be so malicious as to betray his comrades for a well-laid table with a bottle of wine, and that even among our enlightened workers so many let themselves be duped by villains'.[64]

As further details gradually emerged, Willich's own connections with spies came under scrutiny. A police agent, Fleury, offered Willich cash and gifts, which Willich accepted partly because Fleury offered him information on police machinations against the League in Cologne.[65] During the following months, a most peculiar relationship developed between Fleury, Willich and Wilhelm Hirsch, a democratic journalist who, suspected of spying, was expelled from both the CABV and Marx's League.[66] Hirsch convinced Willich that he was still a democrat at heart and was only pretending to serve the police in order to be able to divulge government plots to the revolutionaries.[67] Willich hoped to expose police intrigues, especially those of Fleury, by using Hirsch as a sort of double agent, and to keep up this ludicrous game he even watched silently as Fleury and Hirsch fabricated the so-called 'Minutes' intended to incriminate Marx's followers in Cologne. At the same time Fleury conspired with Hirsch to lure Willich into a police trap, and concocted a fantastic plan to chloroform him in order to ship him to Heligoland and Germany.[68]

This entire bubble burst in November 1852 when Fleury was exposed in the Cologne trial, which in turn forced Hirsch to admit their forgeries. The revelations left Willich in a very bad light. It became public that he had been paid by Fleury, that he had betrayed secrets about emissaries' trips to the Continent, and had let Hirsch escape. Such evidence seemed to imply that Willich was acting consciously for the police and that he was more than merely a victim of their intrigues. Amid recriminations, paranoia and widespread demoralisation, Willich moved the remnants of the CABV to another location. But, in fact, this came close to putting an end to Willich's personal reputation, the club, and Willich's League.[69] Thus Engels recounted that around Christmas 1852, he and Marx mingled '*sans façon* in the Kinkel-Willich-Ruge pubs, something we could scarcely have done 6 months earlier without risking a brawl'.[70] Throughout 1852 Willich also fought a losing battle to keep his ranks from dispersing, with Gebert, Dietz, Schimmelpfennig and Techow emigrating. By November 1852 the CABV's membership had fallen to some eighty artisans.[71] His organisation in shambles, Willich, virtually the last League member to abandon ship, elected to depart for the New World. The move was doubtless a wise choice for him. In New York over 300 people received Willich, giving a banquet in his honour at which Weitling presented him with a sword adorned with a red sash.[72] Despite hopes for continued agitation, he did not resume political propaganda until 1858, and eventually became a major-general in the Union army. During the American Civil War Willich was known to 'put his troops at ease, address them as "citizens", and proceed to a lecture on socialism'.[73] In London, the general exodus caused such disarray that the CABV ceased responding to letters.[74] With this, the history of the Communist League, which had dominated socialist exile politics for over five years, came to an end.

Notes

1 Karl Schapper, 'Gütergemeinschaft', in *Der Bund der Kommunisten: Dokumente und Materialien,* I (1836–49), (reprint Berlin 1983), p. 100 (hereafter cited as *BdK*).

2 Martin Hundt, *Geschichte des Bundes der Kommunisten 1836–1852* (Frankfurt, 1993), pp. 300–11.

3 [K.G.L.] Wermuth and [Wilhelm] Stieber, *Die Communisten-Verschwörungen des neunzehnten Jahrhunderts* (Berlin, 1853), I, pp. 50–1.

4 For details of this and the following see my *Revolutionary Refugees: German Socialism in Britain, 1840–1860* (London, 2003).

5 Marx and Engels, 'Address of the Central Authority to the League', March 1850, in Karl Marx and Frederick Engels, *Collected Works* (London, 1975ff.) (hereafter cited as *MECW*), X, pp. 277–87.

6 'Address of the Central Authority to the League', June 1850, *MECW*, X, pp. 372–3.

7 'Universal Society of Revolutionary Communists', *MECW*, X, pp. 614–15.

8 *Im preußischen Heere! Ein Disciplinarverfahren gegen Premier-Lieutenant v. Willich* (Mannheim, 1848), pp. 28–9, 37–52.

9 [H.A. Rattermann], 'General August Willich', *Der Deutsche Pionier*, IX (no. 11) (February 1878), p. 440; Marx to Weydemeyer, 20 February 1852, *MECW*, XXXIX, p. 42.

10 Engels to J. Marx, 25 July 1849, *MECW*, XXXVIII, pp. 203–4; see also his 'The Campaign for the German Imperial Constitution', *MECW*, X, pp. 196–7.

11 A. Willich, 'Programm der Enterbten', *Freiheit, Brüderlichkeit, Arbeit*, II (no. 12), 18 March 1849, pp. 41–2.

12 F. Engels, 'On the History of the Communist League', in Rodney Livingstone (ed.), *The Cologne Communist Trial* (London, 1971), p. 52.

13 Minutes of the 'Meeting of the Central Authority, 15 September 1850, *MECW*, X, pp. 625–9.

14 'Ansprache vom 1. Oktober 1850', Wermuth and Stieber, *Verschwörungen*, I, p. 267.

15 K. Marx and F. Engels, 'Review, May to October 1850', *MECW*, X, p. 510.

16 *MECW*, X, p. 628; 'Ansprache vom 1. Oktober 1850', Wermuth and Stieber, *Verschwörungen*, I, p. 270.

17 *MECW*, X, p. 628.

18 *BdK*, II, p. 451.

19 Engels, 'On the History of the Communist League', p. 54.

20 'Ansprache vom 1. Oktober 1850', Wermuth and Stieber, *Verschwörungen*, I, p. 266–9.

21 Marx to Engels, 28 October 1852, *MECW*, XXXIX, p. 223; 'Ansprache … 1851', Wermuth and Stieber, *Verschwörungen*, I, p. 275, claims sixty members in four groups.

22 Johanna Kinkel, *Hans Ibeles in London* (Stuttgart, 1860), I, pp. 312–13, 329–50.

23 *Le Banquet des Égaux. Londres, 24 Février 1851* (Paris, [1851]), pp. 22, 24–5; 'Ansprache … 1851', Wermuth and Stieber, *Verschwörungen*, I, pp. 277–9.

24 'Warning to the People', *MECW*, X, pp. 537–9; Engels to Dronke, 9 July 1851, *MECW*, XXXVIII, p. 381.

25 'To the democrats of all nations', *MECW*, XXXVIII, p. 248.

26 'Ansprache … 1851', Wermuth and Stieber, *Verschwörungen*, I, pp. 271–2.

27 Willich to Schimmelpfennig, 17 April 1851, Carl Wilhelm Saegert Papers, Geheimes Preußisches Staatsarchiv, Brandenburg-Preußisches Hausarchiv (hereafter cited as BPH), Berlin-Dahlem, Rep. 192, no. 35.

28 Willich to Becker, 6 December 1850, International Institute for Social History, Amsterdam, Marx-Engels Papers, O 25, copy by Becker.

29　'Ansprache ... 1851', Wermuth and Stieber, *Verschwörungen*, I, pp. 280–1.

30　Willich, 'Doctor Karl Marx und seine Enthüllungen', *New-Yorker Criminal-Zeitung* (hereafter cited as *NYCZ*), 4 November, 1853, p. 339.

31　Willich's and Schimmelpfennig's proclamation, dated January 1851, partly in Wermuth and Stieber, *Verschwörungen*, I, pp. 129–30.

32　Engels to Marx, 23 May 1851, *MECW*, XXXVIII, p. 362.

33　Willich to Kinkel, 21 February 1851, University Library, Bonn, S 2675,28.

34　'An die Deutschen', dated London, 13 March 1851, leaflet in University Library, Bonn, S 2702; reprinted in *New Yorker Staats-Zeitung*, 12 April 1851.

35　'Ansprache ... 1851', Wermuth and Stieber, *Verschwörungen*, I, pp. 280–1; Erik Gamby (ed.), *Edgar Bauer: Konfidentenberichte über die europäische Emigration in London 1852–1861* (Trier, 1989), p. 34.

36　Willich to Schimmelpfennig, 17 April 1851, Saegert Papers, BPH, Rep. 192, no. 35.

37　'Ansprache ... 1851', Wermuth and Stieber, *Verschwörungen*, I, pp. 280–1; Willich to Schimmelpfennig, 17 April 1851, Saegert Papers, BPH, Rep. 192, no. 35.

38　On the fund-raising tour in America see Sabine Freitag's contribution in this volume, Chapter 11.

39　Kinkel remained the leading democratic exile to bridge the gap to the socialists; how the socialists should participate now became one main source of contention between the different democrats.

40　'Agent 0' to Stieber, 14 May 1851, Saegert Papers, BPH, Rep. 192, no. 35.

41　'Agent 0' to Stieber, 29 May 1851, Saegert Papers, BPH, Rep. 192, no. 35; Badisches Generallandesarchiv Karlsruhe (henceforth cited as BGLAK), 49/1021, report of 17 June 1851.

42　'Die revidirten Londoner Statuten vom 10 Novbr. 1850', Wermuth and Stieber, *Verschwörungen*, I, pp. 244–7.

43　'Verhaltungsmaaßregeln für den Bund vor, während und nach der Revolution', Wermuth and Stieber, *Verschwörungen*, I, pp. 293–4. A copy with considerable variations is in *Auszüge aus den von der Polizei in Paris mit Beschlag belegten Papieren des communistischen Complotts* (s.l., s.d.) (copy in Brandenburgisches Landeshauptarchiv Potsdam (henceforth cited as BLP), 10084/1), pp. 6–14.

44　Wermuth and Stieber, *Verschwörungen*, I, pp. 294, 296.

45　Ibid., pp. 295, 297–8.

46　'Forderungen des Volkes im Augenblicke der Revolution', Schapper-Willich file, BLP 8534, f. 115 (slightly different in Wermuth and Stieber, *Verschwörungen*, I, pp. 291–2). This flysheet was produced for the League's congress of July 1851, which was hampered by inefficient preparation and friction with the Parisians and other delegates from the Continent. These 'Demands' were again circulated in 1855–6, and in 1858 the International Association reissued them along with a proclamation by a Mazzini-inspired 'party of action' (Sächsisches Hauptstaatsarchiv, Dresden, Reg. 1893, no. 551, Confiscation of Publications file, IV, f. 104; *Sociale Republik*, no. 23, 25 September 1858, p. 4; Gamby, *Edgar Bauer: Konfidentenberichte*, pp. 418–9).

47 CABV discussion, 18 July 1852, Schapper-Willich file, BLP 8534, f. 101.

48 *Republik der Arbeiter* (henceforth cited as *RdA*), 27 March 1852, p. 103.

49 Meetings of 28 March and 11 July 1852, Schapper-Willich file, BLP 8534, ff. 24 and 73; sometimes only eighteen to thirteen people attended meetings.

50 Central Authority meetings of 13 February (candidates), 2 January (spies), 5 March, 25 June, 11 July, 8 September (money), and 23 January (prisoners) 1852, Schapper-Willich file, BLP 8534, ff. 16, 1, 26, 67, 74, 90 and 7.

51 BGLAK, 48/5212, monthly report from Karlsruhe, 13 May 1852, and Greiff's report, London 30 April 1852, Revolutionary Loan file, BLP 8537, ff. 80–1.

52 They gave a total of 421 Thaler and £30, while Baroness von Bruiningk donated another £30 (BGLAK, 236/8743, weekly report from Berlin, 10 July 1852, no. 18). Northern German groups later gave another £45.6. (report of 1 October 1852, nos. 28, 40).

53 Marx to Engels, 30 August 1852, *MECW*, XXXIX, p. 169.

54 Extract from weekly report, Dresden, 10 June 1852, Revolutionary Loan file, BLP 8537, f. 226; Central Authority meeting, 23 April 1852, Schapper-Willich file, BLP 8534, f. 37.

55 Editors' comment, *BdK*, III, p. 445.

56 Address of the Communist Workers' Association, presented by Willich to the Loan Conference, 22 April, 1852 (Revolutionary Loan file, BLP 8537, ff. 234–5). The address excluded any kind of community with representatives of the non-German 'bourgeoisie', such as Mazzini, with whom Willich, a year earlier, had considered a limited alliance for practical 'action', against some opposition in the CABV.

57 Greiff's reports, 10 and 30 April, 1852, Revolutionary Loan file, BLP 8537, ff. 76–7 and 79–82.

58 *RdA*, 17 April 1852, p. 121.

59 Gamby, *Edgar Bauer: Konfidentenberichte*, p. 76.

60 Friedrich Wilhelm IV to Otto von Manteuffel, 11 November 1850, quoted in Julius H. Schoeps, 'Agenten, Spitzel, Flüchtlinge: Wilhelm Stieber und die demokratische Emigration in London', in Horst Schallenberger and Helmut Schrey (eds), *Im Gegenstrom. Für Helmut Hirsch zum Siebzigsten* (Wuppertal, 1977), p. 75.

61 Report by Saegert, 3 August 1851, p. 12, in Saegert Papers, BPH, Rep. 192, no. 35. These documents became known as 'the Dietz archive' after the secretary of Willich's League from whose desk they had been stolen, and they played a major role in the 1851–2 Cologne trial against Marx's adherents. Copies are in the Dietz file, BLP 11373, ff. 3–51.

62 *RdA*, 27 March 1852, pp. 102–3, and 10 April 1852, pp. 124–5.

63 *RdA*, 3 June 1852, pp. 180–1; Marx, 'Herr Vogt', *MECW*, XVII, p. 56.

64 *RdA*, 5 June 1852, p. 181.

65 Gamby, *Edgar Bauer: Konfidentenberichte*, pp. 59–61, 79–80, 90–1.

66 Hirsch's declaration appeared later in 'Der "demokratische" Mouchard', *NYCZ*, 7 (29 April 1853), p. 66; Marx to Engels, 5 March 1852, *MECW*, XXXIX, p. 59. His police records survived in Hirsch file, BLP 10485, ff. 1–3.

67 Hirsch's 'Confessions' in an undated letter to Willich, University Library Bonn, S 2661, and another version in W. Hirsch, 'Die Opfer der Mouchardie', *NYCZ*, no. 3 (1 April 1853), pp. 2–3, no. 4 (8 April 1853), pp. 32–3, no. 5 (15 April 1853), pp. 42–3, no. 6 (22 April 1853), pp. 52–3.

68 Hirsch, 'Die Opfer der Mouchardie', *NYCZ*, no. 5 (15 April 1853), p. 43; Gamby, *Edgar Bauer: Konfidentenberichte*, p. 91.

69 Marx to Cluss, 14 December 1852, *MECW*, XXXIX, pp. 266–7, and Gamby, *Edgar Bauer: Konfidentenberichte*, pp. 61, 76–97. These were by no means all the police spies who reported on émigrés; Marx himself employed a Prussian informer to spy on Greif and Fleury (Marx to Engels, 10 November 1852, *MECW*, XXXIX, p. 242). There is much material on the supervision of spies in the Prussian police lieutenant Simon's letters to Berlin (Simon file, BLP 11374/1).

70 Engels to Weydemeyer, 12 April 1853, *MECW*, XXXIX, pp. 304.

71 Gamby, *Edgar Bauer: Konfidentenberichte*, p. 53.

72 *RdA*, 12 March 1853, pp. 82–3.

73 Loyd D. Easton, *Hegel's First American Followers* (Athens, OH, 1966), p. 195.

74 *RdA*, 26 February 1853, pp. 69–70.

13

Chartists and Political Refugees

Iorwerth Prothero

London was one of the main European centres for political exiles and refugees. For those among them who persisted in political activity, it offered special opportunities: fewer government and police constraints; the possibilities of open political action, including the unfamiliar British institution of public meetings; and the existence of Chartism, a national, largely working-class movement for democracy unparalleled in Europe at the time in its numerical strength and sustained activity over ten years and more.[1]

Chartism was not constant but evolved over time. Although its programme document, the People's Charter, was drawn up by the small London Working Men's Association in 1838, the Chartist movement initially drew its main strength in the provinces, especially the manufacturing districts. Yet after 1840 London was one of the chief centres of Chartism, and in the mid-1840s it became the headquarters of the movement, when in 1844 the Executive of its national organisation, the National Charter Association (NCA) moved there from Manchester, and the great Chartist weekly newspaper, Feargus O'Connor's *Northern Star*, moved from Leeds.

But Chartism was in decline after 1842 and retreated from nationwide agitation, local activity focusing more than before on educational, cultural, welfare and convivial activities. Led by O'Connor, the NCA promoted electoral participation, cooperative stores, benefit relief, trade unionism and the Land Plan. The *Northern Star* acted less as the national campaigning voice of a movement than as a radical educator, its coverage less exclusively Chartist and including a range of labour movements. The Chartist internationalism of the 1840s must therefore be related to the state of the movement and the trend away from direct efforts to gain the enactment of the People's Charter. Julian Harney was the key figure linking Chartists and foreign refugees in a network concerned less with campaigning than with educating Chartism into wider perspectives and emphases, and changing its intellectual content.[2]

While the current tendency is to place both Chartism and Liberalism within a continuous tradition of British radical patriotism and popular constitutionalism,[3] there were also established minority internationalist elements in nineteenth-century radicalism.[4] The insistence that the many were oppressed and robbed by the few who held power, meant that wars were seen as the work of the tyrannical, corrupt and privileged rulers, and not of the people, who nevertheless bore the cost and did the fighting against those with whom they themselves had no real quarrel. Wars also delayed reform and led to the expansion of oppressive and costly army and governmental establishments. Representative government would stop wars, as the peoples' interests lay in peace. Radicals should therefore work to dissipate national jealousies and prejudices. The rulers also got up wars specifically to check the spread of freedom, such as the British wars against the liberties of France and America. In addition to such general beliefs, British radicals were often enthusiastic over particular developments abroad; there was widespread admiration for the USA as a beacon of freedom, and support for various continental revolutions, in Spain, Greece, Portugal and Belgium. But two causes aroused particular enthusiasm. British radicals particularly looked to France as the hope of democracy through its revolutions of 1789 and 1830. The doomed Polish rising of 1830–1 also aroused tremendous emotion, especially as it was against Russian rule, the Tsar being a particular target of radicals as the bulwark of reaction and an aggressive threat to the whole of Europe. This kind of internationalism was not averse to conflict, or even British armed intervention in support of liberation abroad.

However, these attitudes did not necessitate actual involvement with foreigners, which relied very largely on personal contacts, often fortuitously achieved, and these occurred mainly in London, the chief location of foreign refugees. The Italian Mazzini, head of Young Italy and Young Europe, was in London for most of the 1830s and 1840s, and established an Italian journal and a working men's association to educate London Italians in ideas of a united, independent and republican Italy.[5] British radical disenchantment with the French July Monarchy was confirmed by the various French republican exiles and refugees in London in the 1830s. Marrast, Cavaignac and Cabet were in contact with French Canadian resistance to British rule.[6] Cabet, in London from 1834 to 1839 after exile from France and expulsion from Belgium, also had links there with Polish refugees, got to know Robert Owen well, and was converted to ideas of community of property.[7]

Most of these aspects of radical internationalism were exemplified in the small and exclusive Working Men's Association, founded in 1836 by William Lovett, Henry Hetherington and other ultra-radical artisans. In 1836 and 1837 this issued four declarations on international affairs, in the form of addresses to the Canadian People (supporting their resistance to British policy and drawing a reply from Papineau's committee), and to the Working Classes of Belgium, America, and Europe.[8] The burden of the message was that the working classes were everywhere subjected to oppression and robbery because of their disunity and ignorance of their vital role in society as the true producers of wealth. In reality, all mankind were brethren, all nations had one interest, and they should work together to eradicate the national prejudices and bigotry instilled and used by selfish and despotic rulers.

> Fellow producers of wealth! seeing that our oppressors are thus united, why should not we, too, have our bond of brotherhood and holy alliance? Seeing that they are powerful through your ignorance, why should not we unite to teach our brethren a knowledge of their rights and duties? Perceiving that their power is derived from our ranks, why should not we unite in holy zeal to show the injustice of war, the cruelty of despotism, and the misery it entails upon our species? ... Let us, therefore, brethren, cultivate feelings of *fraternity among nations, and brotherly union in our respective countries*. Let us not be so ignorant as to allow ourselves to be converted into soldiers, police, or any other of the infamous tools by which despotism is upheld, and our brethren enslaved. Let us be prepared to make any sacrifice in the dissemination of truth, and to cultivate feelings of toleration, between Jew, Catholic, Protestant or Dissenter.[9]

These international addresses of the Working Men's Association received much notice and attention, as seeming to mark a momentous departure and presage an age of international working-class solidarity. Actual links, however, depended on personal contacts. Lovett in the mid-1830s got to know Mazzini, whose school for poor Italian boys lay opposite the coffee-house that Lovett ran and resided in, and the Working Men's Association supported his Young Italy movement for Italian liberation and unification in a republican nation-state. Another key figure here was Augustus Beaumont, who had gone with his brother from Jamaica to Paris after the July Revolution and enrolled in the National Guard, and then gone on to Brussels and fought in the Belgian Revolution. In the mid-1830s, when his brother was imprisoned in Paris for his prominent position in the republican Society of the Rights of Man, Augustus established himself as a radical

journalist in London. It was very likely through his contacts that when
the Working Men's Association was formed, its manifesto, constitution and objectives were reprinted in the *Courier Belge*. It was
following this that the imprisonment and fine of a Brussels working-
class leader, Jacob Katz (for trying to hold a public meeting) provoked
the Working Men's Association's address to the Belgian working class,
which Beaumont translated into French. This, the first of the Association's international addresses, was publicised in a number of Belgian
and French liberal journals, including the *National*, and stimulated a
number of meetings in Belgium and a reply to the Association, which
organised a subscription to pay Katz's fine.[10]

In 1838, however, as it was drawn into the rising Chartist movement, the Working Men's Association was challenged by another
London group, who had in 1835 formed the East London Democratic Association, later re-formed as the London Democratic
Association.[11] They condemned its exclusiveness, emphasis on education, failure to condemn the New Poor Law, readiness to work with
moderate and parliamentary 'sham-radicals', and disavowal of physical force.[12] Some were part of an ultra-radical group engaged in
continuous activity, sometimes underground and insurrectionary,
since the last years of the Napoleonic War. A number of these were
Spenceans, who held that no-one had any claim to absolute property
in land, which had been given by God to all and should therefore be
owned in common and let to individuals for rent. They were also
particular admirers of the Irish journalist, James 'Bronterre' O'Brien,
who had made his name as editor of two illegal 'unstamped' radical
newspapers owned and published by Hetherington.

There were two main strands in O'Brien's impact. For him, the
key division in society was between the productive and unproductive members. The former were the working classes, who in a natural
society would receive the full value of their labour, but were in fact
robbed of most of it by the idle unproductive, in various ways. But
of these means of appropriating wealth, by far the most important
was profit, and O'Brien saw it as his mission to displace the traditional radical view that taxes were the main evil and cause of
distress. The worst enemies were not the governors, parsons or even
landlords but the capitalists, the middle 'scheming' classes, who
lived off profits from employing labour in production and from
trading. Democracy was not an end in itself, merely the means to
the necessary complete change of society.

In his journalism, O'Brien reported and commented on events abroad, especially in France, and gave a historical dimension to his analysis, identifying usurers and profit-mongers as the worst enemies of the people. Thus the British middle classes had caused the war against the French Revolution to prevent it from spreading. 'The "Statesmen" who made war on France in 1793, did so only because war was agreeable to the capitalists and profit-hunters, who wanted to put down the French Revolution, that revolution having sought to overthrow the hellish powers of capital and priestcraft.'[13] O'Brien's interpretation of the French Revolution was largely derived from the account by Buonarroti of the 1796 Conspiracy of Equals led by Babeuf, especially his portrayal of Robespierre as the hero of the industrious masses, or 'proletarians' as Buonarroti called them. The second element in O'Brien's influence was thus to establish Robespierre as a champion of full democracy and a new social order. O'Brien insisted that the struggles during the Revolution were the same as those in Britain and France in the 1830s: 'all the evils and horrors of the revolution arose from the fact that it was a middle-class revolution: that is to say, a revolution commenced, conducted, and terminated by and for the middling classes only, the proletarians or labouring classes having had no other share in it than that of fighting, slaving, huzzaing, and starving.' Similarly, he argued that the civil wars in Spain and Portugal between clericalist-absolutists and constitutionalists were of no concern to working men, although he did share in the enthusiasm of a meeting of 'working men and foreigners' when democratic movements briefly appeared in both countries.[14]

The man who rose to the leadership of the Democratic Association, the fiery Julian Harney, came 'to look upon Bronterre as a god',[15] and the Association, with its appeal to the poor 'proletarians', expounded this O'Brienite-Spencean ideology, and interpretation of Robespierre, Babeuf and Buonarroti.[16]

Members of the Democratic Association saw their struggle as having a European significance, Chartist success in Britain being good for continental nations. The chief concern was Poland, whose rising had been strongly supported by O'Brien in 1831 when editor of the *Midland Representative*. It produced nearly 10,000 refugees, the greatest number settling in France, with some 500 coming to Britain. They were, however, divided into hostile factions. Against the aristocratic faction, led by Prince Adam Czartoryski, which formed links with liberals and sought diplomatic pressure in favour of Poland, were ranged a number of more radical groups, which looked to the people for support, and were involved in radical and revolutionary movements in Western Europe.[17]

In London, conservatives were initially dominant, and received much support from fashionable Whig circles through the Polish Exiles' Friends' Society.[18] Each year they commemorated the outbreak of the rising in November 1830, although a small group of more radical émigrés in London held a rival annual commemoration at the Crown and Anchor. In April 1834, however, the father of Polish socialism, Stanisław Worcell, arrived in England after expulsion from France and Belgium, and he and some of the more radical Londoners organised a group of non-noble Polish refugees in Portsmouth into the Polish People, which condemned the Czartoryski group and affiliated to the Polish Democratic Society, founded in Paris in 1832. Also, in May 1836 General Dwerniecki came to England seeking to unite all émigrés around a democratic political programme. He established a Committee of the Polish Emigration, and formed links with radical MPs strongly committed to Polish independence and hostility to the Russian menace. But there was some scepticism among British radicals because of the noble leadership of the 1830 rising and support for the Polish cause from the hated Whigs. Thus at Dwerniecki's 1836 Crown and Anchor commemoration of the rising, two members of the Working Men's Association, Vincent and Beaumont, with the support of the Polish refugee, Major Bartolomei Beniowski, opposed the proceedings. Drawing on a recent pamphlet by Cobden, they castigated the Polish aristocracy for their crimes against peasants, members of the Greek Orthodox faith and Jews. Beaumont noted the selective nature of Whig sympathy for victims of political oppression. 'It is a curious fact, that no sufferers for revolution ever obtained aristocratic sympathy in England but the Poles.'[19] Dwerniecki and other reformers, with the help of the radical lawyer, Edmund Beales, made great efforts to dissociate themselves from the Czartoryski group, establish their reform credentials, highlight the difference between the Polish and Western European aristocracies, and emphasise their commitment to political equality, civil and religious liberty, and abolition of serfdom. They had some success, but their claim to speak for Polish reformers was disputed. By 1837 the Polish Democratic Society had 1,500 members, mostly in France but with a section in London. It was very hostile to the Polish aristocracy, and issued a programme of equality, democracy, provision of education for all, and reform of the privileged social system so that the right to land and other property rested on labour alone.[20]

The London section of the Polish Democratic Society rejected Dwerniecki's group as false democrats.[21] In 1837, again perhaps through Beaumont's links with French and Polish radicals in Paris, Hetherington printed an English version of the Society's manifesto, and it approached the Working Men's Association, which agreed in blaming the suppression of Poland on the privileged nobility that had kept the masses in subjection. The inclusion of the manifesto in a newspaper edited by O'Brien led to a much more enthusiastic response from the East London Democratic Association, which exchanged addresses and held joint meetings with the London section. The Democratic Association now annually commemorated the 1830 rising and interrupted conservative ones, and Harney became a member of the Polish Democratic Society, apparently the only Englishman to do so.[22] But in 1835 the Polish People in Portsmouth had stigmatised the Polish Democratic Society as a tool of the gentry and broken away on a programme of common ownership of land and an alliance of workers in proletarian internationalism. It had two branch communes, one in London, of which Beniowski was a member.[23]

Meanwhile, the Working Men's Association was also contacted by the Committee of the Polish Emigration, which invited them to nominate a member to the Association. It was Harney, during his brief membership of the Working Men's Association, who pressed them to send an address in reply to the Polish Democratic Society, but Lovett had this changed to an address to the working classes of Europe in general and the Poles in particular, and Harney was excluded from a role in composing this address.[24]

Thus the links between Chartists and Polish refugees in London were due to the initiatives of the latter, and were influenced by their divisions. Once the Harney group left, the Working Men's Association seems to have moved closer to the Committee of the Polish Emigration. When Worcell moved to London he took over the leadership of this Committee there, together with Ludwik Oborski and Karl Stoltzman, formerly of Young Poland and Young Europe.[25] These were opposed by the London section of the Polish Democratic Society, to which the Democratic Association remained committed. But it was Beniowski who became the most important Polish Democrat and Chartist in 1839, losing his government pension as a result. He became secretary to the Democratic Association and contributed extensively to its *London Democrat*, and took a prominent role in Chartist meetings. He went down to South Wales in connection with the Newport Rising in November; and was then involved in the conspiracies in London of members of the Democratic Association, and elected to the second Chartist Convention which sought to organise an insurrection to prevent the execution of the Newport rebels.[26]

Nevertheless, these concerns and links were a minor aspect of Chartism in the 1830s, and the situation was not very different in the 1840s. The bulk of the Chartists were committed to the National Charter Association, under the leadership of O'Connor, and showed little interest in foreign causes, and interest did not revive until the decline after 1842.

There was a group of French refugees in London, some part of the French community settled around Leicester Square. A key figure was Nicolas Thiéry, who first escaped to England in 1822, and in addition to belonging to secret societies became a successful footwear manufacturer and dealer, employing several refugees at his big warehouse in Regent Street.[27] In 1839 these exiles held a meeting at the Crown and Anchor to celebrate the fall of the Bastille and sent a communication to the Chartist General Convention.[28] The Bastille commemoration became an annual event, and they set up a French Democratic Society, led by Berrier-Fontaine and Chilman, two veterans of the republican Society of the Rights of Man which had flourished between the Paris risings of 1832 and 1834,[29] and by Auguste Juin, a man of education and letters who had authored a number of works in Paris as Juin d'Allas. In 1836 he fled to England to avoid prosecution for fraud, and was sentenced in his absence in June 1840 to ten years' forced labour. In London he passed himself off as 'Jean Michelot', and, an excellent speaker, he became president of the French Democratic Society.[30] It was this French group that initiated moves towards an organisation of foreign radicals. They had close links with Polish refugees, and working men of different nationalities spoke at their annual Bastille celebrations. In 1844 the French organised help for newly arrived Spanish refugees, and at the Bastille meeting that year it was agreed to set up an organisation primarily to relieve foreigners in distress but also to establish regular communication and understanding between the different groups. Thereafter French and Spanish radicals began attending Chartist meetings.[31] The trend was reinforced by the arrival in London of O'Brien's friend Peter Murray M'Douall, a leading Chartist who had fled to Paris in 1842 to avoid arrest. Here he had been in contact with French socialists, and contributed to Cabet's *Populaire*.[32] Meanwhile the National Executive of which he had been a part had been discredited, and on his return to Britain, he remained detached from the Chartist leadership. He came to London and was an active

Chartist lecturer in the autumn of 1844, the horrors of war being one of his themes, and began a series of penny tracts.[33] Out of his contacts with the French refugees emerged a republican meeting in September 1844 to celebrate the anniversary of the establishment of the First French Republic in 1792. It took the form of a 'banquet', a device used by radicals in France, where public meetings were not allowed and alternatives were found in the form of dinners with toasts that were in effect speeches. M'Douall took the chair and proposed a key toast: 'the democrats of all nations; may they unite in a bond of fraternity to advance the cause of Liberty, and exterminate despotism from the earth.' A leading part was taken by Lovett, who with Hetherington had broken irreparably with O'Connor and remained aloof from the National Charter Association, in a separate small National Association. Their commitment to a largely pacifist internationalism led to support for the Peace Movement, which organised the publication in Paris and London of one of their addresses, opposition to the possibility of war with the United States over Oregon in 1846, and advocacy of the settlement of international disputes through a Congress of Nations.[34] They also retained links with Mazzini and his Polish friend, Worcell, who became a member. In June 1844 they organised a very successful meeting of protest at the official visit of the Tsar.[35] Lovett and Hetherington also helped Mazzini expose the opening, at the behest of the Home Office, of his mail and that of his other close Polish friend, Stolzman, and the communication of their contents to the Austrian government. The scandal became a liberal *cause célèbre*, and the affair did a great deal to arouse British interest in Italian liberation.[36]

There was by now a bigger German refugee presence in London than before. The London based *Arbeiter-Bildungs-Verein* was founded in February 1840 by a few working men, led by Carl Schapper, the watchmaker Joseph Moll, and the shoemaker Heinrich Bauer, and met regularly in a room in the Red Lion, Great Windmill Street. It was partly a social centre for Germans in the metropolis, membership rising to 300 in 1847, with a branch in Whitechapel consisting of 160. It also had educational functions, with a library and a reading room. It remained a plebeian society, and organised help for unemployed members. Every January or February it celebrated the anniversary of its foundation, and every June held an excursion to Hampstead Heath, with beer, and German sausages, bread and songs. It also took ten newspapers, German, English and French, and had political meetings every other Sunday. In opposition to rival London German societies run by clergymen, its line was ultra-democratic. It lasted until 1914, and became best known in London radical circles for its choir. It also threw open its membership to refugees of various nationalities not catered for by organisations of their own.[37]

In September 1844 these Germans held a public meeting to welcome Weitling to London,[38] involving the same people who took part in the subsequent meeting the next week chaired by M'Douall – working men of different nationalities (German, Italian, Spanish and Swiss), French republicans and British Owenites. Most of the speakers at M'Douall's meeting were British, including Lovett, Hetherington, the leading London Chartists Ridley (head of a Chartist benefit society) and Skelton (who invoked Babeuf and Buonarroti), and the Owenites Holyoake, Southwell, Barmby and Bowkett, but the Frenchman Chilman and the Germans Schapper and Weitling also spoke. It was decided to form a committee containing representatives from each national group and from Chartists, Socialists (that is, Owenites) and Complete Suffrage reformers. It was not thus a specifically Chartist group, and was primarily an organisation of refugees, mainly French, German and Polish. But Lovett's National Association supported it, and M'Douall initially persuaded the Metropolitan Delegates, the important coordinating body for the London localities of the NCA, to be represented on the new Democratic Friends of All Nations. But the latter withdrew because of Chartist suspicions of a new splinter group, and this marginalised the new organisation. It was doomed when M'Douall also engaged in a public quarrel with O'Connor early in 1845. Lovett was the main author of an address issued in the new year, but the explicit disavowal of violence offended the continental exiles, who looked to revolution at home, and this led to the rapid demise of the organisation.[39]

The situation was changed by the arrival at the end of 1844 of Harney, as sub-editor of the *Northern Star.* Immediately he set to work to revive a movement for Spencean and O'Brienite ideas of social as well as mere political equality, and recruited former members of the old Democratic Association, many of whom had been inactive since 1839. In December they organised a 'festival of London democrats' to welcome the *Northern Star* to London.[40] But it was in the latter part of the following year that the movement really got under way, Harney's main ally being a close personal friend, Thomas Cooper, the former Leicester Chartist firebrand and committed republican, who on release from prison settled in London and enjoyed enormous popularity through his lectures and writings.

The new 'democratic movement' was punctuated by a series of four 'democratic suppers', at the third of which the Fraternal Democrats was formed.[41] Thus the main factor behind its formation was not internationalism but Harney's campaign for "the Charter and something more."

However, Harney was still committed to the cause of Poland. In Sheffield he had organised an address to the Poles from the Sheffield Chartists, and on his return to London he resumed close links with the leaders of the Polish Democratic Society in London, Worcell, Stoltzman and Oborski (a member of the earlier Democratic Friends of All Nations). But he also drew on the links already established between Chartists and French democrats and their Spanish associates, and at the *Northern Star* festival in December 1844, Chilman was one of the speakers, and the meetings gave three cheers for the democrats of France and Spain. In all the meetings in the latter part of 1845, alongside Harney, Cooper and members of the Democratic Association, foreigners were in evidence, the speakers including the French Berrier-Fontaine and 'Michelot', the Germans Schapper, Weitling, 'Citizen Engels' and Moll, and a Turk, Simmonee. Mazzini and Stoltzman were invited to the third meeting but were unable to attend. In Leeds Harney had met Friedrich Engels at the *Northern Star* office, and the two became friends, Engels contributing two long articles to the paper on German socialism. Engels already knew the leaders of the German refugees in London, and the Fraternal Democrats met at the room, near the office of the Star, used by their society, which Harney and other English democrats soon joined.[42] The first public meeting of the Fraternal Democrats was against the oppression of Poland.[43] It was intended to unite democrats of all nations, and became the most important of all the multi-national organisations during the Chartist period.[44]

The Fraternal Democrats were joined by the German and French Democratic societies, and a number of individuals from other countries, some no doubt already members of the German Society. They met regularly on Sundays, yet aroused in the Chartist leadership the same suspicion and fears of a faction within the movement as had the Democratic Friends of All Nations.[45] They therefore proceeded very cautiously, at first as a loose grouping with no formal structure, and their formation in September 1844 was not even publicly mentioned, although Engels gave a fuller account in the *Rheinische Jahrbücher*.

The success of the Fraternal Democrats was largely due to Harney: through conciliating the main body of Chartists, publicity in the *Star*, and his ideological similarities with the exile groups involved. While Harney no longer called for insurrection in Britain, he strongly supported foreign revolutionary movements, to which the refugees were committed. He also still adhered to the Spencean and O'Brien-ite ideas of the 1830s, in favour of pulling down the present rotten system of social slavery, and saw the grand question, raised by a few heroic opponents of the middle classes in the French Revolution, (such as Robespierre, St Just, Marat, Babeuf and Buonarroti), as the destruction of inequality and selfish individualism.[46]

His outlook had much in common with the views of the French and German radical refugees. Many of the French refugees were veterans of the Society of the Rights of Man, which in the early 1830s had been important in rehabilitating Robespierre. Repression in France in the mid-1830s had brought an end to open republican campaigning, and led to the rise of some clandestine insurrectionary activity in such secret societies as the Families and Seasons – where Blanqui was the leading figure aiming at a seizure of power through an armed coup by a small group; and in this context there was after 1834 growing inter-est in Buonarroti's account of the Babeuf conspiracy. Some of the conspirators were thereby also influenced by Buonarroti's identification of the ideas of Robespierre with those of Babeuf, and won over to the idea of a programme of complete social revolution through the owner-ship of all property by a democratic state (though not collectivisation of production). These Babeuvian ideas had little popular impact, but in May 1839 the Seasons made a disastrous, easily suppressed attempt at a coup. Some of those involved escaped to London, and strength-ened the Babeuvian elements among the French refugees there. Moreover, at the Paris trial of participants in the May coup, several of the accused openly advocated absolute equality of property, and the affair led to more interest in communism. At the same time, there was a reaction against futile secret societies and conspiracies, and the disci-pline, complete obedience to leaders and absence of discussion they entailed. The chief beneficiary of all this was Cabet, whose conversion to communism drew on a cult of Robespierre influenced by Buonar-roti. He returned to Paris in 1839, and a number of former Babeuvian conspirators joined his Icarian movement, which disavowed all conspir-acy and violence, and advocated discussion and propaganda. Cabet won adherents among the London French, including Berrier-Fontaine, and Hetherington began a translation of Cabet's *Voyage en Icarie*.[47]

In the early 1830s there were secret German organisations in Paris, linked to French republicans and Polish exiles (who hoped a revolution in Germany would lead on to one in Poland). These developed in 1836 into the League of the Just, whose branches in Germany distributed a translation of the Working Men's Association's Address to the Belgian workers. In Paris they were closely associated with Blanqui's secret societies, and absorbed Babeuvian communist ideas, Weitling producing a communist programme. Many of the League were involved in the disastrous 1839 Paris coup, and Schapper, Bauer and Moll managed to escape to London, where they founded the German Society.[48] This group was thus also influenced by Babeuvian communism, supported Owenism and Icarianism, and engaged in correspondence with Cabet.[49] There was thus a shared set of ideas uniting these French and German refugees and the democrats around Harney.

In launching the Fraternal Democrats, Harney brought in two British groups. The first was old associates from the Democratic Association (Ross, Ireland, Keen and Waddington). The second was secularists. There was a strong anti-Christian strand in British radicalism, largely based on Enlightenment rationalism. Many of its proponents became active in Owenism, and in the early 1840s, amidst the collapse of the Owenite movement, some Owenite missionaries, led by Holyoake and Southwell, revived anti-Christian propaganda. On release from prison, Holyoake settled in London, and became central to secularist publishing and propaganda. Harney and Hetherington (and the Austrian pantheist Johann Lhotski[50]), were part of Holyoake's network whose ideas were much more receptive to national rights republicanism than the usual patriotic constitutionalism of British radicalism, and they tended to be far more interested in foreign movements. Thus the *Northern Star* report of the 1844 Bastille celebration was copied from Holyoake's *Movement*, which included translations of Weitling's London speeches.[51] Active secularists were prominent in the early fraternal meetings in 1844 and 1845, and of them John Skelton, Ruffey Ridley, Thomas Cooper (briefly), and Edmund Stallwood (London reporter of the *Northern Star*) were members of the Fraternal Democrats.

It would be a mistake, therefore, to exaggerate the ideological uniformity of the Fraternal Democrats, or their support for communism. The ascendancy of such people as Harney and Schapper was reflected in the official declarations and the programme they outlined.

Governments were the tools of the privileged classes, and laws were made to benefit the rich. All hereditary inequalities and distinctions, including monarchy and aristocracy, should be abolished, along with any monopoly of political power and the class rule exercised by money-mongers and the bourgeoisie in Britain, France and America. All men were brethren, and should reject national hatreds, which were manipulated by their oppressors. Under the present system, idlers receive the fruits of the earth and industry, the real producers therefore being social slaves. Because the proletarians were the instruments of the classes above them, especially capitalists, they should act alone for change, and reject the leadership of the middle class. 'Let this great truth be impressed upon every working-man, that it is from the hut and the hovel, the garret and the cellar, must come the regeneration of his order and the social saviours of the human race.'[52] Because the exclusion of the people from the land through monopoly in ownership produced a surplus of labour that kept wages down, all land should become common property and be made available to the people. Labour must receive all the fruits of its labour. But the analysis was not very systematic, and tended to denounce priestcraft, monarchy and national prejudice as much as anything else, as this statement by Harney suggests:

> All schemes of so-called reform: all revolutions not having for their object the emancipation of labour are delusions and frauds; and the pretended reformers who excite the passions of the people for any other purpose, I pronounce the worst enemies of the human race. I mean by the emancipation of labour, not the conferring on the poor man the *privilege* of being robbed by a monopolist – instead of a landlord; not the supremacy of a conventicle Cantwell[53] instead of a privileged parson; not the rule of the *bourgeoisie* for that of the feudalists; I mean by the emancipation of labour that the masses, as the majority, shall rule the state, – that hereditary humbug, and class usurpation shall give place to popular sovereignty; that the laws shall be few and simple and lawyercraft abolished. That those who will have priests shall alone pay for them, and wise men who can be priests to themselves shall suffer neither plunder nor proscription. That those who raise the food shall be its first partakers. That those who build mansions shall live in them. That those who weave linens, cottons, cloths, and silks, shall wear them. That those who make railways and carriages shall have the use of them. That capital, the offspring of labour, shall be its servant and not its master. That equal education shall foster the intellect of all. That none but the idle shall die of hunger, and none but the vicious suffer reproach. And that the absurdities and usurpations of ranks and classes shall disappear, and men be the equal lords of the earth.[54]

The Fraternal Democrats met every Sunday, but remained no more than a 'coterie',[55] viewed with suspicion by the Chartist leadership in the NCA Executive and the Metropolitan Delegates. This was changed by a new attempted Polish rising early in 1846. Harney immediately gave the short-lived revolt in Cracow and Galicia full coverage and support in the *Northern Star*, and particularly welcomed the Provisional Government's proclamation and decree establishing equal social and political brotherhood:

> The Cracow Manifesto proclaims the extinction of serfage, the abolition of class distinctions, the restitution of the land to the nation, and the veritable freedom of the people, by guaranteeing to them the lands they cultivate, and ensuring to each of the patriots in arms a portion of the national domains; the disabled and unfortunate are promised security and national aid; and, lastly, not only the fraternity of all Poles, but the fraternity of all nations, is proclaimed; war is invoked only against those who are the common oppressors and enemies of mankind.[56]

The Fraternal Democrats and the Polish Democratic Society endorsed both rising and manifesto, which the Czartoryski group disowned. Harney was able to allay the suspicions of the Chartist Executive, and the two groups combined with London Chartists and the German and French societies to support the rising and form a Democratic Committee for Poland's Regeneration.[57] This included all of the Chartist Executive, including O'Connor, whose pro-Polish actions went back to the 1830s,[58] the leading members of the Fraternal Democrats, and a number of London Chartists.[59]

While the rising was soon crushed, and the committee was reduced to organising anniversary commemorations in 1847 and 1848, the campaign integrated the Fraternal Democrats and refugees much more into the wider Chartist movement, and widened Chartist participation in the Fraternal Democrats, especially as they also participated in the Chartist campaign against the danger of war with America over Oregon, and to resist being drawn for the militia.[60] Furthermore, Thomas Cooper suddenly espoused nonviolence, and, to Harney's fury, came out against armed insurrection in general, and the Cracow rising in particular. He also engaged in open quarrel with O'Connor, around whom the Chartists rallied to drum him out of the movement. The Fraternal Democrats' opposition to Cooper thus reinforced their favour with O'Connor.[61]

It was only once the pro-Polish movement was under weigh that the existence of the Fraternal Democrats was reported in the *Northern Star*, and they felt able to adopt formal membership (with cards bearing the slogan 'all men are brethren' in twelve languages) and elect six secretaries from the component nationalities.[62] Instead of purely convivial gatherings, their weekly meetings, now every Monday, were political discussions. O'Connor acted as treasurer to them as well as to the

German and French societies, and even came to speak at their first anniversary. They were now joined by the other four members of the Executive and a number of leading London Chartists, including the new middle-class recruit, Ernest Jones, who was fluent in French and German, and became president of the Democratic Committee for Poland's Regeneration. In 1847 they felt able to adopt a code of rules, fixed subscriptions and an elected committee.[63] The Polish agitation also united the radical Polish exiles under the Polish Democratic Society, and a number of them joined the Fraternal Democrats, with Oborski as their unofficial secretary. The Fraternal Democrats opposed other Polish groupings.[64]

Harney also contributed the priceless asset of support from the *Northern Star*, the great Chartist and labour newspaper of which in October 1845 he became full editor. His innovations included greater coverage of foreign news and movements abroad, and he reported the refugee associations, especially the Fraternal Democrats. This was not very welcome to his employer, O'Connor, whose radicalism contained little interest in foreign causes, concerns or groups, or 'democracy' (republicanism and social transformation). But, although he sometimes objected to Harney's policy, on the whole he allowed him a free hand to publicise the Fraternal Democrats.[65]

Thus Harney made the Fraternal Democrats a success through ideological uniformity and the support of the *Northern Star*, but they had no monopoly of Chartist links with foreign refugees. Before 1845, internationalism tended to be stronger among Chartists aloof from the NCA, such as those in Lovett's National Association. These were usually more acceptable to parliamentary and middle-class radicals who supported both repeal of the Corn Laws and the provisions of the People's Charter. Such Chartists persisted in their internationalism after the failure of the Democratic Friends of All Nations. Moreover, while shared ideas facilitated united action among the members of the Fraternal Democrats, they could also alienate other radicals and Chartists. Harney and his allies were strong supporters of a united democratic anticlerical Italian republic free of Austrian domination, and approved of Mazzini's Young Europe movement to unite the movements for national liberation. Mazzini was invited to the meetings that launched the Fraternal Democrats, and although he was unable to attend, he was praised and his health was drunk.[66] But, while he remained on good terms with Harney, Mazzini would have no truck with communism, and held aloof from the Fraternal Democrats, although he did support the Polish agitation. Mazzini in any case valued the friendship of the respectable literary and parliamentary Radical circles he moved in, and their patronage of his school for poor Italian boys and girls, and had no wish to jeopardise them. His two close Polish associates, Worcell and Stoltzman, like him strongly influenced by Lamennais, adopted the same line. Only some secularists joined the Fraternal Democrats, and more stayed aloof from it and the NCA, although Hetherington and Mazzini's friend, the Chartist engraver Linton (a member of Lovett's National Association) were on the Democratic Committee for Poland's Regeneration, and Holyoake was also involved.[67] Their rationalism, enthusiasm for education, anti-clericalism and republicanism also gave common ground with a number of liberal intellectuals, Dissenters (especially Unitarians such as W.J. Fox and Peter Taylor), and London literati, such as Douglas Jerrold. It was precisely such circles that the anti-clerical, anti-Papal and republican Mazzini found congenial.

London was dotted with lectures and classes involving such men as Holyoake, Cooper (after his breach with mainstream Chartism), Barmby, Southwell, Lovett, Hetherington, Fox, Howitt, the radical MP Bowring, Bowkett and Linton, sharing in a common Enlightenment rationalism and humanitarianism, seeing political reform as superficial unless accompanied by a fundamental transformation of people, and often promoting religious and medical reform, feminism, vegetarianism, and rejection of violence and cruelty.[68]

These people, with Worcell, held annual commemorations of the 1830 Polish rising, and had been involved in the Democratic Friends of All Nations.[69] A meeting in April 1846, chaired by Bowring, to protest at the destruction of Poland, led on to a People's International League, in favour of European national self-government, led by Bowring, Mazzini, Cooper, Linton, Jerrold, Fox, Taylor, Howitt and Stolzman.[70] While the Fraternal Democrats attracted mainly Germans and French, the League won over more Italians and Poles. Late in 1847 it began regular lectures, by Cooper and Linton, on Italy and Switzerland (where the *Sonderbund* crisis had created a new radical cause).

The People's International League was contemptuously dismissed by Harney and his allies, but despite the publicity in the *Northern Star*, the Fraternal Democrats may have lost some of their vigour, as in mid-1847 its meetings became monthly instead of weekly.[71] On the other hand, it became more important abroad, and its addresses were inserted in the *Débat Social*, *Réforme* and *Deutsche Brüsseler Zeitung*.[72]

From the start, the German Democratic Society had contained a small, inner, secret group, under Schapper, Bauer and Moll, in the

League of the Just and in contact with Paris and Switzerland. In 1846 the central council was moved from Paris to London, but Weitling left for America. Engels had achieved a rapprochement with them, and in 1845 brought Marx (now based in Brussels) over to London on a visit, when he met Harney, and the next year Marx's German Democratic Communists of Brussels sent a message of support for O'Connor against Cooper.[73] In London, both German and French societies opposed Cabet's suggestion in 1843 of a settlement near Paris, and, especially, his dramatic decision in 1847 to emigrate to America to found a communist colony there.[74] After this split, Marx and Engels took over the League of the Just and transformed it into the mainly German League of Communists with a new programme, and a short-lived journal run by Schapper. In Brussels German refugees and Belgian democrats, including Jacob Katz, also established a Democratic Association for Promoting the Friendship of Nations. Late in 1847 Marx and Engels came over to London for a congress of the Communist League. Marx also attended the Fraternal Democrats, and spoke at a public meeting commemorating the 1830 Polish Rising. He also proposed affiliating the Fraternal Democrats to the Brussels Democratic Association, and the Fraternal Democrats and German Democratic Society agreed to hold a joint conference in Brussels in September 1848. Despite O'Connor's disapproval, this 'plan of democratic progress' was also approved by the Chartist Executive, Metropolitan Delegates and several London Chartist branches.[75]

The events of 1848 disrupted these ambitious plans, but initially the revolution in Paris in February, and the subsequent ones elsewhere, aroused great hopes. An address of congratulation to the people of Paris and the new French Provisional Government was issued by the Fraternal Democrats, and approved by the National Executive, Metropolitan Delegates, German Democratic Society, and a Chartist mass meeting. It was taken across to Paris and presented at the Hotel de Ville: by Harney, Schapper and Moll, on behalf of the Fraternal Democrats, Bauer for the German Democratic Society, M'Grath for the Executive, and Ernest Jones. The French Democratic Society also sent a deputation, and the Polish Democratic Society voiced its hope for an independent, nonaristocratic Poland.[76]

Other Chartist groups were also active. The People's International League also congratulated the French Provisional Government. A meeting at the former Owenite John Street Institution also sent Linton and Collett over to present an address to the new French Republic. On their return, a Democratic Committee of Observation of the French Revolution was formed, which developed into a People's Charter Union, with Thomas Cooper president, and Collett secretary.[77] Members were later active in the Friends of Italy and a Shilling Subscription in aid of European Freedom.[78]

But while there was in 1848 much greater interest in events and movements abroad, there was at the same time a decline in links between Chartists and foreigners. The revolutions meant the departure of many refugees for the Continent, including Schapper, Bauer and Moll. Chilman became active in a revived Society for the Rights of Man and then the Revolution Club, and Michelot ran a political club of the Young Mountain, usually called the Sorbonne Club, until his criminal past was revealed and he went to prison.[79] This meant a decline in the number of political refugees in London, and also of the Fraternal Democrats. Moreover, new repressive government legislation, especially the Aliens' Act, made it dangerous for foreigners to engage in radical politics, and the Fraternal Democrats decided to dissolve and be reconstituted as a wholly British association, to be the main forum for Harney's brand of democratic reform.[80] Thus a chapter in foreign refugee politics came to a close. Mazzini's departure also led to the collapse of the People's International League. Moreover, while Chartism had revived in the first half of the year, with London one of the main centres, in the second half of the year, in the face of government repression, it went into rapid decline, never to recover.

The continental revolutions also met with defeat and this meant the arrival of new, often very poor, refuges in London, the return of some old ones, such as Schapper, and new organisations of refugees. Harney was the key figure in trying to organise support for them, and remained the chief exponent of working-class internationalism, defender of radical refugees against conservative hostility, and organiser of relief.[81]

His efforts were, as before, centred on the Fraternal Democrats, still faithful to the memory of Robespierre and Marat, although Beniowski now opposed his social programme.[82] But their campaign to remodel Chartism failed, and as hopes of renewed continental revolution faded, some of the foreign colonies in London were, with government encouragement, leaving for America. Harney himself left London at the end of 1853, and it was Jones who was to attempt in the later 1850s to unite refugees, including Schapper and Oborski, on a social-democratic programme.

Thus concern for and contact with foreign refugees was not a characteristic of mainstream Chartism, being confined mainly to minority wings, the moral reformers and the social-democratic reformers typified by Lovett and Harney respectively, and to a few individuals with continental experience and contacts, notably O'Brien, Beaumont, Jones and Reynolds. Wider radical and Chartist mobilisation was achieved over the particular issues of the French Revolutions of 1830 and 1848, and the Polish Risings of 1830 and 1846. Even then, common action was strongly influenced by political divisions among British radicals and Chartists, and among the refugees.

Notes

1 For the Chartist movement, see D. Thompson, *The Chartists: Popular Politics in the Industrial Revolution* (New York, 1984); J. Epstein, *The Lion of Freedom: Feargus O'Connor and the Chartist Movement* (London, 1982). For London Chartism, see I. Prothero, 'Chartism in London', *Past and Present* 44 (1969), pp. 76–105; idem, 'London Chartism and the Trades', *Economic History Review* 24 (1971), pp. 202–19; D. Goodway, *London Chartism, 1838–1848* (Cambridge, 1982).

2 For these developments, see A.R. Schoyen, *The Chartist Challenge. A Portrait of George Julian Harney* (London, 1958), Chs. 6–9; H. Weisser, *British Working-Class Movements and Europe, 1815–48* (Manchester, 1975).

3 E.g. L. Colley, 'Whose Nation? Class and National Consciousness in Britain 1750–1830', *Past and Present* 113 (1986), pp. 97–117; J. Epstein, 'The Constitutional Idiom: Radical Reasoning, Rhetoric and Action in Early Nineteenth-century England', *Journal of Social History* 23 (1990), pp. 553–74; J. Vernon, *Politics and the People: A Study in English Political Culture, c.1815–1867* (Cambridge, 1993), Ch. 8; M. Finn, *After Chartism: Class and Nation in English Radical Politics, 1848–1874* (Cambridge, 1993).

4 Weisser, *Working Class*, pp. 4–58; Finn, *After Chartism*, Ch. 1.

5 *Bee-Hive*, 30 July 1864, p. 1; Weisser, *Working Class*, p. 157.

6 Public Record Office, Home Office Papers [HO] 79/4, f.231 (30 January, 16 March 1838).

7 C.H. Johnson, *Utopian Communism in France: Cabet and the Icarians, 1839–1851* (London, 1974), pp. 42–61.

8 British Library [BL] Add. Ms. 37,773, f.19 (25 Oct. 1836); *London Dispatch*, 13 November 1836, p. 65; 30 July 1837, p. 380; 22 October, p. 457; 3 December, p. 505; *London Mercury*, 30 July 1837, p. 665; W. Lovett, *The Life and Struggles of William Lovett* (London, 1967), pp. 80–1, 88–91, 107–11, 125–31.

9 Lovett, *Life*, p.130.

10 BL Add. Mss. 37,773, f.19 (25 October 1836); 27,819, f.45; *Constitutional,* 12 November 1836, pp. 2–4; 22 November, p. 2; 5 December, pp. 2, 3; *London Dispatch,* 13 November 1836, p. 65; 18 December, p. 108; 3 January 1837, p. 123; Lovett, *Life,* pp. 80–2; A.M. Lehning, 'The International, Association (1855–1859). A Contribution to the Preliminary History of the First International', *International Review for Social History,* 3 (1935), pp. 189–91; Weisser, *Working Class,* pp. 67–73.

11 I.D. McCalman, *Radical Underworld: Prophets, Revolutionaries and Pornographers in London, 1795–1840* (Cambridge, 1988); M. Chase, *'The People's Farm'. English Radical Agrarianism, 1755–1840* (Oxford, 1988); I. Prothero, *Artisans and Politics in Early Nineteenth-Century London: John Gast and his Times* (Folkestone, 1979), Chs. 5–7, 14–17; Schoyen, *Chartist Challenge,* pp. 5–12; J. Bennett, 'The London Democratic Association 1837–1841: a Study in London Radicalism', in J. Epstein and D. Thompson (eds), *The Chartist Experience: Studies in Working-Class Radicalism and Culture, 1830–60* (London, 1982).

12 *Northern Star,* 24 March 1838, p. 7; *Operative,* 14 April 1839, p. 7.

13 *Poor Man's Guardian,* 13 September 1834, p. 250.

14 *Poor Man's Guardian,* 27 June 1835, pp. 574–7; *Hetherington's Twopenny Dispatch,* 20 August 1836, pp. 2, 3; 27 August, p. 3; 3 September, pp. 2, 4; *London Dispatch,* 24 September 1836, p.12; 1 October, p.17; *Bronterre's National Reformer,* 15 January 1837, p. 12; J.B. O'Brien, *Buonarroti's History of Babeuf's Conspiracy for Equality* (London, 1836); idem, *Bronterre's Life and Character of Maximilien Robespierre* (London, 1837), p. 216.

15 *Southern Star,* 9 February 1840, p. 7.

16 London Democratic Association Constitution, HO 44/52; *London Dispatch,* 1 July 1838, p. 746; *Northern Star,* 3 July 1838, p. 3; *Operative,* 9 December 1838, p. 84; 16 December 1838, p. 104; 6 January 1839, p. 2; 13 January 1839, p. 10; 3 February 1839, pp. 3,5; *London Democrat, passim.*

17 P. Brock, 'Polish Democrats and English Radicals 1832–1862: a Chapter in the History of Anglo-Polish Relations', *Journal of Modern History,* 25 (1953), pp. 139–46; Weisser, *Working Class,* pp. 118–25.

18 *'Destructive' and Poor Man's Conservative,* 13 July 1833, p. 188.

19 *Weekly True Sun,* 6 December 1835, p. 946; *London Dispatch,* 13 August 1837, p. 378; 29 October 1837, p. 466; *Constitutional,* 29 November 1836, p. 3; 30 November. 1836, p. 3; 1 December 1836, p. 2; 5 December 1836, p. 3; 6 December 1836, p. 3; 19 December 1836, p. 3; 24 December 1836, p. 3.

20 *Manifesto of the Polish Democratical Society* (London, 1837); *London Dispatch,* 10 December 1837, p. 516.

21 *Charter,* 22 December 1839, p. 758.
22 *London Dispatch,* 4 June 1837, p. 300; *London Mercury,* 4 June 1837, p. 301; 6 August 1837, p. 673; *Operative,* 9 December 1838, p. 84; *Charter,* 1 December 1839, p. 713; 22 December 1839, p. 758; Schoyen, *Chartist Challenge,* p. 51; Brock, 'Polish Democrats', p. 144.
23 Brock, 'Polish Democrats', pp. 142–4, 146; *Charter,* 22 December 1839, p. 758; *Northern Star,* 30 August 1845, p. 6.
24 BL Add. Ms. 37,773, ff.69, 70, 84 (3, 4 October, 1 December 1837).
25 BL Add. Ms. 37,773, ff.118, 132 (21 August, 27 November 1838); *Charter,* 22 December 1839, p. 758; Brock, 'Polish Democrats', p. 147.
26 HO 40/44, ff.545, 655, 661, 701, 735, 810, 924, 975; 44/52 15, 19 July, 14, 15 August; *Operative,* 9 December 1838, p. 84; 12 May 1839, p. 16; 9 June, p. 3; 16 June, p. 3; *Charter,* 8 December 1839, p. 721.
27 Alleaume, *Religion Naturelle,* 30 July 1842, p. 440, *International Courier,* 1 December 1864, p. 25; Thiéry entry in J. Maitron (ed.), *Dictionnaire Biographique du Mouvement Ouvrier Français. Première Partie: 1789–1864* (Paris, 1964).
28 BL Add. Ms. 34,245 B, f.78; *Charter,* 28 July 1839, p. 425.
29 Berrier-Fontaine was secretary to the society. Chilman's reports are in Archives Nationales, Paris, CC 616, 1ère. liasse, ff.22–31; see also CC 585, Leclerc interview, and 4 January meeting.
30 *Northern Star,* 21 March 1846, p.1; 18 July, p. 8; *Commune de Paris,* 14 April 1848, p. 3.
31 *Northern Star,* 16 August 1844, p. 8; 24 August 1844, p. 1; 31 August 1844, p. 1.
32 *Populaire,* 19 August 1843, p. 106.
33 *Northern Star,* 28 September 1844, p. 1; 5 October 1844, p. 6; 12 October 1844, p. 1; 26 October 1844, p. 8.
34 Add. Mss. 37,7774, ff.90, 126 (23 May 1843, 18 June 1844); 37,775, ff.24, 49 (10 June 1845, 30 June 1846); Lovett, *Life,* pp. 260–5.
35 *Northern Star,* 15 June 1844, pp. 4,6; Lovett, *Life,* pp. 247–9.
36 *Northern Star,* 22 June 1844, pp. 1,7; 29 June, p. 7; 1 March 1845, p. 1; 8 March, p. 7; 3 May, p. 4; Lovett, *Life,* pp. 247–8; F.B. Smith, *Radical Artisan. William James Linton 1812–97* (Manchester, 1973), pp. 53–8.
37 Harney to Engels, 30 March 1846, and Thom to Harney, 1846, in F.G. and R.M. Black (eds), *The Harney Papers* (Assen, 1969), pp. 243, 75; *Northern Star,* 14 February 1846, p. 3; 21 March, p. 1; 6 June, p. 4; 13 February 1847, p. 6; *Commonwealth,* 17 February 1866, p. 6; Weisser, *Working Class,* p. 127.
38 Lehning, 'International Association', p. 195; Weisser, *Working Class,* p. 135.

39 BL Add. Ms. 37,775, ff.14 (22 October 1844), 14 (28 January 1845); *Northern Star* 28 September 1844, p. 1; 5 October, p. 1; 12 October, p. 7; 19 October, p. 1; 2 November, p. 7; Lovett, *Life*, pp. 256–7; Weisser, *Working Class*, pp. 155–6.

40 *Northern Star*, 14 December 1844, p. 1.

41 *Northern Star*, 16 August 1845, p. 8; 23 August, p. 8; 27 September, p. 5; 15 November, p. 7.

42 *Northern Star*, 25 November 1843, p. 3; 14 February 1846; Harney to Engels, 30 March 1846, in Black, *Harney Papers*, p. 242; Schoyen, *Chartist Challenge*, pp. 129, 134–5; Weisser, *Working Class*, p. 179.

43 *Northern Star*, 13 December 1845, p. 7.

44 Schoyen, *Chartist Challenge*, pp. 135–73, 184, 230; Weisser, *Working Class*, Ch. 4.

45 Harney to Engels, 30 March 1846, in Black, *Harney Papers*, p. 244; Schoyen, *Chartist Challenge*, p. 138.

46 E.g. *Northern Star*, 6 September 1845, p. 5; 26 September 1846, p. 7; *Reynolds's Weekly Newspaper*, 1 September 1850, p. 7.

47 E. Cabet, *Salut par l'Union, ou Ruine par la Division* (Paris, 1845), pp. 9–10; E. Cabet, *Ma Ligne Droite ou le vrai Chemin du Salut pour le Peuple* (Paris, 1847), pp. 64–8; L.de la Hodde, *Histoire des Sociétés Secrètes et du Parti Républicain de 1830 à 1848* (Paris, 1850), pp. 267–81; Berrier-Fontaine to Cabet, 15 July, 20 August, 2 September, 1 October 1847, Bibliothèque Historique de la Ville de Paris, Ms. 1052, ff.20, 22, 23, 26; Harney to Engels, 30 March 1846, in Black, *Harney Papers*, p. 241; *Reasoner*, 30 June 1847, p. 358; 22 September, p. 85; 7 December, p. 16; C.H. Johnson, 'Etienne Cabet and the Problem of Class Antagonism', *International Review of Social History*, 11 (1966), pp. 403–43. For Cabet and his movement, see Johnson, *Utopian Communism*.

48 Lehning, 'International Association', pp. 193–5; G.J. Holyoake, *Sixty Years of an Agitator's Life* (London, 1892) I, p. 96.

49 A. Lehning, 'Discussions à Londres sur le communisme icarien', *Bulletin of the International Institute of Social History* 8 (1953); Schoyen, *Chartist Challenge*, pp. 135–6; Weisser, *Working Class*, p. 126.

50 BL Add. Ms.37, 774, f.10 (16 November 1841); *British Statesman*, 23 July 1842, p. 6; J. Lhotski, *Regeneration of Society the Only Corrective for the Distress of the Country* (London, 1844).

51 Holyoake, *Sixty Years*, I, p. 95.

52 Harney, *Northern Star*, 8 January 1848, p. 1.

53 Harney's epithet for Dr. John Campbell, a noted Calvinist preacher and writer who had criticised the Chartists.

54 *Northern Star,* 26 February 1848, p. 3.
55 Goodway, *London Chartism,* p. 56.
56 *Northern Star,* 20 February 1847, p. 4; 7 March 1846, p. 5; 28 March, p. 1; 26 February 1848, p. 3; Weisser, *Working Class,* p. 141.
57 Harney to Engels, 30 March 1846, in Black, *Harney Papers,* p. 244; *Northern Star,* 21 March 1846, pp. 1,8; 28 March, p. 1; 23 May 1846, p. 8.
58 *Weekly True Sun,* 6 December 1835, p. 946.
59 Harney to Engels, 30 March, and to Engels and Marx, 20 July 1846, in Black, *Harney Papers,* pp. 239, 246; *Northern Star,* 4 April 1846, p. 4; 6 June, p. 1; 18 July, p. 8; 5 December, p. 7; 17 April 1847, p. 7; Schoyen, *Chartist Challenge,* pp. 138–40; Weisser, *Working Class,* pp. 141–3.
60 Harney to Engels and Marx, 20 July 1846, in Black, *Harney Papers,* p. 247; *Northern Star,* 17 January 1846, p. 1; 24 January, p. 7.
61 Harney to Engels, 30 March 1846, in Black, *Harney Papers,* p. 240; *Northern Star,* 14 February 1846, pp. 1, 4, 5; 11 April, p. 3; 25 April, p. 7; 16 May, p. 8; June-July *passim.*
62 *Northern Star,* 21 March 1841, p. 1; Mazzini to Harney, in Black, *Harney Papers,* p. 49.
63 *Northern Star,* 11 April 1846, p. 5; 11 July, p. 7; 26 September, pp. 7–8; 16 January 1847, p. 6; 19 June, p. 8; 2 October, p. 1; Weisser, *Working Class,* pp. 137–8.
64 Brock, 'Polish Democrats', p. 149.
65 O'Connor to Harney, and Harney to Engels, 30 March 1846, in Black, *Harney Papers,* pp. 60, 241; *Northern Star* 26 June 1847, p. 1; *Reynolds's Weekly Newspaper,* 22 December 1850, p. 10; Schoyen, *Chartist Challenge,* pp. 124, 127–8.
66 Mazzini to Harney, in Black, *Harney Papers,* pp. 48, 52; *Northern Star,* 15 November 1845, p. 7; Schoyen, *Chartist Challenge,* pp. 133–4, 137.
67 *Northern Star,* 28 March 1846, p. 1; 23 May, p. 8.
68 There is much information on these in Holyoake's *Reasoner.* See also *Northern Star,* 7 November 1840, p. 5; 25 July 1846, p. 5; Lovett, *Life,* pp. 268–74; T. Cooper, *The Life of Thomas Cooper, written by himself* (London, 1872), pp. 280–1, 296–9; Finn, *After Chartism,* p. 71; J.F.C. Harrison, 'Early Victorian Radicals and the Medical Fringe', in W.F. Bynum and R. Porter (eds), *Medical Fringe and Medical Orthodoxy, 1750–1850* (London, 1987); I. Prothero, *Radical Artisans in England and France, 1830–1870* (Cambridge, 1997), pp. 246–8, 272–80.
69 *Northern Star,* 30 November 1844, p. 1; Smith, *Radical Artisan,* p. 59.
70 *Reasoner* 28 April 1847, pp. 43–4; 29 September 1847, p. 535; Cooper, *Life,* pp. 299–301; Smith, *Radical Artisan,* pp. 59–62; Weisser, *Working Class,* pp. 156–61; Finn, *After Chartism,* pp. 71–2.

71 *Northern Star,* 24 July 1847, p. 7; 8 January 1848, p. 1.

72 *Northern Star,* 24 October 1846, p. 7; 12 December, p. 7; 12 June 1847, p. 8; 8 January 1848, p. 1.

73 *Northern Star,* 25 July 1846, p. 1.

74 *Populaire,* 19 September 1847, p. 374; 3 October, p. 382; Johnson, *Utopian Communism,* pp. 239–40, 246–7, 255–6.

75 Harney to Engels, 30 March 1846, to Engels and Marx, 20 July 1846, and to Marx, 18 December 1847, and O'Connor to Harney, 4 January 1848, in Black, *Harney Papers,* pp. 61–3, 243, 245, 247; *Northern Star,* 4 December 1847, p. 1; 11 December, p. 1; 1 January 1848, p. 4; Lehning, 'International Association', pp. 197–8; Schoyen, *Chartist Challenge,* pp. 137, 142–3, 154–5; Weisser, *Working Class,* pp. 128, 145–9.

76 Harney to Engels, 1848, in Black, *Harney Papers,* p. 248; *Northern Star,* 25 March 1848, p. 5; 1 April, pp. 5,8; 8 April, p. 5; *Reasoner,* 8 March 1848, pp. 202–4.

77 *Reasoner,* March-May 1848; 9 August, p. 174; 6 September, p. 240; 13 September, pp. 250–1; 18 October, pp. 329–30; 22 November, p. 412; C.D. Collett, *History of the Taxes on Knowledge. Their Origin and Repeal* (London, 1899) I, pp. 80–1.

78 *Vanguard,* 29 January 1853, p. 15.

79 *Commune de Paris,* 11 March 1848, p. 4; 16 March, p. 1; 17 March, p. 4; 25 March, p. 3; 14 April, p. 3; *Travail,* 28 May 1848, p. 2; 30 May, p. 2; *Vraie République,* 29 March 1848, p. 1.

80 *Northern Star,* 6 May 1848, p. 8; 27 May, p. 6; Berjeau, *Voix du Peuple,* 3 December 1849, p. 3.

81 Berjeau, *Voix du Peuple,* 3 December 1849, p. 3; *Reynolds's Weekly Newspaper,* 20 April 1851, p. 14; *Vanguard,* 29 January 1853, p. 13; *Beacon,* 9 November 1853, p. 48; 7 December, pp. 102–4; Schoyen, *Chartist Challenge,* pp. 187, 209–29.

82 *Northern Star,* 6 January 1849, p. 5; 5 January, 1850, p. 1; *Reynolds's Weekly Newspaper,* 15 September 1850, pp. 10–11; 5 January 1851, p. 10; 2 March, p. 14; *Beacon,* 16 November 1853, p. 64.

14

Immigrants and Refugees:
Who were the Real Forty-Eighters in the
United States?

Bruce Levine

For many years, scholars described the events of 1848 in Europe as a 'revolution of the intellectuals', 'an explosion of liberal nationalism', a revolution both led and supported primarily by members of the educated, professional middle class. What these middle-class revolutionaries wanted, it was added, was essentially *political* change, especially German unification, increased personal freedom, and greater civic control of the government.[1] This view of 1848, in turn, shaped scholarly perception in the United States of the massive European immigration of the 1840s and 1850s (and especially its large German-speaking component). The effect was to draw a sharp dichotomy between the categories of 'refugee' and 'immigrant' and to minimise the political impact that 'Forty-Eighters' had on American society.

Between 1840 and 1860, about one and a half million Germans left their homelands for the United States. Among them were, to be sure, middle- and upper-class figures – a handful of wealthy, well-connected and influential merchants plus many more middle-sized entrepreneurs and well-to-do professionals (clergy, physicians, attorneys, journalists). But the vast majority of the emigrants were labouring people of town and country. Craft workers composed an imposing sector of this *Auswanderung*. Among those who, for example, left the Grand Duchy of Baden in Southern Germany between 1840 and 1855, between a quarter and one-third worked in the crafts. Of those who left Württemberg a few years later, craft workers composed more than half of the total. The same occupational group accounted for an even larger proportion of those who left Hamburg in the late 1840s and early 1850s. Few historians, however, were willing to believe that the dramatic upheavals in

Germany in 1848 had been influenced by or had even left much of a mark on such people. They were not refugees, who were of course politically minded; they were merely emigrants, who left Germany in search of a higher living standard – an economic motive barely related to the causes, creeds and conflicts of 1848. True refugees, true 'Forty-Eighters', were to be found not among people like these but exclusively among those new arrivals who belonged to the intelligentsia.

These axioms achieved classic expression in an influential article published in 1930 and entitled 'The Revolution of 1848 and the German Emigration'. Its author, Professor Marcus Lee Hansen, was then the dean of immigration studies in the USA. According to him, one had only to glance at 'the crowds of stolid and slow-moving peasants, labourers with calloused hands, and worried and sober artisans' milling about in the American ports of arrival to realise that 'their thoughts were not dwelling on politics or revolution'. A generation later, Professor Hildegard Binder Johnson rendered the same assumptions about the class nature of the revolution and the middle-class character of those it mobilised into a sartorial profile. The *real* Forty-Eighter in America, Professor Johnson explained, 'affected student costume or imitated the style of the romantic hero of the Revolution, Friedrich Hecker, by wearing a broad-brimmed hat, a shirt open at the neck, and a loosely tied scarf ... He was set off from the mass of immigrants, the peasants and the craftsmen, by delicate hands that showed no signs of physical labour.'[2] It was left to Professor Stanley Zucker to specify that true Forty-Eighters in America numbered only some 4,000 individuals, less than three-tenths of one percent of the German immigrants of 1840–60.[3]

The continuing influence of these assumptions is evident even in some of the most recent and sophisticated evaluations of the immigrant experience in America. It is particularly clear in scholarly descriptions of how the veterans of the European upheavals fared in the United States. Although many middle-class revolutionaries experienced an initially difficult adjustment there, it is often said, most eventually came to recognise in their adoptive land the type of society they had always hoped to bring into being in Germany. The most adaptable were therefore able to prosper, win the esteem and admiration of their American-born neighbours, and become staunch patriots and champions of the social and political relations characteristic of the United States. The immigrant politician Carl Schurz captured this view neatly when, in his later years, he congratulated himself and other 'German representatives of the movement of "Forty-eight" who have sought a new home in America' for becoming 'reliable and conservative citizens' there.[4]

This way of telling the story of 1848 and of the emigré Forty-Eighters in America contained part of the truth, but not all of it. It left out a great deal – about what happened in Germany before and during 1848–9, about who left Germany and why in those years, and about what those people experienced and did in North America. Excluded is the social crisis in Germany that yielded political revolution at the end of the decade. Missing as well is the impact of the crisis on the German population, the diverse ways in which common people struggled against their conditions, and the values and goals that informed those struggles and which many of those 'with calloused hands' then carried abroad with them.

By the year 1848, Germans who worked with their hands had been finding their positions drastically undermined for decades. A confluence of economic and demographic forces was accelerating the expropriation, pauperisation and proletarianisation of vast numbers of small producers of town and country. The survival of the estate system of social organisation and the differential privileges it protected, plus the domination of political life by landed aristocrats and repressive government bureaucracies, aggravated all plebeian woes. These conditions had everything to do with the revolution of 1848, its causes and its meaning, as scholars such as P.H. Noyes, Dieter Langewiesche, Jürgen Kocka, Helmut Sedatis, Hartmut Zwahr and Jonathan Sperber have demonstrated: the problems and tensions in Germany that culminated in the 1848 revolutions were not only political but also profoundly economic and social.[5]

It is quite true, of course, that in 1848 most liberal businessmen and their allies in the intelligentsia had a limited view of the changes that Germany required. They hoped to take a nation still fragmented among thirty or so independent states and unite it into a powerful country able to assert itself on the world market and in world affairs. They wanted a constitutional monarchy and a parliament elected by those who owned a minimum of property. This, as one of them (Hesse-Darmstadt's Heinrich von Gagern) put it, would 'assure for the middle class a preponderant influence over the state.' Increased political power for businessmen, they expected, would make government friendlier to economic development. The latter project did not include plans for social levelling or even much social-welfare legislation (which David Hansemann derided as a manifestation of a 'hospital spirit' in politics).[6]

Some craftworkers and others with little or no property, however, clung to a distinct vision of what Germany should become in 1848. They, too, wanted a united Germany. They, too, wanted prosperity and economic growth. But they had their own ideas about how unity and prosperity should occur and who should benefit from them. Hostile to medieval hierarchies (both temporal and ecclesiastical) as well as to the ravages that modern commercial development was imposing upon small producers, such people sought to attain what one German labour leader called 'social freedom and independent existence' for everyone within a society free of exploitation and oppression.[7] Towards that end, they strove to eliminate great extremes of wealth and poverty and substitute a system offering free and universal education, progressive taxation, and social insurance for the sick, widowed and unemployed. Producers' and consumers' cooperatives sprang up, seeking salvation from the transformation of artisans into wage labourers, from their subordination to a small number of 'idlers', and from the appropriation by the latter of a growing share of social wealth. Rather than try to reform monarchy, such people sought a democratic republic based on universal male suffrage.

This radical-democratic constituency in 1848 was large, important and vocal enough to compel liberals to modify their own programme, softening their endorsement of *laissez-faire* policies and abandoning the attempt to base suffrage rights upon property ownership. But even as they tried to placate discontented and assertive plebeians, liberal-led governments also began to repress them and to wax a bit nostalgic about the aristocrats and monarchs who in the past had kept the troublesome rabble in its place. Popular disaffection with the liberals and liberal fears of the populace, mutually reinforcing, opened the door to counter-revolution in 1849.

The tumultuous 1840s left a deep impression on Germany and on those who departed for America in that decade and the next. Working people imbued to one degree or another with radical-democratic and vaguely socialistic values made up a significant (if impossible-to-count) component of the mass *Auswanderung* of that era. In America, some of the new immigrants became farmers, especially in such Midwestern states as Ohio, Illinois and Indiana. But becoming a farmer was neither cheap nor easy, even in the United States. In 1860, as the federal census revealed, about two out of every three Americans who had been born in Germany depended for their survival upon manufacturing or commerce.

What kind of life and labour did such employment imply? In some important ways, of course, it meant a life unquestionably better than the one lived in their homeland. Civic and political rights were incomparably greater in the USA than in Germany. So was individual economic opportunity. Employment levels and living standards were also generally markedly higher. Johann Carl Wilhelm Pritzlaff reported in 1842 that 'you can earn your daily bread better than in Germany, [here] one doesn't live so restrictedly and in such servitude as you do under great estate-owners, you don't have to put your hat under your arm or leave it at the door when you want to have the money you've earned'. And 'if one man works for another, he is not tied [indentured] to any particular time, rather he leaves when he wants to; everyone is his own master'. Even some who made little money could think of themselves as well off, especially in comparison with the extreme privation they remembered in Europe. Ernst Stille of Westphalia, having found work as a brick-maker in Cincinnati in the 1840s, happily informed his family and friends back home that 'a good worker can do his day's work in 10 hours, earn one dollar [for that day] and live well on that with a wife and children, and have such good food and drink like the best burgher in Lengenrich.'[8]

Many of these comparative economic advantages reflected precisely the greater dynamism of capitalist development in the USA than in early nineteenth-century Germany. American commerce and industry were booming in this period; in just a single generation following 1840, goods produced by American industry more than tripled in value. The pace of urbanisation was uneven on a national scale but startlingly rapid in important parts of the North (and most immigrants settled in the North). In 1790, fewer than one in ten Northeasterners had lived in towns or cities. By 1860, the proportion had surpassed one in three in both New England and the Middle Atlantic states (New York State, Pennsylvania and New Jersey). Those who prospered most from such development were, of course, the families who owned the largest commercial, financial and industrial enterprises. But some manual workers, especially those with the scarcest and most modern industrial skills, could also benefit significantly.

That same dynamic capitalism, however, also drove forward changes in the nature of traditional craft production in America (including the growth of wholesale production; stepped-up competition; and the intensification, division, deskilling, and then mechanisation of labour) that were anything but welcome to those dependent upon such work. As populous traditional trades such as tailoring, shoemaking, and cabinet-making succumbed to these changes, native-born youth began to flee, seeking refuge locally in more favoured occupations or moving westward in search of less competitive urban labour markets or independent farming. Immigrant workers, having fewer resources, had fewer options, especially if they were unable to speak English. They often found employment, therefore, precisely in those places and occupations where craft skill, living standards and prospects of eventual self-employment had most dramatically declined.

Here, then, was the meaning of the discovery, made by the author of one Civil War-era survey of American manufactures, that most of those escaping the 'overstocked labour markets of Europe' had 'found a market for their skill and labour in the large commercial cities and manufacturing towns', thereby alleviating 'the drain made by steadily westward migration from the older communities.'[9] The immigrant influx was so great, indeed (as one European visitor noted), that while in earlier years a labour shortage had plagued the USA, by the 1850s 'its seaboard – nay, three or more hundred miles inside it, is now satisfied with labour.'[10] The impact of industrial and demographic change actually extended even further inland than that: newspapers not only in New York but also in Chicago enthused that German craft workers were 'fitted to do the cheap and ingenious labour of the country.'[11] Periods of economic slump made matters considerably worse for working people, of course. In 1854–5 and again in 1857, staggering numbers suddenly found themselves without employment of any kind. The identity of those who suffered most emerges from an 1855 report by the New York Association for Improving the Conditions of the Poor: it was 'the mechanics of inferior character and skill, and especially the lower grade of labourers of both sexes, and their families, chiefly foreigners, that contribute to swell, at all seasons, the number of the permanently dependent.'[12]

A wide chasm thus opened between the ideals and hopes of many German immigrants and the realities that confronted them in America. America had proved no utopia; problems similar to those encountered in Europe seemed to have followed the immigrants to the New World. 'Many of us', recalled a writer for Chicago's *Illinois Staats-Zeitung*, 'were bitterly disappointed … when sanguine expectations proved to be mere bubbles' and we had to wage 'a severe fight for material existence.'[13] Peter Roedel, an immigrant shoemaker, told a receptive crowd in January 1855 that 'in our country we have fought for liberty and many of us have lost, in battle, our fathers, brothers, or sons.' In America, it is true, 'we are free, but not free enough', because here 'you don't get bread nor wood' for your fire, even though 'there is plenty of them ... We want', he exclaimed, 'the liberty of living.'[14]

Nor was dissatisfaction confined to the state of the economy. Hopes of obtaining relief from an even-handed, democratic state actively committed to protecting the weak against the powerful were also disappointed. Most political and economic notables in the USA, convinced that only an unregulated market could allocate resources justly and efficiently, saw neither need nor justification for governmental unemployment insurance or any other kind of public assistance to the poor. Immigrant textile worker Martin Weitz observed at such a moment that for the jobless in the USA 'it is much worse ... here than over there in Germany, because they don't take care of each other here, everyone has to look after himself.'[15] Many of the same politicians, moreover, who left common people to fend for themselves seemed all too ready to cater to the already prosperous. Meanwhile (and with vigorous support from powerful American churchmen) they firmly forbade some of the most cherished pleasures of the poor, such as the consumption of alcoholic beverages and public entertainment on the Sabbath.

What could be done? The solutions that some immigrants now championed drew upon ideals, causes and practical experiences honed in Europe. The society that enjoyed true freedom, they contended, was one that also offered a fairer distribution of labour, wealth and educational opportunities. Political liberties must be used to advance the cause of economic justice, and only greater economic equality among the people could provide a strong foundation for republican government. Once again, religious scepticism grew voluble. Once again groups of German workers sought salvation in producer and consumer societies. The outstanding cooperative advocate in German America was none other than the tailor Wilhelm Weitling, the most important labour leader in pre-1848 Germany.

To the disappointment of Weitling's allies and supporters, however, hopes of blocking the expansion of wage labour in this way proved vain. Fledgling cooperative enterprises simply could not survive in a profit-driven marketplace, and Weitling's once substantial following waned rapidly in the early 1850s. Larger numbers of hard-pressed immigrant craft workers tried instead to defend their condition and interests by fighting on the terrain of industrial capitalism, through the construction of labour unions and the calling of work stoppages. In 1850, 1853 and 1858, German-American workers put down their tools in large numbers and took to the streets, determined to resist attacks on their skills, living standards, dignity, and future prospects. In the midst, and often at the head, of such mobilisations other veterans of the recent revolutions in Europe reappeared – among them Fritz and Matthilde Anneke, Josef Weydemeyer, August Willich and Gustav Struve.

Wage disputes usually triggered such labour struggles, but organised workers also raised larger demands (for example, for collective labour contracts, standard wage rates, and union-shop guarantees) that infringed on the employer's presumed right unilaterally to govern the enterprise. When they addressed themselves to broader issues, unions sought the defence and extension of popular political rights (for example, the direct election and recall of all public officials). They also proposed that government take an active role in safeguarding the interests of working people with laws enacting land reform, imposing maximum-hours and minimum-wage standards, and forbidding child labour. During the economic crises of 1854–5 and 1857, mass meetings (in which Germans figured prominently) demanded that governments provide the jobless with food, shelter and employment on public-works projects, 'not as mere charity, but as a right'.[16]

In the course of these struggles, German-American labour organisations treated the experience of the 1840s (and above all, 1848) as a tradition to which *they* could appeal for inspiration and justification. This was readily apparent during the most dramatic labour confrontation involving German-American workers in this period, the large and violence-marked strike by New York City tailors in 1850. A mass meeting of immigrant working people that filled City Hall Park one day during that summer literally bristled with invocations of 1848. 'Many among us', an immigrant capmaker recalled there, 'have before been engaged in fighting for liberty in [the] Fatherland. Now, brethren,' he declared, '… it is time to fight again.' Yes, a tailor agreed: 'It is now necessary for the millions to rise to put down the despots and aristocrats who get the working men to work in droves for them like slaves and then laugh them to scorn.' A second tailor vowed that 'if necessary we will have another revolution rather than go on to be trodden down any longer.' A third urged, 'My brethren, my friends, my fellow citizens! revolution is the word! We must have a revolution; we cannot go on and submit any longer.' An American newspaper reporter noted that from the 'dense crowd', which had been punctuating this crescendo of Forty-Eighter rhetoric with cheers, there now erupted 'one loud, unanimous, long continued shout of consentient applause' accompanied by prolonged shouts of bravo! bravo![17]

Words and actions like these outraged most of the mainstream press and politicians in America, who insisted that, like all other citizens, industrious workers would reap the full fruits of their individual efforts. Government measures to provide jobs or incomes, they said, were alien to American life and liberty. They would only renew the old forms of dependency, paternalism and unfreedom typical of monarchical Europe. In reply to such strictures, some immigrants asserted that the right to live was a universal right, a right that *all* governments, regardless of their form, must respect. If working people had been able to secure recognition of that right from some of Europe's tyrants, they added, then surely they should expect even more consideration in a free, democratic republic.

This expansive definition of popular rights did little to mollify conservative critics. One writer generally sympathetic to German immigrants fretted over 'the excessive development of some of the worst tendencies of their character', as the result of which 'the earnest and industrious mechanic of Nuremberg grows into the tumultuous haranguer and street-fighter of New York.'[18] An English visitor to the Midwest found the same kind of concerns rife there. 'Skilled, educated, and intellectual,' wrote Isabella Lucy Bird in 1856, the recent German immigrants 'constitute an influence of which the Americans themselves are afraid.'[19]

Forty-Eighter radicalism and the labour militancy displayed by recently landed immigrant workers stoked the fires of an anti-foreign ('nativist') movement that had been growing in the USA, notably in its urban centres, since the mid-1840s. A leader of the nativist party in Ohio thus denounced

> the two extremes of the foreign population that are thrown amongst us, both the adherents of papal despotism on the one side, and disorganising Radicalism on the other – one embracing all that gives body and soul to the dictation and disposal of a temporal and spiritual potentate, who claims his power by Divine right – the other rejecting all authority but their own wild, discordant socialism. The superstitious and idolatrous tendencies of the one, and the atheistical agrarian nonsense of the other, are entirely antagonistic to the American character.[20]

In the opinion of the *New York Morning Express*, the continued growth of a German population of the latter type represented a danger 'infinitely more portentous' than the one represented by the

Irish. After all, 'the Irish, especially the Roman Catholic portion of them, are subject at least to their spiritual authorities.' But 'the German element, on the contrary, is, in the main, subject to no spiritual authority of any sort.'[21] A nativist leader in Pennsylvania complained about the 'very large class of the German immigrants' who were 'imbued with the German philosophy of European revolutionary leaders, and filled with new, strange, and bewildering theories of the destiny of man and of human society.' They spouted 'ultra, wild, and visionary schemes', and in their hands, 'liberty' became 'nothing more nor less than licentiousness' that 'must necessarily lead to a disregard for all law, human and divine.'[22] Nativist New York Congressman Thomas Richard Whitney, too, sounded the alarm about the followers of 'German visionaries and agitators … and especially those of the Red-republican and Socialist school.' 'Generally working-men and tradesmen, respectable in their sphere, and possessing the physical elements of usefulness', they were none the less carriers of a deadly plague – 'Red Republicanism, which by giving the "largest liberty", would paralyze industry, and render both life and property insecure.' 'They are the malcontents of the Old World, who hate monarchy, not because it is monarchy, but because it is restraint. They are such men as stood by the side of Robespierre …'[23]

The pattern of immigrant conduct sketched here and the intense response it elicited was the product not merely of a few thousand émigré intellectuals. Rather, it highlighted the fact that an important segment of a large immigrant generation had been influenced in Europe by the issues and methods of the 1840s. And when migration to a trans-Atlantic republic proved no panacea, many turned once again for inspiration and practical guidance to memories, measures and methods of Forty-Eighter vintage. This broad milieu of plebeian Forty-Eighter immigrants in the USA, incidentally, provided a mass following for many figures prominent in the European revolutions who would otherwise have been consigned in America to the role of isolated, impotent political exile.

The influence of Forty-Eighter radicals proved significant not only in the era's nascent conflicts between free labour and capital. It also became a factor in the struggle over slave labour that erupted in the USA's Civil War in 1861. That struggle spoke to matters close to the hearts and experience of many recent arrivals to American shores. Trade unions, strikes, mass demonstrations, support for the jobless – all such things sprang from and, in turn, reinforced a belief that, despite the many differences that distinguished them from one another, workers in different shops, trades, and even cities, workers from different nations, religions and languages: all of them shared many interests in common and must somehow band together to advance those interests. The principal labour federations that German Americans formed in the 1850s welcomed as members 'all workers who lived in the United States without distinction of occupation, language, color, or sex.'[24]

'Without distinction of ... color.' Those words were rarely heard anywhere in America in the 1850s. The enslavement of Africans and their children had by then been a fact of life in North America for more than 200 years (that is, since the early seventeenth century). To one degree or another, the doctrine that justified this fact, the doctrine of white supremacy and black inferiority, influenced all regions and all social classes in the United States. The organised labour movement was no exception. Few white workers in the North expressed much interest in the future of slavery or in the welfare of black Americans, whether slave or free.[25] More than a few immigrants also proved quick to adopt the racism so prevalent in their new homeland. Many Irish Americans took to it with notorious alacrity. So did some German immigrants. One watchmaker, recently transplanted to New York City from Berlin, did not take long to begin vehemently denouncing African Americans as 'a lazy, stinking race descended from apes.'[26]

But this man's sentiments were not typical, as a recent study of immigrant letters to the old country reveals.[27] German American were evidently much freer from of racial prejudice than were most whites in the United States. A German journalist travelling in North America reported unhappily that 'by treating black men with a certain familiarity and good nature', the German immigrant 'lowers himself even more in the estimation of the [social] circle to which he belongs.' Sometimes, thus, the writer continued, 'in answer to the question, "Was he a white man?" one will hear, "No, sir, he was a Dutchman".'[28] More than a decade later, the *New York Times* was still reporting that 'the only class in this City who appear to be really uninfluenced by [the] intolerant spirit of prejudice against the color of the negro are the Germans.'[29]

German-born labour and democratic activists fought against the powerful current of colour prejudice with particular vigour and for a specific reason. Their experiences in Europe in both trade-union and democratic struggles had taught them important lessons about the meaning and importance of solidarity and had committed them to the belief that civic rights must be made universal. So it was that societies and meetings of German-American democrats placed themselves on record during the 1850s as being against widespread discrimination against free blacks in the free states, a stance until then associated chiefly with free blacks themselves and a modest cadre of mostly Anglo-American abolitionists.

As the conflict in the USA between the free states and the slave states sharpened during the mid-1850s, important organisations and leaders of German-American labour took strong stands against slavery and against the political representatives of the slave-owners. Slavery, such Forty-Eighter immigrants believed, was 'wholly repugnant to the principles of true democracy.'[30] What institution could more easily evoke bitter memories of the European aristocracy (whose culture American planters attempted to mimic) and the system of unequal privilege and unfree labour upon which that aristocracy rested? Slavery, indeed, was 'the worst form in which Despotism appears', noted Gustav Struve. After all, 'Louis Napoleon and the Austrian Emperor leave their subjects their personal freedom, however limited it may be by their tyranny.' Even they 'do not sell men, women and children in the public market.'[31] Former slave and abolitionist leader Frederick Douglass expressed the opinion in 1859 that 'a German has only to be a German to be utterly opposed to slavery. In feeling, as well as in conviction and principle, they are antislavery.' This, Douglass supposed, was the result of their bitter national experience under tyrants at home, which disposed them to recognise 'the value of liberty and to advocate more warmly than [native-born] Americans the equal rights of all men.'[32]

German Americans of the Forty-Eighter immigration were some of the first in the United States to call for and rally to a mass anti-slavery party in the mid-1850s: the Republican Party. A typical case was Franz Arnold, an immigrant mechanic from Frankfurt-am-Main who had worked tirelessly to organise German-American trade unions and cooperative associations, and who proudly styled himself 'a hater of slavery' and 'Southern oppression.'[33] In the presidential campaigns of 1856 and especially 1860, such people appeared in the front ranks of those supporting the new anti-slavery Republican Party. And like the striking tailors of 1850, they commonly summoned their colleagues to action by drawing parallels to the still-fresh memories of 1848. As Gustav Struve, once again, put it: 'Show that it was not the excitement of the moment which drove you on to the course of liberty; that you know for what you fought, for what Robert Blum and other brave ones bled! The great question of freedom takes different forms in the Old and New World. In all its essentials it is the same. Those who beyond the ocean are the aristocrats, are here the slaveholders – those who would reap but not labour.'[34]

Within the Republican Party, furthermore, German-born democrats tended to ally with the radical wing and to oppose those who wanted to make major concessions to the slave-holders. To dramatise the dangers of such conciliationism, they drew a parallel to the ambivalent, half-hearted liberals who had led the Frankfurt Parliament. August Bondi, a young veteran of the revolution in Vienna, made this point as he reflected upon the guerrilla war that erupted in the Kansas Territory during the mid-1850s. Bondi scorned well-to-do northern 'cowards' who had hesitated to confront pro-slavery forces boldly; they 'belonged to that class with whom interest always counts for more than principle, as was the case in 1848 in Germany.' Theodor Hielscher, a schoolteacher who had played a prominent role in Berlin in 1848, fired at the same target with the same type of ammunition. 'In 1848', he reminded his readers, 'during the revolution in Germany, there was [sic] also such men.' Their counsel was no more useful now than it had been there: 'Though others could see that the kings, dukes and princes had formed a secret league in order to overthrow the popular will, these gentlemen boldly asserted that they were "unable" to see the signs of the gathering storm ... And yet I remember having met one of these men who could not see a "reaction", as it was called in 1848, fleeing before the bayonets of the soldiers in 1849, and all he had to say, when I asked him whether he was now able to see the "reaction", was "Who would have thought it possible!"'.[35]

Thus did European experiences in the recent past once again inform conduct in the present. When the Civil War broke out in 1861, German-American labour and allied organisations contributed thousands of volunteers to the Union army. All told, some 200,000 (or roughly 10 percent) of those who served in the Union army during the war were German-born, and 36,000 of these soldiers served in all-German units under German commanders. The socially progressive *Turnvereine* were particularly active in recruiting and organising such forces. *Turners* and former *Turners* alone supplied 7,000 to 8,000 troops and whole army units in Ohio, New York, Illinois and Pennsylvania. A typical example was the case of Cincinnati, where a meeting in *Turner* hall initiated the formation of the all-German Ninth Ohio Infantry Regiment. August Willich was elected adjutant, later major. 'The spirit of 1848', exulted a veteran of the German revolution, 'has once more awakened.'[36]

In January 1863, President Abraham Lincoln finally proclaimed the slave labourers of the rebellious South to be free. That proclamation was highly controversial in the North. But the country's leading organisation of German labour mobilised its supporters strongly to endorse emancipation. Many went still further, pressing the demand, which the Republican Party rejected, that not only slaves but also the great plantations of the former slave-owners should be confiscated, and that this land should be distributed among poor whites and blacks alike.

Victory over the slave-holders in the Civil War that ended in 1865 made possible even faster economic development in the decades that followed. By the 1880s, indeed, the United States was replacing Great Britain as the premier industrial nation of the world. For enterprising individuals, this postwar era abounded in personal opportunity. Compendia of notable German Americans, and many state and city histories published in the late nineteenth and early twentieth centuries, brim over with the names of immigrant artisans, shopkeepers,and professionals whose children and grandchildren climbed the ladders of economic, social and political prominence. As they did so, many became steadily more conservative socially and politically.

Quite a few … but not all. Others associated with working-class Forty-Eighter causes remained loyal to them, and their ranks were reinforced by new waves of immigrant plebeians who carried with them memories of more recent labour and democratic struggles in Europe. Such German-American workers and others who identified with them played important roles in the historic upsurges of organised labour that occurred in the USA during late 1860s, 1870s, and 1880s. These were not among the people whom Carl Schurz would celebrate for having become 'reliable and conservative citizens'. Despite that fact, or perhaps because of it, they left their mark on the history of the times.

Forty-Eighters, to be sure, were not the first people in North America to call for social control over economic life, to assert the right to live and work regardless of the verdict rendered upon them by the marketplace. Nor did these immigrant German Forty-Eighters raise the idea of collective action and trade unions for the first time in North America. But both of these ideas – organisation and collective action among working people and attempts to impose community values upon economic life – came under strong and swiftly escalating attack from the champions of Adam Smith's *laissez-faire* views in the first half of the nineteenth century. The appearance on American soil of these veterans of Germany's turbulent 1840s did much to strengthen resistance to this ideological and practical offensive. The Forty-Eighter-era immigrants described here rejected the idea that 'survival of the fittest', the Darwinian law of the jungle, was also the last word in human civilisation. They insisted that the fight for democracy was as important in the economy as it was in government. And they struggled to teach others the importance of mutual aid and mutual support – in other words, the importance of solidarity.

In all these things, paradoxically, just as in the fight against slavery, the fact that they were 'alien', steeped in a distinctive experience, allowed German Forty-Eighters to play an important role in organising and influencing the outlook of organised labour in America. By clinging to their old ways, they helped change some Americans' notions about what freedom meant, what it required, and who deserved its blessings. Or, to employ the anxious language of their nativist detractors, the 'moral poisons' that the immigrants brought with them into the United States became partially 'infused and incorporated with the body politic here', and 'a considerable portion of our own people' became 'wedded to strange and dangerous doctrines.'[37]

Notes

1 See, for example, Lewis B. Namier, *1848: The Revolution of the Intellectuals* (Oxford, 1946); Charles Moraze, *The Triumph of the Middle Classes: A Political and Social History of Europe in the Nineteenth Century* (Garden City, NY, 1968), pp. x, 290.

2 Marcus Lee Hansen, 'The Revolution of 1848 and the German Emigration', *Journal of Economic and Business History*, 2 (August 1930), pp. 630–1; Hildegard Binder Johnson, 'Adjustment to the United States', in A.E. Zucker (ed.), *The Forty-Eighters: Political Refugees of the German Revolution of 1848* (New York, 1950; rpt. New York, 1967), p. 43.

3 A.E. Zucker, 'Biographical Dictionary of the Forty-Eighters', in Zucker (ed.), *The Forty-Eighters*, p. 269.

4 Carl Schurz, *Speeches, Correspondence, and Political Papers*, ed. Frederic Bancroft (New York 1913; rpt. New York, 1969), V, p. 470.

5 P.H. Noyes, *Organization and Revolution: Working-Class Associations in the German Revolution of 1848–49* (Princeton, 1966); Helmut Sedatis, *Liberalismus und Handwerk in Südwestdeutschland* (Stuttgart, 1979); Jürgen Kocka, *Lohnarbeit und Klassenbildung: Arbeiter und Arbeiterbewegung in Deutschland, 1800–1875* (Berlin, 1983); Friedrich Lenger, *Zwischen Kleinbuergertum und Proletariat: Studien zur Sozialgeschichte der Düsseldorfer Handwerker, 1816–1878* (Göttingen, 1986); Dieter Langewiesche, *Liberalismus und Demokratie zwischen Revolution und Reichgruendung* (Düsseldorf, 1974); Jonathan Sperber, *Rhineland Radicals: The Democratic Movement and the Revolution of 1848–1849* (Princeton, 1991).

6 Donald G. Rohr, *The Origins of Social Liberalism in Germany* (Chicago, 1963), pp. 95–6.

7 Stephan Born, *Erinnerungen eines Achtundvierzigers mit dem Bildnis dem Verfassers* (3rd edn, Leipzig, 1898), pp. 144–5.

8 Both letters reprinted in Walter D. Kamphoefner, Wolfgang Helbich and Ulrike Sommer (eds), *News from the Land of Freedom: German Immigrants Write Home* (Ithaca and London, 1991), pp. 85–6, 306.

9 J. Leander Bishop, *A History of American Manufactures from 1608 to 1860* (3rd edn, Philadelphia, 1868), II, p. 477.

10 Quoted in Kerby A. Miller, *Emigrants and Exiles: Ireland and the Irish Exodus to North America* (New York, 1985), p. 321.

11 *New York Daily Times*, 3 March 1854; *Chicago Daily Tribune*, 7 March 1854.

12 W.J. Rorabaugh, *The Craft Apprentice: From Franklin to the Machine Age in America* (New York, 1986), p. 133.

13 *Illinois Staats-Zeitung*, 26 July 1861.

14 *New York Herald*, 16 January 1855.

15 In Kamphoefner, et al, *News from the Land of Freedom*, pp. 355–6.

16 *New York Herald*, 6 November 1857.

17 *New York Herald*, 27 July 1850; 5 , 7 August 1850.

18 J. D. Angell, 'German Emigration to America', *North American Review*, 82 (1856), p. 265.

19 Isabella Lucy Bird, *The Englishwoman in America* (1856; rpr., Madison, 1966), pp. 119–20.

20 Thomas Spooner, *Report of the President of State Council of Ohio* (5 June 1855), p. 10.

21 *New York Morning Express*, 21 June 1854.

22 John P. Sanderson, *Republican Landmarks: The Views and Opinions of American Statesmen on Foreign Immigration* (Philadelphia, 1856), pp. 219, 225, 227.

23 Thomas R. Whitney, *A Defence of the American Policy, as Opposed to the Encroachments of Foreign Influence* (New York, 1856), pp. 169–71.

24 *Die Sociale Republik*, 29 January 1859, 12 March 1859.

25 See esp. David Roediger, *The Wages of Whiteness: Race and the Making of the American Working Class* (New York, 1991).

26 H. Wobeser to 'mother, brother, and sister in law', 23 June 1864; copy in author's possession.

27 Walter D. Kamphoefner, '"Auch unser Deutschland muss einmal frei werden": The Immigrant Civil War Experience as a Mirror on Political Conditions in Germany', in David E. Barclay and Elisabeth Glaser-Schmidt (eds), *Transatlantic Images and Perceptions: Germany and America since 1776* (New York, 1997), pp. 99–100, 102, 107.

28 Karl Buechele, *Land und Volk der Vereinigten Staaten von Nord-Amerika* (Stuttgart, 1855), p. 279.

29 *New York Daily Times*, 2 March 1869.

30 *State Gazette* (Trenton, NJ), 6 December 1851.

31 *New York Daily Times*, 25 July 1856.

32 Frederick Douglass, 'Adopted Citizens and Slavery', *Douglass's Monthly*, August 1859.

33 *New York Daily Times*, 22 October 1856.

34 *New York Daily Times*, 25 July 1856.

35 August Bondi, 'With John Brown in Kansas', *Transactions of the Kansas State Historical Society*, 8 (1903–4), pp. 278, 285; *Indianapolis Journal*, 21 February 1860.

36 *New Yorker Criminal Zeitung und Belletristisches Journal*, 26 April 1861.

37 *New York Morning Express*, 21 June 1854; An Address delivered by Thomas R. Whitney, Esq., December 23, 1851 ... on the Occasion of the Seventh Anniversary of Alpha Chapter, Order of United Americans (New York, [1852], pp. [10–11].

IV

Women in Exile

15

Keeping busy in the Waiting-Room:
German Women Writers in London following the 1848 Revolution

Carol Diethe

When an estimated 5,000 German émigrés began to stream out of Germany from 1849 onwards in order to escape the *Reaktion* which was swiftly gathering pace, they headed in three principal directions: America if they wanted to build a completely new life, London if they wanted to return to Germany, and Switzerland if they wanted temporary respite in a neutral country which discouraged permanent immigration. Germans who made their way to England, and almost invariably to London, joined a population of German expatriots already numbering roughly 40,000.[1] Since the Hanoverian succession, German culture had influenced English aesthetics – to the point where Händel was adopted as an honorary Londoner. The Romantic movement in the arts and the entry of Queen Victoria's consort Prince Albert of Saxe-Coburg into London life accentuated this cross-fertilisation. However, the 'hungry forties' were a period of misery for the poor in Britain as in the rest of Europe and there were plenty of German families living in London in starvation. The decade saw angry grass-roots reactions to social injustices so that by 1848, when the Chartist monster petition ended in fiasco, writers such as Dickens and Gaskell were warning their readers of the imminent danger of revolution if demands for better social conditions were not met. The freedom to write such things struck the incoming German émigrés, many of whom were writers, as the epitome of political liberty. Their enchantment was invariably swiftly tempered by the shock of discovering the labyrinthine inequalities dictated by the social customs of good society. Bereft of words to describe the intricacies of gentility, they pepper their works with English words for which they feel no German equivalent exists: 'respectable',[2] 'finished young ladies',[3] 'dandies',[4] 'snobs'.[5]

Among the German families exiled in London after the 1848 revolution, the husbands tended to have the education of a gentleman and the income of a butler, a fact which placed great stress on their wives. Single women were even worse off, although there was a demand for German lessons and German governesses were in vogue; there was thus ample opportunity for work which was badly paid but genteel. The two women writers whose work I shall chiefly examine here, Johanna Kinkel, who came to London in 1850, and Malwida von Meysenbug, who came to London in 1852, made their living – initially at least – by giving private lessons: in Johanna's case, piano lessons and in Malwida's case, German lessons. However, I shall begin by discussing the experiences of Jenny Marx, who came to London in September 1849. Born in Trier in 1814, she married her childhood sweetheart Karl Marx in 1843. Like Johanna Kinkel, Jenny was a few years older than her husband. For both women this raised certain problems, but these appear to have been resolved in Jenny's case whereas Johanna Kinkel, in her darkest moments, felt old and ugly in comparison to her splendidly tall and handsome husband, a topic to which I shall return. Jenny Marx became her husband's amanuensis, working her fingers to the bone producing fine copy of Marx's work for the publisher and sublimating any desire she herself might have harboured to write creatively on her own account. A very brief autobiographical sketch by Jenny Marx, the only legacy of writing she left apart from her letters and several rather good theatre reviews,[6] bears witness to the pressure upon her throughout the period covered (the account ends in 1865). Quite apart from revealing the personal difficulties of rearing a young family in cramped conditions, Jenny's account speaks of the destitution of most political émigrés as well as highlighting their tendency to form splits:

> Thousands of fugitives arrived daily; they were all more or less in dire straits, few had any means, all were dependent on others and in need of help. This was one of the most unpleasant periods in our life of emigration. Emigrant committees were organized to assist the émigrés, meetings were arranged, appeals made, programs drawn up, and great demonstrations were prepared. In all the emigrant circles dissensions broke out. The various parties gradually split up completely.[7]

As Jenny Marx goes on to point out, 'the leaders of the factions attacked one another with great viciousness'.[8] It comes as no surprise, then, that Marx attacked Kinkel with open hostility,[9] dubbing him a 'kleinbürgerliche[r] Demokrat',[10] and foaming against his weekly *Hermann*, founded in 1859. Edgar Bauer, a journalist who wrote for the *Rheinische Zeitung*, which Marx edited in Cologne 1842–3 until it was forced to cease publication, was equally damning about Kinkel, whom he thought affected and a womaniser; he comments drily that as far as he has heard, 'Frau Kinkel is actually the man of the house, the real Herr Kinkel'.[11] The Kinkels in turn regarded Marx and his short-lived weekly *Das Volk* (which appeared from May to August 1859) as dangerously radical.[12] Kinkel wisely gave Marx wide a berth, though they had friends in common, not least the ageing Bettine von Arnim (who died in 1859) and Ferdinand Freiligrath, once he had conquered his prejudice against Kinkel (a prejudice orchestrated by Marx). Freiligrath came to London in 1851. When Johanna Kinkel died in 1858 as a result of a fall from a window, he commemorated her death with a poem. The curmudgeonly Marx observed bitterly that Freiligrath had never managed to produce a commemorative poem for a fellow communist.[13]

Soon, the new wave of German émigrés had settled into two opposing camps: the socialists, who streamed in and out of Karl Marx's tiny flat in Chelsea, from 1851 turning to Arnold Ruge's premises when Marx decamped to the British Museum, and the democrats, who regarded the Kinkel household in St John's Wood and later Paddington as their headquarters and made themselves at home there to an extent which greatly impinged on the Kinkels' private life.[14] Understandably, both Jenny Marx and Johanna Kinkel complained of this abuse of their hospitality. The health of both women was affected by their cramped living conditions and by the burdens placed upon them over and above those of performing the duties of *Hausfrau* with minimal domestic help.[15] Like their male counterparts, émigré German women tended to mix mainly with their fellow émigrés; contacts with English people were a secondary consideration. As Betty Lucas revealed, Jenny Marx was virtually housebound for the first few years of her life in London,[16] though when she moved to Hampstead Heath in 1856 she felt she had thrown in her lot with the suburban philistines and that life was now nowhere near as much fun. Most of all, she missed the hustle and bustle of Soho:

> I often missed my long walks in the crowded West End streets after my meetings, our clubs, and the familiar public house with the cosy conversations, which had so often helped me to forget my worries for a while. Luckily I still had to copy out an article for the *Tribune* twice a week, and that helped to keep me *au courant* with world events.[17]

Emigré coteries of every nationality followed the same pattern, though with the Russians, Alexander Herzen's wealth guaranteed hospitality on a grander footing. Nevertheless he, too, suffered from the disruption of a constant stream of visitors, whether from Russia or other countries, notably Poland.[18] Though Jenny Marx, like most of the German exiles in London, at first firmly believed that it was only a matter of time before the family could return to Germany, by the time she had spent a decade in London she had to concede that her children were growing up as English citizens:

> All three children are Londoners body and soul and are completely English in their customs, manners, inclinations, needs and habits. There is nothing worse for them than the terrible thought that they might have to exchange England for Germany, and I must confess that I – even I – dread it ... Expensive though London is, I think we live more cheaply here than we could in Germany ... And we can get credit here and occupy a very cheap little house. Above all, London is so colossal that you can just disappear ... Here one can withdraw oneself into one's shell and nobody will take any notice, while in Germany, every one knows what you had for dinner the previous evening and what your husband earns.[19]

Paradoxically perhaps, the most accurate portrait we have of the life of German émigrés in London in the years following the 1848 revolution is found in Johanna Kinkel's novel *Hans Ibeles in London: Ein Roman aus dem Flüchtlingsleben*, which, though a fictional account, contains much that is demonstrably true, both in terms of the Kinkels' own experience and in terms of generalities, since many of the details, such as the rush among the British poor to emigrate to the colonies[20] if the fare could be found, are corroborated or enlarged upon in Malwida von Meysenbug's memoirs.[21] Johanna Kinkel grew up as a Catholic in Bonn; her brief first marriage ended in separation after six months. In spite of parental discouragement, she funded her own music studies in Berlin by giving private tuition – her innovatory ideas on music teaching were highly regarded at the time. While still a student of music in Berlin in 1832, she was snapped up as resident music teacher by Bettine von Arnim. By the time of her death in 1858, she was a much sought-after piano teacher. She met Gottfried Kinkel in 1839, but they were not able to marry until after the death of Johanna's first husband in 1843, by which time Johanna had converted to Protestantism, though she was fundamentally a sceptic. Apart from *Hans Ibeles in London*, Johanna Kinkel's only other substantial piece of writing is the highly accomplished novella *Musikalische Orthodoxie*, published in the volume *Erzählungen von Gottfried und Johanna Kinkel* in 1849.

Although the discussion about the extent to which *Hans Ibeles in London* is a *roman-à-clef* has unduly crowded out consideration of the work as a literary masterpiece, one has to be clear as to the likely autobiographical details in the novel in order to avoid making incorrect statements about the Kinkels themselves. The heroine of the novel, Dorothea Ibeles née Dewald, is of noble birth (unlike Johanna Kinkel), yet she chooses to fulfil the role of Frau Ibeles, the industrious housewife, rather than mix with other aristocratic émigrés in London such as Gräfin Blafosky. The latter entices the composer and gifted pianist Hans Ibeles into her salon, although he at first agrees with his wife that nothing is more enervating than its waiting-room atmosphere, which feeds the émigrés' hopes for a swift return to Germany and deprives them of the energy to seek meaningful work. Though Dorothea Ibeles shuns the 'cloud cuckoo land into which the disappointed revolutionaries retreated',[22] she watches with concern while her husband Johannes is forced to take on demeaning tasks as music teacher which leave him no leisure to create his own compositions. This was actually the situation in which Johanna Kinkel, as a gifted composer and musician in her own right, found herself in London. With delicate health, she had to battle through a daily quota of private music lessons as well as keep house for Kinkel and her four children (Dorothea has seven in the novel). As Helen Chambers remarks, married life left Johanna Kinkel little time for creative work, musical or literary.[23] By transposing her gift for composing music onto the fictional character Hans Ibeles, and then worrying aloud about the deleterious effect the smothering of his creative genius will have on him as a person, Johanna Kinkel is able to distance herself from a source of deep conflict in her own life, one which perhaps found some resolution through the creative act of writing the novel.

Gottfried Kinkel, trained in theology but by the time of his exile an established writer on cultural topics and art history, was the centre point of émigré German democratic focus and as such was persuaded to make a fund-raising tour to America in 1851–2.[24] His absence appears to have depressed Johanna considerably, though upon his return he was able to establish his reputation in London as a lecturer. People flocked to hear his charismatic delivery. As already mentioned, Johanna Kinkel felt that Kinkel's beauty contrasted with her own singular lack of good looks and in moments of self-doubt she expressed her feeling of inferiority *viv-à-vis* Kinkel's physical attributes,[25] so that it is all the more poignant that the bereaved Gottfried Kinkel, in a letter to his friend Rodenberg, singled out her beauty as one of the qualities he missed most: 'Dear Rodenberg, I am so miserable – and what will become of this life without the beauty, music and glow of freedom which this woman carried in her rich breast?'[26] At the time of her death, some of Johanna Kinkel's friends suspected that she had committed suicide as a result of her husband's philandering. However, there is nothing in Kinkel's biography to suggest that he was a womaniser, although he was certainly the darling of the ladies. There is nothing, either, to suggest that Johanna threw herself from her bedroom window to commit suicide rather than fell, possibly in the grip of a heart attack, in a tragic attempt to gain air. Thus one must conclude that the fictional Hans Ibeles and his wife are only tangentially similar to the Kinkels in their experiences of London exile, as portrayed in *Hans Ibeles in London*, where the resourceful Dorothea wins back her husband's affection after he has been temporarily infatuated with a spiritualist actress Livia. The sexually alluring Livia actually turns out to be none other than Lora O'Nalley, recently pardoned for murdering her husband, in disguise. Although this plot sounds melodramatic, Johanna Kinkel has a genius for spinning a yarn with sufficient realism and humour to keep the reader turning the pages, while all the time we remain aware of the deeper message, that appearances are deceptive and that handsome is as handsome does.

If Dorothea Ibeles' determination to give her children a German education cannot be taken as an accurate account of what Johanna Kinkel actually did, it must surely reflect the attitude of many newly arrived exiles who, convinced that their return to Germany was imminent,[27] wished their children to be prepared for German life. Gottfried Kinkel lamented the fact that he was sometimes too busy to educate his own children.[28] Other émigrés went further than this and thought that too much mixing in English society would be a waste of time. The singer Frau Gerard in the novel is just such a woman. Rather than seek to assert herself in this new society, she retreats into grindingly boring domesticity, mending clothes instead of earning good money through her profession.[29] Thus, though the status of the novel as a *roman-à-clef* can and must be questioned, the ambience of the work nevertheless evokes an unforgettable picture of the struggles of German émigrés as they enter an unfamiliar land of fog,[30] strange customs and incomprehensible vowels.

The Ibeles family are mystified by the determination of every house to boast a pocket handkerchief of garden rather than provide a proper, shared open space for several dwellings, a feature of English life still dear and ineradicable, while the thin lath and plaster walls defeat attempts to drive nails in,[31] and the sash windows are heavy and potentially hazardous. Indeed, the toddler Cilla Ibeles tumbles out of an upstairs window in the story, escaping injury, though the incident chillingly foreshadows the author's own fatal fall two years later.

The all-female Beak family in the house opposite demonstrate a united stiff upper lip when witnessing the arrival of a family of émigré neighbours, but this melts into the equally characteristic English kindness on the occasion of Cilla's fall from the window and, indeed, the novel gives a generally positive appreciation of the English way of life. In a letter written in September 1853 to Carl Fresenius, an old friend of the *Maikäfer* era in the mid-1840s when the Kinkels presided over a small literary salon in Berlin, Johanna Kinkel wrote:'[t]he people here are mostly kind and good and we have nearly always had a friendly reception in exile.'[32] True, such matters as the excessive formality of educational practices are persiflaged in her novel, but rather than attack English customs as irretrievably divisive or just plain wrong, as Malwida von Meysenbug is wont to do, Johanna Kinkel launches her attacks with a much more effective weapon, humour. She makes us laugh at English music lessons in which pupils lose the rhythm by having simultaneously to count 'one two three four.'[33] And though Dorothea Ibeles in the novel is just as shocked by 'idle ladies' as Malwida, Johanna Kinkel the writer recognises their underlying unhappiness behind the trivial social pursuits, as August Bebel would do.[34] Though Dorothea Ibeles finds solace as well as frustration in performing the domestic tasks which the ladies in the Blafosky circle leave to their servants, she comes to realise that her time can be better spent in educating her children, whereupon she hires a second maid. It is worth mentioning that in real life, Johanna Kinkel took herself off to the British Museum to revise her manuscript, demonstrating a level of *de facto* emancipation which ties in with her refusal to portray the overworked protagonist *Hausfrau* as heroic *per se*.

Mention has already been made of the inconsiderate use made of Kinkel's home by his political émigré friends; Hans Ibeles in the novel is similarly inundated, so that 'his tiny house is a meeting place for refugees'[35] and wryly dubbed 'the forum'[36] by his wife

Dorothea. In real life, Baroness Bruiningk appears unwittingly to have abused Kinkel's hospitality; certainly, Malwida von Meysenbug reports in her memoirs that the former friendship between the Baroness and Kinkel cooled.[37] The Baroness then held her own coterie and it has been suggested that the flighty and superficial Gräfin Blafosky is modelled on her in the novel, an assumption refuted by Carl Schurz.[38] Suffice it to say that there is a tone of authorial sincerity in Dorothea Ibeles' complaints about the tyranny of the visitors to their house. Quite apart from the expense of entertaining them, there is the loss of that commodity so precious to the artist: time,[39] a commodity which Malwida von Meysenbug, too, recognised as a 'great capital asset'.[40] Because Gräfin Blafosky resents Hans Ibeles' refusal to flirt with her, she plans a refined revenge on Dorothea, who has decided to boycott Blafosky's time-wasting *soirées*. Gräfin Blafosky takes into her house the aristocratic Hulda von Saintford who, during the 1849 revolution, helped Hans Ibeles to escape from hiding after the collapse of the barricades he had been defending.[41] Ibeles is thus enticed to visit the Blafosky house almost every evening out of gratitude to Hulda, and eventually he does submit to female wiles, though not to those of Gräfin Blafosky or Hulda but the dusky 'Mata Hari' figure of Livia, alias Mrs O'Nalley in brown make-up. It is characteristic of Johanna Kinkel's skill that she unmasks Livia, not through theatricality, but by the more ordinary and believable device of allowing Livia's brown make-up to become smudged. Even then, Livia is dismissed with humanity, her sexuality on view as tawdry and calculating, while with one blistering kiss, which suitably forms the climax to the book and is the more effective for its late arrival, Hans Ibeles puts paid to all his wife's fears about his faithfulness. As the author wryly comments, a kiss can be very persuasive.[42]

If the novel gives us a portrait of an émigré family loosely based on the Kinkel's own experiences, it also provides insights into the unenviable life of governesses in England at the time. Christine Lattek has suggested that Meta Braun's autobiography, inserted into Chapter Eleven as 'Manuscript of the German Governess', was penned as a portrait of Malwida von Meysenbug,[43] and Sabine Sundermann has recently surmised that it might be based on her writing.[44] Ruth-Ellen Boetcher Joeres steers clear of seeking hidden biographical references in the novel to the exclusion of other considerations and simply points out that the fictional portrayal of Meta Braun is the closest Johanna Kinkel comes to describing what would today be called a feminist,[45] though as we shall see, Malwida von Meysenbug's enthusiasm for the women's movement showed a marked cooling once she had left England. I would agree with a remark made by Carl Schurz, a mutual friend of both Johanna Kinkel and Malwida von Meysenbug, to the effect that there is no reason to assume that Meta Braun in the novel is based on Malwida von Meysenbug in real life,[46] especially as Malwida studiously avoided putting herself forward as a governess: 'the lot of a governess is wretched', she wrote.[47] And further: Meta Braun is disloyal to Dorothea Ibeles in a way which would have been quite foreign to Malwida von Meysenbug: Meta engineers Hulda's invitation to stay with Gräfin Blafosky, hoping thereby to keep Hulda well away from Hans Ibeles' friend Dr Stern, with whom she is in love, a tactic which incidentally backfires when Stern and Hulda eventually marry. Meta's emigration to a new life in a new country – Australia – echoes the theme, already touched upon, of emigration to the new colonies as a common solution to British social problems. By the end of her novel, Johanna Kinkel, writing in 1858, is able to report that, as in her own life, the material situation of her émigré family has improved, a trend already documented with regard to Jenny Marx.

Like many Germans before and after them, Jenny Marx and Johanna Kinkel felt *comfortable* in London, possibly because their role as wife and mother awarded them a certain status in Victorian England. This contrasts with the experience of single women such as Malwida von Meysenbug and Amalie Bölte.[48] Both were well educated and from genteel homes,[49] even if these homes had become impoverished, as in the case of Amalie Bölte, Fanny Tarnow's niece. Bölte was not a political exile, having come to England as a governess of her own free will in 1839. She was lucky in that she found several fortunate placements and a circle of influential friends which included the Carlyles. Her voluminous correspondence with Varnhagen von Ense provides a rich source of information (much of it gossip) on the Carlyles and other notables in London at the time.[50] The visit of Fanny Lewald to London in 1850 on what we would now call a publicity tour was something of a coup for Bölte, who undertook to show Germany's leading female writer around. However, the arrangements made were apparently not lavish enough, and Lewald proceeded to Edinburgh, leaving a hostile note of farewell for Bölte which the latter promptly forwarded to Varnhagen von Ense, complaining of Lewald's caprice.[51] Bölte also told him of the antics of the political émigrés, with whom she mixed only on sufferance.

'Good heavens!', she writes. 'If it lay in my hand I would lock them all up as madmen. Their "blood must flow" makes me quite ill.'[52]

By 1851, Bölte had become too ill to continue as governess and she returned to Germany, where she devoted herself to writing. During her time in England, Bölte wrote several pieces of interest to the present study. The tale *Louise, oder die Deutsche in England* (*Louise, or the German Girl in England*) (1846) fires an early salvo at the abuses heaped upon the governess,[53] before delineating the hell of other paid employment open to respectable young women at the time: teaching and needlework. Bölte depicts the horrors of the sweatshop, where the girls labour all night so that ball dresses can be ready for wealthy women, as though such conditons were unique to industrial Britain. However, as Louise Otto was busy pointing out in Germany, which had not yet become an industrialised state, conditions for women who had to earn a living by such work as lace-making were also atrocious.[54] Clearly, Bölte takes a rosy view of German life which is no doubt informed by nostalgia. In *Eine deutsche Palette in London* (*A German Palette in London*) (1846), the descriptions of the snubs Franz Hartung, a budding artist, receives in society imply that artists were tolerated in high society Germany, whereas the snobbery of the *Residenz* in a small German state could be just as philistine. The writer Bruno Gärtner's hopeless attachment to Josephine von Savern in Louise Otto's *Vier Geschwister* (*Two Brothers and Two Sisters*) (1851) provides a fictional example of the situation.

In 'Die Gedächtnisfeier in Oxford' ('The Commemorative Ceremony in Oxford'), the first of four tales in *Erzählungen aus der Mappe einer Deutschen* (*Tales From the Portfolio of a German Girl in London*) (1848), Amalie Bölte gives a detailed description of the tutorial system in Oxford. She criticises the exclusion of women students in this hallowed nexus of academe yet fails to make mention of the similarly parlous state of German girls' education. There is no mention of the moves afoot to better the educational opportunitites of women in England: for example, Queen's College, a teacher-training establishment, was founded in 1848, albeit with male tutors.[55] Bölte highlights the tyranny of the High Church in educational matters: the astronomer Gensen, though recognised as a world expert, is not allowed to take part in the graduation procession because nobody in Oxford can vouch for his religious faith. The disingenuous Ida is astonished to find that the Oxford notables know nothing of Johannes Ronge, the German Catholic firebrand active during the 1840s.[56] Some of her criticism is pertinent: there was anti-Catholic bias in Britain and the first question asked of a governess at any interview usually concerned her religious faith. The English upper-class method of bringing up children, especially boys, was viewed by the incomers as unwarrantably rigid. One should add that even today there is still plenty of criticism of the educational practices in boys' public schools such as Eton – which Bölte spells 'Eaton'.[57] Nevertheless, since Amalie Bölte spent some time working for the family of Sir Isaac Goldsmid, a banker who had helped to found University College, to which was attached the nondenominational boys' school, University College School (which Johanna Kinkel's sons attended), her accounts appear one-sided.

The novel *Eine deutsche Palette in London* is remarkable, not for the opportunities it affords its author to vent her spleen on what she saw as an unwelcoming host country, but for its vignettes mirroring the lives of real people in Chapter Ten (entitled 'Die Notabilitäten'), where the fictional character Franz Hartung visits the Freiligraths and Struves. Freiligrath's wife gives Hartung a warm reception, though the poet himself is not at home. Kinkel's *Otto der Schütz* lies on the table, indicating the cultural pursuits and liberal outlook of the family.[58] A different reception awaits Franz at the Struve household in the suburbs, which Franz reaches by omnibus. The novel has already informed the reader of Struve's interest in phrenology and fanatical devotion to vegetarianism, which he tyrannically imposes on his wife Amalie.[59] Once we are introduced to Struve we find a vain man, the jealous keeper of his much younger wife. Franz is keen to paint Amalie Struve as Judith, but her husband demurs, citing the pressures on their time as an excuse. When Amalie suggests that Franz returns on Sunday, their 'at home' day, Struve objects that a young man like Franz must surely have something better to do.[60] Bölte omits to inform her reader that Amalie Struve is, like her, a writer: Struve's *Erinnerungen aus den Badischen Freiheitskämpfen, den deutschen Frauen gewidmet* (*Memoirs of the Baden Liberation Battles, dedicated to German Women*) and *Historische Zeitbilder* (*Historical Tableaux*) were both published in Germany in 1850. The former work documents Amalie Struve's active involvement behind the barricades in 1848, and, according to Lia Secci, 'offers a complete picture of the developments in Baden, from the earliest beginnings to the final defeat in July 1849 – with the alternating exhilaration and failure, liberation and imprisonment, flight and exile'.[61]

The dedication of Struve's *Erinnerungen aus den badischen Frei-heitskämpfen*, written in London in 1849, contains the same tone of martyrdom detectable in Bölte's work: neither woman could acclimatise to English life and saw England as inferior to Germany in almost every way. As Rosemary Ashton points out, the Struves 'could not make a go of it'.[62] They tried moving to York in 1850 but moved back to London in 1851, and in spite of moral support from friends such as the Kinkels and the Ronges, who were newly arrived in London, they emigrated (or pushed off, as Marx derided[63]) in April that same year to America, where Amalie Struve continued to write and became active in the nascent women's movement. In contrast, Amalie Bölte, like Gaskell and Dickens,[64] thought it quite radical enough to lay bare the circumstances of deprivation and did not feel called upon to provide a solution. This is very clearly seen in *Louise, oder die Deutsche in London*, which ends with the aristocratic yet penniless girl's marriage to a rich lord, a melodramatic ending which ducks the issues raised in the story. This criticism can also be made of the *Visitenbuch eines Arztes in London* (*House Visits of a London Doctor*) (1852). Here the author's mouthpiece is, of course, male, there being no female doctors at this time. The incidents the doctor recounts reveal the limited social and legal protection for women in England, especially in the (rare!) divorce cases where the man is invariably awarded custody of his children since they are 'his property'.[65] Interesting though the anecdotes are, they are too disconnected to add up to an indictment of woman's lot, and, in any case, things were no better in Germany, though Bölte remains reticent on this. Prince Albert had not seen his mother since he was a young boy: she was sent back to her own father after the discovery of her adultery by a husband who had routinely deceived her, yet who remained unpunished. In Germany it was considered right that women should be punished more severely than men for sexual misdemeanours.[66]

Malwida von Meysenbug, a single woman like Amalie Bölte, was born in 1816 in Kassel. Her father was ennobled when she was a young girl; she was therefore from a respectable bourgeois family rather than an aristocrat by birth, though this fact became blurred in her later life when she mixed on equal terms with such women as Cosima Wagner. In 1855, however, when she first met Wagner, himself a German exile temporarily in London to conduct eight concerts for the Philarmonic Society, he was still married to his first wife Minna. The seismic event in Malwida's life prior to her exile in

London had been her love for the 'religiously motivated Utopian'[67] Theodor Althaus, who died in 1852. This love, though not returned, proved fruitful in that he encouraged her to look for social change and to work towards the regeneration of humanity; on a more practical level, he introduced her to a circle of influential men devoted to these ideals, including the Republican Carl Schurz. Schurz became Malwida's close friend in London before pressing on to America, where he carved out a political career for himself. He was Kinkel's student in Bonn and his right-hand man in the democrat upheavals of 1848–9, after which Kinkel was thrown in jail. It was Schurz who audaciously sprang Kinkel from Spandau prison (7 November 1850).

Althaus also put Malwida von Meysenbug in touch with the Republican, Julius Fröbel. Though they never met in person, Malwida was tempted to accept his invitation to emigrate to America with him, but ultimately declined in deference to her scandalised mother's objections. It was thus no accident that Malwida became interested in the educational theories of Julius Fröbel's uncle, Friedrich Fröbel, whose ideas in turn inspired the highly experimental *Hamburger Hochschule*, the equivalent of a teacher training college for girls which existed in Hamburg from 1850 until 1852, administered by Karl Fröbel (Julius Fröbel's brother) and his wife Johanna. Malwida became a teaching assistant and took over Johanna Fröbel's directorial role whilst the latter was pregnant. During the existence of the *Hamburger Hochschule*, Johannes Ronge was also in Hamburg and Malwida had joined the *freie Gemeinde*, helping in an enlightened, nonconfessional Sunday school. In her autobiographical *Memoiren einer Idealistin*,[68] Malwida praises the life of the *freie Gemeinde* 'where church was transformed into school'.[69] After her experiences in Hamburg she definitively and permanently turned her back on organised religion and became what one might call a militant free-thinker.

Though Malwida von Meysenbug ultimately quarrelled with the Fröbels over what she saw as their rigid conservatism, which she believed was directly at odds with their theories, her educational perspective remained fixed on the development of the individual. One of the things she despised most about English life was the place occupied by the Anglican Church in social affairs. She disliked the hypocrisy that this entailed as well as the social deprivation brought about by Sunday observance. One of the main reasons why she determined never to attempt to be a governess was that the first question at any interview invariably related to the candidate's religious persuasion: atheism was almost universally regarded as directly harmful for children at the time, and Malwida was not prepared to tell any lies. When the *Hamburger Hochschule* shut down, Malwida tried to settle in Berlin and it was here, in May 1852, that the police searched her premises and interrogated her. Her brother Wilhelm was furious at her political involvement and tried to take steps to curb her activity.[70] Thus, with no support from her family, she fled from Germany via Hamburg to London, where the only people with whom she had any contact were the Kinkels, though she had not yet actually met them. They became sufficiently close that Malwida was invited to join them on their seaside holiday in Hastings in 1856. From 1853 to 1856 she took over the task of running the widower Alexander Herzen's household, though on the footing of friend rather than governess or housekeeper. With Malwida in charge, visitors were kept firmly to a *jour fixe*. For Malwida, if not for the troubled Herzen, this was the happiest period of her life. The serendipity ended abruptly when Herzen's former friends Nikolaus Ogarew and his wife Natalie arrived and insisted upon Herzen's return to open hospitality.[71]

Wisely, Malwida withdrew from the situation and concentrated on making her living through her pen, having decided that a return to giving private German lessons was simply too strenuous. In the *Memoiren einer Idealistin*, she gives the clearest account of anyone in this chapter of the deleterious effect on German émigrés of hanging around in the waiting-room which London constituted. Her whole account is lucid and, on the matter of émigré coteries, entirely convincing in spite of the high earnestness of her general tone and her irritating tendency to drop names.[72] What she hated were the futile and cynical attempts of the German democrat coterie surrounding Countess Bruiningk to pass the time in idle pursuits. Agreeing with her friend Johanna Kinkel on the matter, she deplored the refusal of this group of émigrés to occupy themselves with meaningful work. According to Malwida, they preferred to nurse a 'sterile anticipation'[73] of a return to their *status quo* as democratic lions once they are able to go back to Germany. Nevertheless, as we see from her lament at the death of the Pole Stanisław Worcell, whom she greatly admired, she grieved genuinely when a fellow exile died far from home. Worcell was buried in Highgate cemetery, as were her other friends, Countess Bruiningk and Anna Schurz.[74] The cemetery would house many more, including Jenny and Karl Marx.[75] (Johanna Kinkel was buried at Woking.)

The main reason why Malwida von Meysenbug's memoirs were hailed as iconoclastic by her contemporaries was the fact that they detailed her attempts to earn her own living at a time when this was still a social taboo. They are also invaluable for the light they shed on ordinary English life in the 1850s. There are several reasons for this. Firstly, though her best friends were the Kinkels, she also mixed freely with the English gentry, gaining access to the circle of Julia Schwabe, the wife of a rich Manchester manufacturer, who took Malwida with her to her estate on Anglesey – where she met Elizabeth Gaskell fleetingly – as well as to Ventnor on the Isle of Wight, also a favourite haunt of the Marx family.[76] The Schwabes were Unitarians, like Gaskell, and were sufficiently established that their circle consisted mainly of aristocrats. Nevertheless, Julia Schwabe had the drive and vision of many other Unitarian women (one thinks of Florence Nightingale); late in life she decamped to Sicily to found a school for poverty-stricken girls. She recognised a kindred spirit in Malwida in so far as both held that girls' education should fit them for life itself rather than for the foppery of the marriage mart; nevertheless, for some reason Malwida did not warm to Julia Schwabe and declined to become her daughters' tutor.

Malwida von Meysenbug's belief that 'the highest task of education is to develop the art of living'[77] set her at odds with the current state of girls' education in England, though to be fair to her she does mention the founding of the girls' secondary school, Bedford College, as an enormous step forward.[78] Throughout the *Memoiren einer Idealistin*, Malwida von Meysenbug provides pertinent comments on the vacuity of the well-bred English girls' education, snorting with contempt over their 'finishing lessons' and shaking her head over the mind-bending indoctrination purveyed in boarding schools. Although she provides a severe critique of the class divisions which arguably still bedevil British society, one always has the impression that Malwida also wanted to be thought of as ladylike, whatever she said about English snobbery. The fact remains that she did not make any particularly close English friend of either sex, though she liked Jane Carlyle and befriended Eugenie Bell when the latter's husband tried to declare her insane for wanting a separation, following a precedent recently set by Edward Lytton Bulwer.[79] Malwida suggests that the outrageous lack of civil rights for married women is a singular feature of British life, but again, matters in Germany were just as bad in every respect except for divorce, which admittedly was much easier (for Protestants).

Malwida's rejection of the humbug of polite society did not, however, make the working class any more endearing to her. Many of the long-standing German émigrés were by now part of London's indigenous poor, and although Malwida, encouraged by her friend Emilie Reeve, made some effort to dispense charity amongst them, this had the effect of turning her even more away from the *Volk*; in fact, the more she saw of the German working class, the less democratic she became. She could see how abysmal poor relief was in England, but was beginning to question the proposed democratic solutions. In her view, the democrats had overturned the old idols but were now setting up the *Volk* as a new false God.[80] For Malwida, this was pandering to the brutalised masses from whom she turned away with horror, even asking herself whether Malthus could possibly be right?[81] She saw nothing but danger in the Democrats' promise to give the *Volk* mastery in society, especially as she had witnessed for herself the failure of the masses to support the 1848 revolutions in Germany which were, after all, carried out largely in their name. She wrote in her memoirs: 'The function of the masses or so-called *Volk* has been, up to now, as we saw in 1848 and 1849, a mere foil in the hands of clever leaders.'[82] Clearly, Malwida's retreat from liberal politics was in full swing and it is therefore scarcely surprising that she held herself aloof from the other great movement which was gathering pace in England, the campaign for female emancipation, which she does not mention in her memoirs even though Mill's tract *The Subjection of Women*, which served as the midwife to the movement as well as its manifesto, came out in 1869 when she was at work on her memoirs.

If her political enthusiasm was swiftly waning during her time in London exile, Malwida's cultural interests were becoming increasingly important to her and these were by no means exclusively German. She was entirely happy in Herzen's Russian household, where she promptly learnt Russian and acquainted herself with Russian writers such as Pushkin. Her friends reflect her drift away from German nationalism: after Herzen, the man she admired most in London was the Italian Giuseppe Mazzini. After Johanna Kinkel, the woman émigré she admired most was the Hungarian Thérèse Pulszky, another leading female figure in London émigré life. It comes as no surprise that when, in 1861, Herzen gave her custody of his youngest daughter Olga (and presumably, judging from her subsequent lifestyle, a large allowance as well), Malwida left London, with its grey skies, stiff politeness and vast underbelly of

suffering poor for the sunnier climate of Italy. She travelled extensively on the Continent, studied art and nurtured her contacts with
interesting friends, finally (in 1877) settling in Rome, where she died
in 1903. If Malwida had entered London exile as a German idealist,
she quitted as a European aesthete for whom the ideas of Arthur
Schopenhauer and later Friedrich Nietzsche and Romain Roland –
the two latter her close friends as young men – were more attractive than political activism.

Malwida von Meysenbug's fortunes allowed her to do what she
had yearned to do when eking out a precarious existence in exile in
London: others were not so fortunate. Amalie Struve died in America
in 1862 without ever returning to Germany. For Johanna Kinkel and
Jenny Marx, early assumptions that a return to Germany would be
possible after a brief spell in the waiting-room were not borne out:
London ceased to be a waiting-room and turned into their permanent home. One could certainly suggest that both Johanna Kinkel
and Jenny Marx wasted their creative energies in scraping money
together to help pay the household bills, so that their obvious talents
were squandered. What these two women shared was a sense of
humour. Jenny Marx made light of her 'intimate acquaintanceship
with the [pawnbroker's] three balls',[83] and Johanna Kinkel, pres-
surised and depressed though she often was, satirised the foibles of
her imaginary English characters with obvious affection. Such good-
humoured criticism of social snobbery, to which, incidentally, the
Germans were by no means immune, never enlightens the pages of
Malwida's tense account. For her, the individual's own life was a
work of art: that was the one thing that mattered. The hardships she
endured in London were arguably small in comparison with the
struggles of Johanna Kinkel or Jenny Marx to bring up a young
family in exile, and a life of leisure lay ahead of her when she left
England. Clearly, Malwida did not really take to London, and in this,
as we have seen, she was by no means alone. Yet she was prepared
to admire England's political liberties, and even had the grace to
miss her place of exile as she sailed away from its shores:

> As Albion's white cliffs gradually disappeared into the green sea, it was
> as though my second home was disappearing. Seven years of exile, full
> of heavy renunciation, hard work, deep sorrows, losses and struggles
> were bound up in this home. But how much love it had provided, how
> much friendship, intellectual progress and growth in the one thing that
> matters.[84]

Notes

1 See Ruth Stummann-Bowert, 'Die politischen und sozialen Erfahrungen Malwida von Meysenbugs in England (1852–1862)', *Malwida von Meysenbug-Gesellschaft Jahrbuch* (1996), pp. 34–49, p. 34.

2 Malwida von Meysenbug, *Memoiren einer Idealistin*, 2 vols (Berlin /Leipzig, ca. 1916), I, p. 298.

3 Ibid., I, p. 338.

4 Ibid., I, p. 286.

5 Johanna Kinkel, *Hans Ibeles in London: Ein Roman aus dem Flüchtlingsleben* (Frankfurt, 1991 [1860]), p. 263.

6 Five theatre reviews, numerous letters (written 1838–1880) and 'Kurze Umrisse eines bewegten Lebens' are found in Renate Schack (ed.), *Jenny Marx. Ein Bewegtes Leben* (Berlin, 1989).

7 Jenny Marx, 'A Short Sketch of an Eventful Life', in Robert Payne, *The Unknown Karl Marx* (London / New York, 1972), pp. 119–39, p. 124.

8 Ibid., p. 124. Jenny herself proceeds to add her penny's worth by attacking Marx's enemies such as the bitter opponent of communism, Karl Vogt, before describing the disappointment she and Marx felt when visited in London in 1862 by Ferdinand Lassalle and his 'poodle', Lothar Bucher (with whom Malwida von Meysenbug had become friendly).

9 Karl Marx, 'Die großen Männer des Exils', in Karl Marx and Friedrich Engels, *Werke*, 39 vols (Berlin, 1956–62), VIII (1960), pp. 235–335. The essay deals mainly with Gottfried Kinkel.

10 Karl Marx to Ferdinand Freiligrath, 6 May 1859, cited in Marx / Engels, *Werke*, XIII (1961), p. 721.

11 Edgar Bauer, *Konfidentenberichte über die europäische Emigration in London, 1852–1861*, edited by Erik Gamby (Trier, 1989), p. 43. Cited by Hannelore Teuchert, 'Neues zur Emigrantenscene in England 1851–1861', in *Malwida von Meysenbug-Gesellschaft Jahrbuch* (1996), pp. 62–7, p. 63.

12 See Carol Diethe, *Towards Emancipation* (Oxford, 1998), p. 93f.

13 See Rosemary Ashton, *Little Germany: Exile and Asylum in Victorian England* (Oxford / New York, 1986), p. 90.

14 See the letter from Carl Schurz to Camille Pitoullet, 1 December 1905, printed in Camille Pitoullet, 'Sur un prétendu roman à clef de Johanna Kinkel "Hans Ibeles in London"', in *Revue germanique*, 3 (no. 4, 1907), pp. 361–407. The letter, pp. 403–7, describes the way Gottfried Kinkel had become 'public property' to his fellow democrats (p. 404).

15 Jenny Marx's mastitis could well have contributed to the death of her son Heinrich (nicknamed Föxchen because he was born on Guy Fawkes night), who was born in 1850.

16 Betty Lucas, 'Noch ein Erinnerungsblatt aus London', in *Leipziger Sonntagsblatt*, 12 October 1862, reprinted in Johanna Ludwig (ed.), *Betty Lucas bei den Familien Freiligrath und Marx. Erinnerungen aus dem Jahre 1852* (Leipzig, 1998), pp. 17–22, p. 17. I was unfortunately not able to find any novels by Betty Lucas (alias Beluty).

17 Jenny Marx, 'A Short Sketch of an Eventful Life', p. 130.

18 Though many of Herzen's visitors were world famous, such as Louis Blanc, the situation was made more complicated for Herzen by his private circumstances – the death of his wife having left him to cope with three children, the youngest of whom, Olga, was barely more than a toddler.

19 Jenny Marx to Bertha Markheim, 28 January 1863, in Bert Andréas, *Briefe und Dokumente der Familie Marx aus den Jahren 1862–1873, nebst zwei unbekannten Aufsätzen von Friedrich Engels*, 2 vols (Hannover, 1962), II, p. 178f.

20 Kinkel, *Hans Ibeles*, p. 253.

21 A brief discussion of the contemporary debate on the merits of emigration as a solution to Britain's social problems is found in Meysenbug, *Memoiren*, I, p. 50.

22 Ulrike Helmer, 'Nachwort' in Kinkel, *Hans Ibeles*, p. 387.

23 Helen Chambers, 'Johanna Kinkel's novel "Hans Ibeles in London": A German View of England', in Peter Alter and Rudolf Muhs (eds), *Exilanten und andere Deutsche in Fontanes London. Festschrift für Charlotte Jolles zum 85. Geburtstag* (Stuttgart, 1996), pp. 159–73, p. 160ff.

24 See Sabine Freitag's contribution in this volume, Chapter 11.

25 See Diethe, *Towards Emancipation*, p. 95f.

26 Gottfried Kinkel to Rodenburg, cited in J. F. Schulte, *Johanna Kinkel nach ihren Briefen und Erinnerungs-Blättern* (Münster, 1908), p. 116.

27 Kinkel, *Hans Ibeles*, p. 91.

28 Gottfried Kinkel to Carl Fresenius, 12 May 1851, cited in Pitoullet, 'Sur un prétendu roman à clef', p. 396.

29 Kinkel, *Hans Ibeles*, p. 74.

30 Ibid., p. 173. London smog would soon become legendary.

31 Ibid., p. 174.

32 Johann Kinkel to Carl Fresenius, September 1853, cited in Pitoullet, 'Sur un prétendu roman à clef', p. 398.

33 Kinkel, *Hans Ibeles*, p. 210f.

34 August Bebel, *Die Frau und der Sozialismus* (Berlin / Bonn, 1980 [1879]), p. 408.

35 Kinkel, *Hans Ibeles*, p. 92.

36 Ibid., p. 171.

37 Meysenbug, *Memoiren*, I, p. 356. See also note 40 below.
38 Carl Schurz to Camille Pitoullet, cited in Pitoullet, 'Sur un prétendu roman à clef', p. 404.
39 Kinkel, *Hans Ibeles*, p. 98.
40 Meysenbug, *Memoiren*, I, p. 267.
41 Ashton, *Little Germany*, p. 197, asserts that Baroness Bruiningk 'took up [Kinkel's] cause and financed his escape from prison'. The fictional Hulda Saintford could therefore be inspired by her as well as Gräfin Blafosky.
42 Kinkel, *Hans Ibeles*, p. 375.
43 Christine Lattek, 'Im englischen Exil 1852–59', in Gunther Tietz (ed.), *Malwida von Meysenbug: Ein Portrait* (Kassel, 1983), pp. 71–110, p. 106 (n. 38).
44 Sabine Sundermann, *Deutscher Nationalismus im englischen Exil: Zum sozialen und politischen Innenleben der deutschen Kolonie in London 1848–1871* (Paderborn/Munich/Vienna/Zurich, 1997), p. 83. This work provides an up-to-date context for the topic under discussion in this chapter.
45 Ruth-Ellen Boetcher Joeres, 'The Triumph of Woman: Johanna Kinkel's "Hans Ibeles in London"', *Euphorion* 70 (1976), pp. 187–97, p. 191.
46 Carl Schurz to Camille Pitoullet, cited in Pitoullet, 'Sur un prétendu roman à clef', p. 407.
47 Meysenbug, *Memoiren*, I, p. 340.
48 Known also as Amely Bölte. I have used the name Amalie because that is the one which appears in her books under discussion in this chapter.
49 Ruth-Ellen Boetcher Joeres, *Respectability and Deviance: Nineteenth-Century German Women Writers and the Ambiguity of Representation* (Chicago/London, 1998), p. 17, writes: 'To discuss German women writers, or German women in general, in the nineteenth century means to acknowledge not only gender but also class, categories that enriched and complicated one another.'
50 See Walther Fischer and Antje Behrens (eds), *Amely Böltes Briefe aus England an Varnhagen von Ense (1844–1858)* (Düsseldorf, 1955).
51 Amalie Bölte to Varnhagen von Ense, 7 August 1850, in *Amely Böltes Briefe*, p. 83: 'Nothing has ever hurt and surprised me more than her [Lewald's] unreliability.'
52 Amalie Bölte to Varnhagen von Ense, 23 April 1850, in *Amely Böltes Briefe*, p. 77.
53 Amalie Bölte, *Louise, oder die Deutsche in England* (Bautzen, 1846), p. 29: 'But what a sad, lonely life a governess in England leads!'

54 Louise Otto's poem 'Die Klöpplerinnen' ('The Lace-Makers') aroused much contemporary interest. It first appeared in the *Oederaner Stadtanzeiger* in 1840.

55 Bedford College, a girls' secondary school founded in 1849 under the directorship of Harriet Martineau, could appoint female tutors.

56 See the influential and much-quoted article by Catherine M. Prelinger, 'Religious Dissent, Women's Rights, and the Hamburger Hochschule fuer das weibliche Geschlecht in mid-nineteenth-century Germany', *Church History* 45 (1976), pp. 42–55.

57 Bölte, *Louise, oder die Deutsche in England*, p. 24. Mrs. Willis's son has a friend at Eton whose genius at the piano has been discouraged, since any attempt to perform publicly would be viewed as not '*gentlemanly*'. The same skills are encouraged in girls, though at the level of dilettantism, and Mrs. Willis boasts that her daughters are '*fond of music*' (p. 44). The words in italics are in English in the original.

58 Amalie Bölte, *Eine deutsche Palette in London* (Leipzig, 1848), p. 177.

59 Ibid., p. 178.

60 Ibid., p. 185.

61 Lia Secci, 'German Women Writers and the Revolution of 1848', in John C. Fout, *German Women in the Nineteenth Century: A Social History* (London/New York, 1984), pp. 151–71, p. 156.

62 Ashton, *Little Germany*, p. 219.

63 Karl Marx to Friedrich Engels, 15 April 1851. Cited in Ashton, *Little Germany*, p. 219.

64 See Raymond Williams, *Culture and Society 1850–1950* (Harmondsworth, 1958), Ch. 5: 'The Industrial Novels'. Williams discusses *inter alia* Gaskell's *Mary Barton* (1848) and *North and South* (1855) and Dickens's *Hard Times* (1854).

65 Amalie Bölte, *Visitenbuch eines Arztes in London* (Berlin, 1852), p. 20.

66 See Ute Frevert, *Women in Germany from Bourgeois Emancipation to Sexual Liberation,* translated by Stuart McKinnon-Evans, (London / New York / Munich, 1988 [1986]), p. 64.

67 Ruth Stummann-Bowert, 'Malwida von Meysenbug und die Demokraten von 1848: Woher sie kamen – wohin sie gingen. Theodor Althaus – Robert Blum – Julius Fröbel – Gottfried Kinkel – Carl Schurz', in *Malwida von Meysenbug-Gesellschaft Jahrbuch* (1994), pp. 71–114, p. 99.

68 This seminal work for German feminism appeared in German in 1876, though the first part had appeared anonymously in French in 1869.

69 *Meysenbug, Memoiren*, II, p. 33.

70 See Wilhelm von Meysenbug's letter to his brother Carl, 27 May 1852, in Karl-Heinz Nickel (ed.), 'Berichtungen', *Malwida von Meysenbug-Gesellschaft Jahrbuch* (1998), p. 199f.

71 Natalie Ogarew immediately took charge of Herzen, his house and his children, disrupting their education which Malwida had been patiently pursuing. She subsequently had an affair with Herzen which produced three children. See Hedwig Völkerling, 'Malwida von Meysenbug und Alexander Herzen im Spiegel der Briefe an ihre Familie', in *Malwida von Meysenbug-Gesellschaft Jahrbuch* (1996), pp. 50–61, p. 57.

72 The fact remains that throughout her life, she forged access to some of the greatest names in Europe, such as Wagner and Mazzini – to name but two. With others, for example, Lord Palmerston, whom she met in a railway carriage (*Memoiren*, p. 296), the acquaintanceship was fleeting.

73 Meysenbug, *Memoiren*, I, p. 302.

74 Ibid., II, p. 62.

75 Jenny Marx died in 1881, leaving a bereft Marx to follow her to the grave in 1883.

76 See A. N. Insole, *Prometheus Bound: Karl Marx on the Isle of Wight* (Newport: IWCC, 1981).

77 Meysenbug, *Memoiren*, I, p. 356.

78 See note 55 above.

79 Meysenbug, *Memoiren*, II, p. 77. Meysenbug mistakenly writes Henry instead of Edward. Ashton, *Little Germany*, p. 199f. argues that the same Mrs Bell flirted with Kinkel at Hyde Park school, a higher educational institution for women and girls, and this could have contributed to the cooling of the friendship between Malwida von Meysenbug and Johanna Kinkel.

80 Meysenbug, *Memoiren*, II, p. 54.

81 Ibid., p. 53.

82 Ibid., p. 54.

83 J. Marx, 'A Short Sketch of an Eventful Life', p. 130.

84 Meysenbug, *Memoiren*, II, p. 161.

16

Jeanne Deroin: French Feminist and Socialist in Exile

Pamela Pilbeam

Jeanne Deroin (1805–94) was a world pioneer in her campaign for votes for women during the Second Republic in France.[1] She contributed to and edited three newspapers for women, organised one of the first women's clubs and set up a network of workers' associations for men and women. This last achievement led to her arrest and imprisonment in 1850. On her release two years later, fearing continued persecution, she retreated into self-imposed exile in London where she spent the rest of her life, teaching, writing, campaigning for women's rights and caring for her family. This investigation is based on Deroin's newspapers, pamphlets, books and letters,[2] and considers her practical achievements as well as her persuasive prose.

Jeanne Deroin was an intensely private person, who believed that people should be judged solely by what they achieve, not by their background and education.[3] Few of her letters survived. It is not unusual to encounter gaps in extant evidence when one is studying women; we know little about huge periods of Deroin's life between 1834 and 1848 and the forty-two years she lived in London. Deroin was apparently writing her autobiography towards the end of her life but nothing was published. A friend, Adrien Ranvier, the son of the communard, Gabriel Ranvier, who knew her in London, wrote articles commemorating her achievements, but died himself before he could complete a biography.[4] Deroin still awaits a full-scale biography.

She was virtually ignored and forgotten for nearly a hundred years before the recent generation of feminist historians began to consider her contribution to the development of feminism, but her role as a socialist has so far received less attention. Michèle Riot-Sarcey, a leading feminist historian in France,[5] and Joan Scott, an American feminist of equal stature,[6] have looked comparatively at the feminism of Deroin and others. Felicia Gordon and Máire Cross in Britain[7] include her in their review of early French feminists and have translated some of her writing and that of other contemporaries. However Deroin remains elusive, summed up by Joan Scott as a paradox. Indeed Riot-Sarcey, who has written most about Deroin and other female feminists of the first half of the nineteenth century, focuses entirely on their ideas and practical achievements and refuses to be drawn into a discussion of their characters, background, family life and friendships.[8]

To understand a writer like Deroin, it is vital to attempt to approach her personality and the life she lived, as well as the context in which she was writing. Deroin becomes far less of a paradox when she is not treated like a fly set in amber. 'Jeanne Deroin is small and thin, with a very pale complexion', wrote the *Gazette des Tribunaux* during her trial in 1851: 'She wears a black silk bonnet with bright pink ribbons around it. She is calm and her responses to interrogation about socialism are erudite and informed.'[9] She was determined, incisive, and at times abrasive. A friend and fellow feminist reformer, Léon Richer, observed that when she addressed a meeting her listeners could have imagined that she was wielding a rifle. Although she was passionate about her politics, she seems to have been rather puritanical in her private life. She condemned the frivolous life-style of many better-off women. Before marriage she apparently hoped to live as brother and sister with her husband and later wrote a pamphlet lauding celibacy. She was loyal to her friends and helped to raise Flora Tristan's orphaned daughter along with her own son and two daughters. She staunchly fulfilled the job of main breadwinner in the family from 1848. She supported her husband through a mental illness when he lost his job as warden of an old people's home because of her radical views. One of their sons, who suffered from hydrocephalus, was totally dependent on her until his death in 1887.

Deroin apparently had a tough early life, though the suffering seems to have been more of the vicarious than the bread-line variety. In a letter to a friend in 1886 she remarked, 'born at the beginning of the Empire, I am aware of the tears of mothers ... Imperial despotism was followed by the despotism of priests ... Poor myself, I saw the suffering of the disinherited at close hand. I suffered more by searching my soul for truth and trying to help others, than by actual material deprivation.'[10] She was a keen reader, especially of Morelly, Mably and Rousseau. Years later, she claimed, in the immodesty of very mature recollection: 'At twelve I had already read everything that had been written on religion, philosophy and theology.'[11] If this was an exaggeration, her educational achievements were impressive, although like a number of her early socialist contemporaries, she probably only acquired a rudimentary literacy in school. That her family background was poor is confirmed by her employment as a seamstress. Her passion for learning was revealed in a unique manuscript account of her beliefs that she wrote at the age of twenty-six when she joined the Saint-Simonians. This forty-four-page *profession de foi* (most new members managed at most a few sentences) was written in a rough school exercise book in the cramped and variable script of someone to whom writing did not come easily. Deroin fought to educate herself, helped by Saint-Simonian evening classes and the support of her local priest. Triumphantly she earned the *brevet*, the state certificate for primary school teachers. She set up and ran a school for poor children during the July Monarchy and for the rest of her life she taught in her own, or in others' schools in Paris and later in Shepherds Bush.

Deroin's feminism and socialism was undoubtedly stimulated by her reading and experience. Olympe de Gouges, who transposed the Declaration of the Rights of Man of 1789 into a Declaration of the Rights of Women, and was subsequently guillotined (though not for her feminism) was a model for her.[12] Deroin related her ideas on the importance of education for all and the need to recognise a right to work to the thinking of two Enlightened writers, Mably and Morelly.[13] Her first acquaintance with practical plans for radical social reform came in 1831 when she was introduced to Saint-Simonianism by her future husband, Desroches. The Saint-Simonian movement was founded by a group of Saint-Simon's associates after his death in 1825. Committed to the 'liberation of women and workers', their ideas appealed to a number of young Parisian women, particularly those working in the needle trades. In her *profession de foi* Deroin asserted that, contrary to common belief, nature made men and women equal. Gender inequalities were constructed by male-dominated society. Paramount was its neglect of the education of girls. 'The education of women is designed to destroy their moral and intellectual faculties. Every possible stratagem is employed to persuade them that they are inferior to men.'

Contemporary marriage consecrated the inferior status of women. Marriage was, she said, a continual conflict between one partner who tried to dominate by his physical strength, the other by her craftiness. 'Most marriages are based on the chance whim of love. Genuine sympathy, respect and equality are absent. It is vain for the law to assert that marriage is indissoluble, a marriage has failed almost as soon as it is made ... Indissoluble unions bind the couple with oppressive chains that are humiliating for the wife. A slave can at least hope for freedom. A wife finds deliverance only in death.' For Deroin the problem lay not merely in the superior physical strength of the male, but overwhelmingly in the codes of law made by men. The French Civil Code of 1804 left the wife utterly dependent on her husband, with no power to control family finances, her children, even her own dowry or other income. Her own lack of education, the absence of career opportunities and the appallingly low wages earned by working-class women exacerbated this slavery. If she took a lover, the law as well as society, condemned her. If her husband had a mistress, the wife could have recourse to the law only if he actually obliged her to share a house with the mistress. This was made even worse by contemporary norms which encouraged the husband to feel he could exercise a roaming eye, and taught a girl to value only 'frivolous tastes and how to exploit her charms and pleasing ways.'

At the beginning of the nineteenth century, Charles Fourier had claimed that society would only be improved when the fundamental equality of women was recognised. He argued that this could only happen by the abolition of monogamous marriage and family ties in small totally communal *phalanges*. The Saint-Simonians also called for liberated 'new' women. Under the influence of Prosper Enfantin their feminism took on a far from egalitarian aspect. Insisting that the basic social unit was the couple, Enfantin propounded the Rousseauist doctrine that men alone possessed rational characteristics, women spoke for the spiritual, moral and artistic side of life. In her *profession de foi* Deroin echoed this standard Saint-Simonian mantra: 'The liberated woman [la femme libre] will be the angel of peace and conciliation whose gentle and powerful influence will unite all the members of the human family in perfect accord and saintly harmony.'

For a fleeting moment Deroin thought that Saint-Simonianism would provide the framework to liberate women. 'Saint-Simonianism has revived my dreams of universal fraternity which I had dismissed as unrealistic … I find myself in accord with the Doctrine, the abolition of the privilege of birth, the liberation of women and the moral, physical and intellectual betterment of the poorest and most numerous social group.' On the other hand, even at the outset, she was alarmed at the hierarchical structure of the movement. She had an uncompromising belief in liberty and equality for all, including women and the poor. 'All people are equal before the law, all must be free, sovereignty belongs to everyone and must never be limited to a single person, or to a narrow segment of society.' In 1831, when France was ruled by an elitist constitutional monarchy, barely reformed after the revolution of the previous year, Deroin expressed the firm conviction that only a democratic republican regime would emancipate the poor from unreasonable labour. She joined fellow Saint-Simonians in rejecting conventional Catholicism, but, like other early socialists, believed that the world was guided by an omniscient spiritual force. 'It is impossible to envisage that countless lifeless atoms could combine together to construct our magnificent universe....in acknowledging the law of progress, we must also acknowledge the presence of a prime moving force [une cause antérieure].'

Disenchantment with Saint-Simonianism was swift. Along with the most enterprising and thoughtful members of the sect, male and female, Deroin deplored the link which Enfantin made between the liberation of women and sexual licence, and resigned. Much later she summarised her disillusionment: 'We want true freedom, not the egotistical drive of the male for immorality [la liberté illimitée du pouvoir de l'egoisme de l'homme pour l'immoralité].' Some of the female Saint-Simonians, she believed, were duped by Enfantin's interpretation of the 'new woman'. 'They [the Saint-Simonians] call upon women to reclaim their rights to accomplish their duties, but to achieve this women must learn to think for themselves. Women are on the threshold of understanding science, but if men are to be the teachers, there is a danger that women will copy their mistakes.'[14]

In 1832 a number of the working-class women who had been drawn to Saint-Simonianism but were disenchanted by Enfantin's ambiguous call for female liberation, united to run the first-ever newspaper for women. Unlike a number of ostensibly male 'artisan' newspapers, this one really was written by workers for workers. It was edited by two young seamstresses, Marie-Reine Guindorf and Désirée Véret (who later married the Owenite, Gay). At first they called the paper *La Femme Libre*. Published from Véret's home, it appeared irregularly, when the editors had enough copy and money to complete a print-run. It sold at 15 centîmes a copy.[15] Jeanne Deroin and other former Saint-Simonians contributed, including Pauline Roland and Suzanne Voilquin. Influenced by Fourier, Guindorf used the paper to condemn the servitude of women and campaign for a woman's right to a living wage. Voilquin argued for equality within marriage, including property rights and authority over children. While the editors privately favoured Enfantin's ideas on 'progressive' marriage, in their paper they defended monogamy. They demanded freedom through the right of association and spoke up for *solidarité* among all women, regardless of class. After a month, in September 1832 they changed the name of their paper, first to the less provocative *La femme de l'avenir*[16], then to *Femme-Nouvelle, Apostolat des femmes,* later *Tribune des Femmes.* One thousand copies of the first issue were printed. The paper survived until February 1834, appearing irregularly, thirty-two times in all.[17] Roland was the only middle-class contributor. To assert their independence from men, they signed their articles with only their first name; for instance Jeanne Deroin signed Jeanne-Victoire.

Disillusioned former Saint-Simonians created Fourierist socialism. Both the working-class women who ran *La Femme Libre* and the middle-class women who had helped found Saint-Simonianism, were the backbone of Fourierism. Fourier's scorn for marriage and a personal god was replaced by the assertion of monogamy and constant references to the Almighty. Jeanne Deroin seems to have devoted these years to her family, to reemerge as a public figure in 1848. However her immediate link-up after the revolution of February 1848 with a number of ex-Saint-Simonian and Fourierist women suggests that she had maintained close contact with them. Immediately after the revolution Deroin joined Désirée Gay, Eugénie Niboyet and Pauline Roland in campaigns for the emancipation of workers and women, focusing on associations, education, civil rights, including divorce and votes for women. They worked through repeated petitions, marches, popular clubs and the press. They hoped that Victor Considérant and the other Fourierist men would support the women's cause.

In 1848 women, like men, formed themselves into numerous associations, which often had overlapping membership lists. Like the mens' clubs they totally ignored the ban placed on associations in the existing Penal Code. Deroin became secretary of the *Société de la Voix des Femmes,* which became the leading women's club. She was a major contributor to its newspaper, *La Voix des Femmes,* which was started on 20 March 1848 by Eugénie Niboyet, another former Saint-Simonian. The contributors included a host of women who had been Saint-Simonians, such as Suzanne Voilquin, Elise Lemonnier, Désirée Gay, Anais Segalas, Adèle Esquiros and Gabrielle d'Altenheim-Soumet. They demanded reforms to the legal status and working conditions for women on the grounds that as mothers women had educational and moral roles within the family. In an address to Ledru-Rollin the paper claimed: 'It is in the name of holy obligations to the family, in the name of the tender ministrations of the mother that we speak to you: yes, like you we have the right to serve our country according to our strength.'[18] Deroin stressed that women had to be liberated because the rearing and moral education of the next generation was in their hands. Maternity not nature demanded that their equality be acknowledged. Deroin and Niboyet petitioned the provisional government to improve women workers' pay, to make women equal in law and to enfranchise them. The tone of their petition was Saint-Simonian: 'the social individual is a union of man and woman. If women are denied the right to participate, reform will be incomplete and lack morality and durability.'[19]

The republicans of 1848 decreed universal male suffrage, expanding the electorate overnight from 250,000 to 9 million men. While all women socialists could agree to press for higher wages for women and better education for girls, Deroin was almost alone in demanding the political enfranchisement of women. 'To all French citizens', she wrote, 'The reign of brute force is over, that of morality and intelligence has begun ... when everything was decided by the sword, it was fair to exclude women from assemblies of warriors ... today we need education and organisation. Women must be called to take part in the work of social regeneration which is just beginning.'[20] The most notable woman socialist, the novelist George Sand, was convinced that other reforms were far more urgent. When Marrast, mayor of Paris, was pressed by a delegation from the *Comité des droits de la femme* that women also be given the vote, he passed the buck to the new Assembly (to be elected by men only). Jeanne Deroin organised and presented four petitions for votes for women to the Provisional Government and published one addressed to all 'citizens', in the *Voix des Femmes*: 'Liberty, Equality and Fraternity have been proclaimed as the right of everyone, why have women been left with only duties to perform, deprived of the rights of citizenship ... Should half the nation be left under the domination of the other half?'[21] Deroin's campaign for votes for women was not taken seriously, but pushed aside as too ridiculous to debate at any length. When some measure of refutation was deemed necessary it was argued that women did not need the vote, that they were represented by their husbands. The *Voix des Femmes* replied that, on such grounds, adult sons should not have a vote.[22] They organised a petition to enfranchise widows and single women, who had no husbands to represent them.[23] The suffragists gained some support from the many popular clubs, but it was often lukewarm. Cabet allowed women to attend his club, but made them sit silent in the gallery. He did not support Deroin's campaign.[24] Considérant was Deroin's most assiduous supporter, but the enthusiasm of his influential newspaper

La Démocratie Pacifique only became pronounced when Considérant had been safely elected to the new Constituent Assembly.

Deroin never abandoned her earlier conviction that unhappy marriages should be terminated and she and her husband drew up a marriage contract before their civil wedding. For her the contract was an agreement to share life, a structured alternative to virginity, but not simply a licence to procreate. Divorce had been legal in France from 1792 to May 1816.[25] There were parliamentary moves to reinstate divorce during the July Monarchy, but each was blocked by the Chamber of Peers. During the July Monarchy individual demands for the reinstatement of divorce became the most common theme of petitions to parliament from both men and women,[26] the most famous being that of Flora Tristan.

Enfantin's trumpeting of trial marriage in the early 1830s led him to the courts and imprisonment on a charge of corrupting public morals. The ensuing scandal made projects to revive divorce legislation seem radical and a threat to society. In 1848 republicans announced plans to reintroduce a divorce law. They presented divorce as a humane reform of the Code, but the project was never prominent, even in the feminist press. On 23 May 1848 Crémieux, Minister of Justice, introduced a bill to restore the right to divorce. He proposed to allow divorce in cases of irretrievable breakdown of marriage after a three-year separation, providing neither disputant was guilty of adultery.[27] In contrast to the parliaments of the July Monarchy, the new National Assembly was hostile to Crémieux's bill. The moderate proposals met a heated, often anti-Semitic response from the right-wing press: Crémieux was one of the first Jews ever to hold ministerial office. The accusations of the journalists ranged from suggestions that other issues were more important to wild assertions that divorce was a diabolical plan to break up families and subvert society in sexual promiscuity and communism.

While the divorce bill was being debated in parliament, supporters in the *Société de la Voix des Femmes* were heckled by men, their meetings disrupted and large crowds of men waited outside to insult them, to such an extent that they had to move to another location. Their newspaper was unable to publish from 29 April to 29 May and the club was obliged to transform itself into the *Club des Femmes*, which met three times a week from the end of May. Their support for socialist candidates in June and for the proposed divorce law ensured that the club and newspaper were mocked mercilessly in the conservative press, in Daumier's cartoons in *Le Charivari* and on the stage.[28]

Daumier portrayed the female supporters of divorce as ugly undesirable hags. They were accused of being hostile to the family and attention was drawn to Niboyet's life apart from her husband, and to Gay's and Deroin's independent life-styles, although Deroin was still with her husband. The Fourierist paper, *La Démocratie Pacifique,* supported Crémieux's proposal. But the bill was dismissed in committee by 13 votes to 4, Crémieux resigned on 7 June and the issue disappeared from sight until 1884.[29]

Media pressure forced the *Voix des Femmes* to cease publication on 18 June and the *Club des Femmes* to close in June 1848. A decree of 26 July 1848 banned women and young people from clubs and denied them a public role. Deroin launched a *cours de droit social pour des femmes* to continue her campaign for equal rights for women. In a brochure publicising the course she summarised her philosophy, which was still fundamentally Saint-Simonian: 'A major reform of society is both urgent and inevitable; but if it is to be complete and lasting, it cannot be solely the work of men. Men can create order in a despotic way, women can contribute the power of maternal love; together they can reconcile order and liberty.'[30] Deroin and Gay broadened their platform, stressing the mutual deprivation of women and workers, much as Saint-Simonians had done in the early 1830s. They set up the *Association mutuelle des femmes* together with a new paper, *La Politique des Femmes* which Gay edited. On 21 August 1848 a prospectus and a preliminary edition of *L'Opinion des Femmes* appeared, edited by Deroin.

The first full issue came out on 1 January 1849. Six substantial eight-page issues were published until August 1849, when an increase in caution money to 5,000 francs forced Deroin to cease publication. The brief of *L'Opinion des Femmes* was to secure the *droit de cité*, political and full legal rights for women. The newspaper referred to political events, but was essentially analytical with an entirely feminist perspective. Its financial backers included the former Saint-Simonian, Olinde Rodrigues. Jean Macé, the pioneer in girls' education, provided keynote articles putting a very measured, somewhat ironical case for equality and votes for women in all but one issue. He repeatedly noted that the vast majority of women were opposed to enfranchisement and that they needed to be persuaded of its merits. Three other themes merited regular articles: 'Mission des femmes', women at work, notably as milliners, actresses and midwives, and the importance of religious belief to socialism. The paper carried lists of associations and brief book reviews.

Deroin also founded an Association of Socialist Teachers, which included men and women. She continued to urge women that it was their duty to demand equal rights, that everyone would gain and that the concept of fraternity was meaningless until their equality had been recognised.[31] 'Working men will never escape the servitude of poverty and ignorance until they liberate their wives.'[32]

Deroin persisted in her lone campaign for the right of women to vote and take part in politics. She stood as a candidate in the 1849 legislative elections and the May issue of her paper was devoted to the campaign of the *démocrates-socialistes* and Deroin's own efforts. She tried to attend the hustings and the workers in Saint-Antoine were sympathetic. Elsewhere she was told that the constitution did not allow women candidates. The *comité démocrate sociale* added her to their list of candidates. George Sand's name appeared on about forty lists, but Sand was still convinced that female suffrage was premature.

Only the Fourierist *La Démocratie Pacifique* and *La République*, owned and edited by the former Saint-Simonian, Bareste,[33] supported her campaign. Bareste was sympathetic to Deroin's claims for equal rights, but found her attempt to stand as a candidate in 1849 'eccentric'.[34] She faced a barrage of insults from the rest of the press. Daumier used the pages of *Le Charivari* to ridicule Deroin's campaign in a series of sharp cartoons.

Jeanne Deroin's demand for votes for women put her at odds with some male socialists, including Proudhon, whose ideas on association Deroin followed closely. In his newspaper, *Le Peuple*, Proudhon launched a campaign against the enfranchisement of women. He insisted that the male citizen qualified as a voter as head of a family. Politics was the concern of families, not individuals.[35] To suggest that women should vote, he claimed, was as foolish as proposing that men breast-feed children. Deroin responded that there were no unique biological characteristics that made voting gender specific. Women, Proudhon asserted, had no place outside the home, except as whores. Deroin retaliated:

> As a Christian socialist, I would say, like you, rather a housewife than a whore if I was convinced that many women become whores to avoid being housewives. Prostitution is the consequence of slavery, ignorance and poverty ... You want to strengthen the family, and you weaken it by demanding the man to the debating chamber or the workshop, the women in the home ... You ask what woman can achieve outside the home? She can help to restore order in the great, but badly-run household we call the state ... no serious and lasting reform can be hoped for

until the rights of women to civil and political equality are acknowledged to be fundamental to our social redemption.[36]

Deroin defended her candidature: 'To the Voters in the Seine department. If, as is your right, you elect a woman to the Legislative Assembly, you will be acknowledging fully our republican dogma, Liberty, Equality and Fraternity for all women and all men. A Legislative Assembly entirely composed of men is no more qualified to legislate for all than would be an assembly of the privileged to decide on matters concerning working people.'[37]

Deroin took issue with others who were hostile to votes for women. She dismissed the claim of the popular historian Michelet that few women actually wanted the vote and that a vote for women 'would mean 80,000 votes for priests'. (Why 80,000? If women were enfranchised the electorate would have doubled.) Others worried about the consequence of giving a vote to the whores of Saint-Denis and whether the vote should be limited to bourgeois ladies. Deroin argued that all would be, like men, simply voters in the republican system. To say women were equal and then deny them a vote undermined the republic itself.[38] To insist that women confine themselves to their roles as wives and mothers, gave these functions 'the stigmata of civil and political incapacity'. No wonder, she exclaimed, that some women escaped from their slavery into a world of good works and 'Christian and angelic piety'.[39]

Although Deroin was scathing about the Church and organised religion, her own feminist convictions always had a strong spiritual base. *L'Opinion des Femmes* ran a series of articles which defined the role of women as a mission and an 'apostolat'. The motherly love that they shared with all women would allow women to transcend class and political boundaries. In public life women would thus be able to replace conflict with concord and fraternity.[40] Deroin was always keen to encourage other women to appreciate their moral and spiritual role as mothers: 'Love, unity and harmony, who better than a woman can inspire these divine sentiments in a man's heart? Who better than a woman can make man understand their power and help him bring the devastation of repeated revolutions to an end?'[41] Deroin gave classes in her Women's Mutual Education Society. In addition she started the Fraternal Association of Democratic Socialists of both sexes for the Liberation of Women. In July 1849 she and Gay were granted 12,000 francs (from the fund set up by the National Assembly to encourage workers' associations) to set up an association of women seamstresses making ladies' underwear.

Deroin devoted the last issue of *L'Opinion des Femmes* in August 1849 to her most far-reaching project, the formation of an *association fraternelle et solidaire de toutes les associations*. Linking together existing workers associations, it aimed to secure the three-fold rights of sovereignty, work and consumption. 'The rights of man can be encapsulated in one sole right, the right to a full physical, intellectual and moral existence ... man's duties can also be summarised in one: to love his brothers more than himself. If these are acknowledged, universal happiness is in reach. The law of God consists of the fusion of solidarity and fraternity.' The association aimed to implement the right to work by providing tools, raw materials and interest-free loans for its worker members. In return for finished goods, members would be given vouchers (*bons d'échange*) which could be exchanged in the association for food and other goods. Farmers were to be brought into the scheme. In addition the association would provide nurseries, schools, vocational training, housing and sickness and old age benefits. The whole organisation would be run on egalitarian and democratic lines.[42] This ambitious project resembled the plans set out earlier by Cabet, Blanc and particularly by Proudhon in his Peoples' Bank. The association of associations was formally constituted on 22 November 1849 and its existence was announced in *La Démocratie Pacifique*, 12 January 1850. It prospered and soon embraced 104 producer cooperatives. Deroin became one of its directors. Plans were made to expand into the *école de commerce* owned by the exiled Ledru-Rollin.

Born in optimism, the Second Republic never secured the confidence of the voters. Control soon passed back to the old monarchist elite, who had no time for socialism and feminism, and who were convinced that worker associations were a threat to capitalism and the 'liberal' economy. After the June Days, 1848, when Parisian artisans rebelled against the government's decision to close the temporary workshops set up after February, the right of association was progressively withdrawn. Deroin's association survived longer than most. In May 1850 their offices were raided and forty-six members, including nine women, were arrested and imprisoned for five months awaiting trial by the *cour d'assise* of the Seine. The trial attracted big crowds. The main charge was not that they were running a workers' cooperative but that they were conspiring against the government and trying to overthrow it by violent revolution. The prosecution claimed that arms and powder were found in the home of one of the accused (not Deroin). One, Mme Nicaud, was accused of having a portrait of Robespierre, which she insisted was Eugène Sue.

The prosecution would not accept Deroin's claim that the association was her idea and that she was the main organiser. Their insistence that the leading men on the committee should be the principal defendants owed nothing to chivalry. Deroin was accused of lesser charges: failing to use her married name, and thus undermining the institution of marriage; standing as a candidate for the Legislative Assembly, and participating in an association which was political and revolutionary, not economic and reformist. Deroin replied that the court represented law made by men and had no right to try her. She explained that she used her maiden name because she did not want people to assume that her husband shared her views. She insisted that she was not hostile to marriage, but to the way in which it was defined in the Civil Code. 'I want to moralise marriage and make it an association of equals in the ways God intended.'[43] The male committee members received sentences ranging from four years to one year and fines of 1,000 to 300 francs. Deroin and Roland were imprisoned for six months: Deroin in St Lazare jail, Roland transported to Algeria. George Sand pleaded for Roland's early release, but the privations she suffered led to her death on the journey home.

Whilst in prison Deroin continued her political activities. She wrote in defence of her association. She also petitioned the Legislative Assembly to maintain the right of women to petition parliament. Petitioning had been almost the only opportunity for women to have a public voice during the first half of the nineteenth century. In 1830 there were seventy-three women out of 2,455 petitioners. After the 1848 revolution there were 174 out of 7,379. Most women petitioned parliament for specific, individual reasons. Jeanne Deroin, on the other hand, wrote a succession of petitions to the Assembly demanding votes for women. In 1851 apparently she was alone in her protest and the abolition of this right of women was passed almost unanimously. Crémieux was one of only two deputies to vote against the measure.[44]

Deroin was released from prison on 3 June 1851. She supported herself by teaching and struggled to gather her family back around her. Her elder daughter had been sent to boarding school and the two younger children had been farmed out to different relatives. Her husband had developed a serious mental illness from which he never recovered. Warned that she was likely to be rearrested for her persistent defence of her association, she fled to England with her two younger children in August 1852. Fellow exiles found her work teaching and embroidering. Her husband developed typhoid fever and died before he could join her. A year later her elder daughter joined her when her education was complete. She was a constant support to her mother and never married. The younger daughter married an Italian hairdresser and died in 1867. Deroin tended her invalid son until his death in 1887.

Deroin remained in London for the rest of her life, living in a respectable middle-class part of Shepherds Bush in Orchard Road, which has now given way to 'improvements', and Cobbold Road, a turning off Askew Road. In 1861 she set up a tiny girls' boarding school, but it did not survive. It was undercapitalised. Deroin charged very low fees and gave free places to girls from poor families. She struggled to pay her subscriptions to French radical papers and was sometimes sent free copies.[45] When most of the exiles returned to France in 1870–1, they persuaded the new republican regime to grant Deroin a pension of 600 francs a year. Deroin never went back home, but she maintained a lively correspondence with feminist reformers in France, sometimes writing during lesson time,[46] and occasionally submitting newspaper articles written on school exercise-book paper.

Half of Jeanne Deroin's life was spent in uninterrupted exile in London. How did her ideas change in this period? Like other early socialists, such as Ange Guépin, she developed an interest in Freemasonry. Guépin joined in the 1860s and quickly became a leading Masonic lecturer. Somewhere around 1859–61 Deroin also applied to join the Freemasons. At the time this was as radical a request as her demand for votes for women had been a few years earlier.

She published three women's almanacs during her exile. She also wrote articles for a number of sympathetic newspapers in France.[47] The first almanac was published in Paris in 1852, the second and third in London and Jersey in 1853 and 1854 respectively. All were published in French and the second also appeared simultaneously in English. Deroin's aim was to promote the idea that women should be guaranteed the same liberty and equality as men. She also stressed the socialist idea of the organisation of work and argued for the abolition of the death penalty. She continued to assert the Fourierist/Saint-Simonian creed that only by liberating women would 'human solidarity' be achieved and that this was God's will.[48] Deroin reprinted the Fourierist Pelletan's review of the Sorbonne feminist professor Legouvé's *Histoire morale des femmes,* with approval. Legouvé's volume was to become the standard reformist account of the position of women in contemporary society. It was translated into all the main European languages. The book began with a historical survey of the role of women. The anti-feminism of the ancient world was noted. Jesus had spoken of the spiritual equality of women, but Christianity denied it in practice. 'Woman is man's crime. She has been his victim since leaving Eden. She still bears in her flesh the mark of 6000 years of injustice.'[49] In present-day society the inequality of women was confirmed by their education. They were taught seduction, not science. Legouvé argued for better education and civil rights for women, but not the vote. He was to be a leading force for reform during the Third Republic.

Deroin's almanacs also included more lighthearted articles on women's clothes, presumably conceived as an antidote to the fashion magazines of the time. Women were advised to abandon impractical clothing and adopt trousers and shorter skirts.[50] Only a few upper-class women like George Sand dared to wear trousers. The corset was condemned as 'un instrument de mensonge'. An article on a woman's right to work was more solemn and demanded better pay and conditions. The 1852 edition also included articles praising nursery schools, a 'letter to Mme. J. Deroin from the reformer Macé' supporting her demand for the vote and a letter from Deroin praising worker cooperatives. The same themes reappeared each year. Deroin also included articles on other subjects that appealed to her, such as temperance and vegetarianism, although she was careful to define temperance as moderation, not abstinence.

The tone of her feminism became increasingly spiritualist. In the 1854 volume Deroin wrote of the need to 'walk in the direction of harmonious progress and accomplishing the law of God, the holy law of fraternal and universal solidarity ... the new Eve, the Virgin, wrapped in her mystical veil, calls humanity to the social religion of Solidarity.' The first step was to set up Solidarité societies to provide education, nurseries and work tools for the 'disinherited'. Women, she asserted, had a crucial role as social evangelists in workers' cooperatives and mutual-aid groups. 'It is down to women, reborn by the spirit of love, liberty and justice, to rebuild society and raise the current incomplete interpretation of social science into a new universal religion which will bind all of humanity in love.'[51]

Deroin sent copies of her almanacs to the Phalansterian library: solidarity was a key concept for Fourierists. Léon Richer, who founded the Association for the Rights of Women in 1870,[52] publicised the almanacs in the *National de l'Ouest* and other newspapers.[53] After 1854 Deroin ran out of funds and no further editions of her almanacs appeared, but she continued to write for French newspapers and always retained contact with reformers such as Richer. Deroin remained in correspondence with him into the 1880s. Through him she made contact with Madame Arnaud.[54]

By 1880 Deroin seemed less absorbed in the spiritualist feminism she had voiced in 1853. She was still intent on combating the 'false pleasures and frivolity' which led women astray. She encouraged Richer's attempts to set up schools that would offer vocational training to children from poor families. She realised that many would think her own efforts had been utopian and thus futile. She remained convinced that education was the key to social progress: 'in future teachers will fulfill the roles of both priests and doctors.' Stripped of moral content, she maintained, 'education is merely oppression and can do nothing to promote human happiness.'[55]

In 1886 she corresponded with Hubertine Auclert (1848–1914), a leading young feminist, but socialist feminism meant very different things to Auclert's generation which was active in the Third Republic. Deroin was aware that her ideas no longer had resonance, although another later feminist, Madeleine Pelletier, was to use her name for a young feminist in the autobiographical novel she published in 1933.[56] Like Pelletier, Auclert justified equality and votes for women from an entirely rational standpoint; there was no trace of the spiritual gender difference evoked by Deroin.

In her eighties Deroin became involved in William Morris's Socialist League, the leading socialist organisation in Britain in the 1880s. The League proclaimed Owenite ideas, which would have pleased Deroin, but she would have been less charmed by Morris's espousal of revolution as a means to promote class warfare. At Deroin's very well-attended civil funeral, William Morris apparently spoke of her dedication to her chosen cause.

What was there to praise? Deroin was almost alone in 1848 in demanding the vote for women. Unlike other feminists, such as Eugénie Niboyet, she was uncompromising in asserting woman's equality. She was convinced that inequality was an invented social construct, with no basis in biology. Although Deroin always maintained the natural equality of women, she always retained the Saint-Simonian idea of the complementarity of the sexes and even she acknowledged that gender difference extended beyond child-rearing. Throughout her life she stressed woman's special role as a spiritual and moral force in the family. This Madonna-type creed was used by her and more moderate feminists as the main lever to try to improve the legal and educational position of women. It recognised that women occupied an important role in society running charities, especially maternal ones, and nurseries. It also implicitly acknowledged that increasing industrialisation deprived middle-class women of economic functions. They were no longer needed to help in the family business, for instance keeping the firm's books. If they did not assert their special moral and spiritual role they risked being left stranded in the nursery. Bonnie Smith's research revealed the significance of this moral role for the middle-class women of northern France during the Third Republic.[57]

Where did Deroin's feminist socialism lead? Her claim for equality was actually based on the glorification of inequality. Her life seems to have been one of fruitless protest. 'I always felt compelled to hammer on locked doors', she wrote to Léon Richer towards the end of her life.[58] Did she advance her 'most holy cause', women's political emancipation? The brutal answer must be 'no'. Although she asserted that women were equal, her espousal of the Saint-Simonian and Fourierist doctrine of spiritual difference and, effectively, moral superiority, carried little conviction. Although she was one of the first women in Europe to demand female emancipation, French women were almost the last Europeans (apart from the Swiss) to secure the vote. She took a leading part in the producer cooperatives of the Second Republic, but the conservative regime eliminated them. She was a vigorous and outspoken feminist journalist who never gave up. She was an example of a virtuous, intelligent, energetic and socially concerned woman. Although her dream of suffrage was not realised until 1945, some of her objectives for the reform of the Civil Code were achieved during the Third Republic: for example, a law permitting divorce.

Deroin seems to have compartmentalised her life between devoting herself to her husband and children and the propagation of socialism and feminism. She was undoubtedly a woman ahead of her times. Although her views on equality and female suffrage were truly visionary, she was beset by the social constraints on women of her younger days, especially seeing spiritual and moral matters as the particular responsibility of women. This was no paradox, but a product of her own unusually heavy family responsibilities, an awareness, that others, such as Olympe de Gouges and Pauline Roland, had paid with their lives for their beliefs and an acute perception of how difficult it was going to be to remove the social and political constraints experienced by women, especially those in their minds.

Notes

1 I am grateful to the British Academy for an award which allowed me to work on the *Fonds Enfantin, Bibliothèque de l'Arsénal,* and on the *Fonds Bouglé* and other printed material in the *Bibliothèque historique de la ville de Paris* and on the Guépin papers in the departmental archives in Nantes (19J1–26). I should also thank the Central Research Fund, University of London, for a grant which enabled me to work on the *Fonds Fourier et Considérant, Archives Nationales,* 10AS. A summary of Deroin's ideas and activities is included in Pamela M. Pilbeam, *French Socialists before Marx: Workers, Women and the Social Question in France* (Montreal and Kingston, 2000). An earlier version of this chapter was presented to the conference 'Women and Brainpower', Royal Holloway, University of London, July 1999.

2 Her 44–page saint-simonian *profession de foi* ... survives, *Lettres de Dames aux Globe* Fonds Enfantin, letter 39, Bibliothèque de l'Arsenal, 7608. The Bibliothèque historique de la ville de Paris (BHVP) holds a good collection of her published work and some of her letters in the Fonds Bouglé. There are letters to and from Deroin in the Fourier and Considérant papers, *Archives Nationales.* These are conveniently, though not always very legibly, available on micro-film.

3 Jeanne Deroin, letters in Fonds Bouglé, BHVP, pp. 42, 47.

4 A. Ranvier, 'Une féministe de 1848: Jeanne Deroin', *La Révolution de 1848, Bulletin de la Société d'histoire de la révolution de 1848,* III (1907), pp.317–55; (1908), pp. 421–30, 480–98; idem, 'Le testament d'une féministe de 1848: Jeanne Deroin', *La Révolution de 1848,* 5 (1909), pp. 816–23.

5 Michèle Riot-Sarcey, *La démocratie à l'épreuve des femmes* (Paris, 1994).

6 J.W. Scott, *Only Paradoxes to Offer. French Feminists and the Rights of Man* (Harvard, 1997); J. Moon, 'The Association fraternelle et solidaires de toutes les associations', *Western Society For French History,* Annual Conference, October 1993.

7 F. Gordon and M. Cross, *Early French Feminisms, 1830–1940,* (London, 1996).

8 Riot-Sarcey, *La démocratie à l'épreuve des femme.*

9 A. Ranvier, 'Une féministe de 1848: Jeanne Deroin', *La Révolution de 1848,* 5 (1907), p. 320.

10 Deroin to Auclert, 10 January 1886, Fonds Bouglé 4247, BHVP.

11 Deroin to Léon Richer, nd [1881]. Fonds Bouglé 4247, BHVP.

12 *Voix des Femmes,* 19 April 1848.

13 'Lettre aux associations', *Almanach des Femmes* (1852).

14 Deroin to Auclert, 10 January 1886, 'chere citoyenne', *see* note 10.

15 L. Adler, *A l'aube du féminisme: Les premières journalistes* (Paris, 1979), p. 41.

16 *La Femme Libre,* no.1.

17 J.S. Moon, 'The Saint-Simonian Association of Working-class Women, 1830–1850', *Proceedings of the Fifth Annual Meeting of the Western Society for French History, Las Cruces* (1977), pp. 274–81.

18 *Voix des Femmes,* 11 April 1848.

19 Quoted in Edouard Dolléans, *Féminisme et mouvement ouvrier: George Sand* (Paris, 1951), p. 2.

20 *Voix des Femmes,* 27 March 1848 (no.7).

21 *Voix de Femmes,* 27 March 1848 (no.7).

22 *Voix des Femmes,* 22 March 1848 (no.2).

23 *Voix des Femmes,* 28 April 1848.

24 E. Thomas, *Les Femmes de 1848* (Paris, 1948).

25 R. Phillips, *Family Breakdown in Late C18 France: Divorces in Rouen 1792–1803* (Oxford, 1980); idem, *Putting Asunder: The History of Divorce in Western Society* (Cambridge, 1989); A. Copley, *Sexual Moralities in France, 1780–1980* (London, 1989).

26 Michèle Riot-Sarcey, 'Des femmes pétionnent sous la Monarchie de Juillet', in A. Corbin, J. Laloutte and M. Riot-Sarcey (eds), *Femmes dans la cité, 1815–1871* (Paris, n. d.), pp. 389–99.

27 W. Fortescue, 'Divorce Debated and Deferred: the French Debate on Divorce and the Failure of the Cremieux Divorce Bill in 1848', *French History 7* (1993). pp. 137–62.

28 "Le club des maris et le club des femmes", in Riot-Sarcey, *La Démocratie,* p. 216.

29 T. McBride, 'Public Authority and Private Lives: Divorce after the French Revolution', *French Historical Studies,* 17 (1992), pp. 747–68.

30 J. Deroin, *Cours de droit social pour les femmes* (Paris, 1848).

31 J. Deroin, *L'Opinion des Femmes,* 28 January 1849.

32 J. Deroin, *L'Opinion des Femmes,* April 1849.

33 Jean Deroin thanked both papers for their support, *L'Opinon des Femmes,* May 1849.

34 *La République,* 13 April 1849 quoted in K.A. Mustafa, '*Republican Socialism and Revolution in France: La République of Eugène Bareste, 1848–1851*' (PhD, Melbourne, 2000), p.107.

35 A. Verjus, 'Le suffrage universel, le chef de famille et la question de l'exclusion des femmes en 1848', in A. Corbin, J. Laloutte and M. Riot-Sarcey (eds), *Femmes dans la cité, 1815–1871* (Paris, n.d.), pp. 401–13.

36 J. Deroin, *L'Opinion des Femmes,* 28 January 1849.

37 J. Deroin, *L'Opinion des Femmes,* 10 April 1849; *La Démocratie Pacifique,* 13 April 1849 (a Fourierist daily, edited by Victor Considérant).
38 J. Deroin, 'Droit Politique des Femmes. A M. Michelet', extract from *L'Opinion des Femmes,* 1 May 1850.
39 J. Deroin, *Du Célibat* (Paris, 1851), p. 13.
40 'Mission de la femme dans le présent et dans l'avenir', *L'Opinion des Femmes,* June 1849.
41 Deroin, *Cours de droit social pour les femmes,* p. 8.
42 *L'Opinion des Femmes,* August 1849.
43 A. Ranvier, ,Une féministe de 1848: Jeanne Deroin', *La Révolution de 1848,* 6 (1908), pp. 423–8.
44 Ibid., p. 484.
45 Letters of Jeanne Deroin, particularly to Léon Richer. *Fonds Bouglé* 4247, BHVP.
46 Deroin to Richer, 2 January 1880, *Fonds Bouglé* 4247, BHVP.
47 P. McPhee, 'Jeanne Deroin', in E.L. Newman, *Historical Dictionary of France from the 1815 Restoration to the Second Empire,* (New York, 1987), I, pp. 321–2.
48 J. Deroin, *Almanach des Femmes* (Paris, 1852), p. 9.
49 Ibid., p. 23: 'La femme est le crime de l'homme. Elle est sa victime depuis la sortie de l'Eden. Elle porte encore dans sa chair le trace de six mille ans d'injustice.'
50 'Réforme des constumes' Eve', *Almanach des Femmes* (Paris, 1852), p. 64.
51 J. Deroin, *Almanach* (London, 1854), pp. 10–31; 'marcher dans les voies providentielles du progrès harmonieux et accomplir la loi de Dieu, la sainte loi de solidarité fraternelle et universelle...la nouvelle Eve, la Vierge, s'enveloppant de son voile mystique, appelle l'Humanité dans la voie de la continence absolue, Religion sociale de Solidarité.'
52 S. Hause, *Hubertine Auclert: The French Suffragette* (New Haven, 1987).
53 Deroin to Richer, 30 March 1850, *Fonds Bouglé* 4247, BHVP.
54 Deroin to Richer, 10 December 1874.
55 Deroin to Richer 10 October 1881.
56 M. Pelletier, *La Femme vierge* (Paris, 1933). Quoted in Scott, *Only Paradoxes to Offer,* pp. 88.
57 B.G. Smith, *Ladies of the Leisure Class: The Bourgeoises of Northern France in the Nineteeth Century* (Princeton, 1981).
58 Deroin to Léon Richer, *Fonds Bouglé* 4247, BHVP.

V

Legacy

17

Home Alone?
Reflections on Political Exiles Returning to their Native Countries*

Ansgar Reiss

The history of exile includes the history of return. The situation of exile itself cannot be described without a phenomenology of the 'longing glance' back to the fatherland left behind. In any attempt to deal with exile, one encounters the frequent wish to return, a long-lasting 'fantasy of return'. This essay, however, deals not with the mere wish to return, but with the actual return to their European homelands of a number of prominent political exiles. Naturally, the hopes and plans nurtured in exile played a crucial part in this. If we look at who among those displaced by the political events of 1848–9 returned home, a number of prominent individuals stand out. Wilhelm Liebknecht and Lothar Bucher could be named for Germany; Gyula Andrássy and Ferenc Pulszky for Hungary; Giuseppe Garibaldi for Italy, and Louis Blanc and Alexandre Auguste Ledru-Rollin for France. But how can these diverse destinies be put together in a 'history of return'? Do their biographies reveal anything about the societies from which they were displaced for decades, and to which they eventually returned? These questions will be investigated here, after a glance at the current state of research, by looking briefly at a number of individual cases. The hope that a uniform phenomenon of sorts will emerge is based on the assumption that a common European revolutionary culture existed in 1848–9, and on the nature of emigration itself.

We shall first address the question of a common European phenomenon. Although there were considerable differences in political, economic and social development within Europe, at least in one area, which we shall provisionally call the 'public sphere', a certain

---

* Translated by Angela Davies, German Historical Institute London.

synchronism had emerged since the Napoleonic era and the Congress of Vienna, as revealed, for example, in the French Revolution of July 1830. International interdependencies in political structures impacted on the character of internal (national) political conflict. The reactions to political conflict were extremely similar all over the continent of Europe. In general, communications made clear progress, and the networks became denser. The development of individual nation-states would have been unthinkable, and could not have happened, without reference to other nations. There was thus a spectrum of common political experiences and a shared political and social vocabulary which made individual national experiences communicable. Finally, European interdependencies were also clearly revealed in the course taken by the revolution, but this cannot be discussed further in this context. Their common experiential context meant that political refugees shared certain political convictions and ways of behaving. After all, before and during the revolution European unity was not merely a rhetorical construct for the liberal democratic movement.

One further proviso needs to be made at this stage. This essay can deal only with 'displaced revolutionaries', not with 'those who were displaced by the revolution'. In other words, it focuses on well-known radical agitators who were forced, by external circumstances, to leave their homelands. If this essay wanted to provide a sociocultural analysis of exile, a much larger framework would have to be selected. However, as the main interest here is European political cultures, and, more specifically, the circumstances under which exiles returned to their countries and what sort of societies they found there, it makes sense to concentrate on exiled radicals. It does not need to be emphasised that there were conflicts between moderates and radicals both at home and in exile. And yet, in exile the political refugees were all, at least to start with, in the same boat despite their differences – and this was in striking contrast to the situation in their home countries.

This tells us something about the nature of exile. Exile was a fate shared by people of different ages and sexes, of different national, social and political origins. Many of these differences, as we have already mentioned, continued to exist in exile, and among the political exiles in particular, new tensions and splits occurred constantly. None the less, contemporary journalists and the governments involved did not hesitate to speak of 'the emigration' as a homogeneous group. The emigrants, too, sometimes saw themselves in this way. This was facilitated by the fact that many of them had known each other before the revolution, even if only by name. Others had met during the revolution itself, or in their first place of refuge, often Switzerland or France. When Switzerland expelled most of the refugees in the autumn of 1849, they met again in London, which thus became the 'capital of the emigration'.[1] Because they had been torn out of their public and private networks, they were receptive to the idea of making new connections. In the run-up to the revolution, and during the revolution itself, much had been in flux politically. Radicals had separated themselves from liberals, liberals had defined themselves as conservatives, etc. In exile, however, it could be said that the political emigrants developed a new view of themselves as a sort of 'European party of revolution'. The common problems of exile came to the fore, and overlaid their differences, at least for a start.

Yet the cohesion of the group was always precarious. The legendary fragmentation among the emigrants has long been seen as something that marked them out as a group that belonged together, but there were also strong processes of erosion at work which threatened to break this bond. Loss of hope that the flame of revolution would soon re-ignite on the Continent, especially after the French elections of December 1851, encouraged the resolve to leave Europe altogether and to settle in the USA. Many who went on to the USA, and some who stayed in Britain, withdrew from politics and attempted to put their private lives in order and to build up a new existence. Others, who were not heavily implicated politically, had not even followed the stream of emigrants as far as London, but had preferred to return to their homelands and, perhaps, accept punishment. No more can be said about them in this essay. Thus the field was diversified in the real period of emigration, the 1850s.

But it is only after the emigrants return to their homelands that the history of the emigration seems to dissolve into a wealth of individual stories. We can almost speak of a recurrence of difference. First of all, nationality once again became significant in this process because the chance to return depended on political developments in the home country and especially on the issue of political amnesty. For those who travelled on from London or England to the USA, the experience of transit in London became, in retrospect, marginal. Their experiences in the USA were crucial. Here we will look only at those refugees who spent the decisive years of their exile in London. There were also prominent refugees who never returned to their homelands, even during the 1860s when many of their fellow refugees did – Lajos Kossuth, Gottfried Kinkel, Karl Marx and Giuseppe Mazzini among them. Those who did not return reveal the many factors, either private or based on matters of principle, which influenced the decision either to return home or to stay in exile.

In the search for reasons, the following issues seem important, in addition to specific life circumstances and the political question of amnesty: (1) the place which returnees believed they occupied in the European spectrum of parties; (2) the weight of national and European arguments, that is, conceptions of the role of their own nations within Europe; (3) their own role within the group of emigrants; (4) how returnees defined themselves *vis-à-vis* this group by their return (the omnipresent question of the 'point of exile'); (5) what role they played, or what role was ascribed to them, after their return; and, finally and perhaps most importantly, (6) how nations dealt with their returning emigrants, what positions they could and did give them.

Four national groups, apart from the older group of Polish emigrants, dominated the emigrant scene in London: French, Germans (with all the problematic implications which this designation contains), Italians and Hungarians.[2] The Hungarians were undoubtedly the most self-contained as a group. Gyula Andrássy and Ferenc Pulszky deserve special mention. Among the French, Louis Blanc and Alexandre Auguste Ledru-Rollin were among the fixtures of the emigration in London. Both eventually returned to France in 1870. Among the Italians, Garibaldi undoubtedly experienced the whole dilemma and tragedy of a returning emigrant most passionately. Among the Germans, two emigrants who enjoyed extraordinary success after their return were Lothar Bucher and Wilhelm Liebknecht.

Andrássy

Count Gyula Andrássy (1823–90), as a Hungarian magnate, lived in a social sphere that was always closed to the other people discussed here.[3] After he went into exile, two of his estates in Hungary were confiscated. On 15 April 1851 he was condemned *in absentia* and his effigy was hanged on 22 September in Pest. But his mother was soon able to send him enough money in exile to allow him to live a life in keeping with his status.[4] He lived mainly in Paris, but Britain held a special position in his political thinking, and it was there that he published his crucial, postrevolutionary programme. Not least his marriage to Katinka Kendeffy, whose family was loyal to the Habsburgs, made it possible for Andrássy to return to Hungary as early as 1857, and fully to reenter Hungarian society.[5]

Andrássy's life reflects not only his social position, however, but also the peculiarities of the Hungarian Revolution. Following in his father's footsteps, Andrássy had initially taken a reforming liberal political course. His connection with Lajos Kossuth in the Pressburg Diet, however, took him beyond this moderate position. In the revolution, Andrássy had first worked for the liberal government of Lajos Batthyány in the provincial administration. When Kossuth took power after the counter-revolutionary troops marched in on 22 September 1848, Andrássy made an appearance at the Battle of Schwechat, the (unsuccessful) attempt to relieve the revolutionary capital, Vienna. A subsequent diplomatic mission took him via Serbia to the Sublime Porte in Constantinople, where he came into contact with, among others, the accredited British ambassador Stratford Canning. Andrássy believed that Britain should take action against the Russian incursion. At least the threatened handing over of the refugees to the Habsburg Empire was prevented.[6] At the end of November 1849 Andrássy left Istanbul, and reached London via Marseilles at the beginning of 1850. There, according to the literature, he did not take part in the emigrants' 'subversive activities, intrigues, and political daydreaming'. However, according to police reports, he was in contact with the emigrants.[7] A short time later Andrássy left London and went to Paris, where he spent most of his time in exile.[8] As early as November 1850, in an anonymous article published in the *Eclectic Review*, Andrássy expressed his renunciation of Kossuth's politics, which aimed for the abolition of the monarchy and Hungary's total separation from Austria.[9] With an eye to the world-political situation, Andrássy proclaimed that it was in Britain's interests to support a free and autonomous Hungary within the framework of a federal Habsburg monarchy. With an eye to Britain's policy of balance, he put Austria clearly at the centre of his deliberations. An end to the repression of Hungary, he argued, was the precondition for a strong and independent Austria. An autonomous Hungary could form a bulwark against Russia, whereas a centralised Austria could exist only by the grace of Russia. Andrássy had one more argument to underline Britain's closeness to Hungary: only Hungary had an 'Old Constitution' like Britain. In Hungary, its expression was the Hungarian kingdom, and it pointed to the 'past and the future'.[10] In the October Diploma of 1860, Austria once again conceded Hungary the right to have a say and its own representative assembly (*Landtag*). Andrássy now returned to politics, but he boycotted the provisions of the October Diploma with reference to the Old Constitution, and called for further-reaching autonomous rights. In concrete terms, Ferenc

Deák's party, which Andrássy aligned himself with, always acknowledged the April constitution of 1848, according to which Hungary was
tied to Austria only in a personal union. Both components shaped
Andrássy's relationship with Britain his whole life long. Since the settlement of 1867, when the Habsburg Empire had been reorganised as the
Austro-Hungarian dual monarchy, and Hungary had received far-reaching autonomy for its part of the Empire, he was clearly orientated by
the *status quo*.[11] His political position in Europe, which marked him
out as a Forty-Eighter, was characterised by an aggressive, sometimes
almost hysterical aversion towards Russia.[12]

The path to the Austro-Hungarian settlement of 1867 cannot be
described in more detail here. In the Hungarian Diet, which assembled
in 1861 after Anton Ritter von Schmerling's February Patent, and to
which Andrássy was elected, he found himself almost exclusively
among partisans of the revolution. As an exponent of moderate politics in Hungary, and carried by a broad national consensus, he had a
unique career among the Forty-Eighters. He became the most prominent figure in Hungarian politics after Ferenc Deák. By adopting as his
own cause Deák's offer to Austria to consider military and foreign
policy, and the accompanying finances, as common matters,[13] he was
able to play a crucial part in the Austro-Hungarian negotiations in the
role, among others, as chair of the relevant *Landtag* committee. When
Austria was defeated by Prussia in 1866, Friedrich von Beust was
appointed Leading Minister in Vienna and there was a reorientation in
Austrian policy, which, finally, resulted in Austro-Hungarian relations
being placed on a new footing in the settlement mentioned above.
Emperor Franz Josef (Francis Joseph) had himself crowned with the
crown of St Stephen in Budapest, thus creating a personal union, and
with the exception of the common matters proposed by Deák, Hungary
received complete autonomy. After Deák had refused the post,
Andrássy became Minister President of the Hungarian part of the
Empire.

One of the coronation presents which Hungary presented to the
Austrian imperial couple is interesting for its relation to emigration: a
silver casket containing 50,000 golden ducats for the widows, orphans
and disabled veterans of the revolutionary army of 1849, the Hovéd
army. In this way the revolution of 1848 was integrated into the
renewed empire, and into the collective memory of its people, at least
as far as its nationalist aspect was concerned. The majority of Hungarians in exile took the opportunity to return to Hungary – a
comprehensive amnesty was declared – and only a small minority,
including Lajos Kossuth, continued to insist on their radical demands,

namely, the abolition of the monarchy and complete independence. Kossuth clearly did not want to give up his role as the leading representative of radical ideas and the 'Party of Revolution', and he did not want to admit defeat by a more moderate course, even though the return of the majority of emigrants meant that, to some extent, he lost his supporters, his 'people' for a second time.

After the founding of the German Empire in 1870–1, which was a serious defeat for Beust's policy, Andrássy was appointed his successor in Vienna, and thus became Foreign Minister of the whole state. Finally he was completely absorbed by European diplomacy – truly a remarkable career for a Forty-Eighter. Although his enmity towards Russia and attempts to form an alliance with Britain largely remained constants, Andrássy completely rejected his revolutionary attitude of 1848–9. Thus, for example, Austria was able to implement the comparatively small success that its Foreign Minister Andrássy had achieved at the Berlin Congress of 1878, namely, that Bosnia and Herzegovina were to be part of Austria, only by a military invasion and brutal and unpopular battles against local freedom fighters (Hadschi Loja was the best known).[14] Without betraying the Hungarian cause, Gyula Andrássy was now, as far his political principles were concerned, on the side of the government.

Pulszky

Ferenc Pulszky (1814–97), by profession a lawyer and by interest a historian and antiquary, was Deputy Foreign Minister in Lajos Batthyány's cabinet in 1848. When he arrived in Britain as a refugee at the end of the year, he passed himself off as the Hungarian envoy. Contrary to his own ideas, however, he did not have an official commission from Kossuth, but acted on his own initiative. He was not authorised until the arrival of a letter dated 15 March 1849.[15] Thus from the start, Pulszky tried to ignore the depressing question of the point of exile by plunging into political activity, and by emphasising a sense of belonging to the group of active revolutionaries.

Like Andrássy, he was condemned to death *in absentia* in his home country. In London and Paris he established many contacts in the international emigrants' community. They included, in addition to his fellow Hungarians, prominent French exiles such as Alexandre Auguste Ledru-Rollin and Louis Blanc, as well as English people who were friendly towards and interested in the emigrants, such as Lord Dudley Coutts Stuart,[16] and Francis W. Newman.[17] With Georg Klapka, Pulszky set up a Hungarian Refugees' Committee in London, and attempted to influence Palmerston.[18] Just as for Andrássy, Hungary's Old Constitution, which was comparable to the British constitution, was a central question for him.[19] But whereas Andrássy took the Hungarian nation born out of the tradition of the aristocratic nation for granted, Pulszky devoted his whole life to constituting the Hungarian nation culturally by academic and journalistic means.[20] Consequently, his revolutionary attitude was always accompanied by plans for a republican educational offensive.[21]

Ferenc Pulszky and Gyula Andrássy probably met in London when Andrássy delivered a letter from Kossuth to Pulszky and László Teleki, dated 12 September 1849. This letter marked the nadir of disappointment for the Hungarians in exile. In it, Kossuth pointed out that at present, the struggle was in vain, and that the time was not ripe for a democratic revolution and an independent Hungary.[22] Pulszky, of course, drew different conclusions from Andrássy. Once Kossuth had regained his courage, Pulszky accompanied him on publicity and fundraising tours through Britain and the USA from October 1851 to July 1852.[23] Like Kossuth, he took less and less notice of public opinion in Britain.[24] With Kossuth, he concentrated on a victorious return to Hungary, which was to be made possible by a revolutionary event that would set everything in motion. Pulszky spent February to April 1853 in the USA again, in order to gain political support and to organise the establishment of a legion in exile.[25] Pulszky's support for an armed rising is shown, among other things, by the fact that he bought weapons in the USA.[26]

In 1855 Pulszky, along with Ledru-Rollin and Mazzini, signed the manifesto of a republican party which proclaimed a holy alliance of all nations, and with whose aid European democracy was to constitute itself as a powerful unit. None the less, Pulszky remained doubtful about purely universal principles of democracy and the freedom of nations, as advocated fervently, with almost religious rhetoric, by Mazzini. After all, Pulszky argued, in the revolution Hungary had firmly defended itself against the Habsburg reaction and against the Russian occupation, and had not pursued some sort of utopian ideals.[27] Nor did Pulszky show any interest in the idea of a confederation of the Danube area, put forward as early as 1849 by László Teleki when he was envoy in Paris, in the appendix to a French publication.[28] Kossuth also supported this idea, first in 1850–1 in Turkey, and especially in 1862, when he put it forward as an alternative to the Austro-Hungarian settlement foreshadowed in the October Diploma. This, he claimed, signified merely a division of power between Austria and Hungary, but not a new, liberal political order.[29] Instead, Pulszky followed a simpler national line, and this was ultimately what made it possible for him to return.

In 1859 the exile scene was in flux. While Hungarians and Italians were brought together in a common cause, namely, their desire to weaken Austria, the German exiles Lothar Bucher and Karl Blind refused to cooperate with Pulszky on a common campaign against Austria. Lothar Bucher thought in 'großdeutsch' (greater German) terms, favouring the idea of including Austria in a greater German empire. For Karl Blind the common hatred of Napoleon III was much more important than an alliance with a revolutionary Hungary.[30] After the first amnesty announced in 1859, the Hungarian émigré community in London began to disintegrate. The Hungarian legion, which had long been firmly established, looked like dissolving itself. Pulszky continued to share Kossuth's view that it was still the duty of the exiles to conspire and then to act in a revolutionary manner.[31]

On 3 April 1860, Pulszky went to Turin as the representative of Kossuth's Hungarian National Directorium in London in order to establish a connection with the Italian independence movement. When he left London, however, it was his intention not to return. It was quickly becoming clear that Cavour would not support the Hungarians in the long term, and on 8 January 1861 Pulszky resigned from his position as Kossuth's intermediary. For the Hungarian community in exile the October Diploma of 1860 was the turning-point. Immediately, room for manoeuvre opened up in Hungary itself, and soon thereafter, 'everyone's services were assessed according to how compromised they were in 1848 and 1849'.[32] It is characteristic that László Teleki was arrested in Dresden in December 1860, and handed over to the Austrian authorities. The latter, however, set him free in return for a promise not to conspire any more.[33]

In a letter to Kossuth, Pulszky explained that the emigration could now either follow the moderate direction of Ferenc Deák (and thus also of Andrássy), or it could take Garibaldi's path and attempt a landing on the Dalmatian coast. The emigrant Georg Klapka, for example, favoured this solution, but Pulszky recognised it as totally unrealistic.[34] Although he had consultations with Giuseppe Garibaldi, who was to act as military commander if necessary, Pulszky then declared his readiness to stand as a candidate for parliament in Hungary. Like many other emigrants, he was elected. However, he was refused a passport, with the result that he could not take his seat until 1867. He joined Ferenc Deák's party. Back at home, the former émigré had the prospect of a comfortable life as a scholar.[35] In 1869 he became Director of the Hungarian National Museum, and in 1872 Director-General of the Hungarian state museums and libraries.

Despite points of contact, Pulszky and Andrássy had gone very different ways in exile. In Hungary, under the 1867 settlement with Austria, however, their paths converged again. For Hungary, whose enemies in the 1848–9 revolution had been found externally, in Russia and Austria, political emigration by no means implied a questioning of the imagined thousand-year history of the nation. In Hungary, therefore, the returning emigrants were able to play an important part in helping the nation to define itself.

Ledru-Rollin

The historical situation in France was completely different. Nation-building itself was not a problem, and there was a great revolutionary tradition. Alexandre Auguste Ledru-Rollin (1808–74), a lawyer like Pulszky and, since the 1830s, known as a representative of radical interests in the legal, journalistic and political fields, was among those who, in February 1848, directed the unrest into a call for the abolition of the monarchy. As Interior Minister in the Provisional Government, Ledru-Rollin soon found himself overtaken by Louis Blanc and other radical democrats and socialists. After the civil war in June, he lost his office and, with Pierre-Joseph Proudhon, Louis-Marc Caussidière and Louis Blanc, was indicted for the events of 15 May 1848. An excited crowd had stormed the revolutionary National Assembly and announced the installation of a new government. Ledru-Rollin had been playing a double game. While he had been placed on the list of members of the cabinet, he also supported Alphonse de Lamartine and others in their attempts to reinstate the legitimate government.

It is typical of Ledru-Rollin's vacillation between pure republicanism and socialism that, although the socialist tendencies of the revolution were restrained in the wake of these events, Ledru-Rollin himself became increasingly well known as a representative of republicanism with a socialist accent. He supported the adoption of the right to work in the new constitution, stood against Louis Napoleon in the December elections, suffered a clear defeat and criticised France's military intervention against the Italian republic.[36] On 13 June 1849 he was crucially involved in an unsuccessful uprising against this policy, and thereupon had to flee to London. The saying ascribed to him – 'I am their leader, I must follow them' – shows how much he had become the prisoner of his own political role. Ledru-Rollin was sentenced, *in absentia,* to deportation. He was excluded from the amnesty of 1857, and even from that of 1869, and was unable to return until 1870, under Emile Ollivier.

In English exile, Ledru-Rollin immediately distinguished himself by bringing out a book that was extremely anti-British.[37] This rejection of a much-praised Britain reflected the old rivalry between Britain and France, and Ledru-Rollin defended France as the motherland of political progress – a defence that became increasingly questionable with Louis Napoleon's plebiscites. Ledru-Rollin was also trying to maintain the feeling of belonging to France among the emigrants. In cooperation with Giuseppe Mazzini, Arnold Ruge and other prominent exiles, he was involved in repeated attempts to organise a European association of democrats, but without lasting success. This turning towards Europe – which, remarkably, always excluded the current host country, namely, Britain – may be interpreted as an attempt to create an 'imagined community' in the face of the threatened loss of the real one through expulsion.

After Ledru-Rollin's return home in 1870, which was very late in a European context, illness prevented him from playing a part in the Government of National Defence which was constituted on 4 September 1870 in the face of the German advance. Elected in February 1871 to the National Assembly that met in Bordeaux, Ledru-Rollin, like other prominent participants in the 1848 revolution, voted to continue the war against Germany, but resigned his seat in protest at the preliminary peace of Versailles of 26 February 1871. Reelected to the National Assembly in 1874, he gave his last speech in support of universal suffrage.

Blanc

Louis Blanc (1811–82), who will be compared here with Ledru-Rollin, spent even longer in exile.[38] Fleeing as early as summer 1848, he went first to Belgium and then to London, when he saw that he was likely to be convicted in the legal proceedings relating to the events of 15 May 1848. He had participated in the violent occupation of parliament and the proclamation of a new, more radical government. Although not a deputy, he had taken the speakers' stand and, like Ledru-Rollin, had been on the list of cabinet members, without, however, playing his double game. Blanc did not return to France until 4 September 1870. Influenced by the Jacobin tradition on the one hand, on the other he was considered an exponent of the Fourierist variety of socialism, to which he had contributed a crucial slogan in his work, *Organisation du travail* (1840). Cooperation was to replace competition, he argued. Blanc was not thinking in premodern terms of small-scale craft workshops; his ateliers are factories with mechanised production on a grand scale. Compared with Robert Owens's 'cooperatism', Blanc brought a stronger political component into socialism. A good part of the *Organisation du travail* was to be the responsibility of the state, a task which had to be organised democratically, and with basic social rights.[39] In stark contrast to Auguste Blanqui, however, Blanc rejected the strike as a means of gaining political demands. He also firmly rejected any form of violence, as is shown by his behaviour in 1848, when he distanced himself from the June revolt, and his rejection of the French Commune of 1871. In principle, what he demanded was state intervention instead of revolution,[40] and a central plank of his manifesto was the demand for people to be educated in a sense of the common good.[41]

Like Ledru-Rollin, Blanc refused to take an oath to the Empire which would have made it possible to return to France. However, he fully supported republicans who returned to France in 1854–6, and participated in French political life again.[42] The amnesty declared in 1859, declared simultaneously with Napoleon III's engagement in Italy, encouraged many to return.[43]

After his return, Blanc, like Ledru-Rollin, became a deputy in the National Assembly in Bordeaux on 8 February 1871, and like Ledru-Rollin, voted for the war to continue. In the by-elections of July 1871, many republicans, and many veterans of the Second Republic, entered the Chamber. In the Third Republic, Blanc supported an amnesty for the Communards, although he had condemned the Commune. He attempted to make contact with a new generation of socialists, such as Benoît Mâlon, but he never achieved real influence again. Yet he was important for radicals such as George Clemenceau. Ultimately, for him, republicanism took priority.[44]

The high honours accorded to Blanc at his funeral in 1882 must not be allowed to obscure the fact that, like Ledru-Rollin, he never became an important figure in the Third Republic. While there was no real alternative to the republic in 1870–1, it must nevertheless be stressed that the republicanism of the 1860s was fundamentally different from Jacobin republicanism.[45] It was a republicanism of parliament, of the press and the law courts, not of conspiracies and grand, demonstrative deeds. Thus the new generation of republicans, who had learned to compromise with the old upper classes under the empire, were not challenged by the returning exiles. During their exile, they had forfeited their influence on the political culture. The nation no longer needed them. In the case of Louis Blanc, it also becomes clear that in the socialist movement in particular, a strong and specific relation with the revolution of 1848 and the emigration existed and was cultivated.

Bucher

Lothar Bucher (1817–92) demonstrates a completely different way of dealing with the past. He was a member of the Prussian National Assembly and, in 1849, was a member of the left in the Prussian Second Chamber. He decided to emigrate to Britain when, on 21 February 1850, he was sentenced to loss of his offices and fifteen months' imprisonment for the comparatively minor offence of spreading the resolution to refuse to pay taxes of 15 November 1848. Bucher stayed in Britain until the amnesty declared on William I's accession to the throne in 1861. He earned his living in Britain mainly by writing for German newspapers, among others, the *Nationalzeitung* in Berlin. In 1864 he was appointed to the Prussian Ministry of Foreign Affairs, and had a career as a confidant of Bismarck's. Because of his past, however, he did not advance as far as the position of secretary of state.[46]

Bucher did not stand out right at the beginning of the revolution. In Berlin, he had initially counted himself among the moderate left, whose goal was the 'rule of the people in the form of the monarchy', and he separated himself from the extreme left, which aimed to achieve a republic by 'the skilful use of social issues'.[47] Early in September, however, he declared his definitive support for the sovereignty of the National Assembly; he did not speak of the sovereignty of the people until 1849 in the Second Chamber.[48] Bucher's position on the issue of the abolition of the last feudal regulations on 9 October 1848 shows a clear awareness of the revolutionary situation. The constituent assembly, he argued, must intervene on the principle of property now, as the future constitution would make this impossible.[49]

In London, Lothar Bucher was in frequent contact with various other refugees, although like Andrássy, he later cast a veil of silence over this episode.[50] The permanent position of correspondent for the *Nationalzeitung* hardly brought in enough to live on,[51] but at least he could stay in contact with part of the German public to which he had related as a politician. In 1851 he had seen English public opinion almost as 'the conscience of Europe',[52] but his opinion soon changed in view of the dominant role of *The Times*, which drowned out all other voices. Thus he increasingly tended to see the press merely as 'published' opinion.[53] This is also the context for his book *Der Parlamentarismus wie er ist*, published in 1855,[54] in which he generalised the insight that public opinion was also subject to manipulation. This is quite clearly the reason for his rejection of political radicalism, but ultimately, this placed a question mark over his job as a journalist.

Another shift allows us to observe Bucher in the Crimean War. At the start, his foreign policy hopes had been vested in Britain, but it became increasingly clear to him that, ultimately, the actions of every nation were dictated by self-interest.[55] From that time on, 'German interests' became the leitmotiv of all Buchner's correspondence.[56] In a letter to Engels, Marx recognised in Bucher the 'Prussian minister-to-be', which could only have been meant derisively at the time.[57]

An extremely positive article about Bucher in the *Neue Conversations-Lexikon*, edited and largely written by the arch-conservative, Hermann Wagener, made the German journalist-in-exile respected in Conservative circles,[58] while the liberals distanced themselves from him.[59] Out of considerations of political power, Bucher went so far as to stand up for Catholic, supranational Austria,[60] and subsequently, he repeatedly fell back on the *Allgemeine Zeitung* as a liberal-conservative newspaper.[61] During the Italian crisis of 1859–60, the idea of a Greater German Reich, that is, one encompassing Prussia and the whole of the multinational Habsburg empire, superseded the primacy of the national idea and all domestic political friction.[62]

If we look at the about-turn in Bucher's journalism, the question arises as to whether he was using his journalism to prepare for his return. The fact that as early as 1857 he felt the Prussian government regarded him in a favourable light supports this view.[63] After his return to Germany in 1862, Bucher was initially politically close to Ferdinand Lassalle. However, he gave up this political friendship when, in the spring of 1863, Lassalle opted to set up an independent workers' party. Also, at this time Bucher had the firm promise of a position in the German Foreign Office.[64]

Christoph Studt attributes Bucher's change of allegiance to circumstances in his private life. An engagement was planned, but it broke up soon thereafter and Bucher found himself in increasing financial difficulties.[65] According to Studt, therefore, Bucher simply became a 'realist'. This could be seen as a consequence of exile;[66] Bucher mutated into a 'monk devoted purely to the state'.[67] Yet how is this biographical change to be interpreted? The contrast with Andrássy's life is striking. Bucher was able to participate in politically shaping his homeland through his work in the German Foreign Ministry only at the cost of disappearing from the public eye and denying his past. Towards the end of his life he assisted Bismarck in writing his memoirs, which tell a story completely different from Bucher's. In Bismarck's conservative assessment emigration seemed to play no important part at all in the 1848–9 revolution.

Liebknecht

Wilhelm Liebknecht (1826–1900), probably the most important Social Democratic figure in the German Reich apart from August Bebel, had his roots in the democratic radicalism of the 1848–9 revolution. Once the revolution broke out, he went to Paris. In September 1848 and the early summer of 1849 he was a supporter of Gustav Struve in Baden. In the summer of 1849 he emigrated first to Switzerland, where he was in contact with Struve and Giuseppe Mazzini in Geneva, but also became increasingly involved with workers' associations. Expelled in February 1850, he went to Britain, where he continued his journalism, becoming a correspondent for Britain. Liebknecht had started writing for democratic newspapers before the revolution, and this work was eventually to lead him to move to Berlin, thus returning to Germany.[68] His journalism, his criticism of Palmerston's policy and of British parliamentarianism, his Russophobia and his 'großdeutsche' political convictions all made him astonishingly close to Lothar Bucher. On the other hand, Liebknecht was also very active in the workers' education movement. This distinguished him from Karl Marx, who, in the 1850s, largely withdrew to concentrate on his academic work, although Liebknecht was personally and politically close to him. In addition to his acquaintance with Karl Marx, Liebknecht particularly cultivated his friendship with Robert Owen in exile in Britain.[69] Although the class struggle was among the central categories of his political convictions, Liebknecht, much more specifically than Marx, put the process of industrialisation into the context of comprehensive social modernisation, which he saw as something positive.[70] This attitude towards British industrialisation also distinguished Liebknecht very clearly from Ledru-Rollin and his purely republican, highly negative image of Britain.

　　Returning to Germany in 1862 – he lived first in Berlin and from 1865 in Leipzig – Liebknecht's British experience fed largely into his work. This applied to the practical organisation of the workers' movement and the trade union movement,[71] and to his wide parliamentary work in the North German Diet, the German Diet and in the Saxon

Landtag.[72] At the same time, he continued to write for the Social Democratic Party press. Liebknecht played a large part in the German
workers' movement association established in Gotha in 1875. In any
case, the emigration was a central element for German Social Democracy, which increasingly developed its own milieu in the Kaiserreich –
it was excluded, but also excluded itself. Karl Marx, an essential refer-
ent for every Social Democrat, stayed in London.

While the bourgeois mainstream in Germany largely ignored the
memory of 1848 and the emigration (with the exception of a figure
such as Bucher, perhaps extreme in this respect), Social Democracy
claimed an exclusive right to cultivate this memory. In 1998, during
the 150th anniversary commemorations of the revolution, it was
pointed out that in the bourgeois memory of the revolution, the
violence had faded, while in the proletarian memory, the goal of a
liberal constitution had faded.[73] This assessment reflects a need for
historical harmony and symmetry rather than the reality of the situation. The memory of the 1848–9 revolution was certainly used to
cultivate a 'bourgeois' fear of violence not authorised from above, and
to underline the aspirations of the 'proletarians' to a democratic state.

The specific fate of the returnee Wilhelm Liebknecht shows clearly
how a positive assessment of the experience of emigration in the awareness of individuals' own biographies and in the perceptions of a Social
Democratic audience relaxed the memory of the 1848–9 revolution. Of
course, a national consensus on these topics in Germany lay in the far
distance future.

The fact that for Social Democrats the experience of emigration did
not end in the 1860s certainly contributed to their positive reception
of the emigration (and the revolution). In 1871, in the newly established German nation-state, Social Democracy was pushed into the role
of 'enemy of the Reich'. The Chancellor of the Reich, Bismarck, used
all available means to cut the ground from beneath its feet and to
suppress it. One of these means was social insurance legislation. The
state insurances for sickness, pensions and accidents introduced
between 1883 and 1889 were intended to inspire loyalty to the new
Reich among the workers and to woo them away from the ranks of
Social Democracy. Another prong of the attack was to place as many
obstacles as possible in the way of the broadly based party work of
the Social Democrats, and the Anti-Socialist Laws of 1878 exposed
Social Democrats to severe state repression. Thus began another period
of emigration, or of retreat underground. With great effort, contact was
maintained between the emigrants and those who stayed at home, or

those who had returned home from the earlier wave of emigration, many of whom had now gone underground.[74] Internationalism was thus taken for granted. The internationalism of the workers' movement had important roots in the experience of the emigrants.

Garibaldi

Finally, a glance at Italy where the cults around Mazzini and Garibaldi, and especially the countless monuments to the latter, are striking and suggest that the émigrés had a positive reception. Giuseppe Garibaldi (1807–82) is, in many respects, difficult to compare with the other emigrants discussed here.[75] Distinguishing features include his humble origins, adventurous life and charisma. London as a place of exile was of minor importance to him. However, the reception that he was given, allegedly by half a million people, in 1864, can be compared with Kossuth's experiences. Garibaldi, sentenced to death *in absentia* in the 1830s, had lived as an émigré since 1834 in various European countries, and later in North and South America as well.

From the mid-1850s, he became an indispensable part of the politics which led to the unification of Italy. By comparison, his participation with Mazzini in the Roman Republic of 1849 seems a mere episode. In fact, Garibaldi's return to Italy – initially, in 1854, to the island of Caprera, north of Sardinia, and then, in May 1859, alongside Piedmont's troops – was made possible by the fact that he turned towards Camillo Cavour's politics, and away from the strict republicanism of Mazzini and the 1849 Roman Republic.

Thus his real exile ended in the mid-1850s. Although Garibaldi was repeatedly taken prisoner and expelled thereafter, he managed to establish a permanent refuge on the island of Caprera. He withdrew to this when he was persecuted or militarily defeated, or just to register his protest against policies which he considered too half-hearted or calculating. The island thus became a symbol, initially of the incomplete nation-state, and later, after Garibaldi's death in 1882 and his burial on the island, of the completed Italian nation-state. In it, therefore, emigration acquired a new and very special meaning. Exile became a fixed element in Garibaldi's biography, and inseparable from him as a figure.

Garibaldi by no means allowed himself simply to be caught up in Cavour's diplomacy. Especially in 1860, the expulsion of the Bourbons from Sicily and southern Italy demonstrated the effectiveness of the republican notion of a volunteer corps, which Garibaldi also used to put pressure on the armies of Piedmont. The ways in which Garibaldi attempted to repeat this success in integrating the later capital, Rome, into the Italian nation-state, and his participation in the Franco-Prussian war of 1870–1 on the side of the French etc. cannot be recapitulated here.

The case of Garibaldi demonstrates how a genuine republican radicalism was able to combine with a modern national movement which aimed less for the glory of a demonstrative individual action, republican virtue, or a Europe of free peoples than for the social modernisation and a lasting position of power for its own nation in competition with other nation-states. A gulf remains between the impulse towards Italian unification among the volunteer corps and the imposition of the Italian state 'from above', which is what happened. And the memory of Garibaldi, his meaning for the Italian nation, is tied completely to the way in which he served the cause of national unification. Garibaldi's life and deeds have become the romantic founding myths of the Italian state, and their memory puts the progress in political culture, which should be associated with '1848', into the background.[76]

In Italy, the enemy of revolution and national unification – as in the case of Hungary – was seen beyond the country's borders, first in the Habsburg monarchy, and then also in the problematic relationship with France. This made internal Italian, and internal Hungarian integration easier, and they were able to integrate the émigrés quite unproblematically. In Italy, of course, the relationship with the Papacy was more difficult. However, the development of the political culture and political institutions ignored the republicanism which had been proclaimed by many of the later émigrés in the first half of the century. This was clear early on in Mazzini's withdrawal from the consensus reached by the Roman constituent assembly in January 1849. And Garibaldi came to terms with the constitutional monarchy, and achieved fame as a military leader and popular hero. However, he played no significant role in the Italian parliament, of which he was a member from 1860.

Conclusion

If we review these biographical sketches of the prominent exiles in London, it becomes clear that the oft-mentioned 'Party of Revolution' was a fiction of the political emigration which simply dissolved as soon as the émigrés made use of the opportunities which arose to return home. However, the fiction of a 'homogeneous party of emigration', as seen from the outside, was not entirely without consequences, for the idea of political parties and internationalism both have roots in it. In concrete terms, the well-developed party solidarity of German Social Democracy can certainly be connected with the experience of emigration. And while Ledru-Rollin and Louis Blanc could not agree with the conditions of the peace treaty of 1871, which also formed the basis of the Third Republic, Liebknecht from the German side was able to vote with them against the annexation of Alsace-Lorraine which was enshrined in it, thus clearly going beyond the limits of national power politics.

But in our context, the issue of how the European nations treated the returning political émigrés is more important than the developing internationalism of Social Democratic political organisations. The pattern that emerges is hardly surprising for the age of nationalism. Where the revolution could be interpreted as an important building block in the creation of a nation-state, whether by bringing a number of small states together or by separation from a transnational state, its political protagonists were later made welcome. In the case of Hungary and Italy, only the most radical positions were excluded in the persons of Lajos Kossuth and Giuseppe Mazzini, neither of whom returned – perhaps deliberately – in order not to destroy the myths built up around them. However, the more domestic political restructuring took precedence over national independence and the latent internal social contradictions which still existed were revealed by the revolution, the more difficult it was for these societies to overlook the wounds which had opened up and to integrate the returnees. For most of the countries of continental Europe, the emigration fell into a period of the most radical social change in the wake of industrialisation. The fact that the returning émigrés found very different societies on their return did not make it any easier for them to assume an important role again. Even in modern London, exile was a sort of standing still for them because it was impossible for them to participate directly in the further development of their home countries. Beyond this, however, the differing receptions which the emigrants received reflect clearly the poles of political development and the frictions within political culture. This perhaps shows itself most clearly in the role of Social Democracy in Germany.

It is striking, too, that something like a tradition of dealing with political émigrés emerged in the various European nations. For example, the émigrés in the states of Eastern Central Europe in the 1990s were in quite a different position from the Social Democrat Willy Brandt, for example, who faced a great deal of hostility in the young Federal Republic of Germany after the Second World War.

Notes

1 For the reasons see the contribution by Andreas Fahrmeir in this volume, Chapter 3.

2 Herbert Reiter, _Politisches Asyl im 19. Jahrhundert: Die deutschen politischen Flüchtlinge des Vormärz und der Revolution von 1848/49 in Europa und den USA_ (Berlin, 1992), p. 261.

3 Eduard von Wertheimer, _Graf Julius Andrássy: Sein Leben und seine Zeit_, 3 vols (Stuttgart, 1912–13); Tibor Simányi, _Julius Graf Andrássy: Baumeister der Doppelmonarchie. Mitstreiter Bismarcks_ (Vienna, 1990); Rainer F. Schmidt, _Graf Julius Andrássy: Vom Revolutionär zum Außenminister_ (Göttingen and Zurich, 1995).

4 Wertheimer, _Graf Julius Andrássy_, I. pp. 56 f.

5 Ibid. I. pp. 69, 72 f.

6 Ibid. I. pp. 22–50.

7 Ibid. I. p. 67.

8 Ibid. I. p. 51; Schmidt, _Graf Julius Andrássy_, pp. 24f.

9 'The Present Position and Policy of Austria', _Eclectic Review_, 28 (1850). Andrássy had first tried to publish it in the _Edinburgh Review_ with the assistance of Pulszky, and had travelled to London for that reason. Wertheimer, _Graf Julius Andrássy_, I. pp. 59 ff.; Simányi, _Julius Graf Andrássy_, pp. 50 ff.

10 Simányi, _Julius Graf Andrássy_, pp. 78 ff., 87. Quotation from Andrássy, ibid. p. 78.

11 Schmidt, _Graf Julius Andrássy_, pp. 80 f.; Simányi, _Julius Graf Andrássy_, pp. 174 f.

12 Schmidt, _Graf Julius Andrássy_, pp. 84 f., 104 f., 128 ff.

13 In the 'Osterartikel' (Easter Article) of 16 April 1865, ibid., p. 32.

14 Ibid., p. 122.

15 Thomas Kabdebo, _Diplomat in Exile: Francis Pulszky's Political Activities in England, 1859–1860_ (New York, 1979), p. 15.

16 Ibid., pp. 100 ff.

17 Ibid., pp. 108 ff.

18 Ibid., pp. 15–23.

19 Ibid., p. 26.

20 Ibid., pp. 39–48, 55 f .

21 Ibid., p. 98.

22 Ibid., p. 61.

23 See the contribution by Sabine Freitag in this volume, Chapter 11.

24 E.g. Kabdebo, _Diplomat in Exile_, pp. 84–6.

25 Ibid., pp. 87 f.

26 Ibid., p. 90.

27 Iibd., pp. 97 f.

28 Ibid., pp. 137 f.

29 A. Kienast, *Die Legion Klapka: Eine Episode aus dem Jahre 1866 und ihre Vorgeschichte* (Vienna, 1900), pp. 1, 7 ff.; Kabdebo, *Diplomat in Exile*, pp. 139 ff.

30 Ibid., pp. 119 f.

31 Ibid., p. 127.

32 Kienast, *Die Legion Klapka*, p. 19

33 Kabdebo, *Diplomat in Exile*, p. 131.

34 Ibid., p. 132.

35 Ibid., pp. 132 f.

36 Alvin R. Calman, *Ledru-Rollin après 1848 et les proscrits française en Angleterre* (Paris, 1921); Robert Schnerb, *Ledru-Rollin* (Paris, 1948); Theodore Zeldin, *France 1848–1945*, vol. I: *Ambition, Love and Politics* (Oxford, 1973), pp. 726–8.

37 *De la décadence de l'Angleterre*, 2 vols (Paris, 1850).

38 Leo A. Loubère, *Louis Blanc: His Life and His Contribution to the Rise of French Jacobin-Socialism* (Evanston, Ill., 1961); Jean-Michel Humilière, *Louis Blanc, 1811–1882* (Paris, 1982).

39 Pamela M. Pilbeam, *Republicanism in Nineteenth-Century France, 1814–1871* (Houndsmills and London, 1995), p. 234; Zeldin, *France*, I, pp. 447 f.

40 Pilbeam, *Republicanism in Nineteenth-Century France*, pp. 175 f.

41 Ibid., p. 177.

42 Ibid., p. 247.

43 Ibid., p. 249.

44 Zeldin, *France*, I, p. 449.

45 This context is discussed by Philip Nord, *The Republican Moment: Struggles for Democracy in Nineteenth-Century France* (Cambridge, MA and London, 1995).

46 Christoph Studt, *Lothar Bucher (1817–1892): Ein politisches Leben zwischen Revolution und Staatsdienst* (Göttingen, 1992); Heinrich von Poschinger, *Ein Achtundvierziger: Lothar Buchers Leben und Werke*, 3 vols (Berlin, 1890–4).

47 Studt, *Lothar Bucher*, pp. 40 f. (Quotation from a letter by Bucher to the *Stolper Volksverein*, 24 September 1848.)

48 Studt, *Lothar Bucher*, pp. 56 f.

49 Ibid., pp. 61 ff.

50 Studt, who largely accepts Bucher's later self-portrait and wants to eliminate any suspicion of radicalism as much as possible (see ibid., pp. 45, 237 and *passim*), mentions this only in passing, or in the notes, pp. 105, 189, 198, note 562.

51 Studt, *Lothar Bucher*, p. 107, note 22.

52 Ibid., p. 139.

53 Ibid., pp. 140, 163 f.

54 Lothar Bucher, *Der Parlamentarismus wie er ist* (Berlin, 1855).
55 Studt, *Lothar Bucher,* pp. 152 f.
56 Ibid., pp.193 ff.
57 Marx to Engels, 18 January 1856, quoted in Studt, *Lothar Bucher,* p. 189.
58 Studt, *Lothar Bucher,* p. 182.
59 Ibid., pp. 183 f. Studt naïvely suggests that from this time, Bucher kept his distance from all parties.
60 Ibid., pp. 196 f.: in the *Drei-Männer-Broschüren.*
61 Ibid., p. 198.
62 Ibid., pp. 203 f. The significance of the idea of the 'Reich' in German history of the 19th and 20th centuries has recently been emphasised by Heinrich August Winkler, *Der lange Weg nach Westen,* 2 vols (Munich, 2000).
63 Von Poschinger, *Ein Achtundvierziger,* III, p. 41. Studt, *Lothar Bucher,* p. 249.
64 This explanation according to Studt, *Lothar Bucher,* pp. 240 and 145. Studt does not attempt to explain Bucher's rejection in the context of his political biography. Bucher's letter in von Poschinger, *Ein Achtundvierziger,* III, p. 85.
65 Studt, *Lothar Bucher,* p. 252: 'solution to an existential emergency.'
66 Studt's summing up is trivial; Studt, *Lothar Bucher,* p. 253.
67 Ibid., p. 255.
68 Utz Haltern, *Liebknecht und England: Zur Publizistik Wilhelm Liebknechts während seines Londoner Exils, 1850–1862* (Trier, 1977).
69 Ibid., p. 25.
70 Ibid., pp. 29 ff., 40 f., 48 ff.
71 Ibid., pp. 46 f.
72 Ibid., pp. 47 f.
73 Manfred Hettling, 'Nachmärz und Kaiserreich', in Christoph Dipper and Ulrich Speck (eds), *1848: Revolution in Deutschland* (Frankfurt/M. and Leipzig, 1998), pp. 11–24.
74 Cf. the essay by Christine Latteck in this volume.
75 Giuseppe Monsagrat, article on 'Garibaldi, Giuseppe', in *Dizionario biographico degli Italiani,* vol. 52 (Rome, 1999), pp. 315–31.
76 Simonetta Soldani, 'Annäherung an Europa im Namen der Nation. Die intalienische Revolution 1846–49', in Dieter Dowe et al. (eds), *Europa 1848: Revolution und Reform* (Bonn, 1998), pp. 124–66.

Index